Showing Off, Showing Up

Showing Off, Showing Up

STUDIES OF HYPE, HEIGHTENED PERFORMANCE, AND CULTURAL POWER

Laurie Frederik
Kim Marra
Catherine Schuler

University of Michigan Press
Ann Arbor

Published in the United States of America by the
University of Michigan Press
Manufactured in the United States of America
♾ Printed on acid-free paper

2020   2019   2018   2017   4   3   2   1

A CIP catalog record for this book is available from the British Library.

Library of Congress Cataloging-in-Publication data has been applied for.

ISBN: 978-0-472-07346-7 (hardcover: alk. paper)
ISBN: 978-0-472-05346-9 (paperback: alk. paper)
ISBN: 978-0-472-12276-9 (e-book)

Acknowledgments

This book has evolved over an editorial collaboration of seven years. We would like to thank our contributors who have stuck with the project through the whole process and so generously responded to many requests for revisions as our conception of "showing" gradually crystallized. We are deeply grateful to LeAnn Fields, Senior Acquisitions Editor at the University of Michigan Press, who recognized the significance of the project, fielded our many queries, and offered invaluable advice along the way. The comments of the two anonymous reviewers markedly shaped and enriched this book; we thank them for their care and insights. Thanks also to our Production Editor Mary Hashman, and to Victoria Scrimer for help with the index. Closer to home, our family members sustained us with their generosity and patience, especially Meredith Alexander, Jehangir and Fénix Meer, and Babbo, Calliope, Emily, Liebchen, Mylo, Pi, Rosie, Shade, Smidgen, Tucker, and Zazu.

When we began this project in 2010, we could hardly have predicted the extent to which *Showing Off, Showing Up* would come to drive our social and political landscape. Ushering the book through production in the final months of 2016 and early 2017, we are compelled to acknowledge both the alarming relevance of certain dynamics of the phenomenon and the need to elaborate some of its other ramifications in the history of cultural performance.

—L.F., K.M., C.S.

Contents

Introduction

Laurie Frederik

> Sometimes glass glitters more than diamonds because it has more to prove.
> —TERRY PRATCHETT, *THE TRUTH*

Showing, a species of performance and action, impacts society with political, economic, and aesthetic effects far in excess of amusing diversion. Phrases such as "on with the show," "let's go to the show," "show me," and "what a show-off" circulate generically in everyday discourse, often without specific reference to art or theater and seemingly without cause for question. Many forms of showing and of heightened performance, however, operate more enigmatically, profoundly affecting the social world, even if our reactions to them are initially flippant or unconcerned because "it's just a show." Examining a wide geographical and temporal range of examples, essays in this volume illuminate how such events foster competition, exaggerate a characteristic, and reveal or expose hidden truths. There is as much to be learned about the power of showing through subtlety and underlying intentionality, just as through overt and showy display. Authors in this volume look at how diverse genres of *showing* are theoretically connected and why they merit more concerted attention.

The implications of showing off and showing up are distinct from the more ubiquitous understandings of performance or performing. The authors in this book focus on the active forms and constructions—verbs and adverbs—and argue that "to show" implies that cultural work is being done through a provocative revealing of signs and symbols, although not always as directly or unambiguously as might be assumed. History may be transformed into "nature" through repeated showing in a Barthesian sort of myth-making

(Barthes 1972), but other times it is transfigured in extraordinary and un-expected ways: messages are communicated through a secret handshake or are suddenly lit up by the momentary appearance of a well-aimed pinspot or swirl of glittering prisms. A door is opened and a perspective is changed, challenged, commercialized, or politicized during or after the experience. The essays in this volume contemplate not only "showing doing" but also the doing of showing, that is, what showing *does* or *generates* in a given circum-stance. Richard Schechner, one of the founders of performance studies, ex-plains that for an artist, "to perform" is to put on a show or a play, but that to perform in everyday life is to show off: to go to extremes for an audience, to underline an action (Schechner 2013, 22). A less scholarly, but more socially embedded perspective is found in moralizing children's books, where show-ing off is condemned as bragging, bossing, or bullying, and showing up is to claim superiority over others (i.e., Berry 1982). Children are warned about the dangers of showing off and the risks of being mean—losing friends, for example—and the practice is discouraged. As adults, however, we have per-mission to show off or up without being reproached, provided we uphold the pretense that we are doing it to demonstrate an exceptional skill or tal-ent gained by years of practice and hard work, or perhaps if our motivation is for positive sociopolitical influence. We are also allowed to show off if we mix the performance with a strong dose of humility and vulnerability, or a bit of humor.

Examples presented in this collection are eclectic in order to illustrate the varied ways in which showing works. Authors ask: What is at stake in the show? What do the participants have to prove? How do performers (as well as spectators) aspire to, live up to, or outdo others for particular rewards or recognition? These heightened and intensified dimensions distinguish showing from other types of performance. Showing attempts to delineate or challenge a definition of authenticity. It suggests an act of pleading for approval or a cause, a provocation or revealing. Showing has the potential to shift ideology, but not necessarily in the same way as performance for social change. Showing is not activist in the usual sense, though its content may be used for similar ends. Spectators think "oh," "aha," "oh my," "humph," or "no way," as they witness or participate in a showing, and performers make demands: "ta da," "see me," "listen to me," "believe me," "follow me," "touch me," "I dare you," or "just leave me alone." Showing requires arousal, be it of ex-citement, offense, anger, frustration, suspense, awe, moral justification, loyalty, camaraderie, or curiosity. The audience has something at stake as well. Showing requires and compels an integral audience of aficionados, members, connoisseurs, skeptics, or hecklers. Hype is usually generated by anticipation or reception and consequent discourse more than by the act of performance itself. Showing oversteps bounds of everyday relations by pushing firmly on an assumption and making viewers hyperaware of its presence, even if just for the space-time of the performance.

A truly effective showing acts on culture and ideology. Experiences labeled "show" hinge on the cultural and historical specificity of artistic and social expectations. An awe-inspiring event in a country with no electricity or running water may consist simply of a play on a designated unraised stage with a single working spotlight (free to all), in contrast to the awesome expectations of a tourist setting out to witness a Broadway musical in Times Square ($200+ a seat) or an Olympic opening ceremony ($1,300+ a seat). Hiding one's hair and face may be an unmarked and mundane performance in an Islamic majority culture, while it becomes an ostentatious and provocative political statement in secularized Europe or terrorist-profiling United States (cf. Phelan 1993). Straddling a horse for nineteenth-century women may have had shock value similar to a publicly screened pornographic film in twenty-first-century Seattle. And the elaborate rituals of a royal wedding may be sacred to the British elite, but they are fair game for shameless ridicule and entertainment in popular media.

Although inherently theatrical, showing is not quite, or rather, not just theater, nor ritual, sport, festival, or spectacle, and the motivations to show off or show up are diverse and often ambivalent. Our examples might correlate in some instances with Debordian spectacle (1967), but their liveness, alternative intentionalities, demands of audience engagement and complicity, and pretensions to sport and art keep them from participating fully in Guy Debord's toxic formulation of mass mediatization and commodification. These instances of showing are not always spectacular or intended for a mass consumer. We consider these showings as particularly thorny examples of cultural performance. As theorized in social science and performance studies, cultural performances reproduce cultural structures with varying levels of authenticity and representativeness. A cultural performance can function analytically as a concrete unit of observation and representative unit of national identity (Singer 1972); as a frame that invites critical reflection on communicative processes (Bauman 1977; Bauman and Briggs

1990); as a counterpoint to everyday life (Kapchan 1995); and, under certain conditions, as a force constructing or deconstructing social status and identities and so considered "performative" (Austin 1975; Butler 1988, 1997). Cultural performance is often a useful distinguishing category for theater studies and theater history, since it refers largely to nonconventional (and non-European) theater forms and may be considered a "point of departure" in which "the artistic performance is created as a special transformation" (Fisher-Lichte 1997, 225). In anthropology, cultural performance has sometimes suggested "folk" or "folkloric," terms that contemporary critical analyses of tourism, heritage, and race have problematized. After the so-called performative turn of the social sciences in the early 1990s, the category of cultural performance became too broad to be distinguishing, since virtually everything could be justified as an example. In this volume, we wish to emphasize the most socially and ideologically efficacious dynamics of cultural performance; what showing—as both a phenomenon and a critical lens—most powerfully illuminates.

To discern showing within the range of other overlapping performance-related terms, we examine its unique forcefulness in cultural performance when it includes factors such as the following:

I. *Hyped Up*: packs a punch, throws into bold relief, exposes core values, hypes up the otherwise humdrum, everyday, or unremarkable;

II. *Competition with Heightened Stakes*: involves competition and judgment, as if sport;

III. *Spectatorship and Vested Interests*: demands more than passive spectatorship and cultivates vested interest, participation, and hierarchy;

IV. *Embodied Excess and New Naturals*: valorizes embodied excess, pushes beyond categories of the "natural," and then generates new physical ideals and typologies;

V. *Hiding, Promising, and Teasing*: reveals social truths and ambivalences by what is hinted at, not shown, hidden, or disguised.

I. Hyped Up: In the case studies of showing contained here, authors investigate different intensities of cultural performances that pack a punch and that are "in it to win it," or rather to win at something or over someone. Dwight Conquergood, another founder of performance studies and an ethnographer, has described performance as cultural processes that produce centrifugal force—part of an energy field. He explains that cultural processes both pull towards a moral center as social dramas are enacted while they simultaneously express themselves outward from the depths of that symbolizing, synthesizing core. That is, cultures throw off forms of themselves—literally "expressions"—that are publicly accessible. (Conquergood 1986, in Johnson 2013, 18)

Conquergood continues: "These heightened surfacing forms throw into bold relief the core values, virtues, and visions of a culture." They are "peaks" of social experience. While we, the coeditors, wholeheartedly agree that cultural values are "thrown off" into "bold relief" in these types of performances, we argue that showing off or up also discloses a particular intentionality. Someone is hyping up the performance or the contentious issue surrounding it in order to draw attention and make waves in society. Participants wish to enhance the energy field or disrupt and redirect it.

II. *Competition and Heightened Stakes*: Showing off and up involves some degree of competition, judgment, and suspense. Its participants may be assessed by class, breed, race, aesthetic, skill, or religion. There is something to prove or disprove and there may be consequences. There is an element of "sport" in the motivation for showing off and up—not necessarily sport as in standard athleticism, but in activities put forth *as if* sport: to display, play, game, divert attention, or perform a style beyond a normal type. The "sport" of showing requires an expectation of or at least the potential for judgment and, thus, confrontation. Standards are contested. The sport of showing off and showing up another, whether principal performers or seemingly ancillary audience members, is taken seriously. Sometimes rewards are more traditional—trophies or monetary awards—while at other times they convey (to one side or the other) a superior value system.

Many analyses of competition focus on war, economics, corporate business, and games. *The Art of War* by Sun Tzu is thought to be the first book on competition's philosophy and technique, a military guide, of sorts, written sometime in the 5th century BCE. Many books with titles containing "The Art of" have since followed (e.g., *Art of Pitching, Art of Chess, Art of Seduction, Art of Leadership, Art of Lawyering*), and these "arts" all lead to being a better competitor in a particular arena (Case 2007, 16). More important for our purposes than the one-on-one game or the precise measurement of strength or speed is the complex system of relationships requiring keen cultural strategy and the accumulation of cultural capital and cultural power. Competition, however subtle and even without prize or accolade, motivates heightened action and dedication. It stimulates persistence, endurance, and poise, and pushes us to work through the particular challenges in our lives. These may be positive elements of competition, but there are also negative—we fear judgment because we are always judging, too, regardless of a performance's level of showiness. This goes for both actors in the scene and fellow audience members. What are we willing to do in order to win? Whose politics are really correct? Should women be wearing a veil? Should we be viewing or making pornographic film? Should we be spending money on the captivity of wild animals? People continually judge each other for choices made, beliefs held, or for what are considered guilty pleasures.

III. Spectatorship and Vested Interests: Standards of judgment are established in line with or as a challenge to the critical eyes of the "consumers" who are not just passive spectators, though they may consider themselves such. Consumption is not just for entertainment, but also for acquisition of expertise by association and accumulation of knowledge. Consumer-spectators often compete with each other as much as the performers—they go to show up in the world, to show off their membership, and to earn more say-so in the club. Showing often goes "over the top" and beyond certain anticipated or accepted boundaries, but frequently this susceptibility is not actualized until the phenomenon is interpreted and hyped up by a group of spectators. These are not "spect-actors" in the sense described by Augusto Boal (1979) in theater of the oppressed, for their participation is not always politically motivated, but these are active spectators whose passionate attentiveness is essential and integral to the show.

Showing off may attempt to demonstrate and define its message and also demonstrate that its members are superior. Audience members have authority in certain spheres, such as a presidential inauguration, the sale of a $130,000 royal hat, or an entire Olympic city built from Soviet ruins. Sometimes spectators understand these power plays, but other times they do not. We delve into how and why this occurs, asking why, for example, some instances of showing off or up become politically hotwired in public view (burqa wearing in France, ethical treatment of killer whales at SeaWorld), while others merely elicit that dismissive and indifferent shrug of "oh, meh, it's just a show" (excessive body makeup for ballroom dancing, ghost tours in Gettysburg).

IV. Embodied Excess and New Naturals: Many essays in the volume describe genres of embodied excess inherent in showing, while others consider the ways in which excess is, in fact, not the point at all, and sometimes not the intention. Performances analyzed in this volume are not "all show" and not always meant "for show," although that may be the result. Acknowledging how performances function as "metacommentaries," we also emphasize the work of the cultural context that affords performers, spectators, and consumers a particular agency. We suggest that showing imparts a unique kind of cultural power through directed intentionality and negotiation. Whether audiences interpret showing differently from theater depends, of course, on scale and the potential for spectator awe, as well as perceived goals. It depends on everyone's expectations of falseness or legitimacy.

Through the agency of producers and consumers, events that show off or up may become "generative" and provide opportunities for "emergence"—that is, new forms of thought, cultural meaning, and performance (see Barber 2003; Bauman 1977; Hallam and Ingold 2008). Showing off or up may be dialectic and dialogic—motivated by market and profit, but also by political maneuverings or opportunities of creative experimentation. There is potential for aesthetic and ideological transformation. The work done by showing may be unintentional, even unfortunate for its participants: elements combine for heightened thrusts of performance (mediated by press, show and competition deadlines, or self-produced), thus resulting in *new* combinations of cultural symbolism and social ideals. Categories of the so-called natural are hypermodified into something different and supposedly better—"pure" breeds are really newer breeds and they are considered a step above what was organically born in their premediated states. This "breeding," biological or cultural, applies as much to humans as to animals.

Authors are concerned with live, modified, and human-made mutations—physical, and conceptual. On a computer screen or monitor, we are keenly aware of these images and realities as airbrushed and photoshopped; we are not perturbed by the process or product. What were once invasions into private lives on reality television shows are no longer surprising or shocking. Digital mediation and rapid technological advances have changed the stakes and made showing and showing off/up into cultural phenomena we take for granted. However, when we experience these showings on a live social stage, surrounded by an invested audience, we are not able to treat the phenomena with the same ease or indifference. Showing something live can provoke swifter reaction and critical reflection. Showing may "hasten into being" (or "hasten out of it") (Aurelius 1907: 64; see also Kirshenblatt-Gimblett 2008) new typologies, values, and social ideals, but this hastening process may be confusing to audiences if they were not around for the historical precedent, and usually no one bothers to stop, look closely, and figure out the riddle. A show may be annual, but it is often ahistorical, experienced without perspective or context. James Fernandez coins the useful yet elusive phrase "edification by puzzlement" (1986, 172–87). He writes that extension, condensation, and revitalization are all products of puzzlement and that "what is brought together is more a stimulated dropping [of] the mediating image, the central term" in our social mythologies (184–85). To further explain, Fernandez quotes Polonius from Shakespeare's *Hamlet*: "By indirections find directions out" (172). In this volume, we examine the puzzling production phases of what society impatiently accepts as codified.

V. Hiding, Promising, and Teasing: Sometimes the work of cultural actors goes unseen and is not considered important until there are attempts to conceal or condemn it. Acts of showing are often powerful for what they do not reveal, at least not at first sight (and not without a fight). Unimaginable visions of ghosts and naked bodies are only granted the stage and spotlight when they are conspicuously hidden and when we are inspired or provoked to search or wait for them. Sometimes an audience does not allow the showing to remain private, even if the performers wish it so. It may be pulled out into the public, never again allowed to go unmarked in the margins. The show may not be "real," but it is not necessarily false. It is always potentially real, a possibly future real, a desired or detested real. In the process of our performative arguments about true or false and right or wrong, we tend to show off our (otherwise undisclosed) ideological and ethical shortcomings. Core values may be grudgingly exposed or misrepresented rather than positively accentuated. They may be shown as problematic and embarrassing, yet also, and sometimes for this reason, marketable or newsworthy, or both. Michael Herzfeld (1997) calls the national engagement with this embarrassment "cultural intimacy" and others write about different aspects of "public intimacy" in and as performance. Sociologist and media theorist Dick Hebdige explains how some segments of society, especially subcultures, are "hiding in the light," and examines how they form "in the space between surveillance and the evasion of surveillance, translat[ing] the fact of being under scrutiny into the pleasure of being watched" (1988, 35). Not all examples of hidden truths in this volume are subcultural, but Hebdige helps to theorize the phenomenon of this kind of ambivalent response—of wanting to remain unseen and unbothered, but also demanding attention or recognition. If certain showings (e.g., performances of racialization or economic elitism, for example) were more publicly shared, they might invite critical debate about controversial practices; however, protected by high-ticket prices and other techniques of limiting access, they too often remain exclusive and private, and thus, their practices go unquestioned.

INTERDISCIPLINARITY AND
THE IMPORTANCE OF ADVERBS

Showing as a concept cuts across disciplinary categories, allowing us to dig much deeper into this ubiquitous and influential mode of manipulating perception and behavior in society: it operates as an analytical frame through which to enlarge understandings of socially consequential dynamics of embodied performance and polemics of representation. When showing is considered as a verb and when "off" and "up" are added adverbially to the formula, authors are able to write from perspectives and through methodologies of various disciplines, as well as across different time periods and cultures. Showing off/up is a robust concept that guides our investigations.

Authors in this collection have departmental homes in theater, performance studies, American studies, Latin American studies, anthropology, women's studies, and English. They gather data through archival research, textual and visual analysis, ethnographic interview, and participant observation. This collection demonstrates how performance studies, in particular, operates analytically as a field of study, and authors attack a widespread and wide-ranging, but also specifically powerful, form of cultural performance— one that must be understood through an international paradigm. The "off" or "up" of showing is hardly just a phenomenon in the United States (although Americans are a particularly competitive bunch), nor is it solely a modern one, but we look at it from a twenty-first-century viewpoint. It is not just the moment of showing off/up itself, but also its reverberations through, on, and in spite of live bodies, and via the digitized and multiple stages of simultaneous commentary and affect.

In stressing the gerund verb and adverbs of "showing off and up," we play with and against more common uses, at least within theater studies, of *show* as a noun, as an artistic text, a dramaturgical project to be deconstructed and teased out. We are usefully provoked by rigorous interrogations of "theatricality" and its relationship to "antitheatricality," which have helped illuminate the foundational question, "what is theater?" Davis and

Postlewait (2003) identify antitheatricalists' condemnatory perception of theater's "take it or leave it attitude" about verification and their deep-seated anxiety that "while theatre reveals an excessive quality that is showy, deceptive, exaggerated, artificial, or affected, it simultaneously conceals or masks an inner emptiness, a deficiency or absence of that to which it refers" (5). That putative emptiness allows for theater to be dismissed as "just a show" at the same time that it threatens supposedly firmer realities and truer faiths. In so doing, of course, the show is far from empty. Contributors to this volume reveal how labels historically deployed as antitheatrical slurs—such as melodramatic, staged, playacting, putting on an act, making a scene, making a spectacle of oneself (Barish 1981, 1; cited in Davis and Postlewait 2003, 5)—point to the very dimensions that make showing off and up substantive and efficacious. If showing off is never an empty gesture, it is even less so when hotly condemned as "cultural banality" and "pseudo-culture" by states protecting national tradition in the face of globalization and tourism (in Cuba, for example, and cf. Adorno 1993). Such state-denounced "pseudo" performances are condemned in the Platonic tradition as devoid of cultural value or authenticity and are repressed as corrupt. Yet at the same time, they are widely *popular* and avidly discussed throughout the population. In their very categorization as "pseudo," they are imbued with discursive power and ideological sway. Showing in market economies and in theater markets may be a bit less concerned with cultural value or truth, but they are still driven by distinct systems of standards: high or low quality, integrity or immorality, powerful or shallow.

Anthropologists often seek out and analyze cultures that express some level of national or ethnic authenticity, but the word "showing" rarely enters the analytical picture since there is an expectation of inauthenticity implied by its use. "Expression" and "representation" are key terms in anthropology, with "spectacle" pertaining to large-scale expressions of national identity and political authority. Spectacle also refers to the competitive commercialism that is part and parcel of American culture. Anthropologist John MacAloon is most famous for his analysis of "meta-genre" and the relationship between spectacle, festival, game, and ritual, but in the end his analysis is still all about "something to be seen," grandeur, echelons, and awe, and how and when one genre encompasses another (1984). The core (or inner box) of the issue is "truth," claims MacAloon, but such a tiny cultural compartment can never be culturally, historically, or theoretically isolated. Spectacle is defined by its degree of publicity, says Don Handelman

(1990), who distinguishes spectacles from "public events," but admits they are most often both. Brazilian anthropologist Roberto DeMatta (1991, 71) uses carnival as an example and classically explains that such spectacles are when "a people reconstitutes itself" (see also Beeman 1993). Showing may be subversively carnivalesque (Bakhtin 1984)—a concept popularly used in analyses of postcolonial and subaltern movements—but more often than not, this is not the case. Showing is ordered and strategic. It is tamed and well rehearsed, like a wildcat in a circus tent or killer whale in a tank, even if it is performing or playing *as if* wild. It is carefully bred like a thoroughbred horse or specially trained to do skillful pseudo-natural feats. Inversions occur, certainly, but not chaotically (at least not intentionally). Subversiveness is inadvertent more often than held as a conceivable prospect.

The word "performance," like show, perceived as a noun, is ubiquitous in theater, performance studies, and more recently in the social sciences, but performance is given more academic respect than show, since it also includes "serious" and activist theater, as well as essential practices and politics of everyday life. Performance, initially defined in a myriad of ways by anthropologist Victor Turner and theater director Richard Schechner, has reached a point now where the term itself remains essential but also becomes increasingly empty, in part, because we rely on it too much. Turner's evolutionary and dramaturgical term *homo performans* (1988) or Diana Taylor's Spanish version, *performar* (2003), call for more recognition of its social action, but these words never took hold in scholarship or practice. Turner asserted that performance was "making, not faking" (1982, 93), and was instrumental in shifting perspectives about performance from *mimesis* (imitation) to *poiesis* (formation) (see also Conquergood 1995). Performance in its verb form, "to perform," is the pivotal force that conjoins imagination and real experience. "To show" animates that conjunction with particular exaggeration and intentionality. Showing is reflexive and self-performing yet highly critical and volatile. It bridges the spectacular and mundane, perhaps compelling our interest most strongly when the tensions in-between are at battle (cf. Palmer and Jankowiak 1996). Adverbially, to show off and up is to perform "Performatively!" with a capital P and an exclamation mark.

Showing is not always performative in the status-transforming sense, but it is never two-dimensional or just temporarily "transporting" either (see Schechner [2010, 117–50] on transforming versus transporting performer and spectator). The act may be one of becoming or asserting. It affects social status as performers and audience increasingly participate in the performance context at hand. People show up, they invest, they accumulate knowledge, they become experts or at least knowledgeable hobbyists, they join the club, they show off, they move up in ranks, they win competitions, they become popular, they begin to believe, others believe them, and they have the influence to change the vote. There is a process, following various phases of action and resulting in increasing intensities of transformative potential. Showing off and up is politically and "pluralistically" performative in that it may also create a *de*-construction of identities and a blasting of expectations ("my god, what a show") (see Butler 1997, 2015; Muñoz 1999; Johnson 2003). It is just as potentially performative when people *don't* show up (for example, congressmen absent from Netanyahu's 2015 speech at the White House, Western leaders absent from the Sochi Olympic Games, participants refusing to sing at a Haitian political rally).

Mark Ronson and Bruno Mars sing this line six times in a row in their current hit song, "Uptown Funk" (www.metrolyrics.com).

If you don't believe me, just watch (come on)
If you don't believe me, just watch (come on)
If you don't believe me, just watch (come on)
If you don't believe me, just watch (come on)
If you don't believe me, just watch (come on)
If you don't believe me, just watch (come on)

By the sixth time, listeners know the words and sing along. Audiences and society members want and need to be a part of the showing. The theatricality must be strong enough to *compel* us to watch ("come on"), to act and believe. Our attention must be seized. It must be repeated more than once and infiltrate our lives in some way, even if only as an obsession.

What does showing do for and mean to performers who are trying to show up others? What does it do to or for those being put on stage (sometimes against their will) and shown off? In this volume, examples of showing are revealed to be self-conscious performances with intention and awareness of an audience, acting within or against social structures. The actors involved may not necessarily have individual or collective agency in the particular dynamic of showing up or off (cf. Bourdieu 1977). Yet, we ask: How can the entire context of performance have agency? What constitutes individual or collective agency? Where exactly is the social power? Who is driving it and why should we care? And what happens next?

ORGANIZATION OF VOLUME

All of the contributed case studies address, in some way, a focused activity enlarged through the dynamics of showing off or up. Section I examines the relationship of "unnatural" spaces and assumptions of "natural" bodies. Essays focus upon the exhibition of animate bodies, including humans and animals. They consider the showing of spectacular bodies in the ring, tank, and cage, and on the floor as if they were in their natural states, but in fact their appearances and behaviors are coached and altered, judged on the new product instead of the one that may have entered the area. Although most of the activities described and theorized here enjoy frequent repetition, their acts of showing are comparatively brief, highly concentrated, hyped, and often competitive. Performances are transformed by performer, trainer, judge, and audiences. In each instance, the showing off of bodies—purebred horse and women riders, Latinized human dancing with un-Latina/o choreography, wildcat and trainer, and (human-)killer whale—takes place in seductively spectacular environments that conceal as much as they reveal.

This section opens with Kim Marra's article, which describes how the showing of beautiful horses and fashionable women at Madison Square Garden displays class privilege, whiteness, Anglophilia, women, and high fashion. Despite its spectacular show of horseflesh and feminine fashion, the horse show was and remains a legitimate sporting event. In contrast to the more familiar and ubiquitous purebred dog show that includes dogs and their "handlers," both the horses and the women who rode them were also spectacular athletes. While horse shows narrativize and commodify nonhuman and human animals alike, the tangible, though perhaps unintended, result of the National Horse Show was to create strong, skilled women. So stunning was their horsemanship (and, it must be admitted, their costumes) that they became the principal attraction in a genre of showing dominated by men. Commodity markets for both horses and fashionable women may have been the horse show's driving force, but they also helped to develop, celebrate, and highlight the complex relationship between horse and human. Marra features the showing—often for profit—of highly aestheticized, domestic(ated) nonhuman animals to coteries of prosperous, predominantly white consumers. She also argues that even as privileged women gained power through horse showing, the activity instantiated beauty standards for the two species in tandem that ultimately undercut human female agency.

Laurie Frederik continues to discuss constructions of the "natural" and the perceived relationship between wild and civilized in a human performance arena that is curiously similar to animal showing. She takes an auto-ethnographic look at how a competitive ballroom dancer becomes so-called Latin American through the manipulation of body, skin, and a set of technically modified rhythms and movements. She analyzes how attempts to show off a particular stereotyped ethnicity and gender are learned and achieved through dance training, physical grooming, and cultural coaching, and questions the supposedly de-ethnicized and de-racialized notion of "polish"—a transracial and homogenizing expectation that all dancing bodies must acquire. She demonstrates how humans, like animals, may be compelled to adapt to an ideal imposed by competitive standards in order to be successful in a highly competitive world of painted and artificially boosted bodies. Dancers are made brown, round, and long-lashed if they are not already, and even more so if they already are, in an unreflexive yet knotty sort of "playing Latino" (see Deloria 1998; Herrera 2015; cf. Bial 2005). One of the distinguishing characteristics of human animals is that we may dwell publicly in the make-believe and the "not-me" (but not not me) for as long as our audiences believe our masquerades to be real. We can learn to play wild, or, in other examples, the "handlers" of the wild. But such theater becomes problematic when minstrelsy—black, brown, yellow, or white, or even Russian— becomes part of the scenario. How does a performer define the ethical lines when choosing to succumb to, and what's more, perpetuate and show off championship standards and elitisms? Who is in charge and to what extent does the showed-off human have choice in the matter? Frederik's essay blurs the lines we assume are self-evident between a trainer and a performer and in cases where readers assume the performer to be the object on display, helplessly "captive" to an aesthetic standard.

Virginia Anderson and Jennifer Kokai consider the showing of undomesticated, "wild," and thus unpredictable nonhuman animals for the amusement of a largely undifferentiated mass audience. In these two essays, the interaction between animal wildness and human tamer is highlighted. Anderson uses Clyde Beatty's big cat show to reveal the dynamics of the human/nonhuman animal relationship in the context of the modern circus. Thousands of years after big cats were first separated from their wilderness roots for human entertainment, they continue to embody nature untamed, and this untamed performance is, in fact, maintained for a reason. In strength, size, splendor, and destructive force, the body of the wild cat surpasses the body of the human trainer who would subdue him—but here the trainer wins. In contrast to lions and Christians in the Roman Coliseum (where the big cat triumphs), the Beatty wild animal show attempts to confirm human mastery over the natural. To tame the big cat—at least to do so on stage—is to assert the superiority of civilization over wildness. The audience for this genre of showing is distinguished from horse shows. Although consumers of the wild animal show may learn something of the exotic animals displayed, pleasurable consumption of such a show requires no specialized knowledge or investment beyond the price of a ticket. The pleasure of watching a wild animal show derives from several sources: the strangeness and natural beauty of the animal, the display of human mastery, and—perhaps most important—the unpredictability of the outcome. Danger and the occurrence of violence, even death, is always a possibility: these possibilities are thrilling and attractive.

Assumptions of the "natural" face off again in Jenny Kokai's article about Shamu and the commodification of killer whales, and nowhere does the showing of a nonhuman animal conceal its purpose more than at SeaWorld. The situation of show orcas is both like and unlike the situation of show horses. In order to sell its product, SeaWorld promotes a line between nature and culture. The binary that academics strive to deconstruct is highlighted as one of their marketing points. Show producers must make the strange familiar (killer enemy to cuddly friend) by aestheticizing nature and romanticizing their nonhuman animals through fantastic linguistic and visual narratives of nature tamed and domesticated. Unfolding in both image and word, the SeaWorld spectacle of exuberant orcas communing like giant Flippers with delighted children seems designed to create a mythology of benign nature. Like beautiful horses and cuddly puppies, the orca is supposedly our friend—a mythology that prevailed until a seemingly affable whale named Tilikum grabbed his trainer, dragged her into his tank, and drowned her before a horrified crowd of onlookers. As Kokai points out, to show the orca as domesticated is deceptive. Not surprisingly, the trainer's death caused producers to change the show radically. If the original show humanized the whale, encouraging spectators to believe in a cuddly, gentle, and even affectionate orca, the new show distances spectators both physically and emotionally from Shamu. The new show, like the old, endeavors to pass itself off as an environmentally sound conservation project, but rather than selling an idea of benign nature, it now employs fountains, music, leaping whales, and dancing trainers.

In contrast to the niche events in Section I, the genres of showing described and theorized in Section II reach out to large audiences over longer, more dispersed periods of time. The authors ask: What did consumers actually receive—materially and ideologically—for the price of a ticket? The essays in this section analyze what might be termed "reality shows" that transpire in and around manufactured events, such as weddings and theater productions, as well as carnivalesque political protests and the festivalization of international sports championships. These are reality shows in that they tend to feature "real" people—amateur, as opposed to professional—performers who trouble conventional audience/performance relationships and thus thwart or rechannel the cultural work of showing. Marlis Schweitzer and Katie Johnson focus on showy objects that take the show beyond the event to audiences in wider arenas. Both draw on new materialist theories of things-in-motion that can script behavior in diverse contexts. Johnson considers the dynamic audience of immigrants, African Americans, white middle and working classes, and moneyed elites who encountered the large, brilliantly colored Strobridge lithographed posters advertising upcoming theatrical productions in the bustling civic space of Cincinnati's Fountain Square in the late nineteenth and early twentieth centuries. "Showing the show" with an image like Eliza fleeing the baying hounds in *Uncle Tom's Cabin* not only whets interest with a heightened visual summary of the action but invites spectators to "collide with pressing social issues" represented both on the poster and in the shared, embodied viewing experience. Schweitzer follows the Philip Treacy bow-shaped hat famously donned by Princess Beatrice at the 2011 Royal Wedding on its dizzying journey into the global mediasphere (cf. Arjun Appadurai's "mediascape") as its cultural work shifts from fashion showing off to Brechtian showing up. Schweitzer looks at how our contemporary display economy privileges excess and the ridiculous over "good taste." She traces the transnational circulation of "a silly thing" across performance mediums to show how serious opportunities emerge for political commentary as well as charitable action. Her article begins by identifying a supposedly static costume item, looks at how it shows up in interaction with a single human body, and then is shown off to billions of people as it virtually circulates on the Internet.

Chelsey Kivland writes of the importance of showing up when "hailed," manifested in a live rally of the Haitian people in order to summon an always ambiguous, undefined reality of "the state." The importance of a large number of bodies, physically amassed together, shows the state that the people have a voice. Organizers question how hardcore, or rather how committed, its citizenship is in its collective performances of resistance. Attending the rally, chanting slogans, singing and marching in carnivalesque processions are risks in their making public and aggravation of an assumption of socio-economic stability. The intended message may only be effectively translated as a political power when there are thunderous voices, loud music, stomping of feet, and swaying of bodies. The potential of the crowd and the possible mass displaying of the people in a specified local space are powerful, but never certain, and not always successful. The showing up of a crowd reveals discontent and disorder, "teetering just short of chaos." The goal is uproar and eventually social transformation, but neither participant nor performer is ever quite sure how it will turn out. Kivland quotes Michael Warner (2005, 114) to explain one of the strategies employed in Haiti: "Run it up a flagpole and see who salutes. Put on a show and see who shows up." But, Kivland continues, what if no one shows up?

Catherine Schuler closes the section by discussing performances of arrogance and the ultraspectacular "illusion" of the Olympics in Sochi as a performance of the modernization of the city and of Russia, or perhaps the masculine vigor of Vladimir Putin himself. Schuler describes the history of Sochi's turbulent development and of the spectacular multimediatized opening ceremonies in all their grandeur, allowing readers to understand the intensity of the experience as if sitting in a stadium seat instead of in front of a television. She analyzes "Sochi" as a type of Wagnerian *gesamtkunst-werk*—a total work of art—not just the spectacle of the opening ceremonies. Like most Olympics, it is not just about ultimate gold medal counts, but about the show of history and of future, and of the construction of memory in a brilliant (but perhaps desperate and doomed, given the political events to follow in Ukraine) international display. Putin's Olympics certainly went well beyond performance and into the realm we are defining here: showing off and up. A longtime researcher in and about Soviet socialism and Russia, Schuler notices the nuanced symbols of "progress" and "modernity" that many visitors take for granted, and in doing so demonstrates how Putin's competitive play with the West was, in some sense, lost in comparisons.

In Section III, showing moves from the private into the public sphere, from intimate to invited. Authors take a different turn on the topic in that their essays describe shows of the intangible, processual, promised, or forbidden, and performances are distinctly mediated. Context becomes an even more crucial marker in the experience. What is generated or "hastened into being" might be highly subjective experiences of the paranormal elicited by competitive guides in Gettysburg, or fervent nationalism in debates over repressing religious clothing in Paris, or tolerance of diverse sexual practices at an amateur porn festival in Seattle. A false start in the performance art scene thwarts contestation as it suspends both artwork and spectators in the process of showing and diverts critical engagement. The possibility of the unexpected is essential to these shows' success. Investigating how these examples push our definitions of showing, the authors question whether shows can be subtle, elusive, or not ever realized, and, if so, are they just as viscerally experienced as the others? The key elements highlighted in this section include potential and possibility, arousing the senses, and the spectatorial dynamics of the performance.

Elayne Oliphant dives into the contemporary and often violent issue of discrimination and misunderstanding of Muslim customs in countries where Christianity is the majority religion. Her example illustrates the explosive dangers of when showing off/up is forced out by hatred and fear. A symbolic costume, such as conservative clothing, turns into an international statement and divisive debate. Oliphant illustrates how fear of both the seen (burqa, performance of Islam) and unseen (individual woman), and the intolerance in the showing up of a politicized symbol has blatant and tragic consequences. She provides an analysis of female performance and passivity (or in this case, perhaps, power) and how it emerges in the politics of selectively displayed religious conventions—conventions not intended to be a display, but which are interpreted as showy and showing off in a new context. Oliphant examines the problematic relationships between religious and secular, intimate and secular, and political and secular through the wearing of the Muslim burqa in France. She uses Judith Butler and William Egginton to back up her argument that the burqa is performative in that it "affects or even produces what it purports merely to describe" (Butler 1990; Egginton 2003). By wearing a burqa, Muslim women hide their hair, faces, and bodies. The French (or generally "Western") interpretation of "hiding" is considered ostentatious showing when it is seen by those who associate the tradition with religious, and thus, political meaning. To hide is to provoke. To effectively assimilate into a new culture requires a lack of showing, or at least not showing a non-Catholic, nonmale, nonwhite, nonliterate, and nonpropertied identity. Oliphant explains that religion, or at least Islamic religion, is too "intimate" to be overtly performed in a secular society. In this case, adherence to modesty and religious tradition becomes a show by accident and was not ever meant to be one. Women in burqas are being inadvertently shown off—though sometimes nowadays also show themselves off—as a political issue and as heated subjects of debate. Men remain unmarked and unremarked upon.

In contrast to uninvited intrusions into the private lives of the burqa'd women in France, Joy Brooke Fairfield's example of the annual HUMP! film festival in Seattle, the "show-and-tell" could hardly be more explicit. Rather than the usual anonymous pornography consumed for the express purpose of arousal and profit, these films are made by and for a local amateur audience who sees them only at the festival and whose response to their neighbor's show is mitigated by the shared vulnerability of their own "tell" when their turn comes. The cultural work of this sharing of showing and telling, argues Fairfield, builds genuine community (benevolent versus malevolent intentions) and fosters a more open, democratic consciousness about usually hidden behavior that insidiously fuels hypocrisy and prejudice. Intimate moments between sexual partners are filmed and framed as "artsy" instead of pornographic, raising questions about the nature of audience receptions of "real" versus theatrical in particular performance spaces.

Robert Thompson and Daniel Sack discuss potentiality and promise and examine how this very uncertainty can constitute the show. Thompson describes how professional ghost tours in Gettysburg offer the possibility of an encounter, the chance of an experience, and it is in this anticipation that spectators are enticed to buy a ticket. "Will I see a ghost tonight"? Certainly you are more likely to see one if you are shown the way by experienced guides who lead you to the authentically haunted spaces, into the backstage nooks and crannies where ghosts are most likely to frequent. If you are lucky, and if you believe it is possible, the ghost may show itself to you. Sightings are most often individual, not collectively experienced, and are emergent only at the sites. Ghosts reveal themselves (maybe) in context and through a live encounter. This performance is three-dimensional and participants must walk down dark streets, duck into basements, and wave away spider webs. They hear the stories told in hushed tones and feel the chill of the evening air. They must go off track and off the beaten path to fully experience the show, whether or not the ghost shows up.

Like Thompson, Sack illustrates the potentiality of performance, but stresses that in a strip show (and also in performance art, or, more elusive still, the two genres superimposed), there may not be a conventional end or an end at all. The audience may experience a series of false starts and incomplete voyages. There may never be a conclusion. Will the stripper ever take off all her clothes? Will the audience be forever suspended in a performance that anticipates a naked body, but never, in the end, sees it? The promise of nakedness, although not necessarily shown, holds audience gazes through the arousal of their imaginations instead of visual actualization, just as the promise of the existence of ghosts is kept alive through stories told in real time and space. Sack shows us his argument textually as he carries the reader through rehearsals, back and forth into the then, now, and maybe. He questions the privileging of sight in showing, and reminds us that there are things we do not see and can never actually touch with our own two hands, but which we must still believe likely. In this way, Sack argues, the work is kept alive.

The essays in Section III address issues of invisibility and live imagery, as well as the performances of signs and symbols, some of which are offensive and threatening, others of which are passive and mainstream, and thus, uneventful. Showing something that is politically charged in one local context may go unnoticed and unmarked in another. Contrasting these essays with those in Sections I and II can enlarge our understanding of just what showing does in societies, and the ways in which shows turn into show*ing* in specific times, places, and ideological structures. Readers will learn to identify proven and potential strategies for social intervention, as they consider these examples of showing off and up and trying not to show. Essays in the collection examine the relationship of agency and structure, of autonomy and socialization in cultural production and consumption. Perhaps the variety of cases offered can help us interpret others that we now experience in a vast, bewildering spectrum. From John Travolta's sizzling disco dancing in *Saturday Night Fever* to Donald Trump's shocking campaign and White House victory, we are often stunned by the influential social sway of showing up and off, and recognize them as timeless categories as we attempt to comprehend our new reality and mobilize our society.

Our contemporary show world is ubiquitous. Many academics are fatigued by continually recited categorizations of performance, which is another reason why we wish to shine a light on these significant dimensions of showing that cut across various spectrums, graphs, and genre divisions. In examining how showing works on society and individuals, how it is culturally and historically specific, and why it is brushed off as "too showy" or "just a show," we emphasize the verb, the adverb, the efficacy, the active force that moves history, and, potentially, critical discourse with a useful form of analytical traction. Showing off and up also offers analytical potential for illuminating this digital and global world in which the power of showing is what travels, regardless of the content. What does the content do and how does it interact in other spheres once disembodied from the original mover?

We hope this collection will interest scholars across disciplines that strive to understand the underlying power of performance as theory and action. What exactly is the spark that ignites our topics of study? "Sometimes glass glitters more than diamonds because it has more to prove," writes Terry Pratchett in his book *The Truth* (2001). And in the end, it if glitters, catches our eye, and makes us pause, it need not be made of diamonds. A mirror ball (also known as disco ball after the 1970s) is an inexpensive assemblage of reflective prisms, giving off random flashes of light, depending on the speed it spins and the intensity of light projected upon it. A small mirror ball that fits in apartment or dorm room spaces may be purchased for just $20 at many suburban shopping malls. Professional party-organizers and nightclubs may choose the larger and higher quality units that cost between $100 and $1,000. The mirror ball is often the ultimate symbol of cultural kitsch, of decorations in nightclubs and at high school dances in American gymnasiums. Sometimes a mirror ball is hung in a church basement or community center event room. It makes us feel both nostalgic and excited. If noted in a nonevent context, our eyebrows raise and we wonder why on earth it's hanging there. We may feel skepticism. When hanging from a ceiling in bright daylight, it is a bit cheesy and pitiful, and, more often than not, simply unnoticed. But when plugged in under the right conditions, the mirror ball delivers an absolutely stunning effect—spinning bursts of multicolored lightning that transforms our worlds, even if just for a moment. We feel the reflective sparkles hit our face, flash in our eyes, and make us blink by its sudden appearance. It is mesmerizing, and it is this moment of transformation that we remember. However humble or grandiose the means of showing, the show off, the glitter, the sudden burst of disruption from what we expect, leaves an impression.

Sources

Adorno, Theodore. (1959) 1993. "Theory of Pseudo-Culture." *Telos* 95: 15–38.

Appadurai, Arjun. 1988. *The Social Life of Things: Commodities in Social Perspective.* Cambridge: Cambridge University Press.

Appadurai, Arjun. 1990. "Disjuncture and Difference in the Global Economy." *Public Culture* 2. 2 (Spring): 1–24.

Aurelius, Marcus. 1907 (1742). *The Meditations of the Emperor Marcus Aurelius Antonius.* London: Macmillan Publishers.

Austin, John Langshaw. (1962) 1975. *How to Do Things with Words.* Oxford: Oxford University Press.

Bakhtin, Mikhail. (1941) 1984. *Rabelais and His World.* Bloomington: Indiana University Press.

Barber, Karin. 2003. *The Generation of Plays: Yoruba Popular Life in Theatre.* Bloomington: Indiana University Press.

Barish, Jonas. 1981. *The Antitheatrical Prejudice.* Berkeley: University of California Press.

Barthes, Roland. (1957) 1972. *Mythologies.* London: Paladin.

Bauman, Richard. 1984 (1977). *Verbal Art as Performance.* Long Grove, IL: Waveland Press.

Bauman, Richard, and Charles Briggs. 1990. "Poetics and Performance as Critical Perspectives on Language and Social Life." *Annual Review of Anthropology* 19: 59–88.

Beeman, William. 1993. "The Anthropology of Theatre and Spectacle." *Annual Review of Anthropology* 22: 369–93.

Bernstein, Robin. 2009. "Dances with Things: Material Culture and the Performance of Race." *Social Text* 27.4, no. 101 (December): 67–94.

Berry, Joy. 1982. *Let's Talk about Showing Off.* Danbury, CT: Grolier.

Bial, Henry. 2005. *Acting Jewish: Negotiating Ethnicity on the American Stage and Screen.* Ann Arbor: University of Michigan Press.

Boal, Augusto. 1979. *Theatre of the Oppressed.* London: Pluto Press.

Bourdieu, Pierre. 1977. *Outline of a Theory of Practice.* Cambridge: Cambridge University Press.

Butler, Judith. 1988. "Performative Acts and Gender Constitution: An Essay in Phenomenology and Feminist Theory." *Theatre Journal* 40.4 (December): 519–31.

Butler, Judith. 1990. *Gender Trouble: Feminism and the Subversion of Identity.* New York: Routledge.

Butler, Judith. 1997. *Excitable Speech: A Politics of the Performative.* New York: Routledge.

Butler, Judith. 2015. *Notes Toward a Performative Theory of Assembly.* Cambridge: Harvard University Press.

Case, James. 2007. *Competition: The Birth of a New Science.* New York: Hill and Wang.

Conquergood, Dwight. 1985. "Performing as a Moral Act: Ethical Dimensions on the Ethnography of Performance." *Literature in Performance* 5.2: 1–12.

Conquergood, Dwight. 1986. "Performing Cultures: Ethnography, Epistemology, and Ethics." *Miteinander sprechen und handeln: Festschrift für Hellmut Geissner*: 55–66.

Conquergood, Dwight. 1989. "Poetics, Play, Process, and Power: The Performative Turn in Anthropology." *Text and Performance Quarterly* 9.1: 82–95.

Conquergood, Dwight. 1991. "Rethinking Ethnography: Towards a Critical Cultural Politics." *Communication Monographs* 58. 2: 179–94.

Conquergood, Dwight. 1995. "Of Caravans and Carnivals: Performance Studies in Motion." *Drama Review* 39.4: 137–41.

Davis, Tracy, and Thomas Postlewait, eds. 2003. *Theatricality*. Cambridge: Cambridge University Press.

Debord, Guy. (1967) 2000. *Society of the Spectacle*. Black and Red Press.

Deloria, Philip. 1998. *Playing Indian*. New Haven: Yale University Press.

DeMatta, Roberto. 1991. *Carnivals, Rogues, and Heroes: An Interpretation of the Brazilian Dilemma*. Translated by J. Drury. Notre Dame, IN: Notre Dame Press.

Diamond, Elin. 1996. *Performance and Cultural Politics*. Routledge.

Egginton, William. 2003. *How the World Became a Stage: Presence, Theatricality, and the Question of Modernity*. Albany: State University of New York Press.

Fernandez, James. 1986. *Persuasions and Performances: A Play of Tropes in Culture*. Bloomington: Indiana University Press.

Fischer-Lichte, Erika. 1997. *The Show and the Gaze of Theatre: A European Perspective*. Iowa City: University of Iowa Press.

Goffman, Erving. 1959. *The Presentation of Self in Everyday Life*. Anchor Books.

Hallam, Tim, and Elizabeth Ingold, eds. 2008. *Creativity and Cultural Improvisation*. Bloomsbury Academic Press.

Handelman, Don. 1990. *Models and Mirrors: Towards an Anthropology of Public Events*. Cambridge: Cambridge University Press.

Hebdige, Dick. 1988. *Hiding in the Light: On Images and Things*. New York: Routledge.

Herrera, Brian Eugenio. 2015. *Latin Numbers: Playing Latino in Twentieth Century U.S. Popular Performance*. Ann Arbor: University of Michigan Press.

Herzfeld, Michael. 2005. *Social Poetics in the Nation-State*. Routledge.

Herzfeld, Michael. 1997. *Cultural Intimacy: Social Poetics and the Real Life of States, Societies, and Institutions*. New York: Routledge.

Johnson, E. Patrick, ed. 2013. *Cultural Struggles: Performance, Ethnography, Praxis (Dwight Conquergood)*. Ann Arbor: University of Michigan Press.

Kapchan, Deborah A. 1995. "Performance." *Journal of American Folklore* 108(430).

Kirshenblatt-Gimblett, Barbara, and Jonathan Karp, eds. 2008. *The Art of Being Jewish in Modern Times*. Philadelphia: University of Pennsylvania Press.

MacAloon, John J. 1984. "Olympic Games and the theory of spectacle in modern societies." *Rite, Drama, Festival, Spectacle: Rehearsals toward a theory of cultural performance* 24180 (1984). Philadelphia: Institute for the Study of Human Issues.

Muñoz, José. 1999. *Disidentifications: Queers of Color and the Politics of Performance.* Minneapolis: University of Minnesota Press.

Palmer, Gary B. and William R. Jankowiak. "Performance and Imagination: Toward an Anthropology of the Spectacular and the Mundane" *Cultural Anthropology* 11. 2: 225–58.

Phelan, Peggy. 1993. *Unmarked: The Politics of Performance.* Routledge.

Pratchett, Terry. 2001. *The Truth.* Harper Torch Press.

Reinelt, Janelle G., and Joseph R. Roach, eds. 1992. *Critical Theory and Performance.* Ann Arbor: University of Michigan Press.

Schechner, Richard. 2010. "Performers and Spectators Transported and Transformed." In *Between Theater and Anthropology, Richard Schechner.* Philadelphia: University of Pennsylvania Press.

Schechner, Richard. 2013. *Introduction to Performance Studies.* 3rd ed. Routledge.

Singer, Milton. 1972. *When a Great Tradition Modernizes.* London: Pall Mall.

Sofer, Andrew. 2009. "How to Do Things with Demons: Conjuring Performatives in Dr. Faustus." *Theatre Journal* 61, no. 1: 1–21.

Tait, Peta. 2012. *Wild and Dangerous Performances: Animals, Emotions, Circus.* Palgrave.

Taylor, Diana. 2003. *The Archive and the Repertoire: Performing Cultural Memory in the Americas.* Durham, NC: Duke University Press.

Turner, Victor. 1982. *From Ritual to Theatre.* New York: PAJ Publications.

Turner, Victor. 1988. *The Anthropology of Performance.* PAJ Books.

Warner, Michael. 2005. *Publics and Counterpublics.* Cambridge MS: Zone Books and MIT Press.

Žižek, Slavoj. 2002. "Big Brother, or the Triumph of the Gaze over the Eye." In *CTRL (SPACE): Rhetorics of Surveillance from Bentham to Big Brother*, eds. Thomas Y. Levin, Ursula Frohne, and Peter Weibel, 224–27. Karlsruhe: ZKM.

Žižek, Slavoj. 2008. "The Spectator's Malevolent Neutrality." Public lecture, June 8. http://www.youtube.com/watch?v=4QhRxhzVU7Y

SECTION I

Race and Breed
Showing Off "Natural Bodies"

Focusing on the exhibition of animate bodies, human and animal, authors in this section examine relationships between constructed, "unnatural" spaces and the purportedly "natural" bodies that perform in them. Their essays consider the showing of spectacular bodies in the ring, tank, and cage, and on the floor as if they were in their natural states, but in fact their appearances and behaviors are coached and altered, judged on the new product instead of the one that may have entered the area. Although most of the activities described and theorized here enjoy frequent repetition, their acts of showing are comparatively brief, highly concentrated, hyped, and often competitive. The presence in the space of performer, trainer, judge, and audience transforms the performance. In each instance, the showing off of bodies—sidesaddled equestriennes and purebred horses, Latinized human dancing, wildcat and trainer, and killer (of human trainers) whale—takes place in seductively spectacular environments that conceal as much as they reveal. Some authors focus on animal performances, but even these essays are really about the humans who reshape their animal subjects to show off. What, we ask, is being shown through the bodies in question? Why are horses, lions, or killer whales symbolically significant in each particular case? How do the actions of human trainers, riders, and coaches upstage their efforts? And who or what is being tamed or liberated?

CHAPTER I

Saddle Sensations and Female Equestrian Prowess at the National Horse Show

Kim Marra

Although horse showing has become a coterie sport now largely ignored in mainstream American culture, the National Horse Show at Madison Square Garden, from its 1883 founding through World War I, commanded vast public attention and influence in New York and across the country as both a social and a sporting event.[1] At that time when horses still powered key parts of the economy, a variety of horsey spectacles were popular in the city, but unlike, for example, Buffalo Bill's Wild West Show or Barnum's Circus, which also played at Madison Square Garden, the National Horse Show offered competition as well as entertainment. Dubbed "The Great Anglo-American Show" by *Life Magazine*, it also exclusively featured formal English-style riding (as opposed to Western cowboy style or circus acrobatics) and displays of aristocratic Anglophile culture and thus gained special ascendancy amid the era's WASP anxieties about increasing immigration from southern and eastern Europe.[2] To finance the venture, a group of prominent, sporting-minded businessmen with names like Vanderbilt, Morgan, Lorillard, Cassatt, and Cheever established the National Horse Show Association of America (NHSA) whose original 920 paying members formed the basis of Louis Keller's first *New York Social Register* in 1887.[3] Modeled on England's prestigious Islington Horse Show and managed by former Westminster Kennel Club Show superintendent Charles Lincoln,

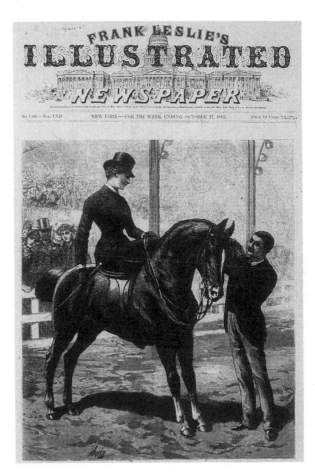

Fig 1.1. "New York City.—The Great Sensational Horse-Show at Madison Square Garden—Decorating a Winner." (Cover of *Frank Leslie's Illustrated Newspaper*, October 27, 1883.)

the event proved immediately successful and soon was installed as an annual fixture in the social calendar.[4] Running for a week in late October or early November just prior to the opening of the opera, the National Horse Show (called simply "the National" or "the Garden") marked the start of the "indoor season" when the affluent returned to the city from their summer estates, and amusement moved inside. Within a decade of the show's founding, the number of competitors grew from 350 to 1,300, and nightly attendance, even in the early years, reached 15,000–20,000. Horses remained at the center of the spectacle, but people were equally on display at the Garden as leading trends in human along with equine appearance and behavior were generated on the arena floor and in surrounding stands. Those trends were quickly disseminated by the major newspapers and magazines, many of which circulated nationally, that covered "Horse Show Week."

Although the event was founded and run by men, and men in these decades still dominated the competition, women emerged as the leading iconic figures of the show. This became vividly apparent in *Frank Leslie's Illustrated Newspaper* coverage in two full-page pictorials published on October 27, 1883, the day after the first Horse Show Week ended. In the first image (fig. 1.1), on the front page, an elegantly attired Anglo lady rider sits sidesaddle on a beautifully crested, highly bred horse in the center of the ring after putting the flashy equine through its winning paces. With her seat pressed firmly in the saddle, she dexterously taps her mount on the haunch with her whip, the signal for the horse to stand squarely on spread legs in proper show pose to receive their blue ribbon. At the rail, a well-dressed gentleman wearing a top hat stands with his right forearm cocked, fingers clasping his cigar, while he gazes at the sensuous curves of the rider raised to eye level over the shapely form of the horse. A finely bonneted woman, presumably his wife, leans into him, expressing concern and placing her gloved right hand over the rail as though to assert her own interest in the scene. On his other side, a younger woman, perhaps his daughter, also fashionably attired, beholds the victorious pair with more than furtive curiosity and the beginnings of a smile. In the second illustration (fig. 1.2), placed opposite a brief article inside the newspaper, another Anglo lady riding aside boldly takes a hurdle on a strapping Thoroughbred, an English breed considered the pinnacle of equine conformation and the most athletic of horses, as fashionable throngs look on from the stands and gentleman experts moving along the rail stop in their tracks wondering at her feat. These equestriennes immediately capture audience attention as the "showiest" riders even though female competitors as of yet only occupied a relatively small portion of the program. Titillating audiences of both sexes, they signal women's arrival into a vast public arena as both skilled athletes in a dangerous sport and arresting beauties at a time when boldness and sensuality in the saddle portended potentially alarming boldness in other areas.

Such demonstrations of female equestrian prowess gain social impact in the peculiar atmosphere of authorized scrutiny and comparison of physical specimens by audiences and experts that the horse show fosters, as evoked in the smaller inset pictures in the second illustration. "Lower" breeds occupy the small drawings, framing the equestrienne and setting off her Thoroughbred's stature and refinement by contrast—above her, the heavy work-

Fig. 1. 2. "New York City.—The National Horse-Show at Madison Square Garden, October 22d—26th," depicting various show scenes. (In *Frank Leslie's Illustrated Newspaper*, October 27, 1883, p. 152.)

horse unhappily tolerating the intrusive examination by six men trying to ascertain his age, muscle tone, and soundness, and below, the pony and the donkey being visited by children. While the men and boys assess the animals' characteristics and test their functionality, the girls reach for their soft equine noses, seeking to make friends. Albeit steeped in the era's sexism, the drawing suggests the historical reality of women forging a different kind of human/equine relationship, one involving a certain empathy and identification based in shared attributes relative to the men who ran the show.

Fancy, expensively equipped horses, along with beautiful, expensively clad women, emerged not only as objects of admiration but also as prime trophies of men's financial and social success. The prize attributes and modes of showing them off developed for the two species in tandem, the one informing the other, as the National "hastened into being" ideal types of horses and humans, especially female humans.[5] This grand institution of showing fostered "good breeding" through both visual display and embodied acts of cross-species mingling, promenading, and, most titillatingly, virtuosic female equestrianism. In and out of the saddle, women competitively showed off their mastery of horseflesh and high fashion, which had decidedly mixed results for their agency: on the one hand, heightened commodification and a more restrictive, racially marked beauty standard; on the other, thrilling empowerment from such public communion with dazzling, thousand-pound equine superathletes felt most directly by the lady riders in the arena but experienced vicariously by the growing numbers of their aspiring sister equestriennes gowned up for evenings in the stands. Illuminating these dynamics of showing at the National requires first historicizing women's riding and mapping the Garden as a unique, multifaceted venue for fashioning humans and equines, and then analyzing female equestrian performance and its ambivalent effects as women increasingly rivaled men in the arts of horsemanship. The hugely public interplay of women's equine-inflected commodification and empowerment at the Garden in these years continued to inform dominant American cultural standards of women's appearance and deportment long after horses faded from the urban landscape and the National Horse Show lost its prominence on the social calendar.

SHOWING UP ON HORSEBACK

The initial appeal of women's riding at the show derived partly from its relative novelty as well as its significance as a manifestation of high-class leisure. Following the Civil War, the growth of the railroad and horse-drawn public transportation made riding in general less of a necessity and more of a sporting pursuit, but whereas riding for sport had been the prerogative of moneyed men for centuries, women only began taking to the saddle in large numbers in the United States in the second half of the nineteenth century. As the urban middle and upper classes acquired more wealth from industrialization and time to spend on leisure, concerns about the health risks of inactive, affluent lifestyles increased. Physicians and advice columnists authorized a burgeoning physical culture movement and singled out certain sports as particularly beneficial to women for both well-being and desirability. "It is not enough," intoned *Harper's Bazaar*'s "For the Ugly Girls" column, "that [girls] know how to dance languidly, and carry themselves in company. To distinguish herself, a young belle must know how to row, swim, skate, ride, and even shoot."[6] Golf was also acceptable; however, she should avoid exercise with heavy weights and "games of strife," such as basketball or hockey.[7] Following the 1885 invention of the bicycle, both men and women avidly took up cycling or "wheeling," but horseback riding, specifically formal English equestrianism, retained a privileged position in the hierarchy of recommended women's sports. *Harper's* asserted: " mothers who make no effort to encourage thoughtless daughters into at least an attempt at riding are overlooking one of the corner-stones of a vigorous constitution. . . . there is really nothing which excels, or even equals, horseback riding. . . . The girl who rides enjoys life and becomes the mother of beautiful children."[8] More than other sports, riding not only fostered good health for reproductive purposes but strengthened abdominal muscles and straightened the back for what was termed a "high-bred" self-carriage—"this noble set of head, this lance-like figure, this easy play of limb"—that was emerging as the physical ideal of modern WASP American femininity.[9]

Properly taught, controlled riding, as opposed to hoydenish cavorting around the countryside, also inculcated desirable character traits. The strict discipline of formal English equestrianism supposedly contained even as it displayed the unavoidably sensual, pulsing up-and-down motion of the woman's body on the horse. For some observers and practitioners, that very containment, exacerbated by corseting and sidesaddle seating, may have made the performance all the more arousing.[10] Still the belief prevailed that as riding disciplined the horse's body, so was the lady rider's body disciplined, and, through her body, her mind; since leading medical authorities understood women's emotions to be deeply embodied (hence frequent diagnoses of "hysteria" meaning literally "that which proceeds from the uterus"), they believed that this bodily discipline could produce mental health conducive to domestic virtue.[11] The National Horse Show would become the largest venue where proper riding, with all of its putative body/mind benefits for women, was exemplified and displayed.

Supporting and feeding into that annual display, an entire infrastructure of riding schools, clubs, and saddlery shops developed that has now almost completely vanished from Manhattan. An illustration appearing in *Leslie's* in 1891 entitled "In the Riding School—The First Lesson" (fig. 1.3) depicts a class of mainly female pupils taking one-on-one instruction from male teachers. The large mirror on the back wall, which helped instill correct form and appearance, shows the self-reflexive performativity of the pursuit. By this time, according to *Harper's Bazaar*, the numbers of riding schools in Manhattan had risen into the dozens.[12] The biggest, William Durland's Riding Academy at Columbus Circle (formerly Grand Circle), featured a large indoor arena and stabling for 300 horses. When it opened in 1887 with a huge evening gala, the *New York Times* commented on the 3,000 people in attendance: "The fact that fully half of those present were ladies showed how popular school riding has become in this city."[13] Pupils took instruction indoors or out on rides in the park.[14] These urban riding schools supplied some of the competitors and many informed and engaged spectators for the National Horse Show. Other competitors and fans came into town from more distant equestrian communities by train.

In this period, knowledge and experience of riding and horses moved across social strata, further widening interest in the show. At the top, membership in the exclusive Gentlemen's Riding Club, whose name had to be changed to the New York Riding Club four years after its 1883 founding to accommodate the increasing numbers of women using the facility, was limited by a hefty entrance fee as well as annual dues and the cost of upkeep for one's horse.[15] At the public riding schools like Durland's, however, one could ride much more economically, even foregoing the cost of horse ownership and just paying for rides or lessons on school horses.[16] These options made the sport more accessible for the swelling numbers of middle-class patrons. And of course one did not have to ride at all to desire to do so or to be interested in horses; for most people, they were an unavoidable part of daily life in the city as they labored to provide the motive force for streetcars, hansom cabs, mills, winches and other machinery for heavy construction, fire wagons, trash collection, funeral biers, freight delivery from ports and rail depots, and other services. In 1900 when 1.85 million humans lived on Manhattan, the island was also home to 130,000 equines.[17] Along with the constant sight of horses working in the streets, members of all classes could consume the frequent spectacle of the affluent riding their flashy saddle horses and driving their carriages in Central Park, especially in the late afternoons and on Sundays. As *Outing Magazine* observed, "All that is loveliest in womankind, all that men envy most in their fellow man, all that is best in horseflesh is represented" against an urban landscape already saturated with horses.[18]

Fig 1.3. "In the Riding School—The First Lesson." In *Frank Leslie's Illustrated Newspaper*, June 13, 1891, p. 317.

THE GARDEN AS SHOW PLACE

The National Horse Show brought that spectacle into a heightened and sustained focus facilitated by the unique layout and spectatorial dynamics of the Garden as a venue. The key features were established in the original building for the National's first seven years and then elaborated upon in the famed Garden II designed by Stanford White where the show played from 1890 to 1920 and reached its apogee of belle époque elegance. *Harper's Weekly* ran an illustration of the building when it was still under construction that offers detailed views of the exterior and interior (see fig. 1.4). At the center where the show horses were exhibited was a large oval 75 feet wide by 200 feet long covered in a layer several inches thick of tanbark footing (a substance akin to mulch composed of bark shavings left over after the tannins were extracted for leather tanning).[19] The track encircling the oval became, in the completed Garden II, the famed promenade, a smooth-surfaced walkway twenty feet wide (enlarged from sixteen feet in the original Garden) to accommodate attendees making what the *New York Times* aptly called "tours of inspection."[20] A post and board fence separated the promenade from the tanbark arena (see fig. 1.5).

Of the throngs moving around the promenade, only those spectators pressed two and three rows deep against the rail could see the action in the arena; the others were strolling to be seen and to see the prominent socialites in the raised boxes around the perimeter. For the full show experience, it was just as important for spectators to have a guide to the boxes as a catalogue of the horses. The *New York Times* obligingly printed a list of the star box holders and their locations in the arena with the prestige of various box positions duly noted.[21] *The Rider and Driver: An Illustrated Weekly Journal of Society and the Horse*, a magazine for urbane equine aficionados, not only chronicled the equestrian competition but provided a detailed floor plan of the boxes, their prices, and their holders' names for readers to take to the show.[22] Sold at private auction for NHSA members, boxes went for prices as high as $550 for the week. Premium reserved seats directly behind the boxes sold for $27–$30 apiece for the week. Less wealthy patrons could buy reserved seats further back for $1.50–$3.00 apiece per day, while general admission for unreserved seats in the upper galleries was $1.00 or less; in at least one year, 1895, admission was offered to those galleries for free.[23] All of the 15,000–20,000 people admitted on a given day could walk the promenade. The National Horse Show truly was "an institution for the dissemination of exclusiveness among the masses," which made active spectatorship and at least visual consumption of that exclusiveness accessible to all.[24]

The NHSA founders who presided over this massive staging declared that their purpose was "[t]o give exhibitions of horses . . . on about the same plan as that pursued at bench shows [e.g., of the Westminster Kennel Club], where the beauty and points of horses, aside from their speed, is [*sic*] to count. It is proposed to exhibit trotters, runners, jumpers, saddle horses, cobs, coach horses, and driving, working, and breeding horses of every description."[25] Bringing all these different types of horses under one roof to be judged was meant to educate people as to the distinguishing features of one type versus another as well as to the optimum features of each particular type, with the larger goal of improving both breed quality and horse management. The stakes for that education went far beyond the horses themselves. As *Rider and Driver* put it in 1895 on the eve of the thirteenth National Horse Show: "What have the Horse Shows taught us? First and foremost, they have created within us a sense of the fitness of things. . . . In place of wild disorder and taste, and rank disregard of what in poetry

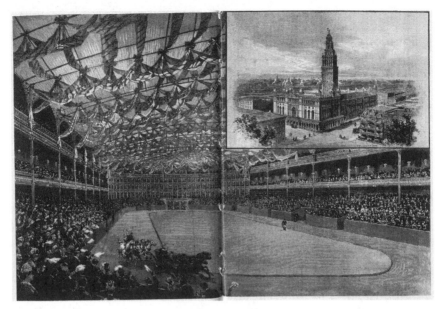

Fig. 1.4. "The New Madison Square Garden Building. In course of construction." (*Harper's Weekly*, April 12, 1890.)

Fig. 1.5. "The Horse Show as Viewed by the Daily Press." (*Rider and Driver* 10, no. 12 [November 16, 1895], 9.)

and rhetoric, in fine arts and in music, and in dramatic composition, would be called the unities, we now have a proper regard for perfection and propriety."[26] Through proper display and judgment of this crucial animal, the horse, American civilization was also being advanced, a nationalistic message reinforced by the hundreds of yards of red and white and blue bunting festooning the Garden rafters.

As to more specific material operations of the "fitness of things," Thorstein Veblen's *Theory of the Leisure Class* (1899), written at the Horse Show's height, is highly instructive. It is difficult to determine whether Veblen ever attended the National Horse Show in Madison Square Garden, but certainly, on what was arguably the largest scale possible in the nation's cultural capital at the time, it exemplified his thesis: "In order to gain and to hold the esteem of men, it is not sufficient merely to possess wealth or power. The wealth or power must be put in evidence, for esteem is awarded only on evidence."[27] Few commodities were as manifestly expensive and visibly powerful as the superior, immaculately groomed, shimmering equines shown at the Garden. Moreover, while some of the breeds on display could pull plows and commercial transport vehicles, most of the show animals were intended for the less useful tasks of pulling private expensive carriages or for riding and thus fit Veblen's key criterion for conspicuous consumption as being "an expenditure of superfluities."[28] Each show horse was listed in the program by its name and the name of its exhibitor or owner, who was usually distinct from the person actually handling or riding the horse in the arena, most often a groom or other paid professional. The owner was usually a box holder conspicuously seated to bask in the reflected glory of his impressive equine. Not every horse shown at the Garden was for sale, but many were, and many spectators came to buy. On the last morning of the show, time was allotted in the arena for the display of equines available for purchase. If the horse placed or especially if it won the competition, its reflected glory—and its price—increased. "Nothing stimulates the value of horseflesh so greatly as horse shows," asserted *Rider and Driver*, and the National Horse Show at Madison Garden remained the marquee venue even as it spawned dozens of similarly organized smaller shows across the country.[29]

From the beginning, the NHSA founders showed off their women as well as their prize equines at the Garden. As the *New York Morning World* reported for the show's opening day, October 22, 1883: "Members of the association, resplendent in silver badges of membership and committee badges, will lead their lady friends around the inclosure [sic] and talk horse and weights to them as though the ladies understood it all."[30] Promenaded on her wealthy man's arm, the lady had to be extravagantly dressed, for, as Veblen noted, "it [is] the woman's function in an especial degree to put in evidence her household's ability to pay."[31] Both on the promenade and in the boxes, the performative display of the ladies gave the National Horse Show its alter ego as "the great clothes exhibition of the year."[32] To some observers, the National proved to be even more a "clothes-horse show" than a horse show. As a New York fashion columnist observed in 1897, "It has really become an established custom that Horse Show Week is the date for winter styles to make their appearance, and the costumes and hats that are seen there are indications of what we are to wear. . . . as a clothes show, it is without rival, and many new points as to the cut of skirts, the trimming of waists, and the new colors are to be found each day."[33] Fashion designers, dressmakers, and their clientele rushed to get their new wardrobes ready for Horse Show Week. No ribbons and trophies were awarded to the clothes horses, but prizes were won in the form of increased social standing, and, for the patriarchs' daughters, desirability on the marriage market; the Horse Show stimulated the value of both prize equines and eligible debutantes, as it affirmed the continuing good breeding and fashionability of the monied men and their families.[34]

Juxtaposing those gorgeous seasonal clothes with the uniquely gorgeous show animals in the special layout of the Garden proved highly propitious for fashion and active spectatorship that spurred consumption. Even the acerbic Veblen contended that although beauty is attributed to other non-industrial creatures (e.g., cats, dogs, and parrots), animal beauty is greatest in the horse whose Classical form was inscribed along with that of the human in foundational Western artworks such as the Parthenon frieze.[35] When walking the promenade, fashionable ladies may not have been able to see the horses unless they pressed for a spot on the rail, but spectators in the boxes and stands saw the ladies on the promenade against the equine spectacle. Horses—especially well-groomed, well-fleshed, well-appointed show horses—are large and commanding enough to be apprehended in some detail even from a distance in a large arena. The arresting beauty of one species accentuated that of the other. Looking at these fine specimens was meant to induce buying. Sixty of the first ninety pages of the three hundred-page *Official Catalogue* for the 1897 Annual Horse Show, for example, are devoted to ads for the latest in sartorial finery, equipage, and other swank lifestyle accoutrements. With so many debutantes showing on the promenade (aka "the Clothes Walk"[36]), the wedding industry was also well represented in the catalogue.[37] More actively consuming spectators on "tours of inspection" were at liberty to walk by and look closely at other spectators as well as equine competitors, for that is what the whole Garden experience invited. The layout put passersby on the promenade in closer and more lingering proximity to each other, and to social lions seated in their boxes decked out in the latest fashions, than was generally possible at other venues, such as theaters.

WOMEN'S FASHIONABLE SHOW OF PASSIONATE EQUESTRIANISM

Even as some commentators (mostly male) continually asserted that women attended the National more for the clothes than the equines, insisting that women did not really know about horses and weren't interested in them, the two passions—fashion and equestrianism—became mutually reinforcing for a growing number of women. Perhaps most obviously, the exercise of riding helped women look better in their clothes. But there were more complex reinforcements as well. The 1895 Horse Show issue of *Rider and Driver* featured over its "Notes for Women" column a drawing (fig. 1.6) entitled "Two Hearts that Beat as One" depicting in two intertwined panels a fancy horse in harness and a lady in haute couture.[38] The drawing connotes strong sympathy and identification between the two: both are valued in the patriarchal economy for their beauty and "breeding"; both are served by others but are still themselves cast in a subservient role; both are wearing trappings of what Veblen called "vicarious leisure," leisure performed "for the behoof [*sic* (!)] of the reputability of the primary or legitimate leisure class," that is, "the economically free and self-directed head of the establishment," that is, the male head of household.[39] The horse's harness and docked tail equate to the woman's ensemble, especially, to use Veblen's terms, "the high heel, the skirt, the impracticable bonnet, the corset," all of which restrict natural movement, even breathing, limit productive "vulgar" labor, and cause discomfort, which supposedly guarantees that the leisure is "vicarious," that is, performed for someone else's pleasure.[40] Yet through horses as well as fashion, women would find multiple ways to make their performance of this leisure more than "vicarious" as they began deriving their own pleasure and power from these activities as expert consumers and practitioners.

Fig, 1.6. "Two Hearts Beat as One." (In "Notes for a Woman by a Woman," *Rider and Driver* 10, no. 13 [November 23, 1895], 21.)

Much of that pleasure and power women would take still at the expense of horses, but horses also benefited from a sympathy that had to be based on more than certain shared circumstances in the economic structure. Generally smaller in stature than men and conditioned as nurturers rather than aggressors, women learned to exercise their will through greater patience and kindness. This approach harmonized with changes in training methods since the Renaissance from more severe physical punishment and ostentatious shows of dominance to a reward-based system more in concert with the rising interest in animal protection and welfare.[41] Women often achieved better communication and developed more companionate relationships with horses than their male contemporaries did. As depicted in figure 1.3, "In the Riding School—The First Lesson," women acquired equestrian knowledge from men and then pursued it on their own to better and better effect. The "gentler sex" soon spectacularly rivaled and even surpassed men at implementing the newer, gentler methods on the National Horse Show stage.

With horses as with fashion, women gained pleasure and a certain economic and cultural power through intense acquisition of expertise. Steeped in tradition and ceremony, formal English riding and carriage driving demanded a preoccupation with precise detail—the proper equipment, exact fit of its myriad components, highly refined mastery of technique—similar to that required in mastering the art of finding and wearing suitable haute couture. Just as there were articles in women's magazines such as *Godey's*

about what to look for in fashion, so there were articles in those same magazines about what to watch for in a lady's horse and in women's riding and
driving.[42] Women's participation in the sport was sufficient by 1884 to occasion the publication of *The American Horsewoman* by Elizabeth Platt
Karr, the first book-length equestrian manual written by and for American
women.[43] Well-done English equestrianism, like fine fashion, both makes
a powerful overall impression and works as a subtle art that compels close
scrutiny. Having initially learned from men, women proceeded to produce
and consume their own knowledge of how to practice these arts themselves
and scrutinize others doing so. They took their existing knowledge of horses
and fashion into Madison Square Garden and made it their business to acquire more "hippic wisdom" as well as sartorial acumen during Horse Show
Week. With a slight turn of her head, the lady standing to see above the
social conversation in her box and looking through her lorgnette in figure
1.7 can shift her gaze back and forth between the competitors in the ring and
the fashion plates moving along the promenade below, extracting a world of
information from each. Moreover, she is both looking and performing looking, fashionably showing off how to look for the benefit of other spectators.
Writing about the Horse Show in her "Outdoor Woman" column for *Harper's Bazaar*, Adelia K. Brainerd reported that she "saw numerous other attentive pairs of eyes, and many gloved hands busily inscribing notes."[44] Space
for these jottings was conveniently provided under the printed header "Visitor's Notes" in the right-hand margins of the 160 catalogue pages devoted
to detailed listings of individual equine entries. Although official judging
remained exclusively the province of men at the Garden until 1916, women
were rapidly becoming adept performers of expertise and discerning judges
of horseflesh as well as fashion in these early decades.[45]

For numerous female spectators, it was not sufficient to view the horses
from a distance. In a November 1895 installment of a regular fictional column in *Harper's Bazaar*, "Mrs. Wouter Van Twiller Saturdays," depicting the
various activities of a circle of fashionable New York ladies, the female narra-
tor writes of attending the Horse Show with Miss Van Auken and foregoing
their usual perch in the boxes:

We have tried a new way of going this time—in with the rabble that
buys no seats, and stands close pressed against the railing enclosing the
tan-bark ring—as near to the horses, in fact, as it is possible to be. You
can get all the play of their splendid muscles while standing there, the

Fig. 1.7. "An Evening at the Horse Show, Madison Square Garden, New York." (*Harper's Weekly*, November 19, 1892.)

fine fire in the eye as one more spirited than another races about the ring, his head within a foot of your own as he dashes past. You see the splendid running of the grooms. They and the superb unharnessed stallions with whom they run side by side are as stunning as any bit from a Greek frieze.[46]

As fascinating as they found the horses in the ring, these ladies, like many of their real lady contemporaries, also relished going down to the lower level to visit the horses in the stabling area where they could stroke their silky coats, sidle up to a Mrs. William C. Whitney or a Mrs. Potter Palmer in a gorgeous gown also stroking favored steeds, maybe steal a close peek at her fine cape or jewelry, and ply the grooms for intimate details about their charges.[47] The *New York Times* reported that at the 1888 National: "The ladies were not the least afraid of the horses and boldly invaded the boxes. They did not hesitate to request the grooms to remove the blankets and when this was done they discussed the several points of the horses with an earnestness and wisdom that were quite entertaining to the masculine lookers-on."[48] While men may have expected and even wished that the ladies were more afraid of horses, women were cultivating a familiarity with the animal on their own highly fashionable terms and demonstrating it publicly for others to see and be inspired by.

Seeking to better their own horsemanship, or simply curious about members of their own sex venturing into so demanding and thrilling a sport, lady spectators were particularly attuned to the female competitors and their horses. Of women who competed in the show, the greatest number did so as exhibitors who, like most of the male exhibitors, enlisted others, usually grooms or paid professional riders, to handle their horses in the arena, including horses that they themselves rode or drove in carriages outside the show in the riding schools, parks, or hunt fields. Even if they were showing in their husband's name and employing professional riders and drivers, their entries could still by extension evoke their own expertise as horsewomen and teach their female friends, all while manifesting women's authority over hired help.[49]

But the most thrilling lessons and sensations of showing came when women exhibited the horses themselves. As impressive as women's carriage driving was to spectators, women's riding inspired more admiration and trepidation because of the greater bodily contact with the horse and the special athletic challenges of sitting sidesaddle. In the carriage, the lady driver, albeit wearing a gown, was still seated in more or less the same pose as her male counterpart. Not so for the lady riding aside whose position purportedly kept her respectable by preventing her from spreading her legs over the horse. Practiced in a sporting context rather than for any necessity of transportation in this period, sidesaddle riding epitomized Veblen's "vicarious leisure." It was patriarchally imposed, torqued the body in what Elizabeth Platt Karr in her foundational manual deemed unnatural and artificial ways, required a corset, and often caused pain and discomfort, especially if not done well.[50] The sidesaddle rider had to find her balance in an asymmetrical position and hold herself in place by squeezing her legs together between brackets or pommels mounted on the saddle that kept both legs on the horse's left side. These pommels provided security, which enabled ladies seated sidesaddle to ride at speed over varied terrain and over jumps, but they also compounded the danger because if the horse fell, the rider had a more difficult time than if she were seated astride of breaking free from the saddle to avoid being crushed. If the rider fell from the horse, she was always at risk of her long skirt catching on the pommels and being dragged. In spite of these well-known dangers, ladies were still required to ride sidesaddle at the trend-setting Garden and in polite society until 1915. As one prominent English riding master explained, "the side saddle is the most decorative, dignified, and graceful method, and pleases the male eye, which prefers the ultra-feminine woman to the type which emulates the male in attire or atmosphere."[51]

Yet sidesaddle also became a quintessential example of how women took a visible expression of men's authority and desire and derived their own power and pleasure from it. The riding habit constituted its own fashion genre which women scrutinized with the same intensity and expertise as they did the gowns on the promenade and in the boxes. There was considerably less latitude in style changes from year to year in riding attire as opposed to daily and evening wear, but the habit's consistency was part of its strength and allure. Correctness of form on the horse was inseparable from correctness of dress, and both the habit and the way of riding were supposed to reflect a "classic" formal elegance devoid of frills. Working dialectically with Parisian couture, equestrian fashion kept the show's cultural aspirations grounded in English Protestant simplicity while its classic lines showed off the feminine form to best advantage in the saddle. In spite of the requisite skirt, those clean, formal classic lines also recalled the sport's masculine and militaristic history. Riding habits, in fact, were typically made from the same fabrics as men's suits and early in the nineteenth century were furnished by men's tailors rather than dressmakers. Even after women's clothiers began providing them, the jackets retained a crisply tailored masculine cut.[52] This aspect of the styling resonated beyond mere functionality; a woman riding a horse, even ladylike aside, was still adopting a traditionally very male position of command, which only became more apparent as she put the horse precisely through its paces in the show ring before a crowd of thousands.

Moreover, the sidesaddle rider, no less than a rider astride, still feels the tremendous power and excitement of "all the play of [the horse's] splendid muscles" through her body, beginning with her seat. Elizabeth Karr, like most experts on the subject, stresses "the absolute necessity of a good seat" for effective riding.[53] This comes from developing balance and suppleness and engaging abdominal, thigh, and buttock muscles in rhythm with the horse's movement. Subtle shifts of weight forward or backward, pressing one seat bone down more firmly than another, tipping the pelvis—these are powerful means of communication with the horse. The lady rider's extension of her right thigh forward to hook her knee around the top pommel actually puts more surface area of her bottom in contact with the saddle than would pertain astride. This magnifies the possibilities of using her seat, which she must exploit in order to compensate for the absence of her right leg on the horse. She carries a riding crop to reinforce the communication when necessary, but the major signals to her mount come from her lower body. With her legs together on the left side obscured by the skirt, the lady sidesaddle, when riding properly, appears to be very poised and doing almost nothing while a profound exchange of energy and sensation pulses between her and the horse.

Radiating beauty and intrigue, sidesaddle riding emerged as a premier feature of the Garden showcased in the prime-time evening slots. By 1895, the class for Ladies' Saddle Horses in which ladies were required to ride drew twenty-nine entries, some of whom also competed against men in open Saddle Horse and Hunter classes, prompting *Rider and Driver* to declare: "One result of the Horse Show has been to accentuate the superiority of women generally over men in riding and managing the horse."[54] Most of the women who graced the Garden tanbark in the 1890s and early 1900s were amateurs, that is, wives and daughters of wealthy men who were not paid a salary to ride but who had the means and opportunity to pursue the sport seriously.[55] While women's participation steadily increased, women riders remained much fewer in number than the male competitors at the National in this period, which is partly why these equestriennes commanded special focus. Male spectators, even horsemen, for whom sampling sidesaddle would have been akin to donning drag, were amazed by the excellent performances these ladies got from their horses with such little apparent effort and seeming lack of crucial means of control. More knowing female spectators, bent on extracting lessons for improving their own technique, could better perceive the subtle signals their sister equestriennes gave their mounts in the show ring. Increasing numbers of these women attended the Horse Show with saddle sensations fresh in their seats from rides earlier in the day in the park or at one of the riding academies. Watching breathlessly as the lady competitors remained perfectly poised while guiding their dazzling mounts over five-foot fences on the tanbark, these women transformed Veblen's "vicarious leisure" into their own vicarious thrill. Those sensations had effect beyond the show and the saddle. As Belle Beach, who became the most well-known professional lady rider in this period, wrote so evocatively about rid-ing for women, "it is of all the exercises the one best adapted to keep them in condition, to restore the glow of health, and to key up the whole system to respond to all the delights of life."[56]

Along with enhancing their ability to experience pleasure, the sensa-tions of riding, whether felt directly or vicariously, emboldened women to advance in other arenas, but at a long-term cost. In its "Notes for Women," *Rider and Driver* observed, "Besides gaining 'nerve' and habits of decision and control, which are likely to prove of service in after days, a girl who is taught to ride early generally develops into a graceful and well-proportioned woman."[57] As learned and shown at the Garden, women's riding inculcated a particular physical type whose grace and proportions were keyed to those of the Thoroughbred horse, the English horse par excellence, supreme product of British breeding programs imported to America, which *Rider and Driver* proclaimed "the perfection of equine conformation."[58] Veblen articulated its significance for his economic theory: "In horses—more particularly in sad-dle [as opposed to carriage] horses—which at their best serve the purpose of wasteful display simply—it will hold true in a general way that a horse is more beautiful in proportion as he is more English; the English leisure class being, for the purposes of reputable usage, the upper leisure class of this country, and so the exemplar for the lower grades."[59] With their putatively greater sensitivity and patience than most men, women were temperamen-tally especially well suited to this most sensitive and spirited of breeds, as Mrs. Clarke noted in her 1848 series "Hints on Equestrianism for the Fair Sex" in *Godey's Lady's Book*.[60] Writing later in the nineteenth century, Eliza-beth Karr insisted that the bodies of horse and rider must be aesthetically compatible as well. The Thoroughbred's tall, graceful, finely chiseled features called for a rider of like conformation; "[t]he naturally slender, symmetrical figure, when in the saddle, is the perfection of beauty," she asserted.[61] These horse and rider combinations were showcased in the ladies' classes in the evenings at the Garden.

The same features that Karr specified as necessary to fit the lady rider to the most regal of horses became codified in the American Girl, the na-tion's first mass-produced visual stereotype of ideal female appearance and deportment. Her primary creator, the commercial illustrator Charles Dana Gibson, was a box holder and regular fixture at the National Horse Show. Iconically etched in pen-and-ink, the Gibson Girl, aka the American Girl, debuted in *Life Magazine* in 1890, the year the National moved into Garden

Fig. 1.8. Charles Dana Gibson, "Are you exhibiting at the Horse Show this year?" (*Life Magazine*, 1897.)

II and entered its belle époque.[62] Gibson's first major biographer, Fairfax Downey, offers this description of her classic features: "a tall, radiant being, her gaze clear, fearless and direct, her nose slightly and piquantly uptilted. Her lips fine-modeled and alluring. Her soft hair crowning a serene brow and caught up into a dainty chignon. The graceful column of her neck rising from the décolletage that barely concealed her delicately rounded bosom. Her slim waist emphasized by the bodice cut of her gowns."[63] It is well established that Gibson synthesized this Girl from the features of beautiful women whom he observed in WASP high society, including the statuesque Irene Langhorne who led the Grand March of the Patriarch's Ball and became his wife and companion in the Horse Show box.[64] But his visual vocabulary was also informed by the spectacle of beautiful, well-bred horses. He traded indelibly on human/equine correlations, as illustrated in figure 1.8, where two patriarchs exchange the following dialogue: "Are you exhibiting at the Horse Show this year?" "Yes, I am sending my daughter." The height of this progeny; her long, graceful neck and limbs; the strong, well-defined jaw; the high brow; even the uptilted nose, which correlates with the finely dished equine facial profile of its Arabian progenitors—all are distinctively Thoroughbred features. Her gaze might be "clear, fearless, and direct," like that of the lady and her horse jumping in figure 1.2, were she to open her eyes. But here she demurs in favor of the patriarchs' gaze, epitomizing the tension between the WASP cultural desire for women's horsey athleticism and power for purposes of "good breeding" and anxieties about maintaining male dominance. Women were emboldened and sensually awakened as riders, but those to whom doors most readily opened as they sallied boldly forth from the saddle into the human political and professional arenas would be those who best embodied the well-bred Thoroughbred type with all of its prescriptions for beauty, power, and containment. The cross-species dynamics of showing at the Garden pushed these heightened, contradictory qualities to extremes and hurled them outward into the wider culture and forward into the twentieth century.

Notes

The research and writing of this essay began during a residency at the University of Iowa's Obermann Center for Advanced Studies in fall 2011.

1. The National Horse Show ran for more than a century in four successive incarnations of Madison Square Garden; however, with the Depression and the decline in widespread interest in the horse as the animal was supplanted by the internal combustion engine, the show did not continue to hold the same degree of wide cultural focus after World War I. Since 1989, the show has moved to different venues, including Meadowlands Arena in New Jersey; Wellington, Florida; and, most recently, the Kentucky Horse Park in Lexington. It has continued to be a premier event on the horse show circuit even as its social profile has shrunk.

2. "Was It a Horse Show?" *Life* 24, no. 622 (November 29, 1894), 350.

3. Kurth Sprague, *The National Horse Show: A Centennial History, 1883–1983* (New York: National Horse Show Foundation, 1985), 9.

4. "Arranging for a Horse Show," *New York Times*, June 21, 1883, 8; "The Coming Horse Show: A Novel Exhibition to Be Given in October," August 30, 1883, 8. The Westminster Kennel Club Show, also held annually in Madison Square Garden, dates from 1877.

5. This notion of "hastening" is from the introduction to *The Art of Being Jewish in Modern Times*, ed. Barbara Kirshenblatt-Gimblett and Jonathan Karp (Philadelphia: University of Pennsylvania Press, 2008), 11.

6. "For the Ugly Girls: No. XXII," *Harper's Bazaar* 6, no. 52 (December 27, 1873), 826.

7. William Inglis, "Physical Culture for Young Girls," *Harper's Bazaar* 44, no. 2 (February 1910), 119.

8. "The Riding Class," *Harper's Bazaar* 25, no. 40 (October 1, 1892), 799. See also Adelia K. Brainerd, "The Outdoor Woman: Horseback-Riding," *Harper's Bazaar* 30, no. 42 (October 16, 1897), 863, and "Horsewomen in Brooklyn: The Riding Season about to Commence—the Horse Has Downed the Bicycle Again," *New York Times*, October 30, 1898, 20, for accounts of the resurgence in popularity of horseback riding among affluent women after the initial bicycle craze.

9. "For the Ugly Girls: No. XXII," *Harper's Bazaar* 6, no. 52 (December 27, 1873), 826.

10. See, for example, Valerie Steele, *The Corset: A Cultural History* (New Haven: Yale University Press, 2001), 35, 114–15, on the erotic ambivalences of corseting.

11. Jennifer Mason, "Animal Bodies: Corporeality, Class, and Subject Formation in *The Wide, Wide World*," *Nineteenth-Century Literature* 54, no. 4 (March 2000): 522–23; Carroll Smith-Rosenberg and Charles Rosenberg, "The Female Animal: Medical and Biological Views of Woman and Her Role in Nineteenth-Century America," *Journal of American History* 60 (September 1973): 334–35.

12. "The Riding Class," *Harper's Bazaar* 25, no. 40 (October 1, 1892), 799.

13. "A New Riding School: Thrown Open Last Night with a Brilliant Show," *New York Times*, February 10, 1887, 5.

14. See, for example, "The Riding Class," drawn by T. de Thulstrup, *Harper's Bazaar* 25, no. 40 (October 1, 1892), 796.

15. "The Riding Club," *Harper's Bazaar* 20, no. 11 (March 12, 1887), 184.

16. "Horses and Their Keep," *New York Times*, April 28, 1895, 6.

17. Clay McShane and Joel A. Tarr, *The Horse in the City: Living Machines in the Nineteenth Century* (Baltimore: Johns Hopkins University Press, 2007), 16.

18. James W. Tuckerman, "Park Driving," *Outing* 46 (June 1905), 259, quoted in McShane and Tarr, *Horse in the City*, 89.

19. Sprague, *National Horse Show*, 29.

20. "The Coming Horse Show: A Novel Exhibition to Be Given in October," *New York Times*, August 30, 1883, 8.

21. "Society and Its Horses: Both on Exhibition at Madison Square Garden This Week: A Guide to the Occupants of the Boxes," *New York Times*, November 10, 1895, 11.

22. "The Box Sale for the Horse Show," *Rider and Driver* 10, no. 11 (November 9, 1895), 8.

23. "The Coming Horse Show," *New York Times*, October 20, 1895, 19; "Horse Show Seats in Demand," *New York Times*, November 8, 1895, 6; Classified ad, "Horse Show, Madison Square Garden," *New York Times*, November 12, 1895, 7; "Horse Show Makes Profit of $50,000," *New York Times*, November 21, 1910.

24. "Horse Show Week Opens Social Season," *New York Times*, November 12, 1905, SM1.

25. Quoted from the *New York Times*, June 5, 1883, in Sprague, *National Horse Show*, 8.

26. "The Fruits of the Horse Show," *Rider and Driver* 10, no. 11 (November 9, 1895), 7.

27. Thorstein Veblen, *The Theory of the Leisure Class: An Economic Study of Institutions* (New York: Vanguard Press, [1899] 1928), available in the Hathi Trust Digital Library, http://babel.hathitrust.org/cgi/pt?view=image;size=100;id=coo.31924013756204; q1=English%20leisure%20class;page=root;seq=1, 36. All subsequent citations are to this edition.

28. Veblen, *Theory of the Leisure Class*, 96.

29. "Horse Shows as a Stimulant," *Rider and Driver* 10, no. 12 (November 16, 1895), 8.

30. "The Great Horse Show," *New York Morning World*, October 22, 1883, quoted in Sprague, *National Horse Show*, following 46.

31. Veblen, *Theory of the Leisure Class*, 180.

32. A. T. Ashmore, "Fashions at the Horse Show," *Harper's Bazaar* 33, no. 48 (December 1, 1900), 1975.

33. "New York Fashions: Horse Show Costumes," *Harper's Bazaar* 30, no. 46 (November 13, 1897), 939.

34. Veblen defines "gentle blood" as "blood which has been ennobled by protracted contact with accumulated wealth or unbroken prerogative," *Theory of the Leisure Class*, 55.

35. Veblen, *Theory of the Leisure Class*, 143–44.

36. "What Is Doing in Society?," *New York Times*, November 13, 1898, 16.

37. *Official Catalogue: Annual Horse Show*, vol. 13 (New York: National Horse Show Association of America, 1897), 44.

38. "Two Hearts that Beat as One," "Notes for Women by a Woman," *Rider and Driver* 10, no. 13 (November 23, 1895), 21.

39. Veblen, *Theory of the Leisure Class*, 59.

40. Veblen, *Theory of the Leisure Class*, 181. In *Victorian Fiction and the Cult of the Horse* (Burlington, VT: Ashgate, 2006), 96, Gina M. Dorré correlates the painful severity of "gag" bearing reins used to make carriage horses hold their heads unnaturally high for a more spirited look with the tight lacing and high bustles of late Victorian dress.

41. Jennifer Mason, "Animal Bodies: Corporeality, Class, and Subject Formation in *The Wide, Wide World*," *Nineteenth-Century Literature* 54, no. 4 (March 2000): 513.

42. "Hints on Equestrianism for the Fair Sex by a Well Known Lady Equestrian" [Mrs. J. Stirling Clarke], *Godey's Magazine and Lady's Book* 37 (November 1848), 45–48, 108–9, 169–71, 240–42. For later examples, see "Scenes at a Horse Show," *Harper's Bazaar* 22, no. 11 (March 16, 1889), 191–92, for advice on the qualities of a lady's horse; and C. de Hurst, "How Women Should Ride," a *Harper's Bazaar* series whose first part appeared in 24, no. 33 (August 15, 1891), 626.

43. Mrs. Elizabeth [Platt] Karr, *The American Horsewoman* (Boston: Houghton Mifflin, 1884).

44. Adelia K. Brainerd, "The Outdoor Woman," *Harper's Bazaar* 29, no. 47 (November 21, 1896), 978. Marlis Schweitzer analyzes this intense female scrutiny of fashion in

the theater in *When Broadway Was the Runway: Theater, Fashion, and American Culture* (Philadelphia: University of Pennsylvania Press, 2009), 96–99.

45. "Woman's World: The Pioneer Woman Judge of the National Horse Show," *Fulton Evening Times*, January 15, 1916, 7, reported that Lady Beck, an Englishwoman who had competed at the Garden the previous year and was known as an expert at fox hunting, had become the first woman invited to judge at the show. She officiated with Mr. James G. Marshall of New York's Riding Club in judging the class for "undocked saddle horses of the thoroughbred type."

46. "Mrs. Wouter Van Twiller Saturdays: The Horse Show," *Harper's Bazaar* 28, no. 47 (November 23, 1895), 946.

47. "New York Fashions: At the Horse Show," *Harper's Bazaar* 25, no. 48 (November 26, 1892), 955.

48. "Horses of All Degrees: Continued Interest in the Great Show," *New York Times*, November 7, 1888, 8.

49. Adelia K. Brainerd, "The Outdoor Woman," *Harper's Bazaar* 29, no. 47 (November 21, 1896), 978.

50. Elizabeth Platt Karr, *The American Horsewoman* (Boston: Houghton Mifflin, 1884), iv.

51. Lt. Colonel F. C. Hitchcock, *Saddle Up: A Guide to Equitation and Stable Management* (New York: Scribner, 1937).

52. Alison Matthews David, "Elegant Amazons: Victorian Riding Habits and the Fashionable Horsewoman," *Victorian Literature and Culture* (2002): 182.

53. Elizabeth Platt Karr, *The American Horsewoman* (Boston: Houghton Mifflin, 1884), xi.

54. "Notes for Women by a Woman," *Rider and Driver* 10, no. 13 (November 23, 1895), 21. In Saddle Horse classes, there was no jumping; the horse was judged on the quality of its gaits for park riding. Hunter classes were supposed to show off skills for fox hunting, including jumping.

55. "Big Evening Crush at the Horse Show," *New York Times*, November 23, 1901, 3; "Horse Show Week Opens Social Season," *New York Times*, November 12, 1905, SM1; see also Sprague, *National Horse Show*, 65.

56. Belle Beach, *Riding and Driving for Women* (New York: Scribner's, 1912), 3.

57. "Notes for Women by a Woman," *Rider and Driver* 10, no. 12 (November 16, 1895), 10.

58. "Horse-Show Judging: A Quick Glance at the Most Important Features to Be Taken into Consideration When Selecting Prizewinners—How Every Spectator May Do His Own Judging," *Rider and Driver* 10, no. 11 (November 9, 1895), 10.

59. Veblen, *Theory of the Leisure Class*, 144–45.

60. "Hints on Equestrianism for the Fair Sex by a Well Known Lady Equestrian," [Mrs. J. Stirling Clarke], *Godey's Magazine and Lady's Book* 37 (November 1848), 169.

61. Karr, *American Horsewoman*, 7.

62. Carolyn Kitch, *The Girl on the Magazine Cover: The Origins of Visual Stereotypes in American Mass Media* (Chapel Hill: University of North Carolina Press, 2001), 37.

63. Fairfax Downey, *Portrait of an Era as Drawn by C. D. Gibson: A Biography* (New York: Scribner's, 1936), 100–101.

64. Kitch, *Girl on the Magazine Cover*, 39. See also Martha Banta, *Imaging American Women: Idea and Ideals in Cultural History* (New York: Columbia University Press, 1987), 81.

CHAPTER 2

Painting the Body Brown and Other Lessons on How to Dance Latin

Laurie Frederik

ESCAPE FROM ACADEMIA

Ballroom dancing was my escape from the analytical. A purely physical and artistic activity, it offered reprieve after long hours of reading, writing, and thinking. In contrast to more devised and potentially narrative dance forms, I was able to detach ballroom dance from academics since it was exhilarating and felt good to *do*, but to me it did not *mean* anything intellectually. Anthropologists have always been deeply concerned with "meaning" and the ubiquitous Geertzian "webs of significance" that we, as cultural beings, have spun for ourselves. At age twenty-seven, I had just started graduate school, so I had plenty of significance and semiotic analysis in my daily life and really just wanted to feel the exuberance of artistic movement, stretching musculature, and good old-fashioned sweat. I did not attribute meaning to ballroom in the same way I did with other artistic forms because I believed it was about action, not representation. My "experiential reality" was not about meaning (cf. Downey 2005, 19) because I did not deem it so. My dance reality was about training, technique, and proper presentation on the floor. It was about moving freely, powerfully, and expressively to vibrant music as if it were in my blood and making the complex, highly technical, and nuanced look easy. The superficiality and showiness of ballroom was its very attraction—an otherworldly and sparkly realm that promised to alleviate the stress of my scholarly obligations. Ballroom was an over-the-top dance form, playful and fun, but the higher I rose in the competitive ranks, the more I had to play up and intensify the physical falsification. The more seriously I considered it as a sport, the more I had to transform into the domain of masquerade. Everything I had to do to myself (or pay someone to do to me) involved applying some manmade item labeled "fake."

One important requirement of competitive ballroom performance was "tanning." My body had to be stained a darker hue with a liquid lotion or spray containing DHA (dihydroxyacetone or glycerone). The chemical smell of these lotions was intense, unpleasant, and lingering, and my skin burned a little when applied. For pale skin, the tanning process had to begin several days before an event. The intensity of tanning or "browning" in competition ballroom is only really noticed by audiences if the lotion or spray is applied badly. Professional judges and other dancers are able to pinpoint problems with physical presentation, but regular spectators may not know how to articulate the exact reason for their unease, just that the dancer looked sloppy or perhaps a bit ill—an orange hue shadowing her face, or extra-darkened splotches or streaks running down legs, arms, or backs. Tanning should appear "natural" in the ballroom setting—naturally ethnic or acquired poolside—though the painted on shade likely looks severe and abnormal in daylight. Tanning was the most tedious part of the preparation ritual, but there were other expectations.

My eyelashes had to be replaced with long glued-on synthetics. My short, plain fingernails were disguised with long and flashy daggers. My face became a freakishly exaggerated version of the more ordinary palette I was born with, eyes contoured with heavy makeup through black lines, red swirls, white glittery smudging, and striking artificially colored accents. A nearly full bottle of hair spray shellacked every follicle of my "up-do," including elaborate extensions held into a massive bun with sculpted swirls and finger waves. I was smothered from head to toe in rhinestones and bright neon colors. Sometimes the stones were even glued to my hair, scalp, and the skin near my temples. Earrings were kept in place with a dollop of spirit gum (a resin/alcohol liquid adhesive used in theater for attaching facial hair and fake noses) so they did not fly off during spins. Nothing exposed to the spectator gaze was left unpolished, except, perhaps, if I was careless, the skin between my fingers or the palm of my hand. The extreme showiness of the form freed me from attempted analyses, or so I initially thought.

In this essay, I focus my analysis on competition dance, also known as "dancesport," and the International Latin category within the larger ballroom umbrella (hereafter "Latin-ballroom"). I examine competitive ballroom dancing phenomenologically as an individual and collective cultural practice. This is an auto-ethnographic look at how dancers experience an expressive form that shows one thing (standardized technique, athletic skill, and artistry), and may appear to show off another (Latin Americanness or "other" ethnicity), but is really a dynamic and ever-changing indication of creative innovation, hybrid genres, and decontextualization. The potential fracture in consistent and accurate analysis of competition Latin-ballroom dance is in the divide between the *intention* of the dancer and the *perception* of the image generated for an outsider audience, including informal and official judges. I agree with the notion that the showing of ethnicity, gender, and identity is not as it appears or even as we feel we perform our own. Thanks to a generation of articulate scholars, we are conscious of the complexity and politics of identity construction, but are still not necessarily aware when our "appreciation" of a cultural form transgresses into categories of inappropriate or "appropriated" in a given society (see Johnson 2003). We may not realize when we are problematically "playing" or "acting" a particular ethnicity (Deloria 1999; Bial 2005), when we are disidentifying (Muñoz 1999), or, as in my case, identifying with something altogether different, known only to insiders. Considering this process of Latinization (whether cultural, ethnic, or based in movement technique) in terms of showing off and up helps to clarify the stakes of the competition and its role in a participant's life. It also shows us how analyses of perform*ing*—as distinct from performance—shed important light on any form of expressive culture.

Unlike other scholarship on dance forms, Latin-ballroom as a cultural world cannot be well understood through an analysis of movement or performance context. "Meaning" is not usually the contentious issue in competition ballroom dance, especially since the same bodies are performing between five and ten differently coded, culturally specific dances in a single competition, all back to back in less than ten minutes. In the Latin category, dancers begin the round in carnival mode, bouncing and curving *voltas* traveling down the length of the floor, emoting happy celebration in a Brazilianesque *samba*. Ninety seconds later, they change face and body action to Cuban *cha cha*, staccato and precise, smaller steps aggressively stabbing at quick lines and hitting hard on the "four-and-one" in flirtatious pursuit of the partner. Another quick turnaround in music cues dancers that it is time for a slow loving rumba with longing, graceful, and balletic stretching movements, interspersed with sensuous figure-eight hip action. Jumping briefly back over the Atlantic to Spain, dancers shift into a Spanish *paso doble*, where the man is the primary attraction, the fearless matador. The woman, thus, becomes the bull (or the cape, or the gypsy flamenco dancer, depending on the choreography), dancing intensely to the death, the final musical "crash" often ending with her literally lying on the floor under the imposing eyes of the victor. Then suddenly, as competitors quickly wipe the sweat from their brows between dances, any semblance of Latin-ness is completely shed for the American style *jive*, feet flicking and kicking, bodies bouncing up and down, dancers silently thinking the words and feeling the *tick-a-tick-a-tick-a-tick*. Audiences are invited to imagine 1950s era poodle skirts swirling, and even the hardcore feminists among them may temporarily forget gender politics and male-female typecasting in the display of athleticism and the joy of big band beats. The full five-dance round is over in less than eight minutes. These quick changes of danced intention and mood are one of the biggest challenges of ballroom dance. Transformational acting techniques come in handy: be sassy, be aggressive, be romantic, be angry, be cheery, as each dance demands. The immediate requirements of character-making then make the body *feel* and thus show those very things in the dance.

Latin-ballroom is a genre hodgepodge, but it is consistent in its physical aesthetic and in certain foundational movement techniques, particularly hip, foot, and leg action. Whether or not a dancer is culturally Brazilian (samba), Cuban (cha cha, rumba), Spanish (paso doble), or African American (jive) is completely irrelevant; the authenticity of ballroom performance is measured in different ways. Physical bodies are carefully crafted to become Latin-ballroom dancers and to conform to the rest of this movement community—not a linguistic, ethnic, or racial community—if only for the hours in which they are dancing on the ballroom floor. Its actual practitioners differ in surprising ways from its ostensible cultural reference (Latino), especially recently, since, in fact, *Russians* have been the most impressive and successful ballroom dancers in the United States for the past decade. They win U.S. National Championships and then go on to world competitions to compete as official representatives of this country. Dancers who identify as Lithuanian, Polish, Slovenian, Italian, and South Africans are also high-level U.S. and world champions ranked at the top in the world standings. When considering the demographics of who is representing this dance form on the most influential stages, it is evident that Latin-ballroom dancers perform a professional ideal rather than national model. In social clubs and while living in Cuba, I wanted to dance Latin like a Latin American. In competitions, I wanted to dance Latin like a Russian.

Fig 2.1. Lydia Petrigova, professional Latin dancer and owner of a dance school, DC Dancesport Academy, teaches her highly popular Latin technique class, ongoing and fully attended for ten years. On her website, the text written over this photo reads: "Dance like everyone is watching." Petrigova is from Russia, now living in Virginia. Her students are from a variety of ethnicities and nationalities. Image courtesy of Lydia Petrigova.

FROM BALLROOM TO "DANCESPORT": A SHORT EXPLANATION

Competitive ballroom dance in North America includes four distinct styles, which are judged as separate events:

International Latin: samba, cha cha, rumba, paso doble, jive
International Standard: waltz, tango, foxtrot, quickstep, Viennese waltz
American Rhythm: cha cha, rumba, bolero, swing, mambo
American Smooth: waltz, tango, foxtrot, Viennese waltz

Each of the four styles features a syllabus that describes different levels of mastery: bronze (newcomer and basic) to silver (intermediate) to gold (advanced). The syllabus for each level contains a list of dance steps, outside of which a competitor cannot legally venture without disqualification. Beyond gold is the "open," also called "championship," level, in which dancers may utilize any choreography, including elements of contemporary, jazz, hip-hop, African, flamenco, or whatever else, as long as the performance is judged as categorizable in rhythm, foundational steps, and general flavor of the dance at hand.

The term "dancesport" refers to ballroom dance competition (in contrast to social dance) and has been in use since 1990. The move from ballroom to dancesport increased in popularity when the International Dancesport

Federation applied for, and was granted, recognition by the International Olympic Council in 1997. Nearly all competitions nowadays are labeled "dancesport."[1] For the past decade, a campaign to include competition ballroom dancing in the Olympics has continued and has been a popular topic of discussion in ballroom circles. However, in order for the dance form to be standardized enough to fit the model of an Olympic sport, it will have to lose some of its showiness and create calculable units of measurement and degrees of difficulty: skills must be recognizable not only to judges, but also to audiences. As is, dancesport has been deemed too artistic and too hard to judge—too subjective. Defenders have tried to equate it to figure skating and ice dancing, but ice-skating competitions are solo exhibitions, performed one by one or pair by pair, with "tricks" that are identifiable and scored. In contrast, dancesport competitions feature all dancers (all pairs or couples) on the floor at the same time. The master of ceremonies announces to the competitors and public, "your next dance is the cha cha" (or paso doble, or waltz), and with this cue, loud music emerges from the speakers like a gunshot and the starting gate bursts open. Poised and waiting, dancers erupt into action when the musical beats hit the air and do not stop moving until the music ends. It is a race, a series of sprints, each lasting ninety seconds long with a fifteen-second break in between. Yet the dancers don't always sprint ("travel") in the same direction. Part of dancesport's artistry is to avoid collision while traveling fast in a variety of directions, sometimes inverted, other times spinning. The scene is often raucous, audience members yelling out names or numbers (pinned on the male competitor's back) at the top of their voices (Go Krystian and Irina! Go #52! Awesome #12! Woop woop!), and they also boo loudly at unpopular results. A ballroom competition is not unlike a hockey or football game. Experienced couples are forceful and do not give up their space on the floor willingly; expressions of territory claiming may appear to be part of the choreography. Arms outstretch a little bit more when another couple gets too close, and champions are recognized as those who never shrink in size or slow their speed to let another pass, nor do they say "excuse me" when passing in return. Aggressive showing off and up in competitive ballroom dancing is accepted and essential to the game. The ultimate goal is to prove, surpass, win, and stand on the highest podium.

Joanna Bosse (2015) describes a much softer "self imaginary" in ballroom dance and says that the drive to learn dancing is inspired by a transformational and emergent process of "becoming beautiful." Bosse, however, focuses on social dance and not competitive ballroom, which is an important

Fig. 2.2. 2011 World Dancesport Federation, World Latin Dance Championships, podium of finalists, held in Singapore 2011. 1st place: Zoaran Plohl and Tatsiana Lahvinovich—Croatia; 2nd place: Andrei Zaitev and Anna Kuzminkaja—Russia; 3rd place: Nino Langella and Kristina Moshenskaja— Italy; 4th place: Martino Zanibellato and Michelle Ablidtrub—Denmark; 5th place: Gabriele Goffredo and Anna Matus—Moldova; 6th place: Pavel Pasechnik and Francesca Berardi—Italy.

distinction. Social dance implies "for fun" and to mingle in a partner dance party setting. In the movements, arm stylization is subtle, less exaggerated and enclosed in the invisible circle of the duo; dancers' facial expressions are limited to smiling and raised eyebrows. In social dance, steps are led and followed (rather than the practiced measures of memorized choreography), and sparkling or feathered attire is limited. Dancers are unpolished: they show up to a class or party after work, in crumpled business casual or sneakers and jeans. Social dance is to relax, and as the name implies, to socialize, but mostly it is to dance. No conversation is necessary and partners alternate. I often danced with fifteen different men in a single party, saying no more to them than "yes, let's" and "thank you."

Someone might want to show *off* during a social dance, but normally showing *up* one's own partner or others who dance in the local community is frowned upon. Showing up another dancer in a social setting is impolite, and may be considered grotesque behaviorally as well as aesthetically. While questionable in etiquette, people still admire accomplished moves and overt acts of display. Social dance may be for enjoyment, community-building, and physical fitness, but for some it is also a way to attract sexual partners. Attraction requires standing out from the crowd. Nonconformity, at least aesthetically, is much more acceptable here than on a competition floor.

Polishing the Body

Moving from the social into dancesport world is a fairly significant transition. Presentation of steps and body action must be accentuated and exaggerated to an extreme. Movements must be intentional and big: stretching and extension, kicks, arm reaches, foot turn out, punches, impulses, twisting, angling. Ballroom competitors are also famous for their facial expressions, which match the bodies in intensity. Another adjustment is physical presentation. "Polished" is an often-used descriptive word in dancesport, along with "finished"—a continuous cultivated surface from head to toe, both in body and costume. Any one detail left out may result in an incongruous costume, for a performer cannot wear thousands of rhinestones and brightly colored gowns with scuffed shoes, messy hair, unpainted faces, or bare-naked blotchy skin. A Midwestern white girl with green eyes and freckles had to be transformed completely in both categories to be taken seriously, not into a *Latina*, necessarily, but from plain to polished, raw to finished. For all of us, it was really more about shine than shade, although both were important. Women with dark eyes and black hair had an impressionistic advantage, even though they may have had no more Latina ancestry than lighter complexioned competitors and they still had to fully polish up before performing. Some African American dancers were also instructed to tan, to their shock and frustration—though most often they shrugged it off with no real protest, other than a raised eyebrow or grumble. Regardless of one's origins as Greek, Italian, or Persian, everyone had to polish and to pass as a Latin-ballroom dancer, just as I had to in order to fit into this world, "fitting in" meaning, more accurately, to become a champion. Questions I routinely asked my coaches and fellow dancers during competition preparation were; "Does this dress have enough rhinestones?" or "Is my face done?" or "Am I tan enough yet?"

When confronted with the question of tanning, most female dancers explained that tanning simply made them look thinner and made their legs, arms, and back look better, that they looked "healthier." It was chalked up to gaining "the look" in ballroom dance. They never said that tanning made

Fig. 2.3. Latin-ballroom dance costumes are brightly colored and full of thousands of individually glued rhinestones, beads, tassels, and feathers. This is an example of a fully finished polish job. (Photo by Stephen Marino.)

them feel more authentically *Latina*, though one admitted that it made her feel less culturally *White*. If Latinization was the goal tanning of Latin-ballroom dancers in the 1950s competitions, the association had since fallen out of practice and consciousness. Tanning, among other bodily ornamentations, was tiresome, but it was one of the unquestioned rituals necessary for the ideal aesthetic and how a competition dancer learned to conform.

Based on over twenty years of competing in Latin-ballroom, I do not believe that dancers are pretending to be "other" in the way intellectuals analyze in similar circumstances, or at least not anymore and not for competition dancers. I began to compete in Cape Town, South Africa, in 1993: a region where ballroom was very popular and danced more by "coloured" and black South Africans than by white. I have also lived and competed in

Latin-ballroom in Atlanta, Seattle, New York City, Chicago, Toronto, and Washington, DC, and I competed in two Latin World Championships in Spain and Finland with my Japanese-born dance partner. In years of formal and informal interviews with participants, I have learned that dancers are not trying to brown-body or brownface with the same ideological motivations as blackface minstrelsy, although that may be what is visually performed through the act of painting skin. Can motivation and actualization be separated? That was one of the essential questions I struggled with, caught between shame and defensive justification of my own practice. Kathy Davis describes a similar feeling of shame as a feminist scholar dancing the male dominant Argentine tango in her book, *Dancing Tango: Passionate Encounters in a Globalizing World* (2015). She asks, as did I: Was I trying to have my (politically correct) cake and eat (dance) it too? (188).

Regarding blackface in Latin-ballroom, dance scholar Juliet McMains (2001, 57) gives a scathing account of the industry aesthetic and points out,

> While the current visibility of dancesport in the United States does not approach the popularity attained by American blackface minstrelsy (1830s–1930s), the parallels between these two entertainment forms are striking. In both practices, lighter-skinned performers paint their body darker in order to talk our behavioral stereotypes ascribed to an ethnic group with darker skin and less social, political, and economic power.

McMains, following Coco Fusco (1995), also writes about the general misunderstanding of "Latino" as a racial category: "Latinos are white, black, brown, and dozens of mestizo shades in between," yet "the fiction of a generic 'Latin' identity is fostered through dancesport" (56) Although I do not fully believe (nor do I want to) that tanning and polishing is a form of minstrelsy, I agree that there is a lot more going on in this cultural world than meets the eye. Painting the body brown is something that has caused me physical and ideological distress over the years, but in contrast to McMains, or perhaps in addition, I would argue for another interpretation. Dancers today are not trying to become Latin or Latina/o, thus their performative intention is not to brownface, which implies ethnic othering. They try to use this polished disguise to find a heightened, theatricalized, and competitive version of themselves. Dancers do not necessarily want to become characters, someone apart from themselves. Instead, they want to show off a new *self*, to shed their normal public mask, or at least become what they wish or imagine themselves to be through the dance. They want to be professional looking so that they conform to industry standards.

A full polish job is not cheap (head to toe: skin, face, hair, nails, dress, jewelry, shoes), which means that serious competitors have commitment and resources. Competition ballroom is largely dominated by the upper socioeconomic classes. Within the community, there are smaller pockets of poorer participants who are addicted and thus willing to go into debt to feed their "dance habit"—a frequent joke, even among the wealthier dancers. As a graduate student, I had much more commitment (and obsession) than resources. I worked extra hours at a restaurant to pay for my dancing, and even then I was only able to afford one private lesson every two weeks. On off weeks, I practiced alone or with a partner in free university spaces. For the first several years, I borrowed and rented competition dresses and wore old dance shoes, the scuffmarks covered up by staining them with black tea. I did not look professionally polished in those early days, but I was learning how to *become*—to move from one cultural realm into another. There was a discovery of self in those years, and new performances of both academic and dancer. I could not be quiet or humble in either category if I wanted to be successful. I had to be assertive, confident, take risks, and use failure as a stimulus to work harder. I had to go against my otherwise introverted "nature" and show off in spite of my fear and uncertainty. Sometimes, I had to fake it. Performances of my intellectual self were raw and exposed as I attempted to climb the grueling steps to an ever-elusive ivory tower, but in Latin-ballroom, scantily clad, cleavaged, leggy, fully embellished and bejeweled, I was liberated by my alter ego into a seemingly hyper-theatrical but very real world.

McMains explains that ballroom dancesport displays itself at an almost grotesque level as participants aspire to show "glamour," but that dancers have the potential to engage in Bakhtinian carnivalesque: "The grotesque body exceeds normative expectations, bulging, protruding, and excreting beyond its own limits" (2006, 43). The ballroom dancer makes a spectacle of herself, says McMains, but that excessive body is no longer a spectacle, nor is it grotesque, once inside the ballroom. The competition audience does not usually see the dancers' presentation as grotesque, especially those who are dancers themselves. Personally, I only felt grotesque or out of place when I left the venue (hotel, convention center, event hall) and went beyond into the nonballroom world to buy dinner or snacks. Outside the context of ballroom dancing, there were double takes, raised eyebrows, and even occasional comments, making it clear that my appearance aroused suspicion and critical appraisal. To these viewers, I was clearly showing off something, though they did not realize that thing was ballroom dancing.

Every time I left the hairstylist and makeup artist chair and went into the practice room for warm up, I felt the synthetic enhancements attached to my body: Lycra seams, hairpins, dried hairspray, nail glue, bra cups, clip-on earrings, bangles, shoe buckles—foreign sensations, some quite uncomfortable—on my face, scalp, eyes, fingers, and feet. I could smell the intense chemical aromas of the lotions, sprays, and adhesives, a sensory experience that did not end until the layers melted away under a long hot shower, late into the night after the dancing was done. In the pliant and specially designed high-heeled ballroom shoes, my balance pitched slightly forward and my perspective on the world was 2.5 inches higher. Pulled, pinched, painted, tucked in, and pushed out, I held my head and walked differently. I was always conscious of the gazes of other competitors as I made my way down the hallways toward the ballroom and on to the floor. At first, I felt *like* a Latin dancer or *as if* a Latin dancer, and then after many years of training, *as* a "real" Latin dancer.

Ballroom dance appears to be a transparent form of cultural expression, aggressively promoting unambiguous archetypes. It does not attempt to hide the processes that construct the stage persona. Ballroom dancer identity is openly constructed, even "forced," as one informant stated, and born without obvious precedent in some instances, in which case it becomes interesting for performance studies scholars. Fakery is superimposed upon talent and hard work until it is no longer fakery, but rather is integral to performance—all the chemical polish becomes soldered to the dancing body. Dancers prove they are serious, not content with just social dancing, in part by painting their commitment onto and into the pores of their skin. Some of the paint and glue wash off with a long shower, while others linger on the body for days afterward. The ideological transformation remains for years or for a lifetime.

Dramatic Irony at Work and Play

For as many years as I have been ballroom dancing, I have been conducting research about how Latin American cultures express national and ethnic authenticity. "Representing" and "performing" one's national or ethnic identities are popular ways of analyzing the phenomena, but the word "showing" rarely enters the picture at any level of analytical deconstruction. For me, ballroom dancing was two-dimensional and shamelessly so, and this is why I liked it—I thought that I did not have to analyze it. In contrast, my focused academic investigations were about "realness," authenticity, and perceptions of cultural purity. Perhaps I unconsciously blocked the implications of my dancesport actions from myself as a scholar so as not to taint the hobby that gave me so many moments of joy outside academia. For me, ballroom dancing focused on the body and movement, musicality, creativity, and modern reinterpretations of our grandparents' dances: dancing evoked nostalgia and tradition, and the challenge of modernizing a dance style, rather than pushing me to consider highly polemic performances of race, class, and gender. Scholars have recently begun to write more critically about contemporary ballroom and specifically dancesport, including its history of racial politics. There are fascinating analyses of intimacy (Ericksen 2011), glamour and beauty (McMains 2006; Bosse 2015), costuming (Marion 2008), whiteness and whitening (Martin 2010), and exotic fantasy (Picart 2006). Writings have also discussed the potential for control or power over one's partner, endorsement or rejection of feminism, the internal politics of the dancesport industry, accumulating cultural capital, and the effects of mass media. I read everything I could find on the subject with great interest, yet these analyses left out a crucial dimension of what I was experiencing.

Latin-ballroom dance demanded that I show myself and was shown by my coaches as a certain specimen of dancer: racialized, heterosexualized, and commercialized. But that surface reading was not what my body felt or what I believed I was showing to others or myself as I practiced and attempted to remold my actions and emotional "projection" in performance. When I danced, I felt more "me," not more "other." The paint and polish were masks of sorts, but I wanted to be a champion ballroom dancer and aspired to reach the professional level. My motivations and goals were very narrowly defined. The irony was that to feel more "me," I had to practice and pay for hours of coaching. I had to learn and master very precise steps and technique through rigorous training and practice, but I was also instructed to be "wild," to "let loose," and dance "uninhibited," to emote and project. I was routinely criticized for being "too square," "too technical," and "too reserved." Coaches spent hours trying to teach me to dance International Latin more "naturally," to pull out the "inner Laurie."

Throughout my academic career, I had studied postcolonialism in Kenya, apartheid in South Africa, the African diaspora in the Caribbean, and the plight of *mestizaje* and *los indios* in Latin America. I taught about the performance of identity and disidentity, as well as performance of nation. In my university classes I routinely critiqued examples of blackface and brownface and used them as historical markers for societal shifts in the perceptions of race and as instances of discrimination and exoticism. I wrote and lectured about nineteenth-century Cuban blackface minstrel shows called *Teatro Bufo* (Frederik 2001, 2005, 2012, see also Lane 2005) and the 1960s debates about the theatrically browned faces of Natalie Wood and George Chakiris in the film *West Side Story*. I did all of this while pulling the sweater down over my arms to hide the splotchy fading of ballroom tanned skin on each postcompetition Monday morning when I was back on the University of Chicago campus for classes and advisor meetings, and later as a professor at University of Maryland and advisor to my own graduate students. I had to show myself off differently in the university—mind, not body—and in that setting I also had to perform myself as gender neutral as possible.

The Art and Sport of Being Seen

Competitors in ballroom dance out-show other couples performing at the same time in the same space. I cannot think of another sport with the same competitive setup: 12–18 couples or 24–36 people on the floor, simultaneously dancing as hard as they can to grab winning attention, with rhinestones, beads, and feathers flying off dresses from aggressive movement, sweat flowing, eyes flashing, arms reaching, feet hitting the floor, *taka-taka-taka-taka*, no ambiguity, no question. It is crazy and exhilarating. In my early years as a competitive dancer, I resisted the extreme theatricality of this aesthetic, convinced that it was more important to subtly show off my technical skills and body movements and that I should not submit to trends. In my contemporary dance years, I wore black leotards, simple ponied hair, and focused on extension, line, timing, and execution. Why did I need all the fluff and hoopla? However, as I rose in the ballroom ranks and worked with better partners and teachers, I was forced to conform, lest I not look polished and professional, not look like a champion, and thus not win. I disliked tanning and preening, and primping, which were extremely time consuming and uncomfortable. But the longer I competed, my coaches required me to comply with the industry standards, and I was sent off the floor before my heats if I was not deemed up to par. The word "serious" came into play. Dancers who did not show up as sparkling and polished were not considered serious—not prepared or well coached—and the first impression of judges and fellow competitors was that they probably were not very good and not a threat.

Competition Latin and ballroom dancing is unabashedly self-indulgent. It is about joy and the power to compel. Ballroom dancers are flamboyant and seek to shine, eyes up and staring directly and provocatively into the eyes of the spectators and the judges. "Look at me, you must look at me, I dare you to look away, you cannot look away," it says. "I am showing off, look at me!" As an industry, ballroom dance does not attempt to be symbolic or "artistic," although aesthetic judgments are still made for high financial and reputational stakes. Dancers are evaluated instead of interpreted—judged by quality of movement, technique, musicality, appropriate characterization of the dance, and choreography. No manifest political message lies behind the genre's painted bodied racialization, at least not in the realm of ethnic authenticity or from the dancer's perspective. The politics in competition Latin dancing is often internal and often has to do with the results, the winners and losers, and who profits along the way. Politics in the ballroom dance world swirls around the one couple that the judges cannot stop watching, as well as the couple that is slashed off the score sheet by a single stroke of the adjudicating pen. Those who are able to heighten their performance and emote electricity are seen on the floor. In competition, it is not important if the dancers are the most culturally representative of a particular heritage, at least not for non-Latino dancers. Latin dancesport competition is not a commentary about violence, war, inequality, or injustice, nor is it about love and romance (although it's true that sex is a central theme). It will not change the world or be a widespread revolutionary sensation like salsa or hip-hop, for it cannot be pinned down as having one particular directional or cultural focus. Yet it works intensely on the bodies and ideologies of its community.

Latin-ballroom is not about "embodying"—it is about showing off impeccable dancing. Competitive Latin dancers fear being forgettable and seek to be "scored," that is, attracting enough attention from the judges to make cuts during the preliminary rounds and place as high as possible (at least in the final top six, better yet, the top three). Passing, or, worse, "disappearing" on the floor is a fatal flaw that no competitor would want. A dancer may be an excellent technician, but still not stand out among others dancing alongside her or him. For this reason, a dynamic visual element is crucial for success; dancers must project a presence that is larger than their rivals on

Fig. 2.4. Yulia Zago-
ruychenko, nine-time
World Champion
in Latin Dancesport
with partner, Ricardo
Cocchi, started her
own tanning lotion
brand, NUD. This
is an advertisement
on her professional
website. The model in
the photo is Zagoruy-
chenko.

the floor. The practice of conforming to an ideal in Latin-ballroom yet also standing out is a complex negotiation.

A competitive realm of professional judgment and standard-making further complicates the process. Producing this ideal aesthetic is not only physically uncomfortable, but also, under close examination, ideologically discomforting. Latin-ballroom is a hyperstylized, hypergendered, and hyper-racialized dance form, and as a result the experienced reality is elusive and inconsistent. We think we understand the performances, since the dancers do little to hide their exaggerations and are not ashamed by the showing off. Certainly, the usual critiques of "Western" and "hetero" affinities are easy to categorize and critique. But no one apologizes for these problematic tenden-cies in the ballroom community, which is a relatively isolated dancer-realm that has its own rules, social networks, and hierarchies. Nor are internal trends drastically changing with increased critical consciousness in society.

Ballroom dancing is pure exhibition: a stage on which talent, physical skill, and intense, long-term training are demonstrated, but also one on which a heightening of traditional gender roles is performed, not in everyday life, but for a seated and highly critical audience. I did not feel any more *Latina* when I competed in full costume, but it is true that I felt more like a "woman"—the one defined by society–when I was prepped and dressed for showing off to an expert panel of judges. In this context, I was performing my gender "correctly" (cf. Butler 1988, 1990). I danced better when I looked the part, or rather, when I *felt* the part. Feeling more like a woman in a sparkly dress, makeup, and high heels is socialized into many of us from toddlerhood. The child princess becomes an adult queen. So, by this logic, one finally reaches the pinnacle of successful femininity in ballroom dance competition. For me, being fully costumed in ballroom was a drag performance of sorts—a cisgender (tomboy, academic) woman becoming a more polished and performatively "woman" (or since I was showing off, "Woman!"). Here, perhaps, was a performative context in which gender stereotypes could be revved up without people becoming critical or feeling absurd. Perhaps it was this bizarre surface (and slightly subepidermal) layer that *enabled* me adequately to perform the necessary repertoire of movement and give me the confidence to pull it off. Part of the intensity of the experience were the overall sensations of competition, including a cacophony of color, smell, thundering musical amplification, painful straining of muscle, and the chill of the ballroom air. In the physical action of vigorous dancing, sweat begins to run down a dancer's chest, back and legs, forcing cheaper variants of tanning fluid to streak, just like running mascara down one's cheeks after a good cry. Nothing matters. Adrenaline suppresses intellectualizing without missing a beat.

HOMOGENEITY AND ERASURE

What becomes evident, especially when one alternates between contemporary dance and ballroom dance scenes, is that ballroom produces a particular kind of physical and visual homogeneity, an erasure of diversity. Body shapes may be very diverse in Latin-ballroom (in contrast to the lean, skin-and-bones expectations of a classical ballerina), but ideally one's skin is all painted a similar hue, lest a body stand out as unfinished, and thus, unprofessional. An African American dancer laughed at the thought of tanning and said: "We're all the same color out there!" (Debbie Clyne, interview with author, Atlanta, December 2015). All ballroom dancers try to achieve "the look" and we all understand what that means without further explanation. Through the homogeneity, however, one must still show up the others, achieving through performance rather than appearance. In other words, the "It" quality, examined by Joseph Roach (2007), must be recognizable and reproducible:

> Although the perception of It must be excited by some extraordinary perturbation in the looks and personality of the adored, the aura that It broadcasts arises not merely from the singularity of an original, as Walter Benjamin supposed, but also from the fabulous success of its reproducibility in the imaginations of many others, charmed exponentially by the number of its copies. (177)

And herein lies the challenge of winning ballroom dance competitions—how to show off the "it" but also show up like one of them. How does a dancer conform to a standardized ideal, show off a heightened expertise and precisely defined technique, but also promote a unique stylistic hype that will be remembered, seen through the crowd, and thus scored as better than all the others?

One example of the ballroom industry's recognition of twenty-first-century it-ness happened in 2009, when *Dancing With the Stars* TV personality Carrie Ann Inaba was slated to attend the U.S. National Latin-Ballroom Amateur Dance Championship as a guest judge. Dancers protested heatedly against her involvement weeks before the event began, claiming that she knew nothing about ballroom dancing and, what's more, would be judging for an important competition in which U.S. titles were at stake (the top two placements at nationals move on to world championships). So organizers changed her role to a judge of "star quality," her vote not affecting placements, and she gave an award to one couple in each national championship category for being the most charismatic and having the most star potential. Those winning this honor (not always the overall winners) were interviewed on video by Inaba and given a special trophy. My partner, Gary, and I did not win the "star quality" award, and in some ways it stung a bit more than not winning the national title that year.

TRANSNATIONAL LATIN DANCERS

Statistically, few Latin-American-born dancers participate in ballroom competitions, and very few have ever achieved high standings in the national or

Fig. 2.5. IDB Ballroom Camp, held annually in Rockville, Maryland. Dance partnership in class getting competition styling coaching in July 2015. (Photo by Stephen Marino.)

world rankings. Dominican-born and New York-raised Jose DeCamps won the American Rhythm division with his Polish-born partner, Joanna Zacharewicz, from 2007 to 2010. And Haitian-born Emmanuel Pierre-Antoine won with his Russian partner, Liana Churilova, in 2014. No Latin American or Caribbean champion dancers appear in the Latin divisions on recent record, although dancers with Latin American surnames in past years include Ron Montez with Elizabeth Curtis (1979–85) and Rick Valanzuela with Melissa Dexter (1991–92). Assessment by surnames alone does not reveal origins or the self-identifying nationality of the individuals, and the politics of being and claiming Latino heritage in the United States today has changed. Those non-ballroom-dancing Latin American and Latino dancers I have encountered scoff at the ballroom cha cha, samba, and rumba, dismissing the dancesport versions as "incorrect" and "inauthentic." Helena, a Cuban-American ballroom dancer, told me that when her Cuban-raised mother watched her take a rumba lesson, she stood up angrily and asked the instructor, "What's this shit?" (Helena Kostik, interview with author, New Jersey, January 2016). Helena also admitted that she feels like a "white girl" when dancing in Latino clubs, now that she is highly trained in Latin-ballroom.

Latin-ballroom dance differs from the kinds of social and show dancing done by Latinos in various ways, especially timing, basic steps, arm styling, and attitude. In fact, I have not met many Latinos who are willing to perform Latin American dances in a ballroom way. The president of the University of Maryland Latin Dance Club thanked me for my offer to help coach their performance team, but said that my style was "too ballroom" and "not street," which was what they danced (Marcella Goldring, in personal conversation, College Park, Maryland, October 2015). Many Latinos also become frustrated at the ballroom industry because it is not interested in legitimacy or in their authorized opinions. They complain that ballroom continues to unabashedly misuse the names and misrepresent the dances. One Latina informant admitted that she was afraid to be criticized that *she* was not doing the cha cha correctly by mostly white (and nowadays, often Russian) ballroom judges: How could that be, given her Latin American descent? Then again, other Latinos have exclaimed that it is beautiful; different yes, but beautiful, and a Latino performance team director in Delaware, Joe Figueroa, admitted that the ballroom aesthetic and stylization was being increasingly adopted in salsa competitions.

Therefore, critical rejection is not across the board. Context is important. When dancing in a Latin competition within the ballroom world, one must dance Latin-ballroom, not Latin American. It is a transnational arena where dancers from all over the world come together to compete. In World Championship dancesport competitions, dancers hold signs with their country name as they walk onto the floor (two couples per country). There is one brief moment of recognition for their national qualifying status, but once the signs are put away, they are all ballroom and cannot (or should not) be distinguishable. The dances themselves are also denationalized: Samba is no longer Brazilian, Rumba not Cuban, and Paso Doble not Spanish. A new cultural territory is created in this sphere.

I have experienced the other side of this perspective. When dancing with a professional group called Ballet Folklorico de Atlanta in the mid-1990s (salsa, merengue, cha cha), my fellow performers—all born in Mexico, El Salvador, Colombia, and Cuba—openly questioned whether I could really learn their dances if I did not have any Latin American blood. Several of the group's members resented my presence for this very reason, especially whenever I was given a front-row position in a new routine. When spectators found out my ethnic status after a performance, they were surprised, and I was grudgingly told that I danced "pretty well for a *gringa.*" These post-performance responses made me doubt my dance ability. They believed that I was a Latin dancer while I was dancing, my body apparently showing off *Latinidad,* but close up, I was unmasked, my hidden truth disclosed, my status lost. My supposed authentic showing off of Latin dance became a "Latin number" instead, as Brian Herrera might suggest (2015), or perhaps, "Latinoid"—neither here nor there. In the end, this was true, not only for me but also in the group's overall performance of their cultural and national selves. Having trained in Latin-ballroom and competed in dancesport for

Fig. 2.6. Crowded competition floor, filled with Latin-ballroom dancers. (Photo by Stephen Marino.)

Fig. 2.7. Advertisement for Donna Inc., custom ballroom dress designer based in Wilmington, Delaware. (Image courtesy of Donna Inc.)

Fig. 2.8. Garry Gekhman, born in Russia and raised in Israel, now a U.S. citizen and professional competitor and instructor in Virginia. Teaches at the IDB Dance Camp in Rockville, Maryland, July 2015. (Photo by Stephen Marino.)

several years by this point in my life, I was never trying to pass as authentically Latina in ballet folklorico, just as a good dancer. This experience made me forevermore suspicious of my own justifiable place in these Latin American(ish) worlds.

Fred and Ginger Go . . . Latino?

After fifteen years as an International Latin-ballroom dancer, I began to compete in the "American Smooth" category. "Smooth" is the American style of the traditional Standard dances: Waltz, Tango, Foxtrot, Viennese Waltz, and Quickstep. Dresses are long, elegant, and full, and meant to show off the flowing movement of the pair of dancers moving quickly across the floor.

Long pieces of fabric called "floats" are sometimes attached to gloves and shoulders to accentuate speed and fluidity. American Smooth was the contemporary version of Fred Astaire and Ginger Rodgers's foxtrots and quicksteps in 1930s Hollywood films. By moving into this Astaire and Rodgers-like category, I assumed I would not have to tan and was greatly relieved by the prospect. Finally, I could just show my body's usual paleness and not feel so anxious about performative misidentification.

This style has never carried connotations of Latin American. The dances were a representation of whiteness and the leisure class, of pearls, champagne, and butlers. Yet, as I neared my Smooth competition debut, my coach, Mazen Hamza, notified me that, yes, I was expected to be tan in the same way as necessary for the Latin category. I looked at him in shock and confusion. Only one dance in Smooth is originally Latin American (the tango from Argentina) but the International Latin aesthetic has carried over. The body aesthetic is no longer—if it ever was—about trying to be a different ethnicity for performance, regardless of ballroom dance style; the aesthetic has come to be identified with professionalism and perceptions of *ballroom* perfection. The modern-day Fred Astaires and Ginger Rogers are ultrafit athletes, their costumes show torsos and have slits up to the hip, and any feathers added to the woman's costumes are intended to sexualize and intensify more than soften.

The argument that tanning makes a body symbolically Latin American would not apply to the Smooth or Standard divisions, in theory or performance. In fact, historical modifications and alterations to the style of Smooth dance moves (in waltz, tango, foxtrot, quickstep, and Viennese waltz) were made to distance the practice from "blackness," to rein in the alleged wildness of African American popular dance and the unpredictability of improvised kicks and dips, and to inculcate morality and control (see Martin 2010, cf. Desmond 1999 on Hawaiian dance and "soft primitivism"). Many of the modern-day rules were defined and institutionalized for competition by the British Official Board of Ballroom Dancing in the 1930s.

I consider these movements as particular colors painted upon the dancing human, as examples of "invented traditions" so famously defined by Eric Hobsbawm and Terence Ranger (1983). They are based upon historical precedents, but have been transformed by elements outside the reality of chronologies and documented facts. The cultural practices are now part of a *ballroom* aesthetic, not Latin American or any other, traditions separated from their imagined origins. After years of brown-bodying, the

Fig. 2.9. Emmanuelle Pierre-Antoine and Liana Churilova performing for "Dance Legends," a New York-based professional show, featuring national and world champion partnerships. (Photo by Ryan Kenner.)

original motivation, or at least the perceived origin of performing Latin Americanness, dropped out of the dance population's artistic consciousness, thus allowing the practice to expand from the Latin-ballroom category into Smooth without question from participants. The memory of the model seems to have been with each subsequent generation of competitors and even more so as it was catapulted into popular reality television programs. By looking at competition dancing phenomenologically, from the "inside out," not only cultural knowledge but from the experience of the body (Downey 2005), I contend that the modern ballroom competition aesthetic has little to do with tanning in order to become another race or ethnicity. But it does have to do with nationality and a new twenty-first-century show of Russian dancers, or more importantly, Russian dance champions.

The Latin Americanness of Russian Champions

After 1990, a flood of Russian and Polish dancers began to teach and compete in the United States. Trained in Latin ballroom from childhood during the Soviet era, they were serious competitors with strict rehearsal discipline and flawless technique. Surnames of those making the final (top six) of national events are increasingly multisyllabic, and top-level female dancers often go only by their first names: "Irina" (Sarukhanyan) or "Natalia" (Pomaranov), or "Izabella" (Jundzill). My dance heroes are named Yulia Zagoruychenko, Natasha Skorikova, and Lydia Petrigova, not Maria Torres or Lorena Hernandez. Indeed, my own dream is to be an authentically *Russian* Latin dancer. I had to learn to dance like a Russian Latin dancer. I had to paint my body brown like a Russian Latin dancer. I had to dress like a Russian Latin dancer. I could, with training and the right preparations, become a Russian Latin dancer.

This phenomenon is an example that shows off how racial and cultural mixing takes social turns that do not seem to make sense and do not necessarily follow the political consciousness of the time. These trends in the competitive ballroom industry may constitute a new form of transracialization and whiteness, some observers argue, but I disagree, since which category is moving "trans-" another is unclear, and everyone in the industry is tanning, rather, "polishing up," not just white into brown. Asian, Latino, and African Americans also "tan" themselves. Even my Lebanese coach, Pakistani husband, and African American partner tanned and polished themselves up for competition. Transnationalism is certainly a central part of the industry, but the showing off and up in worldwide ballroom communities is not necessarily about an exoticization of another culture, at least not a culture or race that is routinely recognized by any official census.

When I tried to critique my dancesport using critical theory, I usually found that the experience of showing up and off at dance competition was, in many ways, showing up the theory too. The answers were continually "yes, but" or "yes, and," or "no, not quite." The label of the show is inconsistent with what is experienced. Audiences see and judge, dancers see and feel, outside media see and interpret for mass consumption, and the ballroom world continues to spin in its own way. Performance is key, especially when we try to grasp the frustrating yet fascinating incongruity of performative signals. Ballroom has always been a spectacle, once only for an internal crowd that generated clout and profit regardless of outsider perception, but now also for millions of TV viewers around the world who are instructed to be mostly concerned with whether or not a couple did an illegal lift (feet off the floor), jeopardizing their potentially perfect "10" score. Who will win is the central question and seems to be the only thing at stake.

Fig. 2.10. Max Sinitsa and Tatiana Seliverstova, professional American Smooth competitors, based in California. Modern costuming and choreography are no longer typically reminiscent of Fred Astaire and Ginger Rogers. (Photo courtesy of Joe Gaudet Photography.)

Competitive Latin-ballroom illustrates the ever-changing and complex ways that race, ethnicity, and identity are performed and conceptualized. Sometimes these performances change over time with social and political turns or revolutions, commercial expectations and demands, or shifts in population (immigration, for example), but sometimes the change happens unexpectedly and fast and is completely unhinged from our predictions as well as our own experience. Thousands of dancers, especially those who wholly embrace "the life," have learned to perform themselves in ways that were once completely foreign to their preballroom social, physical, and ideological dispositions. Ballroom dance breaks down and reforms one's personal tendencies and also society's expectations of their particular social performance. The ordinary may become "extra-ordinary" through strategic agency (training, intention, passion), which potentially leads to a new generation of practice, revealed especially when one spins out under the heat of the bright lights and takes a bow.

Notes

1. For example, Virginia State Dancesport Championship, Capital Dancesport Championship, Colorado Dancesport Championship, Emerald Ball Dancesport Championship, and U.S. National Dancesport Championship.

Sources

Bial, Henry. 2005. *Acting Jewish: Negotiating Ethnic Identity on the American Stage and Screen.* Ann Arbor: University of Michigan Press.

Bosse, Joanna. 2015. *Becoming Beautiful: Ballroom Dance in the American Heartland.* Urbana: University of Illinois Press.

Bourdieu, Pierre. 1977. *Outline of a Theory of Practice.* Cambridge: Cambridge University Press.

Bulman, Robert. 2006. "Shall We Dancesport? The World of Competitive Ballroom Dancing." *Contexts* 5, no. 1 (Winter): 61–63.

Butler, Judith. 1988. "Performative Acts and Gender Constitution: An Essay in Phenomenology and Feminist Theory." *Theatre Journal* 40, no.4 (December): 519–31.

Butler, Judith. 1990. *Gender Trouble: Feminism and the Subversion of Identity.* New York: Routledge.

Davis, Kathy. 2015. *Dancing Tango: Passionate Encounters in a Globalizing World.* New York: New York University Press.

Deloria, Philip. 1999. *Playing Indian.* New Haven: Yale University Press.

Desmond, Jane. 2001. *Staging Tourism: Bodies on Display from Waikiki to Sea World.* Chicago: University of Chicago Press.

Downey, Greg. 2005. *Learning Capoeira: Lessons in Cunning from an Afro-Brazilian Art.* Oxford: Oxford University Press.

Ericksen, Julia. 2011. *Dance with Me: Ballroom Dancing and the Promise of Instant Intimacy.* New York: New York University Press.

Frederik, Laurie. 2001. "The Contestation of Cuba's Public Sphere in National Theater and the Transformation from Teatro Bufo to Teatro Nuevo." In *Gestos,* año 16, no. 31.

Frederik, Laurie. 2005. "Cuba's National Characters: Setting the Stage for the Hombre Novísimo." In *Journal of Latin American Anthropology,* vol. 10, no. 2.

Frederik, Laurie. 2012. *Trumpets in the Mountains: Theater and the Politics of National Culture in Cuba.* Durham: Duke University Press.

Fusco, Coco. 1995. *English is Broken Here: Notes on Cultural Fusion in the Americas.* New York: The New Press.

García, Cindy, and Ramón H. Rivera-Servera, eds. 2014. "Latin@ Dance: Conversations across the Field of Dance Studies." Special issue of *Society of Dance History Scholars* 34.

Hanna, Judith Lynne. 1988. *Dance, Sex, and Gender: Signs of Identity, Dominance, Defiance, and Desire.* Chicago: University of Chicago Press.

Hebdige, Dick. 1979. *Subculture: The Meaning of Style*. New York: Routledge.

Herrera, Brian Eugenio. 2015. *Latin Numbers: Playing Latino in Twentieth-Century US Popular Performance*. Ann Arbor: University of Michigan Press.

Hobsbawm, Eric, and Terence Ranger, eds. 1983. *The Invention of Tradition*. Cambridge: Cambridge University Press.

Hodgkinson, Paul. 2002. *Goth: Identity, Style, and Subculture*. Oxford and New York: Berg.

Johnson, E. Patrick. 2003. *Appropriating Blackness: Performance and the Politics of Authenticity*. Durham: Duke University Press.

Lane, Jill. 2005. *Blackface Cuba: 1840–1895*. Philadelphia: University of Pennsylvania Press.

Marchand, Trevor H. J., ed. 2010. *Making Knowledge: Explorations of the Indissoluble Relation between Mind, Body, and Environment*. West Sussex, UK: Wiley-Blackwell.

Marion, Jonathan. 2008. *Ballroom: Culture and Costume in Competitive Dance*. Oxford: Berg.

Martin, Christopher. 2010. "How the Waltz Was Won: Towards a Waltz Aesthetic." PhD diss., University of Maryland, College Park.

Mauss, Marcel. 1973. "Techniques of the Body." *Economy and Society* 2, no. 1: 70–88.

McMains, Juliet. 2001. "Brownface: Representations of Latin-ness in Dancesport." *Dance Research Journal* 33, no. 2: 54–71.

McMains, Juliet. 2006. *Glamour Addiction: Inside the American Ballroom Dance Academy*. Middletown, CT: Wesleyan University Press.

Muñoz, José Esteban. 1999. *Disidentifications: Queers of Color and the Performance of Politics*. Minneapolis: University of Minnesota Press.

Olson, Laura. 2004. *Performing Russia: Folk Revival and Russian Identity*. London and New York: Routledge.

Pesman, Dale. 2000. *Russia and Soul*. Ithaca: Cornell University Press.

Picart, Caroline Jean. 2006. *From Ballroom to Dancesport: Aesthetics, Athletics, and Body Culture*. Albany: State University of New York Press.

Richardson, Philip J. S. 1946. *A History of English Ballroom Dancing: 1910–1945: The Story of the Development of the Modern English Style*. London: Herbert Jenkins.

Rivera-Servera, Ramón. 2012. *Performing Queer Latinidad: Dance, Sexuality, Politics*. Ann Arbor: University of Michigan Press.

Roach, Joseph 2007. *It*. Ann Arbor: University of Michigan.

Schechner, Richard. 1985. *Between Theater and Anthropology*. Philadelphia: University of Pennsylvania Press.

Schneider, Rebecca. 1997. *The Explicit Body in Performance*. New York: Routledge.

Strathern, Andrew. 1996. *Body Thoughts*. Ann Arbor: University of Michigan Press.

Taylor, Diana. 2003. *The Archive and the Repertoire*. Durham: Duke University Press.

CHAPTER 3

Shamu the (Killer) Whale and an Ecology of Commodity

Jennifer A. Kokai

On February 24, 2010, at the SeaWorld Orlando amusement park, an orca named Tilikum grabbed trainer Dawn Brancheau, pulled her into the water, and drowned her. This was not Tilikum's first act of violence, nor was such behavior exceptional in the history of the orca display at the park. In 1971, an orca bit a bikini-clad trainer on the leg and the whale had to be pried off of her so that she could go to a hospital. In 2006, a whale dragged another trainer underwater and nearly drowned her. According to a widely reprinted article, California investigators declared that "it was only a matter of time" before a whale killed a trainer ("Garcia and Jacobson 2010). After the 2006 incident the investigators reportedly encouraged the use of lethal force against the whales if they went "out of control" and were "not responding to other control measures" (Perry 2007).[1]

Brancheau's death forced SeaWorld to reenvision certain aspects of their presentation of the whales. The parks eliminated *Believe*, a show that represented whales as kindred spirits to humans and showed humans dancing and swimming with the whales and riding on their backs. *One Ocean*, which requires whales to interact with elaborate fountains rather than humans, replaced *Believe*. In essence, SeaWorld producers created *One Ocean* in the aftermath of *Believe* in order to maintain the presence of whale shows at the park and to renew the artificial and commoditized relationship between humans and whales constructed by SeaWorld. In the competitive theme park industry, SeaWorld has distinguished itself through its brand as an ecological theme park relying largely upon a heightened display of killer

Fig. 3.1. "Shamu"
jumping at SeaWorld,
San Antonio, 2011.

whales and showing off human dominance over them to do so. The performances of *Believe* and *One Ocean* are not just performances, they are a
metonym for the entire SeaWorld product: an experiential blend of pseudo-
environmentalism, environmental domination, and environment as entertainment that Tilikum's actions put at risk.

There is a long-standing tension at SeaWorld between whale shows invented by producers and the nature of the whale. SeaWorld wants to show
off the whales as tamed, friendly, educational, inspiring, and thrilling, to
maximize profit. Their narrative has little to do with the whales' desires and
needs, and the whales often don't comply. Tensions between the stories of
whales sold by the parks and the whales as creatures of nature mean that
SeaWorld must constantly revise its shows in order to keep profits high.[2]
In this essay, I describe and analyze the material and ideological practices
I witnessed at SeaWorld (both live and in tourists' recordings). I contrast
the new performance strategies adopted after Brancheau's death with the

old as SeaWorld attempted to maintain its overall message: killer whales are human friends and ambassadors to the ocean. Dramaturgically analyzing the theatricalized showing of orcas in an artificial environment reveals an underlying ideology about relationships between human and nonhuman animals and the presumed dominion of the human animal over the seas. As opposed to a more clinical scientific or factual idea of nature, the SeaWorld performances use spectacle and display to construct for patrons a utopian version of "nature" as a location separate from and outside of human culture that nevertheless remains under and benefits from human control. Through the orca shows with their narratives, trainers, and mises-en-scène, showing as a force allows SeaWorld to confirm for us what we want to believe about the world and humans' place in it. The material harm done to whales and the adverse ecological impact of humans on the oceans are occluded by a show that tells us a much more pleasant story: that we are loving guardians of the sea and all its creatures.

While this is most visible through animal performances, and especially the killer whale displays, the "show" at SeaWorld is not just the performance itself but rather the myriad practices that frame and present the performance to the audience. The chain of SeaWorld amusement parks brings together shows, rides, thematic scenery and landscaping, and, most important, human and sea animal interactions. The park claims an educational purpose: visitors have opportunities to hear factoids about the animals, to witness them doing spectacular feats (like jumping high out of the water), and to interact with sea creatures (feeding dolphins dead fish, for example). The main menu of the webpage presents four categories—Parks, Conservation, Education, and Blogs—in a layout that suggests they carry equal weight. For an additional fee, the park allows patrons to interact with the sea animals or to have "up close tours" ("Attractions" 2013).

"SHAMU" AND THE SHOWING OF KILLER WHALES

The orca, or killer whale, show is the most popular and publicized attraction at the park. The park mascot, "Shamu," is ubiquitous in the advertising, merchandise, and decoration. Shamu is everywhere. SeaWorld has spent decades promoting Shamu the whale as docile and fun. In the 1980s, a television commercial promoted "four-ton killer whales that [a]re actually cuddly" (1980s Sea World Commercial 2009). Vintage commercials regularly showed small children hugging the orcas. Trainers rode the whales, spectators waved at them, and fans voted on baby names. Before you enter the parking lot at SeaWorld San Antonio, you are offered the opportunity to purchase "Shamu's preferred parking." When you enter the gates you enter under a large stained glass image of an orca. In the plaza at the entrance you can pose with a human dressed in a giant Shamu mascot uniform who literalizes the promised "cuddly" whales and hugs you tightly while cameras flash. Through all of these actions, Shamu is configured as a friend to humans.

Paradoxically, no live whale named Shamu appears at the park. The SeaWorld website clarifies that Shamu is the "stage name" given to any performing whale, male or female (Seaworld, "Ask Shamu" 2013). A whale at SeaWorld has many names, indicating the degree to which humans want mastery, via multiple Adamic acts of naming, over this powerful and mysterious creature (Derrida 2008, 15). First, the whale has a scientific name, *Orcinus orca*, then several common names, "orca," or "killer whale." Then the captive animals at SeaWorld are given individual names (Tilikum, for example). Finally, the animals are referred to collectively as "Shamu." Each of these names is an effort to classify and control the whale, whose actions—dying quickly in captivity, drowning trainers, killing foolish pelicans—evade the script SeaWorld writes for them.

The name "Shamu" acts as a microcosm of the whole show's desire to domesticate and commodify the whale. SeaWorld sells an idea of a huggable, touchable whale, like the stuffed animal "Shamus" clutched by children around the park. The SeaWorld website suggests a possible origin for the name "Shamu": "Friend of Namu," that is, a friend of one of the first captive orcas at the original park displayed in 1965 (a young male who died quickly when caged).[3] The new whales are then placed into a genealogy of human possession and control of orcas; each new whale is a "friend" of one of the first whales captured. The naming practices create orcas that were made, literally through breeding, and figuratively through naming and character development, by SeaWorld.

"Shamu" is, most importantly, a friend to all people. While one can imagine, given tiger or lion taming shows, that SeaWorld could have constructed a park around the dangers of the orca, an apex predator, the company has taken a different route to reach families and maximize potential profit. To differentiate itself from other theme parks, such as Disney World or Six Flags, who also compete for family tourist dollars, SeaWorld has

Fig. 3.2. Cuddly "Shamu" loves children. SeaWorld, San Antonio, 2011.

constructed a park that touts education and environmentalism and thus offers a moral halo to visitors. The shows, advertisements, and website imply
that purchasing a ticket to SeaWorld will teach visitors something about
the oceans *and* do good in the world, making consumerism appear to be an
act of environmental conscience. The choice to make "Shamu" a friend to
humans, and to imply that the park merges education with entertainment,
differentiates SeaWorld from other theme parks that only entertain. The
tricks that Shamu and other animals perform also increase the spectacle
and differentiate the park from zoos, which claim to educate and entertain
as well. Given this mythos of environmental education through friendly encounters with marine animals, more than anything else that could happen
at SeaWorld, Shamu killing a human is a nightmare. It forces the public to

Fig. 3.3. "Shamu's
Preferred Parking."
SeaWorld, San Anto-
nio, 2011.

think harder about whether or not the park is educational (do the typical
nondeadly performances really show us the truth about orcas?) and whether
or not buying a ticket is act of environmentalism (are we helping orcas or
driving them crazy?).

Going to SeaWorld is an expensive proposition; patrons tend to be
middle class to upper class, and predominately white (Desmond 1999, 220).
Ticket prices vary from park to park, but in Orlando they are on par with
tickets at Disney World, Busch Gardens, and other major theme park attractions. In the 2013 summer season, tickets in San Antonio cost $65 for adults
and $55 for children. In Orlando tickets cost even more: $80 for adults and
children. These figures don't include refreshments (no food can be brought
into the park), souvenirs, or fish to feed to dolphins.

Given the cost of attendance, visitors expect more for their money than
a conventional fish-swimming-by-behind-glass aquarium experience. Along
with the roller coasters, brightly colored kids' rides, and overflowing sou-

venir booths, SeaWorld must also provide an encounter with its putative focus—sea animals—that transcends a simple "display" of nature. SeaWorld shows up other aquariums' more placid entertainments by constructing animal performances that provide special thrills, such as splashing spectators and shocking them with the sight of a human trainer's head entering the mouth of an apex predator, but all while reassuring tourists that, like a roller coaster, this was ultimately harmless and "just for show."

THE LIMITS OF THE SHOW

Brancheau's death and Tilikum's actions revealed the elements of orca behavior and agency that SeaWorld did not want to show off. Her death occurred during a special event where visitors could pay extra to "Dine with Shamu." That is, her death occurred in full sight of, and was caught on camera by, park visitors who had just been enjoying watching the trainer play with the 12,000-pound whale. SeaWorld quickly moved to suppress this incident, removing the videos through the threat of a lawsuit and working in concert with Brancheau's family to try to seal the official video, which should have been public as a matter of course ("Dawn Brancheau Death Video Ruling" 2013). SeaWorld makes hundreds of videos of "Shamu" jumping, flipping, and snuggling with humans available on their website, but the video of Brancheau's death and other videos that display typical orca hunting behaviors are elided from histories of the parks and performances.

Though the park had legal grounds to prevent Brancheau's death from appearing online, other videos of hunting behaviors have remained, for example, one showing a whale killing a pelican that foolishly landed in the tank ("Killer Whale Kills Pelican & Eats It During Show" 2011). The pelican's death was, of course, a foreseeable action given orcas' predatory nature, but it is one that SeaWorld does not care to show at the parks and only appears when tourists interrupt SeaWorld's carefully crafted depiction of "Shamu" (SeaWorld, "Killer Whales: Diet and Eating Habits" 2013).[4] By filming these violent events and releasing them to a wider audience through the Internet, spectators are not just watching or participating in the performance; they are actively dismantling the show and the ideological narrative of human/whale friendship they ostensibly paid for. This damages the desired effect of the whale show and impedes SeaWorld's ability to market their park as environmental and educational, their key draw for a family-friendly attraction.

For this reason, though SeaWorld allows tourists to post millions of videos publicly of Shamu behaving as the Park desires, the corporation suppresses videos that reveal the edges and seams of the show.

With or without the tourist videos, Brancheau's death made international news, as did the lawsuits that followed. Animal rights organizations, such as People for the Ethical Treatment of Animals (PETA), used this as an opportunity to once again call for SeaWorld to cease keeping the whales in captivity, arguing that it was immoral, unnatural, and unhealthy for all: "It's not surprising when these huge, smart animals lash out. This is not the first incident in which a trainer has been harmed by an animal who has been deprived of any semblance of life" ("SeaWorld Whale Attacks, Kills Trainer" 2013). On October 25, 2011, PETA filed a lawsuit in the U.S. district court in San Diego contending that whales are being unfairly kept as slaves in violation of the Thirteenth Amendment ("PETA Lawsuit Seeks to Expand Animal Rights" 2013). Following the trainer's death, PETA, in spite of its controversial tactics,[5] garnered more supporters, which put SeaWorld on the defensive. The book, *Death at SeaWorld* by David Kirby, and documentary, *Blackfish*, released in 2013, increased the pressure. *Blackfish* reached a wide audience, making over $2 million in ticket sales. Both works document the long history of orca violence at the parks as well as make compelling arguments that keeping orcas in captivity is a morally problematic and foolhardy activity. While this evidence was available and well known to whale researchers and those who sought it out, these two sources synthesized the information in an engaging way for the general public.

Initially the local police told the public that Brancheau had slipped or fallen into the water and drowned. This claim contradicted eye-witnesses who saw the whale pull her into the water ("Killer Whale Fatally Attacks Trainer" 2010). When it became clear that the official version of the story could not withstand scrutiny, SeaWorld reported that the whale pulled Brancheau in by her hair. This too is questionable. Websites such as "The Orca Project" filed Freedom of Information Act requests and obtained footage from tourists present at the attack. Based on this evidence, the website's authors maintain that Tilikum dragged Brancheau in by the arm and that SeaWorld misrepresented the event in order to implicate Brancheau for leaving her long hair down. This tactic allowed the park, now requiring trainers to wear buns, to make it seem as if stricter safety requirements were already in place ("SeaWorld Trainer Death Theory Debunked as a Ponytail Tale" 2013).

Public outcry and concern forced SeaWorld to change their shows quickly. They had to reassure the audience that no human would be killed in front of their children. They had to argue forcefully against the position of animal rights organizations that orcas should not be in captivity, which suddenly resonated with the general public. They had to separate their mascot, Shamu, from the actions of one whale, Tilikum. The power of "showing" at SeaWorld is not simply to entertain but to restructure the basic relationship between humankind and nature. While Brancheau's death would not necessarily compromise sales of the show itself (SeaWorld could, after all, continue to charge admission to see the whales in a tank), it could easily destroy the far more profitable second product: a mythology of whales as cuddly friends who serve as our ambassadors to the ocean.

In *Believe*, SeaWorld shows the whales as essentially tamed friends, presenting humans as rightful masters of the oceans and its denizens. Brancheau's death caused spectators to become more skeptical of that depiction, which in turn caused SeaWorld to alter their presentation of the imaginary relationship between human consumers and nonhuman commodities. *One Ocean* offers more modest claims than *Believe* about human and orca relationships. Unlike *Believe*, which implied that whales and humans understood each other, the stated goal of Shamu's new performance is to encourage audiences to "care" about "his world." Both shows claim a commitment to ecology and education, but emotional arousal through extravagant spectacle seems more to the point. Both shows also distort and mischaracterize the relationship between human and ocean, while encouraging passive spectatorship.

BELIEVE AND THE LIMITS OF BELIEF

I first saw *Believe* in person at the San Antonio, Texas, SeaWorld on March 21, 2010, after Brancheau's death in Florida. It was clear that *Believe* was not being performed as intended; there were large portions of time where nothing much happened (perhaps the producers hoped that lighting effects would compensate for the lack of action in the water). The trainers stood off to the sides of the whales and despite musical crescendos and lyrics exhorting the audience to feel "greater," the show felt generally flat and dull. At that viewing, I overheard a couple remarking that they hoped all of the trainers would survive this performance, but the trainers stayed well clear of the whales and were never in any danger. Brancheau's death clearly ghosted this performance, even months later with different whales and in a different city.

Unlike many parts of the park, which are packed with rides, lurid colors, and flashing lights, SeaWorld has tried to make the orcas' space appear as a utopic version of nature, a space undomesticated by human intervention. The tank extends outside of the arena, preventing spectators from gauging its true size. The audience can imagine the expanse of the arena's water flowing into another huge body of water or even into the ocean itself. The sides of the arena are painted with soft pastel blues, pinks, and greens that give the impression of sunrise or sunset and make the roof of the arena look like a gentle sky. The roof shields the audience from the unrelenting Texas sun, making it a far more pleasant place than the actual outdoors. There are large video screens on either end that constantly show images of animals— orcas and others—swimming freely in the ocean and contribute to the feeling of the arena space as a "natural" environment. Even the music is generally soothing, or emotionally stirring in the manner of light rock (in contrast to the modern hip-hop or pop music heard in other parts of the park).

Although Shamu Stadium is far from natural, SeaWorld has taken care to make it seem gentler and more natural than other parts of the park. As Susan G. Davis argues, spaces at SeaWorld are made to appear "effortful (that is, polished by labor and held under control) and effortless (green, shady, abundant, and freely growing) at the same time" (1997, 83). In Shamu Stadium, this is particularly noticeable. SeaWorld attempts to show us that "nature" is relaxing and entertaining, better than the "wilds" of human daily life or the orca's ocean. At SeaWorld, "nature" doesn't have traffic *or* bugs.

Although the performance of *Believe* that I saw in San Antonio had far fewer tricks than in previous versions, watching the whales leap from the water is, nonetheless, an awe-inspiring spectacle. The whales' sheer size is astonishing, and their ability seemingly to defy the laws of physics by leaping enormous heights and somersaulting their great bulk through the air rightly causes spectators to gasp. Their movement transcends human capability. Their bodies are sleek, with distinct black and white areas, and their eyes seem to radiate intelligence.[6] San Antonio is landlocked, hours away from the ocean and even farther away from orcas' natural homes. The opportunity to see creatures that the average person would otherwise never encounter relatively close up feels like a privilege. The auditorium is enormous. Spectators who choose to sit outside the "splash zone" are hundreds of feet away from the orcas. Still, given the number of Shamu vid-

Fig. 3.4. Shamu's Stadium at SeaWorld, San Antonio.

eos filmed and uploaded on YouTube by tourists, and the message boards where people share their experiences of the shows, simply being in the same space as the orcas is most of the attraction for people. As one tourist stated in a review on the travel site Trip Advisor, "Getting soaked to skin by Shamu, what a privilege."[7]

Anyone with Internet access can view the Shamu videos for free online, but the willingness of hundreds of thousands of visitors from the United States and abroad to buy expensive tickets indicates that they value the direct experience of live orcas and other animals. If tigers have "It," according to Joseph Roach, because of their "personality-driven mass attraction" and "air of perceived indifference" (2007, 3–5), the same can be said of whales, who dwarf their human trainers, and charge the spectacle with danger; however, unlike the tiger shows, SeaWorld constructs the human and whale relationship as one of communication and play. The act of showing allows SeaWorld to heighten some aspects of the whales while minimizing others so that spectators can be awed by Shamu's size and power, without worrying about the whale's relationship to people.

If awe is what spectators go to experience, then a live performance is far superior to a video. Still, fans record the shows and post them on the Internet as a memento of their visit and an inferior way to witness the orcas. While fan videos are not the same as a live performance, they allow a historian to capture the shows at different moments in different parks. For example, in video performances recorded in 2006–7, I saw a very different *Believe* than the live show I saw in 2010.[8] Like other Orca shows, *Believe* starts with prerecorded video footage—but rather than whales, we see humans: in this case a young boy, wearing a carved whale tail necklace, who spots a wild whale in the ocean. As the boy runs off camera, a male trainer runs out from behind the screen onto the main stage wearing the same necklace and carrying a kayak paddle, just like the boy in the video. The intimation is clear: the boy in the video grew up to be a whale trainer at SeaWorld. Starting with footage of a human spotting a whale sets up a relationship between spectator and trainer, not spectator and whale. Like the boy in the video, we are human beings waiting for and hoping to spy a whale. Like the trainer, we could also control an orca.

The action abruptly shifts to real time, where another trainer, sometimes male and sometimes female depending upon the show, is interacting with a whale on a side stage. The trainer is wearing a black and white suit, echoing the colors of the whale and emphasizing the relationship between the humans and the whales. He allows the whale to spit water in his face and splash him, and the audience laughs at the whale making a fool of the trainer. This carefully calibrated scene is effective and touching. Another trainer caresses and appears to care deeply about the whale. The whale adopts a series of submissive poses, shaking fins with the trainer and bobbing her head side to side in the water while the trainer strokes her. As the music swells the trainer kisses the whale and the whale allows him to hug her. Although trainers exaggerate their movements and gestures so that the audience can see this supposed show of affection, the giving of a food reward, the actual stimulus for the whale's proximity, is minimally visible.

The whales leap and flip, beach themselves and swivel around, receiving a constant stream of fish as rewards. Then a female trainer joins the whale in the water. The whale allows the trainer to ride on her back, and then turns around, allowing her to float on her stomach. Accompanied by a recorded female voice singing about how we are all "a part of something far greater," the two are a picture of relaxation and ease. Alone center stage in the spotlight, whale and trainer twirl around in a pas de deux, their bodies inter-

Fig. 3.5. A female trainer, her hair in a bun, in the "One Ocean" show in 2011, rewarding "Shamu" with fish.

twined while the singer reaches a crescendo in volume and pitch. Her lyrics instruct us to "come take our place in the dance in the sky, the land, and the sea." Again, watching this, spectators likely identify with the trainer, wish to take her place, and to experience swimming with an orca.

Just as SeaWorld must negotiate selling environmentalism for capitalistic gain, the park also participates in a complicated history of enticing tourists through shapely trainers in tight body suits while keeping parks family friendly. Built in San Diego, California, in 1964, the first SeaWorld drew inspiration from two other parks: Weekie Wachee in Florida and Aquarena Springs in San Marcos, Texas. These parks used their locations at natural springs and built theaters that allowed spectators to see beneath the water's surface. In an era before the 1968–72 documentaries of Jacques Cousteau, the sea and its creatures fascinated tourists. However, both of these parks also relied upon the spectacle of women dressed as mermaids to lure tourists and add glamour to the water, and initially SeaWorld was no different. Originally, the major draw at SeaWorld was the "Sea Maids," attractive, college-age women who swam in the tank with the fish. In newspaper cover-age, the women and not the marine life often received top billing. Though women's bodies are often used to sell entertainment, the practice is particu-larly notable for water-based entertainments because Ecocritics have long pointed out the cultural associations between women and water. As Sara Ahmed writes, "In most cultures, water as the primal fluid—purifying, re-generating, creating, and destroying—is closely intertwined with women's roles as bearers and nurturers of life" (2006, 81). For all of these reasons, the decisions by the park to use women trainers probably arose organically. To audience members, women would seem more naturally at home in the water with the whales.

Sociologist Stephen J. Fjellmen argues that "the culture of late capitalism has seen the spread of commoditization into perhaps the last two available domains—the unconscious (pornography, psychotherapy, fantasy) and na-ture (wilderness parks, zoos, and anthropology)" (1992, 6). All three parks began as perfect blends of these two domains: commoditization of a kind of fantastic soft-core pornography (mermaids) and commoditization of the water. Although now much larger in scale and scope, SeaWorld still privi-leges performance. While the women in fish tails have disappeared, the vid-eos that accompany the whale shows often feature attractive young women. Female trainers who work with the whales embody a more (post)mod-ern image of mermaids as powerful swimmers at home in the sea. Today, SeaWorld's videos and trainers are just as often populated with attractive, well-groomed young men. Whether live or mediated, SeaWorld employees rarely talk. Like the whales, they are bodies to be looked at. If understand-ings of gender, entertainment, and aquatic environmentalism have evolved, the spectacle of attractive trainers still remains a part of the performance. Regardless of their appearance, their presence helps reinforce the idea that SeaWorld shows are safe and that orcas and other animals are friends.

At the end of their dance, the female trainer embraces the whale and kisses it, and then encourages the whale to vocalize. This vocalization gives the impression that the whale is talking with the trainer about their duet, that they have a relationship, that swimming together helps the trainer to understand and communicate with the whale through a shared language ("Seaworld- Somethin Far Greater" 2007). Kissing and cuddling contin-ues throughout the performance. Though this interaction is intended to reinforce the narrative SeaWorld crafts—that whales are harmless and love people—after Brancheau's death it was difficult to watch the videos without fixating on the female trainer's long ponytail hanging so near the whale's mouth.

Believe anthropomorphized the orcas, alleging a fundamental harmony between human and whale. Many performance choices suggested that the whales were essentially tamed and that humans were/are the masters of the ocean and all of its creatures—even the 10,000-pound mammal sitting atop the food chain. The lyrics of the songs reinforced SeaWorld ideology. In "Something Far Greater" the refrain told us that "every creature walking the land, and dancing the ocean, or learning to soar tells us we're part of something far greater, something far more." Paradoxically, the song asked human animals in the audience to embrace water, sky, and nonhuman animals as equals, while also justifying SeaWorld's dominion over the whales and commodification of the whale-human relationship. By swimming in the water with the whales, the trainers became "far more" than mere humans and the whales become far more than mere whales.

Showing off the whales and the humans who are the masters brings into sharp relief the complex and contradictory relationship between environmentalism and capitalism in contemporary culture. Through our domination of powerful nonhuman animals like orcas, and their conditional submission to us, we show ourselves as "far greater" than millions of other sentient animals on the planet. This perception of human superiority impacts choices made toward the environment; we feel entitled to resources and spaces as the planet's most intelligent species. SeaWorld as a business promotes itself as helping consumers feel not only as masters of the planet but also as protectors of it. The show contains, markets, and updates "nature" into something that consumers want repeatedly to purchase. "Nature," of course, would often best be preserved by leaving it untouched and therefore unmarketable. These incompatible goals combine to create a performance that requires constant upkeep in order to show only what SeaWorld wants.

The version of *Believe* performed after Dawn Brancheau's death was a shadow of the former display. Audience response to the trainer's death and ensuing legal problems compelled SeaWorld to ban all close contact with the whales and all "water work," as they call direct interaction between human and whale in the water. Although the usual video and music remained, gone were the seemingly intimate moments between whales and humans. Gone was the spectacle of humans riding on the whale's back. Before Brancheau, trainers selected one child from the audience to pet an orca. In the revised version, children were selected and brought on stage, but they had no contact with the whales. Instead, they were asked about their "dream ca-reer."[9] Given the ease with which Tilikum killed Brancheau, audiences can no longer *believe* that trainers understand and can control killer whales; the show was no longer effective. SeaWorld had hubristically set out not just to display human mastery over smaller sea animals, as other aquariums do, but to show off that it could master orcas.

SeaWorld protested the Occupational Safety and Health Administra-tion (OSHA) bans, but the orders were reinforced by a state court case in 2011 and federally in 2013. There would be no more contact between people and whales at the parks. *Believe* rested heavily on water work, on showing humans swimming with and commanding orcas. As the tourists' comments and the lack of activity demonstrated, *Believe* was now a show devoid of spectacle, allowing room for the dramatic events in Orlando to seep in and ghost the performance. In order to seize control of the narrative, prop up Shamu as friendly and not murderous, and get the show back in working order, SeaWorld would have to do something.

ONE OCEAN (RULED BY SHAMU)

In the summer of 2011, the parks announced with fanfare the creation of a brand-new show, *One Ocean*. The transition from *Believe* to *One Ocean* dem-onstrates in performance where the show ends and reality intrudes and re-veals the limits of human commodification and control of nature. In order to maintain the park's ideology that humans and whales have a warm, mutually nurturing relationship, which is the underlying message of the park, Sea-World producers had to create a new production that underscored points of cross-species connection while discouraging any close interactions. This was different from any show they ever had to make before.

One Ocean has a limited narrative plot that is similar in important ways to *Believe*. In San Antonio, the narration of the performance takes place pri-marily on enormous video screens positioned at either end of the arena the-ater.[10] For the duration of the show, the lighting turns the water from a uni-form blue to a spectrum of shimmering colors, while a pulsing soundtrack builds and quiets the crowd's enthusiasm. The show commences with a video stating that we are "one world, connected by one ocean" and exhorting us that "if we love something we will cherish it, and if we cherish it, we will protect it." The first section ends with a display of the show's official graphic:

Fig. 3.6. "Shamu" flips while humans hold the world in their hands. "One Ocean," San Antonio, 2011.

a child's hands hold two orcas jumping as water streams behind them toward the earth. The message is blatant, hubristic, and simplistic. We are the masters of the world, we must protect the ocean and its creatures, and the best way we can do that is by making children love Shamu. Images and references to children are a frequently recurring feature of the show.

The next segment presents a montage of images of children who are profoundly affected by meeting marine life. There is no dialogue, only music playing, and the live whales are not in the theater. Even video images of children are kept separate from live whales. A young girl on a hike with her father spies killer whales swimming freely in a bay, and is so entranced by this memory that when she grows up she decides to work with whales. A young boy meets a dolphin and then grows up to work with dolphins. A young girl visiting an aquarium sees a whale mimicking her motions. Each sequence of images underscores the idea that seeing a whale is a profound gift to your children and that whales welcome interactions.

SeaWorld struggled with the media after Brancheau's death, and this segment in particular works to repair the damage done to the park's image. By representing multiple types of whales and not just an orca interacting with children, the producers reverse the effects of marketing "Shamu" as a unified character. Another strategy was to persuade all of the news outlets that covered the story to differentiate the actions of one whale—Tilikum— from SeaWorld's traditional practice of calling all orcas "Shamu." Complicating the narrative and introducing new characters, the show has changed in an effort to avoid the perception of Shamu as dangerous or a villain.

The segment in *One Ocean* where children encounter whales reminds the public of the relationship imagined, constructed, and promised by Sea-World. We may no longer be "part of something far greater" in our one-on-one relationships with whales as *Believe* argued, and children may no longer be allowed to cuddle with them, but *One Ocean* maintains that, at SeaWorld, the whales' primary function is still to help humans understand the ocean and choose careers. After the long video introduction, the music swells and the video screens turn to a backdrop of sky and clouds. A live orca leaps center stage with no humans present live or on-screen. This show continues to separate even mediated images of humans from live orcas. As prerecorded singers sing and whales leap and jump spectacularly throughout the arena, live trainers remain silent. Wearing blue uniforms that allude to the ocean rather than the black and white suits that referenced the whales, trainers run about the arena, from platform to platform, signaling the whales to perform their tricks. The trainers bop and dance their choreography to a cheerful tune about how we are "on our way to a brighter day." Unlike *Believe's* songs, the lyrics of songs in *One Ocean* seem to argue that humans and whales have had a rough patch, but that things are going to look up now.

At the conclusion of this segment, the whales exit the stage and previously invisible large fountains mounted on the edges of the arena and aimed inward suddenly spout enormous streams of water. The audience cheers for the fountains almost as loudly as they do for the jumping whales. Although equating mechanically moving water to the extraordinary feats of the whales might seem odd, these fountains are designed to replace humans in the arena and interact with the whales in our stead. A fountain, after all, is water tamed—water conducted through pipes built according to human specifications and aesthetics. In fact, fountains have widely been used as a commodified spectacle; large quantities of water move under human direction in a splashy show that glistens under lights. Although far less danger-

Fig. 3.7. Fountains at SeaWorld, San Antonio, 2011.

ous than the stunts in *Believe* and therefore less thrilling, the fountains that substitute for humans seem to satisfy SeaWorld audiences. The whales still interact with humans, though now through a far safer surrogate.

Today, particularly in drought-stricken central Texas, showy fountains used purely to entertain, even with recycled tank water, signify excess and decadence, a fitting representation of human intervention into nature. Advance press for the show claimed that the whales would engage with the fountains, but the orcas mostly ignore them. Working in unison with the music and lights, the fountains jet out larger or smaller amounts of water depending upon how much energy the show wants to create. During one popular part of the performance, when Shamu splashes the crowd, the fountains rise to their peak levels, the music swells, and the crowd cheers as the whale douses eager overheated spectators. This is supposed to be a huge spectacle of human control—of water and whales moving on human cues— rationalized by the repeated message: there is *One Ocean* and it is the responsibility of humans to protect it. Whatever the substance of the environmental rationale, a recalcitrant whale can show up the show, thwarting not just human control over nature, but human choice over what is highlighted and what is kept offstage, the very premise of the SeaWorld enterprise.

If SeaWorld shows constantly exhort the audience to protect the future of the ocean, they offer little guidance for doing so. Apparently just by coming to SeaWorld we have already done something proactive for the ocean. Even more important, by bringing children to see whales, we have somehow changed the whales' dire ecological situation for the better. The show also tells us that, like humans, whales learn by observation; thus we should model actions for our children like "eating sustainable seafood." Despite all the rhetorical posturing, the show is virtually devoid of educational content concerning whales, environmental protection, or concrete action steps.

The performance is full of rhetorically empty sentiments: for example, "It is such a privilege for all of us at SeaWorld to work with Shamu and all of the other amazing animals in the park. It inspires us to make a difference, all of us working together to celebrate and care for our animal world. When we care for our oceans, we're securing the future for the next generation." This statement implies that the nonhuman animals at SeaWorld have a choice whether to be there or not, that SeaWorld cares about the animals that live there, and that any of this has a positive impact on the ocean, miles away from the park. Participating in this imagined construction of human-whale relationships means that we are buying into the idea that we have done our environmental duty, that we are stewards of the planet and are teaching our children to value it. The high cost of a ticket to SeaWorld must buy the spectator something of value beyond just an opportunity to see whales. Sea-World's narrative implies that the park has done many good things with visitors' money; thus the cost of admission buys them environmental absolution. There is no need to do anything else for the ocean and wild whales.

CONCLUSION

In the aftermath of Dawn Brancheau's death, many asked what Tilikum was thinking.[11] This interest in Tilikum's mental state was heightened by the film *Blackfish*, which presented him as a mistreated and emotionally damaged creature. Yet Tilikum remains at SeaWorld Orlando, and is still a part of the show. He appears alone under a pouring waterfall, with no trainers visible. But even though this strategy works to decouple the whale and his drowned trainer, spectators will probably wonder about his intentions for the rest of his life. Was he playing with Brancheau's long ponytail, like he might a new toy? Was he aware that dragging her below the surface would kill her (like the whale and the pelican)? Given the way SeaWorld anthropomorphizes whales and characterizes their relationships with humans, these questions took on great importance to SeaWorld fans.

Fredric Jameson claims that nature is one of the last commodifiable things left. SeaWorld's market empire commodifies and creates demand for orcas and human-orca relationships. Like appliances and junk food, Sea-World's packaged nature displays a kind of planned obsolescence. Captive whales die much sooner than wild whales. According to zoologist Randall E. Eaton, "Orcas have survived about ten years on average in aquariums, no matter how old they are when captured. . . . we know that one orca died in the wild at an age of at least 140 years old, then by accident. Some estimates run 70 years for males, 100 years for females in the wild" (2003, 448). To be born a SeaWorld whale is to be born into a very different and briefer life than an ocean orca. And as OSHA so clearly stated, whales endanger their human trainers. Working closely with them will and has inevitably ended in human death.

SeaWorld purports that "Shamu" makes us care more about the ocean and the world. If it were true that Shamu's sacrifices improve the lives of large numbers of orcas, perhaps it could be said that this trade-off is ethical. What *One Ocean* actually does, however, is to show relationships between human and nature in terms of human mastery. The novelty of somersaulting orcas reigns at SeaWorld, and individuals like Brancheau and Tilikum matter little beside the imagined and shown-off relationship between "Shamu" and humans. As Eaton observes, "Profits and enlightenment don't mix when the latter must be given up for the former" (2003, 448). SeaWorld executives know that they are not following best practices with their orcas. As early as 1979, orca scholars had already begun urging aquariums to change the way they kept and cared for orcas, but to little avail.

SeaWorld's assertion that "if we love something we will cherish it, and if we cherish it, we will protect it" may contain some truth, but the orca shows lull spectators into believing that their mere presence at the performances will protect the whales. As a *New York Times* article on PETA's lawsuit recounted, "Jenny Raymond, 47, who was visiting from Switzerland, said she was delighted by the show and does not buy the argument that the orcas are slave laborers. 'I think they are in better conditions here than in the wild'" ("PETA Lawsuit Seeks to Expand Animal Rights" 2013). Despite well-known statistics that whales die in captivity decades before they would in the oceans, and that captive orcas exhibit signs of severe mental agitation and stress, that numerous serious human injuries and deaths have resulted from keeping orcas in captivity,[12] SeaWorld performances have convinced many patrons that humans can better care for orcas than orcas themselves.

In 2015, SeaWorld announced "The Blue World Project," another change to the way it shows off the orcas. With plans to open in San Diego in 2018, SeaWorld frames the new style of tanks, which allow humans to view orcas from above, below, and the side, as an end to orca shows at that park; however, the tank will still be roughly the same size as their current enclosure, and will likely still show off dazzling orca tricks by calling them "behaviors" that keep the orcas from being bored. What will be gone is the heightened spectacular performance, the obvious showing off with lights, narrative, fountains, and songs that has been the hallmark of the orca display for so long. Major changes, or even the cessation of the show, won't happen because Shamu is not just an orca, and the orca display is not just a performance. Audiences who buy a ticket to the show, and then buy the show's message, carefully crafted through the publicity, the park, the landscaping, the things shown off and the things kept hidden, as millions do, will believe that all "Shamu" really needs is a hug, and that human interventions and impositions on flora and fauna are an inherently good thing. The true effects of showing orcas as a product to be bought, and nature as something that can be mastered and sold, may be to assure our mutual destruction.

Notes

All photographs were taken by the author for nominative use and not endorsed or authorized by SeaWorld. Portions of this material can be found in a revised and extended version in the fourth chapter of my monograph, *Swim Pretty: Aquatic Spectacles and the Performance of Race, Gender, and Nature* (Carbondale, IL, Southern Illinois University Press, 2017).

1. Indeed, the Orlando park has been embroiled in a court battle with OSHA that found them liable of negligence and assessed them a large fine in 2011. As of July 2014, their last option is to petition the Supreme Court ("SeaWorld Fights OSHA Findings in Trainer's Death" 2013).

2. An outstanding history of SeaWorld is found in Susan Davis's book *Spectacular Nature* (Berkeley: University of California Press, 1997). This article is in many ways building upon her excellent foundation and discussing later performances and events. In my larger book project, I concentrate more on how SeaWorld is a continuation of a his-

tory of underwater spectaculars in U.S. culture and how their evolution demonstrates our changing gendered and raced notions of human relationships with water.

3. Though orcas can live for up to 100 years in the wild, Namu, a relatively young male whale, died after only one year in captivity. See Moorby, Lisa. 2009. "Center for Whale Research: One of These Killer Whales Is Almost 100 Years Old . . ." Center for Whale Research. http://whaleresearch.blogspot.com/2009/05/one-of-these-killer-whales-is-almost.html

4. It is important to note that this information actually comes from SeaWorld's website, but is not included in any of the Shamu shows, nor is it available to be read at Shamu Stadium, and so the information is not accessible to SeaWorld visitors.

5. For a typical critique of PETA's use of women's bodies, see "PETA and a Pornographic Culture" by Cathleen McGuire and Colleen McGuire and published in *Feminists for Animal Rights* 8, nos. 3–4 (Fall-Winter 1994–95).

6. Orcas, and cetaceans in general, are considered by scientists to be as or more intelligent than humans, although their intelligence is clearly different and often inscrutable to us. For more on this, see Lori Marino, Richard C. Connor, R. Ewan Fordyce, Louis M. Herman, Patrick R. Hof, Louis Lefebvre, and David Lusseau, et al., "Cetaceans Have Complex Brains for Complex Cognition." *PLoS Biol* 5, no. 5 (2007): e139. doi:10.1371/journal.pbio.0050139.

7. "Fantastic Dine with Shamu—Review of SeaWorld Orlando, Orlando, FL—TripAdvisor," 2014. Accessed July 3. http://www.tripadvisor.com/ShowUserReviews-g34515-d102412-r4073651-SeaWorld_Orlando-Orlando_Florida.html

8. All show descriptions that were not personally observed or recorded come from the following YouTube videos: ("Sea World—Believe Pt. 1" 2006) ("Sea World—Believe Pt. 2" 2006), ("Sea World—Believe Shamu Killer Whale Show Part 1" 2008), ("Sea World—Believe Shamu Killer Whale Part 2" 2008), ("Seaworld- Somethin Far Greater" 2007).

9. At one show that I attended, the child wanted to be a fashion designer—which certainly contrasts with the trainer in the video who dreams of working with whales as a child. The old moment, where a child was selected to pet "Shamu," was definitely more in line with the overall narrative the park presents, and this new moment indicates how far from the message the postdeath *Believe* show had become.

10. I attended multiple performances of the show at SeaWorld San Antonio on June 25, 2011. All analysis comes from these shows and my personal video recording of them.

11. As an example of concern about Tilikum's intent, see "Diary of a Killer Whale: What Motivated Tilikum's Attack on Dawn Brancheau?" Tim Zimmerman.com, July 8, 2010. http://timzimmermann.com/2010/07/08/diary-of-a-killer-whale-what-motivated-tilikums-attack-on-dawn-brancheau/

12. Since SeaWorld opened in 1964, there have been dozens of attacks leading to serious injuries and several deaths caused by human interactions with orcas. A few well-publicized injuries include: in 1971, SeaWorld secretary Annette Eckis required 200

stitches after an orca she was riding for a publicity event seized her body, and in 1987 trainer John Selick had his back, leg, and pelvis broken (Johnson 1987). Deaths include: in 1999, Tilikum found with the body of a man named Daniel Dukes who had broken into his tank after hours (Wallace 2016) and in 2009, a trainer named Alexis Martinez was killed by an orca at Loro Parque, a SeaWorld owned park in Spain. Tilikum was also previously one of the whales responsible for the drowning of trainer Keltie Byrne in 1991 at SeaLand of the Pacific before he was acquired by SeaWorld. There are many, many more well documented incidents of whales severely injuring humans (Zimmermann 2011).

Sources

1980s Sea World Commercial. 2009. http://www.youtube.com/watch?v=HEhTwamxF 9Q&feature=youtube_gdata_player

Ahmed, Sara. 2006. "Flowing Upstream: Negotiating Gender and Equity in Water Policy and Institutional Practices in India." In *Water: Histories, Cultures, Ecologies*, edited by Marnie Leybourne and Andrea Gaynor. Crawley: University of Western Australia Press.

"Attractions." 2013. SeaWorld Parks and Entertainment. Accessed May 6. http://seaworldparks.com/en/seaworld-orlando/Attractions

Chaudhari, Una. 2007. "Animal Rites." In *Critical Theory and Performance, Second Edition*, edited by Janelle G. Reinelt and Joseph R. Roach. Ann Arbor: University of Michigan Press.

Davis, Susan G. 1997. *Spectacular Nature: Corporate Culture and the SeaWorld Experience*. Berkeley: University of California Press.

"Dawn Brancheau Death Video Ruling: Dawn Brancheau: Judge Rejects Family's Bid to Seal Death Video, Photos." 2011. *Orlando Sentinel*, September 15. Accessed May 6, 2013. http://articles.orlandosentinel.com/2011-09-15/news/os-dawn-brancheau-death-video-ruling-20110915_1_dawn-brancheau-work-with-killer-whales-whales-without-adequate-protection

Debord, Guy. 1994. *The Society of the Spectacle*. New York: Zone Books.

Derrida, Jacques. 2008. *The Animal That Therefore I Am*. Edited by Marie-Louis Mallet, translated by David Wills. 3rd ed. New York: Fordham University Press.

Desmond, Jane C. 1999. *Staging Tourism*. Chicago: University of Chicago Press.

Eaton, Randall E. 2003. "Orcas and Dolphins in Captivity." In *The Animal Ethics Reader*, edited by Susan J. Armstrong and Richard G. Botzler. New York: Routledge.

Fjellman, Stephen M. 1992. *Vinyl Leaves: Walt Disney World and America*. San Francisco: Westview Press.

Foucault, Michel. 1982. "The Subject and Power." *Critical Inquiry* 8, no. 4 (Summer).

Garcia, Jason, and Susan Jacobson. 2010. "Animal Trainer Killed at SeaWorld." *Los Angeles Times*, February 25. Accessed July 21, 2016. http://articles.latimes.com/2010/feb/25/nation/la-na-seaworld-death25-2010feb25

Johnson, Greg. 1987. "Unlike Now, 1971 Injury Was Out in Open." *Los Angeles Times* December 8. Accessed July 21, 2016. http://articles.latimes.com/1987-12-08/business/fi-27610_1_sea-world-employee

"Killer Whale Fatally Attacks Trainer." 2010. ABC News. February 25. http://abcnews.go.com/GMA/AmazingAnimals/whale-kills-trainer-sea-worlds-shamu-stadium/story?id=9932526

"Killer Whale Kills Pelican & Eats It During Show." 2011. http://www.youtube.com/watch?v=Irx7g6OVzJo&feature=youtube_gdata_player

McGuire, Cathleen, and Colleen McGuire. 1994–95. "PETA and Pornographic Culture." *Feminists for Animal Rights* 8, nos. 3–4 (Fall-Winter).

Moorby, Lisa. 2009. "Center for Whale Research: One of These Killer Whales Is Almost 100 Years Old." Center for Whale Research. http://whaleresearch.blogspot.com/2009/05/one-of-these-killer-whales-is-almost.html

Perry, Tony. 2007. "Killer Whales Endanger Park Staff, State Says." *Los Angeles Times*, March 2. http://articles.latimes.com/2007/mar/02/local/me-orca2

"PETA Lawsuit Seeks to Expand Animal Rights." October 25, 2011. Yahoo! News. Accessed May 6. http://news.yahoo.com/peta-lawsuit-seeks-expand-animal-rights-222219887.html

Roach, Joseph. 2007. *It*. Ann Arbor: University of Michigan Press.

Save the Whales. "Captivity." 2013. Accessed May 6, 2013. savethewhales.org. http://www.savethewhales.org/captivity.html

SeaWorld. 2013. "Ask Shamu." Seaworld.org. Accessed May 6, 2013. http://www.seaworld.org/ask-shamu/faq.htm

SeaWorld. 2013. "Attractions." Seaworld.org. Accessed May 6, 2013. http://seaworld-parks.com/en/seaworld-orlando/Attractions

"Sea World—Believe Pt. 1." 2006. http://www.youtube.com/watch?v=ttq2ou8XuSU&feature=youtube_gdata_player

"Sea World—Believe Pt. 2." 2006. http://www.youtube.com/watch?v=UKe77D1Di0k&feature=youtube_gdata_player

"Sea World—Believe Shamu Killer Whale Show Part 1." 2008. http://www.youtube.com/watch?v=fIisP8EZvCM&feature=youtube_gdata_player

"Sea World—Believe Shamu Killer Whale Show Part 2." 2008. http://www.youtube.com/watch?v=8LMCBpEIFkc&feature=youtube_gdata_player

SeaWorld. 2013. "Killer Whales: Diet and Eating Habits." Seaworld.org. Accessed May 6, 2013. http://www.seaworld.org/animal-info/info-books/killer-whale/diet.htm

"SeaWorld Fights OSHA Findings in Trainer's Death." Sept 19, 2011. DeseretNews.com. Accessed May 6, 2013. http://www.deseretnews.com/article/700180503/SeaWorld-fights-OSHA-findings-in-trainers-death.html

"Seaworld- Somethin Far Greater." 2007. http://www.youtube.com/watch?v=qvdwbHHyXDc&feature=youtube_gdata_player

"SeaWorld Trainer Death Theory Debunked as a Ponytail Tale." 2011. The Orca Project.

April 20. Accessed May 6, 2013. http://theorcaproject.wordpress.com/2011/04/20/seaworld-trainer-death-ponytail-theory-debunked/

"SeaWorld Whale Attacks, Kills Trainer; Involved in Two Previous . . ." 2013. Zimbio. Accessed May 6. http://www.zimbio.com/Tilikum+the+Orca/articles/TBEV-42CirGf/SeaWorld+whale+attacks+kills+trainer+involved

Thacker, Christopher. 1970. "Fountains: Theory and Practice in the Seventeenth and Eighteenth Centuries." *Occasional Paper (Garden History Society)* no. 2 (1970).

Wallace, Benjamin. 2016. "Seaworld, Breached." *New York Magazine*, May 4. Accessed July 21, 2016. http://nymag.com/daily/intelligencer/2016/04/seaworld-tilikum-orcas.html

Zimmermann, Tim. 2010. "Diary of a Killer Whale: What Motivated Tilikum's Attack on Dawn Brancheau?" Tim Zimmermann.com, July 8. Accessed May 6, 2013. http://timzimmermann.com/2010/07/08/diary-of-a-killer-whale-what-motivated-tilikums-attack-on-dawn-brancheau/

Zimmermann, Tim. 2011. "Blood in the Water" Outside, July 15. Accessed July 21, 2016. http://www.outsideonline.com/1886916/blood-water

CHAPTER 4

Hyping Clyde Beatty and His Wild Animal Show

Virginia Anderson

The circus means thrills, excitement, snarling jungle beasts. The circus means fun
for young folks and old. But under the big top you see only part of the story. The
real drama comes behind the scenes, where five hundred people live as one family,
where Clyde Beatty constantly risks death in the most dangerous act on earth.
This master of the big cats has journeyed to Africa and India, hunting down his
beasts in their native jungle. All of this is part of the Clyde Beatty story![1]

Jubilant calliope music swells, preparing a listening audience for another
promised breathtaking adventure in the life of the celebrated animal trainer.
By the early 1950s when this language introduced a popular radio program,
Clyde Beatty (1903–65) had become a household name. The diminutive but
lithe figure had captured the popular imagination with a daring wild animal
act that combined seemingly ferocious lions and tigers, and was constantly
adding elements of danger so that it might never be surpassed. Through
comic books, radio, and film, Beatty's tales of adventure with the jungle cats
circulated widely among an enraptured public. During the Great Depression, the Second World War, and the early years of the Cold War, Beatty
achieved celebrity status in America virtually unheard of in the circus world.

The time was right for Beatty—or, perhaps more accurately, for the
persona he projected. His was a special case among animal trainers; with
nearly mythological roots as a Midwestern boy who ran away with the circus
and made something of himself from the poorest of backgrounds, Beatty
embodied the patriotic courage and charisma promoted within American
popular culture during times of economic hardship and frightening global

conflict. He managed the media as he managed his cats, creating a show on and off stage of confidence and keen insights into the operation of the beasts before him. The wild animal act was a key draw for competing circuses during these years. Much was at stake culturally and financially for both proprietor and performer, which made the celebrity animal act an event worthy of energetic marketing. Audiences found reflection, escape, and even hope under the big top, along with affirmation of enduring ethnic and gender prejudices.[2] The more apparently dangerous the act involving triumph over supposedly "natural" enemies, the greater the cultural affirmation—and the greater the demonstration of a show's superiority over rival acts.

To an extraordinary degree, Beatty's wild animal show asserted human mastery over nature and civilization over savagery in a seemingly unpredictable, highly dangerous setting. While training wild animals, his act also inspired American media to promote circus shows, already over-the-top in displays of skill and apparent risk, in yet more hyperbolic ways to great cultural and commercial effect. Clyde Beatty's career prompts us to explore the relationship between the culture industry and popular imagination; with the wild animal act, he tapped into the fears of a shaken American populace, and audience consumers hungrily paid for the reassurance he provided.

WILD ANIMALS, EMOTIONS, AND ADVERTISING

In *Wild and Dangerous Performances: Animals, Emotions, Circus* (2012), Peta Tait describes the emotional values with which animal performances were imbued throughout the twentieth century. Tait insightfully considers the role of human emotions in the mimetic reproduction of familiar signifying actions, and stereotypes assigned to gender, location, and species. This essay expands on Tait's work, demonstrating that advertising executives exploited the triumvirate exchange among human, animal, and consumer to sell commodities. I trace the dynamics of this exchange in relation to the cultural signification of Beatty's animal acts—and the animals themselves—within the popular imagination, from early ads for breakfast cereals to a boom in linkages between the strength of the wild beast and the power of gasoline, batteries, and tires. Beatty's celebrity throughout the twentieth century invited advertisers to draw not only upon his testimonials but also on the ways his particular shows hyped power plays between human and animal. If hype means to stimulate and work up, the adrenaline rush aroused in the snarl and tangle of barely contained beasts circling the ring threw off centrifugal waves of potent marketing potential.

Precisely because wild animals often represent danger and a lack of control, they carry considerable emotional weight during periods of financial depression, war, and other instability. John Stokes describes the desired effect of the wild animal act as "that of a complex whole, depending upon a combination of proximity and distance, a mixture of dominance and vulnerability, of harmonious certainty and the ever-present risk" (2004, 144). Drawing on the literature of animal studies and celebrity, I endeavor to reveal relationships between Beatty's spectacularization of live wild animal acts and developments in modern marketing, both of which relied for their effect on emotional manipulation steeped in current cultural ideologies and together compounded economic growth.

By the time Beatty took the ring, he was able to build on the glamour of the wild animal trainer's profession that had already been established for generations. Early twentieth-century product marketers began to look to the circus virtuoso for his link to the imagination and therefore potential to manipulate the emotions of likely consumers. A 1907 advertisement for Grape-Nuts cereal places the viewer inside a cage with four lions and a muscular male trainer, perhaps modeled on Edwin Henry Landseer's iconic paintings of Isaac Van Amburgh (1811–65), the first wild animal trainer of modern times. The trainer in the ad stands calmly poised with one arm cocked on his hip and the other extended with a whip he appears to have just brought down on the head of a female lion who cowers at his feet. A crowd of well-dressed spectators looks on from the other side of metal bars lining the wall. The limited text reads simply: "Perfect Control: It takes steady nerve and a clear brain to do that kind of business. You can 'tame the lion' of this world if your food gives you the clear brain and nervous vigor. 'There's a Reason' for Grape-Nuts."[3]

As the traveling circus grew into a major popular entertainment by the 1920s and provided inexpensive relief, escape, and even employment during the Depression years, advertisers pushed this heroic motif to further profit. Increasing attention to the emotional exchange between trainer, animal, and viewer as described by Tait coincided with a similar investment in emotion in advertising. "Since the 1920s," observes Jean Kilbourne, "advertising has provided less information about the product and focused more on the lives, especially the emotional lives, of the prospective consumers. This shift coincided, of course, with the increasing knowledge and acceptability of psychology, as well as the success of propaganda used to convince the population to support World War I" (1999, 71). Illustrating these developments, the Ethyl Gasoline Corporation launched a popular series of advertisements in 1932 featuring anonymous animal trainers that show specific, power-based relationships between person, animal, and viewer in order to cultivate an emotional reaction toward its product. This implied relationship becomes explicit in one ad that reads: "Ethyl makes Gasoline Behave. Watch the lion tamer enter the cage. Your own eyes prove his mastery over the king of beasts. Seeing is believing. And now, for the first time, you can *see* the difference Ethyl makes in gasoline. You can see *how* it tames and controls the burning of gasoline inside the engine." The accompanying image features a male trainer approaching a ferocious lion baring its claws and teeth, a pistol and whip in his hands. Drawn from the trainer's point of view, the image places the viewers' gaze on the beast before them to be tamed; the forceful language and the involvement of their own eyes as commanded by the text empowers them to feel heroic. If they buy Ethyl gasoline additive, they, too, can experience the rush of confronting danger and gaining control—much needed during this time of so much economic uncertainty.[4] This psychological, consumer-based approach to advertising, in turn, surely helped to motivate live and depicted animal acts over the decades that followed.

In this process, advertisers moved from using anonymous trainer figures to employing named celebrities, a transition that Beatty's popular image galvanized. His popularity raises questions about his public and private personae. Who was he "really" and what did he (and his act) represent that sparked the imagination of advertising executives, inducing them to invest small fortunes in his endorsements? Obviously, they saw something different—something extraordinarily marketable—in this circus star's career. Beatty surpassed others on the U.S. circus circuit in developing and showing wild animal training as a legitimate profession and heightening its charge in a shifting media-landscape.

THE CULTURE OF CELEBRITY

Modern celebrity exploded with what historian Daniel J. Boorstin has termed a "Graphic Revolution" involving new technologies in printing, telegraphy, photography, moving pictures, and television that fostered widespread diffusion of information and images (Ponce de Leon 2002, 12). An increase in leisure time in the 1920s provided new opportunities for mass consumption of these materials. The rising culture of leisure also challenged older, nineteenth-century values of hard work, self-restraint, and deferred gratification and placed more emphasis on novelty, excitement, personal fulfillment, and self-expression, qualities celebrities seemed to embody (60). Amid this transformation, a wide spectrum of media, from sensational tabloids and glossy weeklies to serious newspapers, portrayed celebrities as "real human beings" with whom readers could identify (6–7).

During the hardships of the Depression and war years, which spanned the height of Beatty's career, large segments of the U.S. population sought solace and distraction through the new image-laden media. Many people were consumed not only with the glamour of celebrity life but also with the ways in which they could feel close to it. Success stories that were redolent with seemingly real personal detail yet shaped by familiar mythic patterns proved the most appealing. As Terry Cooney (1995) writes of the 1930s, "Magazine biographies told time and again of a man—for it remained a male myth—who had gone to work as a boy (most likely with only a limited education, preferably with a rural background) and risen through effort, merit, and a touch of good fortune to financial success or public distinction. Articles by the score insisted that America was still the land of opportunity" (61–62). Young Clyde Beatty offered a prime and timely example of the American success myth on which both he and advertisers could capitalize.

Like many children of his generation, Beatty was fascinated by the circus when it came to his hometown of Bainbridge, in rural Ohio. As a boy, he developed animal shows featuring dogs, cats, guinea pigs, and even a raccoon he taught to perform tricks. An academically indifferent student, Beatty worked several jobs to support his mother and three sisters.[5] Not surprisingly, before completing high school he ran away with Howe's Great London Circus; for five dollars a month, Beatty cleaned cages, all the while closely observing the noted animal trainer Louis Roth. [6] Even in the early stages of his career, Beatty's enthusiasm caught the eye of circus colleagues and, within two years, he was granted a bear act of his own. He made it clear that he was also willing and able to take on big cats; thus, when an opportunity arose at the Hagenbeck-Wallace Circus (the acting cat trainer had a heart attack), management asked Beatty to step up. Providing charismatic and capable performances, Beatty, then in his early twenties, quickly received top billing for his "single-handed battle with the most savage jungle beasts known to man" (fig. 4.1).

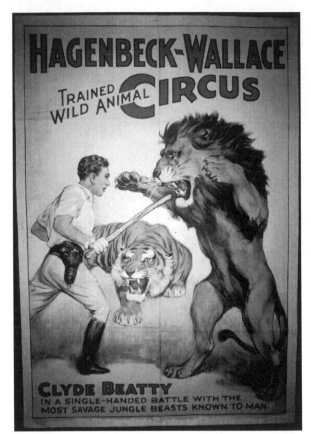

Fig. 4.1. "Clyde Beatty Greatest Wild Animal Trainer of All Time." (Circus Posters Collection (TC093); circa 1850–1973, Graphic Arts Collection, Department of Rare Books and Special Collections, Princeton University Library.)

If celebrity status, as Charles L. Ponce de Leon (2002, 6) argues, is created through the "strategic presentation of personas," Beatty achieved this both by conscious planning and agile exploitation of happenstance. Beatty deliberately courted the public's favor semiotically through his costume. Although he employed military dress for a brief period, he created his enduring image in the garb of an adventure-seeking African explorer: knee-high boots, a pith helmet, and white breeches and shirt. But it was his nearly fatal accident in April 1930 that first captivated broad public attention. The *New York Times* reported:

> Attacked by a tiger, Clyde Beatty, trainer, owes his life to Prince, giant lion and veteran circus trouper.
> Beatty was conducting a dress rehearsal and preparing for the opening

show of the season when Trudy, a new tiger, knocked him down, clawed and bit him.

Prince, one of the lions and tigers in the cage with Beatty, jumped at Trudy, hurled her across the arena, beat and chewed her.

Other trainers intervened to save Trudy's life. Beatty was sent to the hospital with a mangled arm and other injuries.[7]

Other newspapers across the country ran the story, filling in more details, including that Beatty himself managed to arise and drive other agitated animals from the cage into the runway before he staggered outside and collapsed. Prince, who was later known as Nero, would become a celebrity in his own right for his loyalty to Beatty (Joys 1983, 112). The widely reported attack established a nationally recognized, enduring image of the fearless young trainer with powers both to wrangle and seemingly induce the cooperation of these huge, potentially violent animals.

Beatty's recovery became paramount in the public consciousness, as the media recycled it and wove it indelibly into his mythic story. Circus historian John Culhane describes the tense weeks that followed the accident:

> Radio and newspapers kept the nation informed as Beatty fought to recover. Six weeks after the lion attack, Beatty said he was about ready to leave his wheelchair and reenter the big cage. He was determined to make a return engagement with the Ringling show when it opened in New York that April. Once again, the circus was functioning as a metaphor for America. In this Depression year of 1932, Clyde Beatty seemed to express the national longing for recovery, and the belief that an American boy could overcome the "Law of the Jungle." The New York date had to be delayed, but Clyde Beatty did make it to the Garden in 1932, as well as in 1933 and 1934. These were the days in which Franklin D. Roosevelt would firmly assert that "The only thing we have to fear is fear itself." Was there a better example than Clyde Beatty? (Culhane 1990, 210)

These events capture Beatty's development, during the darkest days of the Depression, into "a symbol of winning out against great odds" (208). Joanne Carol Joys explains how the well-publicized relationship in this incident stuck "during the first seven years of his career, [and] writers and publicists even gave him a trusty sidekick, Nero. . . . Although Beatty claimed Nero's actions were those of an arena boss protecting his domain, the story enhanced the appeal of the performance at a time when Tarzan and his animal helpers also were garnering audience enthusiasm" (1983, 105–6).

Beatty also engaged the popular imagination as the victorious underdog by publicly challenging previous employers who had tried to take advantage of him. Although he quickly came to serve as the chief draw for the circuses for which he worked, he was not proportionately paid. Beatty left Ringling Bros. and Barum & Bailey Circus and merged forces with the Cole Brothers. Their joint circus moved into the Hippodrome, becoming, according to a *Time* magazine cover story, "Cat Man," in 1937, "the first important tent show in a generation to challenge 'The Greatest Show on Earth' not only by playing New York, hitherto practically a Ringling monopoly, but playing it before Ringling got there, and playing it under a 'permanent top' (a building as distinguished from a tent)." Complicit with the media in showing his on- and offstage selves, Beatty emerged from the story as a successful entrepreneur with a beautiful wife as well as an adventurer who traveled the world and faced danger every day—and always came out the victor. He smiled from the cover, dressed in business attire (fedora and suit) and holding a young wildcat in his arms over the caption "Clyde Beatty and Captive." Only the cat distinguished him from *Time's* largely white, middle- and upper-middle-class readership of the magazine. In the context of other articles in the magazine, Beatty provided both the sense of danger and the reassurance of normalcy its editors surely knew their audience sought after reading about mounting international conflict.

THE POWER OF SHOWMANSHIP

While conceiving of and creating his acts, Beatty was ever conscious of his audience's desire to see him as much as the big cats, and he put his charisma to use; "I want people to see me close," he said in another *Time* magazine story, "close enough to smell the cats. . . . When I'm in there, I don't know if there are a hundred or a thousand in the audience. It doesn't matter. I'll give them anything; I'll give them everything" ("King of the Beasts" 1965).

Hardly a reference is made to Beatty without mention of his superior theatrical sensibilities. He constructed his act for maximum dramatic tension, asking audiences to believe in the reality of his constant peril. He trained the cats to snarl and bare their claws in a hyperbolic show of aggression, one heightened and exaggerated to produce strong feeling. His characteristic props included a whip, a chair, and a blank-loaded gun, which he used to prod his cats to the "attack." Hoh describes an audience favorite that required Nero to "knock the chair from his hand and drive him from the arena, from which Beatty would 'escape' in the nick of time, slamming the cage door behind him. Pausing to review the situation and wipe his brow, Beatty would then reenter the cage to thunderous applause, and subdue Nero merely by a hypnotic stare into his eyes" (Hoh and Rough 1990, 226). This "hypnotic stare" served as Beatty's trademark and was even the title of one episode of his television serial. As documented by Joys, popular magazines of the time such as *Field and Stream* and *Literary Digest*

> called the highpoint of his act the stare-down of Nero after he backed the trainer against the bars, disarmed him with a sweep of his mighty paw, and roared in fury. Beatty stopped the charge by suddenly taking a step toward him, leaning forward until his face was within a foot of his and staring him into submission. Nero, with a baleful look, gradually stopped roaring, snarled, shook his head in baffled rage, and backed away to return to his pedestal. It was a masterful performance. (1983, 113)

If some viewers were suspicious of hypnosis itself as a form of hype in its most negative sense, that is, as a sham, in a performance context, especially one as exotic as wild cat taming, it invoked the force of the Svengali who could infuse his own will and desire into another being and hold her (or him) in thrall. Indeed, Beatty performed the subjugation of seemingly wild and ferocious animals with the precision of an expert showman and maestro imbued with special powers keen to keep the show suspenseful and mysterious to amp up the excitement.

The audiences' emotional investment in Beatty's live performances became a rich resource for advertisers seeking to invoke similar states of mind. Throughout the trainer's career, his promotional marketing promised to reward that intense consumer desire for the thrill of apparent danger and reassurance of demonstrable control. Before Beatty lent his name to their enterprise, the Cole Bros. Circus used his image (in 1934) to hype their enterprise (fig. 4.2). A muscular lion springs from a high stool, teeth bared and claws outstretched as a youthful, rosy-cheeked Beatty raises a whip, controlling the beast with a confident gaze. His biceps bulge through his fitted shirt and his holstered gun and flexed stance indicate that he is embracing the dangers before him. The slightly curved lines of the chair that Beatty tightly clasps and thrusts from his waist provide just enough sexual imagery to fur-

Fig. 4.2. "Clyde Beatty in single-handed battle with the most savage jungle beasts known to man." (Circus Posters Collection (TC093); circa 1850–1973, Graphic Arts Collection, Department of Rare Books and Special Collections, Princeton University Library.)

ther enhance his virility. From the lower left corner, a tiger, teeth and claws bared, poses a threat to both Beatty and the lion, its natural enemy. The image indicates Beatty's control of the situation while heightening the dangers to which he comes so perilously close. A banner along the bottom boasts the circus's star performer: "Clyde Beatty, Greatest Wild Animal Trainer of All Time."

When Beatty finally acquired his own circus, his act's advertising reflected his mastery of both animal and enterprise: showing acts of bravery in the lion's cage apparently led to financial fortune. Several aspects of the poster emphasize Beatty's celebrity, especially the extra bit of enticement: "In Person." Wide distribution of Beatty's image exemplified the dynamic his contemporary, Walter Benjamin, described in "The Work of Art in the Age of Mechanical Reproduction" (1968); in an increasingly mediatized society, the aura of his actual presence carried its own capital, which in turn lured ticket-buying spectators to the show. Furthermore, the poster hypes the potency of Beatty's act, as dozens of snarling lions and tigers surround him. At the peak of his career, Beatty put on a show of managing more than forty mixed animals in a cage at once, more than any other trainer in America, and this widely publicized achievement fueled his fame and fortune.

SPINNING OFF CIRCUS HEROICS INTO POPULAR MEDIA

Beyond newspaper accounts and interviews concerning events with circus animals, Beatty first penetrated American homes in 1933 through tales of "close calls" in and outside of the ring in his first book, *The Big Cage*. Written, as celebrity books often are, with a coauthor (Edward Anthony), the book covers Beatty's training techniques and "tricks," offering readers a vicarious glimpse into his world. Beatty even devotes a chapter to his fan mail, subtly encouraging continued written adoration by suggesting that his fan base informs his act.

As time went on, emerging media entertainment venues persuaded Beatty to play "himself" in a number of radio, film, and television programs. The first such performance happened in a 1933 film adaptation of *The Big Cage*, in which a twelve-year-old Mickey Rooney played the trainer's young admirer. The film enjoyed wide success, which encouraged the production of comic books and children's books that allowed young audiences to relive Beatty's adventures again and again. Upon the release of his follow-up film, *The Lost Jungle* (1934), the *New York Times* reviewer referenced a popular dime novel hero when he called Beatty the "Frank Merriwell of the big top, the shy lover, the scourge of the black-hearted, the one man jungle safari . . . bashful young man who finds sanctuary from the terrors of the everyday world with his frisky pets in the big cage. . . . He saves everybody in sight, from everything in sight" ("Lions, Tigers, and Mr. Beatty" 1934). Beatty had become a cultural icon.

Although hardly accounting for his entire audience, children occupied the heart of Beatty's fan base—a fact well known to marketers. Less inhibited in their spontaneous reactions, children tended to erupt with more emotional expression than adults under the big top, and they were more prone to imitation in their daily lives. Through his animal acts, Beatty showed the value of American ruggedness and bravery; seeking to emulate their role model, children could pretend to be Clyde Beatty at home. Not only was Beatty's face emblazoned on circus souvenirs, but kids could save Quaker Oats box tops and send away for Beatty-authored home circus instruction guides, jungle-themed jewelry, or even their very own trainer's bull whip so that they, too, could show their allegiance to the values Beatty represented (fig. 4.3).

Beatty's celebrity status allowed him to break in to radio, a significant achievement for a performer whose show ostensibly relied for maximum effect on the physical presence of trainer and animals. Even during the Depression, radio was considered a staple of American culture and the success of a radio show—like live animal acts and marketing—depended on a listener's emotional engagement with a story. Billed as "[t]he world's greatest wild animal trainer Clyde Beatty with an exciting adventure from his brilliant career," and targeting younger audiences, the thirty-minute show employed professional actors who voiced Beatty and the other roles in fifty-two episodes from 1950 to 1952. In plots elaborated from anecdotes in Beatty's books or wholly invented, such as "Amazon Adventure," featuring Beatty fighting a voodoo cult, or "Danger in the Deep," portraying Beatty locked in an underwater battle with an octopus, the show hyped Beatty's heroism into fantastical realms. The medium itself abetted hyperbole, as soundscapes without visuals allowed listeners' imaginations to run wild. Historians William and Nancy Young note that "unlike movies or plays, radio gave the illusion of being free [of cost]. Once the receiver was paid for, no other costs were involved or so it seemed. Advertisers quickly grasped the importance listeners placed on radio and were willing to put their dollars into commercials: ad spending went from slightly over $3 million in 1932 to well over $100 million by 1940" (2002, 207–8). Radio brought instant attention across America to hundreds of performers, hyping their celebrity in both material and imaginative ways that live performance simply could not. Beatty's particular stardom as an exotic adventurer benefited from radio hype to an extraordinary degree.

Beatty put his vast celebrity to use boosting American morale through implied support for the troops overseas in Korea. In one episode of his radio show, Beatty and his wife Harriet travel to South America in pursuit of animals for his act. After passing through customs, as the character Beatty explains in his expository narration, they went straight to the American consulate. Beatty asks his heavily accented Brazilian driver to wait for them so that he might take them to their hotel:

Fig. 4.3. From the 1935 Quaker Oats Company publication, "How to Teach Your Dog Tricks," written by Beatty. (Reprinted with permission from Quaker Foods.)

BEATTY: Coming Harriet?

HARRIET: Right behind you, dear. Oh, there's the flag! You know, Clyde, I always get a thrill out of seeing our stars and stripes when we're so far from home.

BEATTY: Oh, so do I, honey. Comforting to know that whatever country we may be in there's a little bit of the United States nearby ("Amazon Adventure" 1950).

The nostalgic and patriotic tone of this moment permeated Beatty's public persona and fed into popular sentiment; American soldiers were fighting overseas in a war to contain the spread of Communism. His "Amazon Adventure" may have acquired extra significance as the exotic animals coupled with strange "voo-doo" forces came to symbolize a dangerous, potentially metastasizing foreign enemy. To show off his manly human strength and power over the inchoate and unknown, concepts exacerbated by the unseen medium of radio, was to show off *American* strength and power over threats posed by increasingly murky foreign enemies.

SHOWING OFF TO SELL

Both before and after radio enlarged his celebrity, Beatty pursued stardom in Hollywood, where fans emulated film stars and advertising executives were quick to capitalize on that connection. As Samantha Barbas notes, "though sometimes costly, imitating the stars often fostered excitement, fulfillment, and strong feelings of self-worth. By the early 1930s, the link between the movies and consumer products was successfully forged" (2001, 81). In Beatty's case, sponsors like Rolex and Studebaker were betting that his fan base extended beyond the children's market.

A 1937 advertisement for Studebaker automobiles (fig. 4.4) celebrates Beatty's entire circus business as much as the car:

They packed the Hippodrome in New York at their opening last month, famed Clyde Beatty and the Coles Bros. circus. Interviewed in his dressing room after a performance, Beatty "most celebrated trainer of lions and tigers in the world," was asked what he did for relaxation from the tenseness of his moment in the cage. "Why nothing much, I suppose, except to drive my Studebaker," he answered. "That's what I call real re-laxation!" Beatty and his charming wife, long-time Studebaker admirers, chose the air-curved, gleaming 1937 Studebaker for their personal car in preference to any other car of the year.

Photographs of Beatty in and out of his circus gear show the cool confi-dence of a man to whom audiences could relate (clowns and trained dogs interacting with the car served as foils for Beatty's suave presence). Although Beatty thrived in the public spotlight, he also benefited from an aspect of celebrity generated from the exposure of "real selves" that are presumed to lie behind the public face (Ponce de Leon 2002, 5). Such revelation itself became a form of hype, as Beatty crafted home scenes in his autobiographi-cal writings of the 1930s and 1940s that later inspired performances of the "private" Beatty by actor Vic Perrin in the 1950s radio show. Iconic moments showed the famous big cat conqueror at home with his seemingly sweet and gentle wife, Harriet (played by Eve McVeagh), who was in reality a former Russian dancer who entreated Beatty to teach her to train wild animals, which he did, but she only performed at his behest.[8] Beatty's persona of a hard-working "regular" guy who comes home after a long day to a devoted helpmate—and just happens to have a job epitomizing bravery, excitement, and adventure—served him well because it fostered audience identification with these seemingly more real aspects of an otherwise remote—if highly visible—superhero (Ponce de Leon 2002, 13). A caption accompanying a photograph of Harriet and Clyde Beatty standing on either side of a Stude-baker occupied by big cats plays on Beatty's highly constructed private as well as public selves: "Cats don't like an act like this. But Beatty, pictured here with his wife, made them like it." The description and accompanying images show not only the strong domestic patriarch but also the courageous solo adventurer.

Moreover, these dual personae fostered the additional hype that if fans were like Beatty in his more ordinary aspects, perhaps they could emulate him in some of his extraordinary ones as well, or at least aspire to do so. Advertisers capitalized on and compounded that desire, especially among middle-class, white men with whom Beatty enjoyed considerable popu-larity. In its September 10, 1938, issue, the *Saturday Evening Post* featured a hypermasculine Eveready battery ad starring the celebrity circus trainer (fig. 4.5). The banner line reads, "Murderous 'Jungle Fever' was in their Eyes.

Fig. 4.4. An advertisement for Studebaker automobiles: "Life Photographs of New Clyde Beatty Show Find Exciting 1937 Studebaker in Spotlight." (From the author's collection.)

Clyde Beatty, Caged with Snarling Jungle Cats, Faces Blackest Moment of Death-defying Career." The reader holds his breath as Beatty confides how the Eveready batteries in his flashlight saved his life:

> And then, with that cage full of mixed cats raging at me and each other . . . the lights went out! In the flicker of an eyelash the huge glaring big top went dead black! In the dark the snarls of the beasts sounded twice as loud. Green eyes glowed. In an instant they would leap for me! I jumped back, pressed hard against the steel bars of the cage. I whipped out my flashlight, flung the beam square in the startled face of the nearest cat, then gave it to another and another. In a moment, (a mighty long moment) the trouble was repaired, the lights flashed on again and a tremendous sigh rose from the crowd. I was still alive. The power of fresh DATED "Eveready" batteries had held at bay the fury of the jungle!
>
> (Signed) *Clyde Beatty.*

The imagery used in the advertisement shows Beatty, still strong and masculine in a moment of confrontation with devils of the jungle, his flashlight revealing a particularly sharp-fanged lion and other beasts. The bars standing between Beatty's experience and the reader's play an important role: although readers may never experience Beatty's acts of "death-defiance" directly, the act of buying his batteries allows them a share in his power.[9]

Beatty and all that he represented proved to be a powerful marketing tool for decades to come. Kellogg's Rice Krispies became the featured sponsor of *The Clyde Beatty [Radio] Show* in the 1950s. By 1965 Beatty served as spokesman for Rolex watches. In one print advertisement, an obviously aged, but still grinning, Beatty dressed in safari gear holds up two kittenish tigers. The banner reads, "Clyde Beatty wears two tiger cubs . . . and a Rolex." The text describes him as capable, successful, assured, organized, well traveled, and adventurous: "In the capable hands of Clyde Beatty, these two squirming additions to his famous menagerie will soon be star performers under the Big Top. The Rolex DATEJUST chronometer on Mr. Beatty's wrist is a star performer, too. Whether traveling on safari, handling the big cats, or coordinating the 1001 details of the largest tented circus in the world, Clyde Beatty depends on his Rolex to tell him the right time—every time—under all conditions—everywhere in the world."

Fig. 4.5 "Murderous 'Jungle Fever' was in their Eyes," an advertisement for Eveready batteries featuring Beatty. Printed in the *Saturday Evening Post*, September 10, 1938. (Reprinted with permission from Energizer Brands, LLC.)

CONCLUSION

Over the decades that followed, as the circus declined, so, too, did Beatty's thunderous celebrity. In *Wild Tigers and Tame Fleas*, Bill Ballantine includes an anecdote, set in a muddy field in the "Southern boondocks," that captures the end of Beatty's performing career: "The matinée had just started as I picked my oozing way across the sloppy backyard to the Big Top's side entrance alongside the bandstand. There were more seats than people in the grandstands, but Beatty was giving his all just the same" (Ballantine 1958, 116). An air of nostalgia colors the trainer's response to the largely vacant stands: "I'd like nothing better . . . than to turn over my years of experience to some kid. I'll never stop looking, but I don't think I'll ever find one with what it takes. . . . Anyhow, these days the kids all want to make money crazy quick, like Elvis Presley—or else they want to be scientists, engineers or rocket men—fly to the moon" (Ballantine 1958, 138). Indeed, the cultural values that furnished a foundation for Beatty's trajectory in the 1930s, '40s, and early '50s had once again changed. The new cultural climate did not favor a Beatty protégé.

Although he had survived more than one hundred attacks by wild cats during his career, Beatty finally lost a battle with cancer. On July 30, 1965, *Time* magazine eulogized Clyde Raymond Beatty in a two-page spread. A photo, taken in 1945, captures his early charisma and lithe physique; his whip sails through the air as the lions and tigers perched behind him on ladders bearing his initials glare menacingly. "Last week in Ventura, Calif., at about the time the matinée would have started, cancer finally clawed to earth the man who could never abide being called an animal tamer. 'If they are tame,' he always said, 'there is no act'" ("King of the Beasts" 1965). In her introduction to this volume, Laurie Frederik writes: "The pleasure of watching a wild animal show derives from several sources: the strangeness and natural beauty of the animal, the display of human mastery, and—perhaps most important—the unpredictability of the outcome. Danger and the occurrence of violence, even death, is always a possibility: these possibilities are thrilling and attractive." Always keenly aware of the efficacy of "showing," Beatty understood this. He also understood marketing and money.

For nearly thirty years, Clyde Beatty showed his animal act in ways that complemented core American values. His daring performances with wildcats and emotionally seductive commercial testimonials sold a powerfully appealing persona of virile masculinity. He and his marketers hyped an image that resonated with audiences; what was not shown—the less market-able women and foreign trainers—may have further magnified his celebrity.

Circus trainers, animals, and audiences still negotiate complicated power relationships, but the circus, particularly the wild animal act, has changed dramatically since Clyde Beatty first entered the big cage. Many circus acts have eliminated wild animal acts altogether in favor of routines featuring rescued shelter dogs or other domesticated animals. Human use, exploi-tation, and showing of animals reveal shifts in cultural values: today large carnivores seem less mysterious and dangerous. Often portrayed sympa-thetically (as in the case of Cecil the lion killed in Zimbabwe by American dentist Walter J. Palmer in 2015), they have become essential not to circus acts, but to urgent conservation efforts. In this environment, circus train-ers caught physically abusing animals may cause potential ticket buyers to boycott, and eventually cause the circus to close permanently. The embodied show of battling exotic creatures as Beatty knew and practiced it may indeed be over, but the dynamics of media hype that he and his promoters and advertisers practiced so well continue to spin with new technologies and "othered" enemies into the twenty-first century.

Notes

1. "Tiger Escape," *Clyde Beatty Show*, 1950 (Commodore Productions, Radio of Yes-teryear, CD-DH0569), 0:16–0:43.

2. Frenchman Alfred Court (1883–1977) and Vienna-born Roman Proske (1898–1972), tiger trainers, faced cultural obstacles to achieving celebrity status during parallel years of increased patriotism. Although most circuses with wild animal acts featured fe-male trainers by the early 1920s, Canadian-born Mabel Stark (1889–1968) was different from most. She was not married to a circus man and, though written opinions vary, she does not seem to have been a conventional beauty like many circus women. Her femi-ninity was nevertheless accentuated in the public eye by the fact that, unlike her male contemporaries, Stark was always unarmed, working without a gun, whip, iron fork, or chair (Durant and Durant 1957, 196). A public fear and fascination with the strong female controlling males or masculine symbols found double representation when Stark served as a body double for Mae West in the film *I'm No Angel*. See Tait 2012 for analy-sis of these trainers' careers.

3. "There's a Reason for Grape-Nuts," Postum Cereal Co. Battle Creek, Michigan, 1907.

4. "Ethyl Makes Gasoline Behave," Ethyl Gasoline Corporation, New York, 1932.

5. Little information is available concerning Beatty's father. Katharine Wilkie's biog-

raphy, written for children, portrays Clyde as the only male in the household to support his mother and sisters.

6. The amount of Beatty's first wages varies among sources. He may have made as much as three dollars a week as a cage boy. He was also granted room and board for his efforts.

7. "Lion Saves Man from Tiger: Trainer Knocked Down at Kokomo, Rescuer Storms Attacking Beast," *New York Times*, April 27, 1930, 26. See also Joys 1983, 112.

8. The *Clyde Beatty Radio Show* episode "Beauty and the Beast" is based on material from Beatty's 1941 book *Jungle Performers* relating how he taught Harriett to become a wild animal trainer.

9. In an interview with Bill Ballantine, re-created in Ballantine's book, *Wild Tigers and Tame Fleas*, Beatty recounts presumably the same incident. There is no mention of a flashlight.

Sources

"Amazon Adventure." 1950. *The Clyde Beatty Show*. October 26. Commodore Productions. Radio of Yesteryear. CD-DH0569.

Ballantine, Bill. 1958. *Wild Tigers and Tame Fleas*. New York: Rinehart.

Barbas, Samantha. 2001. *Movie Crazy: Fans, Stars, and the Cult of Celebrity*. New York: Palgrave.

Beal, George Brinton. 1938. *Through the Back Door of the Circus*. Springfield, MA: McLoughlin Brothers.

Benjamin, Walter. 1968. "The Work of Art in the Age of Mechanical Reproduction." In *Illuminations* edited by Hannah Arendt, translated by Harry Zohn. New York: Shocken Books.

A Brief Biographical Sketch of I.A. Van Amburgh, Now Traveling with his Menagerie Throughout the New England States. N.d. Broadside. Harvard Theatre Collection, Houghton Library, Harvard University.

"Cat Man." 1937. *Time*, March 29, 44.

Cooney, Terry A. 1995. *Balancing Acts: American Thought and Culture in the 1930s*. New York: Twayne.

Culhane, John. 1990. *The American Circus: An Illustrated History*. New York: Henry Holt and Company.

"Death in Stateroom B." 1950. *The Clyde Beatty Show*. November 16. Commodore Productions. Radio of Yesteryear. CD-DH0569.

Durant, Johan, and Alice Durant. 1957. *A Pictorial History of the American Circus*. New York: A. S. Barnes and Company.

Fox, Charles Philip, and Tom Parkinson. 1985. *Billers, Banners and Bombast: The Story of Circus Advertising*. Boulder: Pruett Publishing.

Hoh, LaVahn G., and William H. Rough. 1990. *Step Right Up! The Adventure of Circus in America*. White Hall, VA: Betterway Publications.

Joys, Joanne Carol. 1983. *The Wild Animal Trainer in America*. Boulder, CO: Pruett.

Kaplan, Abraham. 1966. "The Aesthetics of the Popular Arts." *Journal of Aesthetics and Art Criticism* 24, no. 3 (Spring): 351–64.

Kilbourne, Jean. 1999. *Can't Buy Me Love: How Advertising Changes the Way We Think and Feel*. New York: Simon and Schuster.

"King of the Beasts." 1965. *Time*, July 30, 55.

"Lions, Tigers, and Mr. Beatty." 1934. *New York Times*, June 8, 18.

Pfening, Fred D., Jr. 1965. "Forty Years in the Center Ring." *Bandwagon* 9, no. 4 (July-August): 4–8.

Ponce de Leon, Charles L. 2002. *Self Exposure: Human-Interest Journalism and the Emergence of Celebrity in America, 1890–1940*. Chapel Hill: University of North Carolina Press.

Speight, George. 1980. *A History of the Circus*. London: Tantivy Press.

Stokes, John. 2004. "'Lion Griefs': The Wild Animal Act as Theatre." *New Theatre Quarterly* 20, no. 2 (May): 138–54.

Tait, Peta. 2012. *Wild and Dangerous Performances: Animals, Emotions, Circus*. New York: Palgrave.

"Tiger Escape." 1950. *The Clyde Beatty Show*. April 13. Commodore Productions. Radio of Yesteryear. CD-DH0569.

Young, William H., with Nancy K. Young. 2002. *The 1930s*. Westport, CT: Greenwood Press.

Power and Presence The Politics of Showing Up

The essays in section II take up even more willfully instrumental acts of showing. In contrast to the essays in section I, which endeavor to expose the ideological in seemingly apolitical acts of showing, section II examines explicitly political modes of showing off and up. Objects and events described here show off in the interests of people, nation, or state. They are intentional, though circulation through new media and technologies may alter not only the original creators' intentions but also the audience response. The show after the show (the circulation of Princess Beatrice's hat), the showing of the show (Strobridge posters), the show of protest (Haitian carnival), and the show within the show (Sochi's Opening Ceremony) transpire in and around manufactured events, such as weddings, theater productions, carnival, and international sports events. Whether manufactured by state or people, these shows transform quotidian things and places—a hat, theater posters, decaying cities—into symbols and signifiers of political movements, nation building, and state planning. They promote (sometimes accidently) an image of national culture, asking spectators and participants to invest emotionally, and often financially, in it.

CHAPTER 5

Princess Beatrice's Ridiculous Wedding Hat and the Transnational Performances of Things

Marlis Schweitzer

This is a chapter about a hat. Not just any hat but a hat seen around the world by an estimated two billion viewers. Yes, *that* hat, the bow-shaped Philip Treacy fascinator worn by Princess Beatrice of York at the Royal Wedding of Prince William and Kate Middleton.[1] And so, given its silly subject, this essay is silly. But it also aims for something else. By following the transnational circulation of a silly thing across multiple performance platforms, this chapter sets out to show how moving objects can provoke less-than-silly opportunities for political commentary and charitable action. As such, it sees an important correlation between the advancement of political movements and the movement of objects, images, and ideas via mediascapes—the term coined by Arjun Appadurai to describe the global outlets, that is, newspapers, websites, and television that facilitate the flow of information.[2] As a circulating thing in itself, already shaped by the thoughts and questions of multiple readers, this chapter also calls for a different kind of performance history, a history that acknowledges the centrality of objects in human lives, especially where performance is concerned. Such a history seeks to decenter the human subject by examining moments when quotidian objects—objects that the human subject "looks through" in order to understand the world or herself, or both—become something else, slippery things that the human subject relies upon for the performance of self.[3] When an object breaks, when it ceases to function properly, when it "misfires" (to extend Judith Butler's useful term to describe moments when speech acts fail to achieve their intended effect[4]), it enters the world of things, calling atten-

Fig. 5.1. The "ridiculous" hat. (Photo: Boris Roessler. dpa picture alliance archive/Alamy.)

tion to "subject-object relations."[5] By studying such moments, this chapter maintains, theater and performance studies scholars might arrive at a different understanding of human subjectivity and begin to chart very different genealogies of performance.

In an essay published in *Theatre Historiography/Critical Interventions*, Margaret Werry advocates a "new materialist" approach to theater and performance historiography, one that resists the binaries of object/subject, human/nonhuman, sociality/ materiality by focusing less "on what things are" than on "how they happen, where they go." Such an approach refuses to see objects as merely part of the background, the "set" as it were, and "admit[s] other cultural formations of performance, and the political rationalities they incarnate, into our disciplinary imagination."[6] New materialism—which encompasses many of the ideas promoted by "thing theorist" Bill Brown, whose own theories extend those of Martin Heidegger—presents an alternative method for analyzing the formation and perpetuation of oppressive ideologies (by, for example, examining how the organization and layout of racist imagery in children's books directs readers both emotionally and physically[7]); it also provides a way to identify moments when things challenge existing perspectives and facilitate positive change. More pressingly, it presents a strategy for rethinking human relationships with the rest of the material world as the world's population exceeds the seven billion mark and the realities of global warming and other ecological disasters affect the lives of all species.

Working from a new materialist perspective, this essay looks at how fashionable objects worn on the body perform with and alongside human subjects within a display economy that privileges excess and the ridiculous over "good taste." In addition to situating Princess Beatrice's "hat trick" within the history of sartorial escapades, I draw from the work of Bill Brown, Robin Bernstein, and others to consider the extent to which the extreme fascinator scripted the immediate and wide-ranging responses it received. Rather than interpret the hat as a static object with a fixed physical location, I see it as a mobile, mutating thing, a thing-in-process that took on a life of its own and occupied multiple locations simultaneously. Responding to Arjun Appadurai's call for scholars to "follow the thing,"[8] I track the hat's movement from Treacy's salon to the Royal Wedding and out into the vast entanglements of the World Wide Web—to the blogs that made it a star, to Facebook, where it has its own page, and to eBay, where the original Treacy creation made its final appearance as an auction item. I argue that as much as Princess Beatrice breathed "social life" into the showy hat when she decided to wear it, it was ultimately the hat in its many mutations that transformed the princess from a fashion failure into an inspired and inspiring philanthropist.

PERFORMING HATS/PERFORMING THINGS

Hats are showy objects with the potential to upstage those who wear them. As actors, magicians, jazz dancers, and clowns know, a successful "hat performance" requires not only finding the right hat but also spending enough time living and rehearsing with it until it becomes a fluid extension of the body. Most frequent theatergoers have witnessed moments when hats take over, when they misbehave or refuse to act as they should, leaving their performing human partners looking under-rehearsed or incompetent. In these moments, the hat takes on a life of its own: it is as much of a performer as the embarrassed clown or dancer who scurries to pick it up.

Hats are rarely static objects. Within the theatrical universe, their function continually shifts in relation to the performer's body and may often be seen as an extension of that body. Tossed aside (e.g., hung on a hat rack), a hat becomes part of the mise-en-scène; removed but still held by the performer, a hat transforms into a prop[9] (e.g., the magician removes his hat, places it on a table, and pulls a rabbit from it); left on the head, a hat remains part of the costume, an ensemble player of sorts. In this respect, hats perform with, through, and alongside the humans who wear them. They afford insight into a character's personality, status, or motives and at times assume a life of their own (e.g., Lucky's hat in *Waiting for Godot*).

Though hats cease to function as signs of signs outside the theatrical frame, they continue to perform in complex ways as they move along the production-consumption continuum. In the hands of a milliner, for example, a hat is the product of creativity and labor, a newly assembled thing made from an assortment of wire, fabric, feathers, and other trimmings. In the hands of a clerk, a hat is a commission, a possible raise, a promotion. In the hands of a customer, a hat is a promise, a projection of a possible self—no longer a (visible) product of labor but an enticing (fetishized) commodity waiting to become personal property. Once purchased and placed on the head of a new owner, a hat becomes part of a clothing ensemble—comparable at times to a string quartet, at others to a band of misfits; it conforms to the shape of the body even as it enhances or extends that body's shape, speaking to or yelling at the clothes beneath it. And, of course, hats do many other things: they protect the body from other objects (e.g., hard hats); they shield it from the elements (e.g., a rain hat, toque, or sun hat); they signal affiliation with a specific group or community (e.g., religious, national, sports); they represent professional expertise (e.g., a police officer's hat); they symbolize status (e.g., a crown); they project ideas about the subject's identity (gender, race, class); they attract attention. But some hats attract more attention than others; these hats cross over from the realm of object-hood into the world of "things."

In her award-winning article, "Dances with Things: Material Culture and the Performance of Race," Robin Bernstein outlines the difference between things and objects in order to emphasize how certain things script human behavior. Drawing from Martin Heidegger and "thing theorist" Bill

Brown, among others, she defines an object "as a chunk of matter that one looks through or beyond to understand something human." By contrast, a thing "asserts itself within a field of matter."[10] Bernstein uses the example of a knife to illustrate her point. In the hands of the amateur, the knife is merely an instrument used to complete a specific task: it is a means to an end. In the hands of the chef, however, the knife is a critical tool, an extension of the self, "with potential and stubbornness, with past, present, and future motions of slicing and chopping." The knife as thing scripts the chef's actions, leads her to perform certain tasks, and in so doing "forces a person into an aware-ness of the self in material relation to the thing."[11] Such things disrupt the boundary between humans and objects by calling attention to the processes whereby human subjectivity is constituted through an engagement with objects. As Bernstein elaborates, objects cross over into thing-hood when they "trigger what Joseph Roach calls 'kinesthetic imagination' as a 'faculty of memory—as when a knife cuts a finger and the person to whom that finger is attached . . . performs a dance of pain that is stylized through its citation of gender, class, age, race, and other categories of analysis."[12] In other words, when human interactions with objects lead to specific performances that go beyond the everyday, objects become things.

Though hardly a thing theorist, milliner Philip Treacy understands how hats can influence or direct human behavior through the emotions they evoke. Born in Ahascragh, County Galway, Ireland, in 1967, Treacy began sewing at age six for his sister's dolls, attended the Royal College of Art in the 1980s, and entered the world of high fashion in the 1990s through the mentorship of outspoken fashion editor Isabella Blow. "She introduced me to everything I know," Treacy explained in a recent interview with *The Ob-server*. "She invented me. . . . I made the hats, she wore them."[13] Treacy credits Blow with introducing him to the "magic of the hat" and for encouraging him to reimagine how hats might look and behave on the human body, specifi-cally the bodies of the wealthy white women who make up his clientele. Not surprisingly, many of Treacy's most famous designs draw inspiration from, or play with, real-world objects not normally associated with millinery; his memorable creations for Blow (both his model and muse) include an eighteenth-century French ship, a castle, sheep horns, and a pheasant (Blow was buried wearing the pheasant hat after committing suicide in 2007).[14] In Treacy's hands such objects became magical things that appealed to a younger (though still predominantly white and upper-class) demographic, overturning the long-held association of hats with old ladies.[15] "Everyone has a head so everyone has a possibility to wear a hat and you feel good in a hat," Treacy has vehemently argued. "People feel better for wearing them . . . [they] make the heart beat faster."[16] For Treacy, then, hats operate on both an affective and a physiological level to change how a person feels and presumably how that person behaves. And some hats go beyond this to affect the feelings and behavior of all who come into contact with the hat. This was certainly the case with Princess Beatrice's "ridiculous" fascinator.

THE "RIDICULOUS" HAT

When the twenty-something Princesses of York, Beatrice and her sister Eugenie, stepped from their elegant carriage onto the red carpet outside Westminster Abbey, their flashy wedding ensembles stood in sharp contrast to the more muted (if still colorful) outfits worn by the other guests. Yet while Eugenie's electric blue suit and matching fascinator were undoubtedly bold, it was Beatrice's head-to-toe appearance in a color reminiscent of Crayola's original and much-maligned "flesh" that attracted the most attention.[17] Why? Yes, it was outlandish and silly. But when compared with many of the bizarre hats Treacy has made for other clients, including his more recent creations for pop diva Lady Gaga (remember the surreal silver lobster?), the princess's fascinator seems rather tame. And Beatrice was hardly the only guest wearing a Treacy creation at the Royal Wedding: Victoria Beckham, Zara Phillips, the Duchess of Cornwall (Camilla Parker Bowles), and over thirty other women, many of them established Treacy clients, also made splashy appearances in his designs.[18] Indeed, Treacy has been a royal favorite for well over a decade. "[I make] hats for royalty from all over the world because they wear hats," he explained in an interview with online magazine *Fashionetc.com*, "and I've worked with them for fifteen years."[19]

Given Treacy's long-standing relationship with royalty—he praises Queen Elizabeth for keeping "hats alive in the imagination of people all over the world"[20]—his collaboration with Princess Beatrice was hardly unusual.[21] In fact, Treacy later revealed that he had hoped to *emphasize* the princess's royal ancestry through his unique design. In a post-wedding interview with the *Manchester Guardian*, he claimed that he had been inspired by Beatrice's resemblance to her "great, great, great, great" grandmother Queen Victoria. Rather than remake Beatrice into a modern monarch (and risk the ire of the princess's grandmother), however, Treacy opted to turn her into a doll. "I thought of her as a beautiful, exotic, Victorian doll," he explained. "I thought I was making a hat with a bow on it."[22] Though the idea of a royal tribute is lovely, Treacy's disturbing characterization of Princess Beatrice as a Victorian doll suggests that he saw his client as an object to manipulate (like the dolls he had designed clothes for as a child) rather than as a fellow participant in the design process. Such comments (inadvertently?) invoke the Pygmalion myth of the female object made whole through a masculine touch; the ballet *Coppelia,* based on the stories of E. T. A. Hoffman about a man obsessed with his lifelike doll; and the lengthy history of women called upon to signal familial status through sartorial display and other forms of "conspicuous consumption."[23]

Yet when considered alongside other forms of royal spectacle and showmanship, the doll comparison is remarkably apt. When she donned Treacy's oversized bow, Princess Beatrice participated in an elite and elitist performance tradition that goes back as far as the institutionalization of Ladies' Day at Royal Ascot. Established in 1711 by Queen Anne to showcase royal sportsmanship, the four-day horse race quickly became an important annual event in the royal social calendar. In 1807, Regency-era dandy Beau Brummel turned Royal Ascot into a fashion parade when he "decreed that men of elegance should wear waisted black coats and white cravats with pantaloons."[24] By the mid-nineteenth century, society ladies and royalty spent vast sums of money on dresses for the four-day event, reserving their most "sumptuous toilette" for the third day when the Gold Cup was awarded.[25] In the twentieth century, Ascot attendees with a flair for the theatrical continued to promote an economy of excess with outlandish hats representing animals, fruit, buildings, sporting equipment, and a wide assortment of other objects. Such hats celebrated the beautiful and the bizarre and ignored or denigrated the purely functional, marking the bodies of those who wore them as wealthier, better bred, and more sophisticated than those around them.

It is no surprise that Phillip Treacy has become a staple designer at Royal Ascot. In 2008, he helped launch the event by photographing a model wearing one of his (now) iconic asymmetrical hats. His influence was also notable at the tercentenary (300th) Ascot held in June 2011, where the most eye-catching creations included an elaborate eighteenth-century pompadour (a tribute to Queen Anne), a bed of daisies, and a feather-plumed iPad.[26] As these examples suggest, Royal Ascot continues to function as a staging ground for elaborate performances of wealth and privilege, where much of the excitement for the average observer comes from watching what happens *off* the racecourse.[27] The recent popularity of Treacy's whimsical fascinators among the royals and other members of the social elite in Britain further demonstrates how white female bodies are positioned within a display economy of excess. As the name suggests, the fascinator is less a functional head covering than a frivolous creation of feathers and jewels intended to *fascinate* others; this emphasis on the fascinator as active subject (that which fascinates) has the rather peculiar effect of representing the woman who wears the fascinator as a passive yet spectacular object of desire, a stage for the active doing of the hat.

In light of this history of royal excess and Treacy's role in its development, what seems to have distinguished Beatrice's sartorial spectacle from previous performances was less the hat itself than the context in which it was worn—a Royal Wedding may draw a similar audience to Royal Ascot but it is most definitely *not* a horse race—and its difference from the other Treacy hats. Unlike Eugenie's leaf-shaped hat, which resembled many of Treacy's other Royal Wedding creations, Beatrice's "bow" was a major departure from the overall aesthetic: a hat among hats that did not frame as much as perform a handstand on the princess's head.

Beatrice's soap-opera-like family history may also have been a factor in the hat backlash. In their post-wedding responses, journalists, bloggers, and commenting readers accused the princess and her mother, spurned royal Sarah Ferguson, of trying to upstage the wedding couple. American blog *PopEater* cited an unnamed source who suggested that the Duchess of York had "helped pick out those hats" for her daughters in order to exact revenge for being excluded from the wedding events. "The one thing Sarah hates more than anything is being ignored," the friend reportedly stated, "and this was her way of saying f-you to the family who would rather pretend she doesn't exist."[28] While farfetched if not entirely impossible, Beatrice's striking physical resemblance to her disgraced mother (*not* Queen Victoria) seemed to corroborate this account of millinery subterfuge, playing into cultural fantasies of fairy-tale weddings and ugly stepsisters consumed by jealousy. Indeed, one of the most popular Photoshopped images to travel the Internet after the Royal Wedding was a comparison of the Princesses of York with the ugly stepsisters from Disney's *Cinderella*.[29] Sarah Ferguson had turned the royal family into a very different kind of show with her bourgeois antics and now her daughters appeared to be following a similar path towards gauche self-spectacle.

Online responses to Princess Beatrice's hat were swift and often cruel.

Fig. 5.2. The *Cinderella* comparison.

Bloggers referred to it as a toilet bowl ring," a "flying spaghetti monster," a pretzel, ovaries and fallopian tubes, an antelope, a spider, and the severed head of Medusa.[30] Not all the feedback was negative—some fans dedicated songs to the hat and posted them on YouTube—but most observers agreed that the princess had committed a fashion faux pas: 80 percent of *Huffington Post* readers declared it "the worst ever."[31] As a result, images of the hat appeared everywhere—newspapers, blogs, Tumblr, eBay, and Facebook pages. A week after the wedding, the Facebook page "Princess Beatrice's Ridiculous Royal Wedding Hat"—one of at least a dozen Facebook pages devoted to the hat—had already received over 12,000 "likes" (as of August 27, 2011, the page had 140,920 "likes").[32] Visitors to this page and others shared Photoshopped parodies of the "ridiculous" hat. For example, amateur "shoppers" turned it into the Eye of Sauron, a doorway for a tabby cat, and spaghetti for Disney's *Lady and the Tramp*; others transplanted it to the heads of world leaders, animals, children, and fictional characters (fig. 5.3).[33]

As these examples suggest, Princess Beatrice's hat functioned very much like other Internet "memes," quirky images or videos that rapidly circulate through multiple media channels in a viral-like manner. "A meme," explains cultural critic Malcolm Gladwell, "is an idea that behaves like a virus—that moves through a population, taking hold in each person it infects."[34] Evolutionary biologist Richard Dawkins originated the term in his 1976 book, *The Selfish Gene*, in which he defined memes as units of cultural transmission comparable to genes.[35] Though popular in the 1990s, meme theory has since fallen out of favor in academic circles, criticized by many as offering an overly simplistic explanation for the transmission of complex ideas within

Fig. 5.3. A collage of several of the Photoshopped images inspired by the hat.

and across human populations.[36] The term has nevertheless been enfolded into North American popular culture, where it is most often used to describe media-fueled phenomena like Princess Beatrice's hat.[37] These memes hold the public's attention for a few days, occasionally a few weeks, and, like most fads, their potential for affecting political change or personal transformation appears rather limited.

However, I'd like to argue that Princess Beatrice's hat was different—that while its circulation through Internet channels resembled that of other memes, it ultimately did more than provoke a giggle or guffaw. As it spiraled through the global mediascape, Princess Beatrice's hat became a thing that facilitated political commentary and charitable action. In what follows, I look more closely at several of parodies of the "ridiculous" hat before discussing Princess Beatrice's decision to sell the Treacy original on eBay.

POLITICAL FASHIONS

Hats perform and so do photographs. I refer specifically to the widely circulated image of President Barack Obama, Hillary Clinton, and other members of the Security Council anxiously waiting in the White House "Situ-

Fig. 5.4. The Photoshopped "Situation Room" photo.

ation Room" while U.S. military forces capture and kill Osama Bin Laden. The photograph first appeared on the White House's flickr page—a site frequently used by the social-media-savvy administration to offer visitors "backstage" access to the president's daily routine—and was soon picked up by media outlets around the world.[38] As a propaganda image, the photograph labors hard to demonstrate that the president and his advisors had authorized Bin Laden's death and witnessed it live via streaming video. It credits Obama with the terrorist's death while showing the emotional toll on those involved. Released just days after the Royal Wedding, the photograph was also an obvious target for Photoshop parody. Enter the hat.

In figure 5.4, all thirteen government officials don Princess Beatrice's hat. The doctored image is well composed, presumably made by someone with better than average Photoshop skills. Upon close examination, one notices that the creator has adjusted the size and angle of the hat to suit the individual wearer, giving the impression (almost) that the rooms' inhabitants have staged the photograph themselves. But, of course, this was hardly the case. So what can be made of this image? What does it do? One response is that it trivializes the death of Osama Bin Laden and turns U.S. government officials into silly, clown-like figures. A more generous reading is that it invites critical reflection on the severity of the event and on Obama's refusal to circulate photographs of the dead al Qaeda leader despite loud calls from media outlets and American citizens for "proof" of his death.[39] It also calls attention to the staginess of the original "Situation Room" photo, to its use as propaganda. The thirteen transplanted Beatrice hats transform Obama and his advisors into dramatic characters and raise troubling questions about the frequency with which they rehearse their war games. In this respect, it is the ultimate *verfremdungseffekt*. It has succeeded, as Brecht outlines, in "turning an object from something ordinary and immediately accessible into something peculiar, striking and unexpected"—although, of course, the photograph was far from ordinary to begin with.[40]

Princess Beatrice's hat promotes a similar *verfremdungseffekt* in "Hats for Kate," a publicity stunt arranged by the Canadian-based action organization Environmental Defense to coincide with the Duke and Duchess of Cambridge's tour of Canada in July 2011. The online exhibit opens with a photograph of a Kate-look-alike wearing an enlarged, maple-leaf printed adaptation of Princess Beatrice's fascinator—"the hat that got us talking hats—even far away in Canada."[41] There is nothing overtly political about the "Mapleleaf Beatrice" hat; rather, it serves to entice visitors to continue clicking to the next hats in the series, where the exhibit's political objective becomes all too clear. Two clicks away, visitors are confronted with "Tar and Feathers," a black veiled hat topped by two tar-covered ducks. The caption beneath the photograph reveals that the hat was made to "mark the day Canada achieved infamy when a flock of ducks mistook a massive toxic lake in the [Alberta] tar sands for a good place to land."[42] Other hats in the exhibit comment in similarly provocative ways on Canada's exploitation of natural resources and its reluctance to support international climate agreements. A text box at the bottom of each page invites visitors to find out "what's *really* going on" by clicking through to the Environmental Defense page. There, the organization reveals the real purpose of the campaign, namely to show the royal couple "how much Canada has changed since Will's childhood visit."[43]

This clever publicity stunt exploited public interest in the royal couple, particularly interest in Princess Catherine's own symbolic fashion choices (she wore a maple leaf fascinator on Canada Day) and familiarity with the Princess Beatrice debacle. Though it's impossible to know whether the stunt had any direct effect on the royals or online visitors, it nevertheless succeeded in drawing attention to Environmental Defense at a time when royal mania in Canada was reaching a fever pitch. Moreover, by parodying the rather ridiculous genre of the fascinator itself, the campaign exposed the white, upper-class privilege that dominates the fashion world and challenged those "fascinated" but living outside that world to think more carefully about how their actions and the actions of government were affecting the world they lived in.

CHARITABLE PERFORMANCE VIA EBAY

If Princess Beatrice was hurt by those who compared her hat to a toilet seat or uterus, she managed to reclaim her pride when she put the hat up for sale on eBay. Interestingly, it was her mother, the rumored coconspirator Sarah Ferguson, who first mentioned the princess's decision during a May 11, 2011, taping of the *Oprah Winfrey Show*.[44] The princess confirmed news of the auction in a later press release, announcing that all proceeds would go to UNICEF and Children in Crisis through her newly founded charity, the "Little Bee Initiative." "I've been amazed by the amount of attention the hat has attracted," the princess formally stated. "It's a wonderful opportunity to raise as much money as possible for two fantastic charities. I hope whoever wins the auction has as much fun with the hat as I have."[45] Phillip Treacy also issued a statement, subsequently posted on eBay, in which he declared that he was "delighted, flattered and touched by HRH Princess Beatrice's decision to donate the hat to charity. . . . I hope that people all over the world will be generous and that this hat will benefit many."[46] With this announcement, the much-reviled hat, now described as a "unique sculptural celebratory headpiece,"[47] and the princess bold enough to wear it, appeared to the public in a very different guise (fig. 5.5). Koy Thompson, chief executive of Children in Crisis, lauded the Princess for using "the power of her world famous hat through online auction and social media to create the iconic charity event of the year."[48] No longer the ugly stepsister, Princess Beatrice emerged as a generous, media-savvy woman; her hat and the reaction it had received had made her a better person, at least according to the new media spin.

In the ten-day bidding period that followed, the hat attracted over half a million viewers to eBay and bids from thirty-one potential buyers from the United Kingdom, Canada, Australia, Singapore, Bulgaria, Sweden, and the United States.[49] Public figures from UNICEF U.K. ambassador and entrepreneur Duncan Bannatyne to children's entertainers the Wiggles submitted bids and urged others to join the auction. Celebrity Tweets from Victoria Beckham, Lady Gaga, Stephen Fry, and Cat Deeley likewise urged Twitter followers to check out the auction and drive up the bidding. It was this aspect of the auction, more than anything else perhaps, that distinguished it from previous auctions of royal clothing, such as the June 1997 Christie's auction of Princess Diana's dresses held just months before her death. By using the (arguably) more democratic auction site, Princess Beatrice invited

Fig. 5.5. The hat photographed for the eBay auction block. (Photo: Mike Stone/ Alamy.)

fans and collectors from around the world to participate in her charity event as observers (eBay posted the bids as they came in) and performers (the bidders themselves). Of course, the actual bidding process only worked to mark, yet again, the economic disparity between those capable of bidding and those who could merely watch it happen, not to mention the Children in Crisis for whom the money was intended. Center stage once more, the hat did not disappoint: it eventually sold for £81,100 (over US$130,000) to an unidentified bidder.[50]

The story of Princess Beatrice's "ridiculous" hat offers one example of how showy objects can influence human behavior in deep and meaningful ways, challenging traditional binaries between humans and nonhumans. "The story of objects asserting themselves as things," writes Bill Brown, "is the story of a changed relation to the human subject and thus the story of how the thing really names less an object than a particular subject-object relation."[51] For as much as humans "encode things with significance" or give life to them through physical contact or usage (i.e., putting *on* the hat), it is "the things-in-motion that illuminate their human and social context."[52] Although originally designed with the goal of showing off Princess Beatrice as a young, vivacious, and possibly rebellious young royal, the hat-in-motion showcased different relationships. Leaping metaphorically off the princess's head to enter the global mediascape of eBay, Facebook, and Tumblr, it invited humans to react in many different ways: to laugh, to ridicule, to parody, to give, to aid, and ultimately, to celebrate.

Notes

1. The term "fascinator" is widely used within fashion circles to describe lightweight millinery that sits on the front of the head, either over the forehead or on the side of the crown.

2. See Arjun Appadurai, *Modernity at Large: Cultural Dimensions of Globalization* (Minneapolis: University of Minnesota Press, 1996).

3. This definition of "thing" comes from Bill Brown's article "Thing Theory," *Critical Inquiry* 28, no. 1 (Autumn 2001): 1–22.

4. Thank you to Natalya Baldyga for to suggesting this application of Butler to me.

5. Brown, "Thing Theory," 4.

6. Margaret Werry, "Interdisciplinary Objects, Oceanic Insights: Performance and the New Materialism," in *Theatre Historiography: Critical Interventions*, ed. Henry Bial and Scott Magelssen (Ann Arbor: University of Michigan Press, 2010), 227–28. For an overview of recent developments within "new materialism," see the introduction to my edited collection with Joanne Zerdy, *Performing Objects and Theatrical Things* (Basingstoke: Palgrave Macmillan, 2014). See also the collection *New Materialisms: Ontology, Agency, and Politics*, ed. Diana Coole and Samantha Frost (Durham: Duke University Press, 2010). Other key theorists on objects or things, or both, include Arjun Appadurai, ed., *The Social Life of Things: Commodities in Cultural Perspective* (Cambridge: Cambridge University Press, 1986); Bill Brown, "Thing Theory," *Critical Inquiry* 29, no. 1 (Autumn 2001): 1–22; Alice Raynor, *Ghosts: Deaths' Double and the Phenomena of Theatre* (Minneapolis: University of Minnesota Press, 2006), esp. chap. 2; Sara Ahmed, *Queer Phenomenology: Orientations, Objects, Others* (Durham: Duke University Press, 2006).

7. Robin Bernstein, "Dances with Things: Material Culture and the Performance of Race," *Social Text* 27.4, no. 101 (December 2009): 67–94.

8. See Appadurai's "Introduction" to *The Social Life of Things*.

9. I'm working with Andrew Sofer's definition of "prop" here, whereby objects onstage become props through their interaction with actors. See Andrew Sofer, *The Stage Life of Props* (Ann Arbor: University of Michigan Press, 2003).

10. Bernstein, "Dances with Things," 69. Bernstein offers a more extensive exploration of the "scriptive thing" in *Racial Innocence: Performing American Childhood from Slavery to Civil Rights* (New York: New York University Press, 2011).

11. Bernstein, "Dances with Things," 69–70.

12. Bernstein, "Dances with Things," 70.

13. Kate Kellaway, "Philip Treacy: 'I Like Hats That Make the Heart Beat Faster,'" *Observer*, July 10, 2011, http://www.guardian.co.uk/lifeandstyle/2011/jul/10/philip-treacy-milliner-interview, accessed September 2, 2011; "Philip Treacy: Hat Designer," Design Museum, http://designmuseum.org/design/philip-treacy, accessed September 2, 2011.

14. "Philip Treacy: Hat Designer." Treacy's imaginative hats made him an industry favorite and by the mid-1990s he was collaborating with Karl Lagerfeld, Alexander McQueen, and Gianni Versace.

15. It is also worth noting the importance of hats to many communities of African American women, who wear lavish hats or "crowns" to attend church on Sunday. See Michael Cunningham and Craig Marberry, *Crowns: Portraits of Black Women in Church Hats* (New York: Doubleday, 2000); Samuel G. Freedman, "A Generational Divide Worn on Their Heads," *New York Times*, April 19, 2014, A18, http://www.nytimes.com/2014/04/19/us/a-generational-divide-worn-on-their-heads.html?_r=0, accessed July 16, 2014.

16. "Philip Treacy: Hat Designer."

17. In 1962, Crayola renamed its "flesh" crayon "peach" in response to complaints that the name "flesh" failed to acknowledge the complexity of human skin tones.

18. Erin Donnelly, "Royal Wedding Hats: Princess Beatrice and More Philip Treacy Toppers," *Fashionetc*, April 29, 2011. http://fashionetc.com/news/fashion/1670-royal-wedding-hats-princess-beatrice-philip-treacy, accessed September 2, 2011.

19. Ibid.

20. Kellaway, "Philip Treacy: 'I Like Hats That Make the Heart Beat Faster.'"

21. Erin Donnelly, "Philip Treacy Talks Royal Wedding, Lady Gaga, and Why Kate Should Wed in McQueen," *Fashionetc*, April 24, 2011. http://fashionetc.com/fashion/influencers/1591-philip-treacy-talks-royal-wedding-lady-gaga-and-why-kate-should-wed-in-mcqueen, accessed September 2, 2011.

22. Kellaway, "Philip Treacy: 'I Like Hats That Make the Heart Beat Faster.'"

23. Thorstein Veblen famously coined the term "conspicuous consumption" in his 1899 treatise, *The Theory of the Leisure Class* (Boston: Houghton Mifflin, 1973).

24. "Royal Ascot at 300," *Telegraph*, April 19, 2011. http://www.telegraph.co.uk/sponsored/travel/enjoy_england_trips/8404369/Royal-Ascot-at-300.html, accessed September 2, 2011.

25. Duchess of Marlborough quoted in "Royal Ascot at 300."

26. "Hats and Fascinators at Royal Ascot 2011 in Pictures," *Telegraph*, June 14, 2011. http://fashion.telegraph.co.uk/galleries/TMG8575063/Hats-and-fascinators-at-

Royal-Ascot-2011-in-pictures.html., accessed September 2, 2011. Interestingly, Princess Beatrice's wore a "remarkably understated nude hat" to Royal Ascot 2011.

27. Joel Kaplan and Sheila Stowell, *Theatre and Fashion: From Oscar Wilde to the Suffragettes* (Cambridge: Cambridge University Press, 1995), 11.

28. Kat Angus, "Sarah Ferguson Catches Flak for Princess Beatrice's Wacky Hat," *Vancouver Sun,* May 3, 2011, http://www.vancouversun.com/news/royal-visit/Sarah+Ferguson+catches+flack+Princess+Beatrice+wacky/4718967/story.html, accessed September 2, 2011.

29. It's worth asking whether Treacy intended to invoke the reference to the ugly step-sisters when creating his hats for the Princesses Royal. Given his reputation for creating playful hats that recall everything from fine art to popular culture, he may well have aimed for something Disney-like.

30. See for example, Katie Rogers, "Prince Andrew's Daughter Princess Bea's Royal Wedding Hat Looks Like . . . Caption This!," *Washington Post,* April 29, 2011, http://www.washingtonpost.com/blogs/royal-wedding-watch/post/prince-andrews-daughter-princess-beas-royal-wedding-hat-looks-like—caption-this/2011/04/29/AFFlzMFF_blog.html; Sasha Slater, "Mad Hatter: It's Not Just Beatrice's Wedding 'Pretzel'—Do Philip Treacy's Crackpot Creations Look Good on ANYONE?," *Mail Online,* May 23, 2011, http://www.dailymail.co.uk/femail/article-1383648/Royal-Wedding-Princess-Beatrices-hat-looked-like-pretzel-Philip-Treacys-creations-look-good-ANYONE.html; Asher Moses, "Princess Beatrice's Hat Takes Royal Wedding Viral Crown," *Sydney Morning Herald,* May 2, 2011, http://www.smh.com.au/technology/technology-news/princess-beatrices-hat-takes-royal-wedding-viral-crown-20110502–1e3ys.html, all accessed September 2, 2011.

31. "Princess Beatrice's Hat: Worst Ever?," *Huffington Post,* April 29, 2011. http://www.huffingtonpost.com/2011/04/29/princess-beatrice-hat-worst_n_855657.html, accessed September 2, 2011.

32. "Princess Beatrice's Ridiculous Royal Wedding Hat," http://www.facebook.com/pages/Princess-Beatrices-ridiculous-Royal-Wedding-hat/203705509669392; Rob Leigh, "Princess Beatrice's Royal Wedding Hat Attracts Thousands of Facebook Fans," *Mirror,* http://www.mirror.co.uk/news/royal-wedding/2011/04/29/princess-beatrice-s-royal-wedding-hat-attracts-thousands-of-facebook-fans-115875–23095674/, accessed September 2, 2011.

33. "Princess Beatrice and Her Hat," http://princessbeatriceandherhat.tumblr.com/, accessed September 2, 2011.

34. Malcolm Gladwell, quoted in *Public Health for the 21st Century,* ed. Louis Rowitz (Sudbury, MA: Jones and Bartlett, 2006), 370.

35. C. B. Davis, "Cultural Evolution and Performance Genres: Memetics in Theatre History and Performance Studies," *Theatre Journal* 59 (2007): 585–614, quote at 596.

36. Wendy Arons provides a helpful overview of meme theory in her chapter, "Beyond the Nature/Culture Divide," in *Critical Interventions in Theatre Historiography,* ed. Hen-

ry Bial and Scott Magelssen (Minneapolis: University of Michigan Press, 2010). Arons offers some suggestions for how meme theory may be used by theater and performance historians.

37. See, for examples, the Internet Meme Database at knowyourmeme.com, http://knowyourmeme.com/

38. Jolie O'Dell, "White House Releases Situation Room Images from Bin Laden Raid," *Mashable.com*, May 2, 2011, http://mashable.com/2011/05/02/situation-room-pics/, accessed September 2, 2011.

39. Martha Raddatz, Jake Tapper, and Jessica Hopper, "Release Bin Laden Death Photos? CIA Director Thinks It Will Happen," ABC News, May 3, 2011. http://abcnews.go.com/Politics/osama-bin-laden-death-photo-sought-911-families/story?id=13516795, accessed September 2, 2011; Oliver Tree and Neil Sears, "White House Will NOT Release Gruesome Pictures of Bin Laden's Mangled Corpse," *Mail Online*, May 1, 2011. http://www.dailymail.co.uk/news/article-1382828/Osama-Bin-Laden-dead-picture-White, accessed September 2, 2011.

40. Bertolt Brecht, *Brecht on Theatre: The Development of an Aesthetic*, ed. John Willett (New York: Hill and Wang, 1964), 143.

41. "Mapleleaf Beatrice," http://www.hatsforkate.ca/, accessed September 2, 2011.

42. "Tar and Feathers," http://www.hatsforkate.ca/, accessed September 2, 2011.

43. "Canada You've Changed," http://wfc2.wiredforchange.com/o/8298/p/dia/action/public/?action_KEY=6405; http://environmentaldefence.ca/about, accessed September 2, 2011.

44. "Princess Beatrice to Auction Off Wedding Hat on eBay," *People.com*, May 11, 2011. http://www.people.com/people/package/article/0,,20395222_20488576,00.html, accessed September 2, 2011; Wendy Leung, "Princess Beatrice's Ridiculous Hat Hits eBay: Um, Any Takers," *Globe and Mail*, May 11, 2011, http://www.theglobeandmail.com/life/the-hot-button/princess-beatrices-ridiculous-hat-hits-ebay-um-any-takers/article2019003/, accessed September 2, 2011.

45. Lauren Paxman, "A Pretzel or Toilet Seat? Beatrice's Royal Wedding Hat Looks More Like a Piggy Bank as Charity Bids Top £18,000," *Mail Online*, May 18, 2011, http://www.dailymail.co.uk/femail/article-1388251/Princess-Beatrices-Royal-Wedding-hat-charity-auction-bids-18k.html.

46. Treacy quoted in "Ridiculous Royal Wedding Hat Fetches $131K for Charity," *CNN.com*, May 22, 2011, http://articles.cnn.com/2011-05-22/entertainment/beatrice.hat_1_royal-wedding-hat-auction-listing-auction-benefit?_s=PM:SHOWBIZ

47. eBay listing, quoted in "Princess Beatrice's Royal Wedding Hats Gets a £75,000 Bid on eBay," *Guardian*, May 21, 2011.

48. "Over Half a Million View Princess Beatrice Hat Auction for UNICEF and Children in Crisis," *Unicef.org*, http://www.unicef.org.uk/Media-centre/Press-releases/Over-Half-a-Million-people-view-Princess-Beatrice-Hat-Auction-for-UNICEF-and-Children-in-Crisis/, accessed September 2, 2011.

49. Ibid.

50. Belinda White, "Princess Beatrice's Philip Treacy Hat Sells for 81,101 on eBay," *Telegraph.co.uk*, May 22, 2011, http://fashion.telegraph.co.uk/columns/belinda-white/TMG8529823/Princess-Beatrices-Philip-Treacy-hat-sells-for-81101-on-eBay.html, accessed September 2, 2011.

51. Brown, "Thing Theory," 4.

52. Appadurai, quoted in Brown, "Thing Theory," 6.

CHAPTER 6

Strobridge Posters and Late Nineteenth-Century Melodrama

Katie N. Johnson

Over one hundred years ago, the Strobridge Company, a powerhouse lithographer, created astonishingly beautiful posters for America's top performers. With its new technology and low-paid immigrant labor, the Strobridge Company mass-produced stunning posters about American popular entertainments that dominated the poster market. From lowbrow circus acts to Belasco extravaganzas, Strobridge posters were the ultimate "show off" in advertising blockbusters and flops alike. Moreover, by employing famous artists, the posters constituted some of the most striking artwork of its day. What does it mean to "show" the show? *How* does a poster show the show?

This essay examines Strobridge theatrical posters as fascinating snapshots of promoting late nineteenth-century U.S. popular culture.[1] Having surveyed dozens of posters in Cincinnati Public Library's Strobridge Poster Collection, I move beyond an analysis of Strobridge lithography as a purely aesthetic achievement that boosted profits, considering also the hidden dividends of reading the artwork as a repository of cultural conversations. The essay also reveals how citizenship is "showed" through printed artifacts, which by no means invites passive spectatorship or consumption, but rather active, critical engagement. For the purposes of this essay, I have chosen posters that portray nonnormative citizenship, gender subversions, and ruptures in hegemonic discourses—those theatrical posters in which the melodramatic climaxes hinge upon figures that exceed their prescribed bounds. In such renderings, it is striking how nonwhite and female characters bear the burden—but also the pleasures—of defying normative constraints and the extent to which Strobridge artists capitalized on these blockbuster, if not utopian, moments. Women are often portrayed as fleeing (either literally or symbolically) ideological confines: crossing frozen ice patches into freedom, swinging from trees to the rescue, or challenging white patriarchs. Ethnicity and race also play a central role in this visual landscape, whether the posters portray racial performativity, negotiations of North and South in postbellum America, or what Daphne Brooks has called "bodies in dissent."[2] From anxieties regarding the legacy of slavery in *Uncle Tom's Cabin* to the "flying gals" in *Down in Dixie*, Strobridge posters can be seen as a visual synecdoche for how late nineteenth-century Americans negotiated constructions of race, gender, and citizenship. My central claim is that the posters that packed the most punch were those that distilled polemics in U.S. culture.

Given this rich visual archive, Strobridge posters serve as the basis for two case studies that chart the intersection of "showing," performance, and cultural identity. My analysis begins by considering the first-ever lithographic billboard, which premiered in Cincinnati in 1881. On one level, the billboard—tellingly called "Eliza Pursued by Bloodhounds" and which promoted the latest touring theatrical version of *Uncle Tom's Cabin*—was a technological innovation that packed audiences into the theater; on another level, the billboard "scripted" public space by inviting spectators to interact critically with the Ohio River, mixed-race public spheres, and the legacy of slavery in this border city. My second case study examines Strobridge posters designed for American melodramas that depicted pressing cultural issues, such as the struggle between Northern and Southern identity and female power.

As has been well documented by theater scholars (see especially Bruce McConachie and David Grimsted), melodrama dominated the American stage for decades in the nineteenth and early twentieth centuries.[3] Like Hollywood blockbusters today, nineteenth-century melodramas were immensely popular but also characterized by populist sentiments, with a focus on spectacular thrills, crimes to be solved, victims to rescue, and action-packed rescue scenes. While many of them were utterly forgettable, their posters are not. At first glance, these posters appear to tug on emotional heartstrings in predictable ways. They excelled in featuring heightened action scenes—usually, the play's climax—frozen, like a snapshot. The challenge for the poster artist was to condense key plot elements into a single two-dimensional space in exciting visual ways. A good lithographer had to understand not only graphic design and drama but also high-stake issues and events from U.S. culture. Strobridge artists did exactly that—showed the show, but also showed the nation.

Before delving into these case studies, I would like to first contextualize the development of the Strobridge Company as a major producer and distributor of lithographs. Like many beginnings, the Strobridge Company began as something else.[4] While at first printing solely stationery, the business quickly turned to all kinds of lithography, including calendars, maps, portraits, and posters. By the 1880s, Strobridge was known nationally for its lithography, making its home in the German immigrant section of Cincinnati called Over-the-Rhine.[5] The Cincinnati area had no less than four powerhouse lithography companies, all of which were competitors: Russell-Morgan Print, Cincinnati; Strobridge Lithograph Company, Cincinnati; Inquirer Job Printing Company, Cincinnati: and the Donaldson Lithograph Company, of Newport, Kentucky (right across the Ohio River). The Cincinnati area therefore became known for having four of the largest printing establishments in the world, as well as for inventing a new kind of lithography.[6] Lithography played an important role in the commercial printing industry, especially in the development of posters.[7] Before the invention of lithography, wood engravings were used for theatrical promotional materials. Given the capital and labor-intensive process of producing woodcut posters, limited quantities of just twenty-five or thirty posters were distributed to advertise theatrical engagements in a given town. Lithography, by contrast, was far more cost effective and became the emerging technology, allowing advertisers to use more posters to "show" the show. Color lithography was another Strobridge technological invention facilitated by preparing separate stones for each of the colors in the design. Strobridge began producing color prints by the early 1860s. Their posters used six to eight different colors, thus giving the company a competitive edge. As art historian Kristin L. Spangenberg has observed, "The posters were designed to delight and amaze audiences, young and old, who were unfamiliar with art and its conventions, and exposed them to these pictorial delights for the first time.[8] By the turn of the century, the Strobridge Company had the reputation for being the largest producer of circus, theater, and magic posters in North America.[9] Known also as the "Tiffany of Printers," Strobridge was credited by admirers as embodying "the standard of perfection in artistic theatrical lithographing," as one article put it in 1895.[10] Moreover, because the Queen City was ideally situated on the Ohio River and on major railway lines, it had an efficient distribution system (the same system that would bring touring theater and circus companies to Cincinnati).

While producers of popular entertainments had long used various visual forms of advertising, the development of the poster—more specifically, the poster as an art form—began in the middle of the nineteenth century.[11] Aesthetically, many of these posters engaged with emergent technologies of photography, scenic design, and silent film, while others drew on Romantic realistic painting. French artists like Jules Chéret, who was "hailed as the creator of the modern poster," and Henri de Toulouse-Lautrec, with his iconic posters for the Moulin Rouge, paved the way for other artists to take up what many had previously considered a quotidian art form.[12] It was not just on the continent that well-known artists sketched posters: English artist Aubrey Beardsley produced striking, if controversial, posters for British plays such as Oscar Wilde's *Salomé*. And Czech artist Alphonse Mucha was much praised for his iconic Art Nouveau theater posters for Sarah Bernhardt. In the United States, artists such as Harry Ogden, Matt Morgan, and Paul Jones joined the Strobridge firm, which became world famous for its colorful, detailed, high-quality designs. Noted artist and lithography historian Joseph Pennell observed in 1898 the impressive reach of the "House of Strobridge":

> In a word, we shall not be far wrong in saying that lithography in America was for a long time wholly commercial. And yet the great Cincinnati firm of Strowbridge [*sic*] was a sort of cradle for many of the more distinguished younger American artists, who as journeymen lithographers received their first training.[13]

A 1907 article in *Theatre Magazine* characterized poster production as an admirable artistic industry: "the leading firms of American lithographers work independently of the outside artist. They have their own staffs of forty or more competent artists," with recognizable artists primarily in charge of design.[14] As in Europe, the use of well-known artists by U.S. firms— particularly by Strobridge—made a former vulgarity now newly aestheticized. According to *Theatre Magazine*, "The new poster artist has proclaimed Art everywhere, and has made it his mission to touch the ugly necessity of the trade with the ennobling brush of beauty."[15] Citing the remarkable improvement in poster aesthetics, the author continued, everyone "must admit that the theatre poster now stands in the foremost rank" as an art form.[16]

Significantly, most of the visual examples mentioned were by Strobridge artists, though Strobridge was never explicitly named.

With a large staff of what we might call "trench artists" as well as a reserve of well-known lithographers, Strobridge could churn out posters with relative speed and superior quality. Regrettably, few posters credit any of the artists or technicians who worked on them. As Therese Hayman notes in *Posters American Style,*

> Strobridge was a sort of cradle for many of the more distinguished younger Americans, who received their first training there as journeyman lithographers. It is not easy to trace their individual designs, for names never appear upon the[m].[17]

Matt Morgan, a star of the Strobridge stable, is exceptional in this regard, in part because he became head of the company's art department, but also because he had a distinguished artistic career as a sign painter and cartoonist before joining Strobridge. In a 1916 book about scenic painting and poster art, Frank Atkinson recalled, "Matt Morgan, in his day, won the distinction of being America's greatest poster artist; he was formerly a sign painter" as well as a cartoonist for *Leslie's Weekly*.[18] Moran's painterly pedigree was palpable, as Christopher Kent has observed: "The pictorialism of his [Morgan's] posters, often depicting a central scene from the play with several vignettes of other scenes, perfectly captures the scenery-driven values of the nineteenth-century theater."[19] If spectacle-driven theater influenced posters, then the reverse was also true, as "the priorities of poster publicity even drove the scenery itself on occasion."[20] This performative loop between scenography and theater advertising is unmistakable in my first case study: iconic posters for *Uncle Tom's Cabin*.

TECHNOLOGICAL INNOVATIONS ON THE RIVER: *ELIZA PURSUED BY BLOODHOUNDS*

In 1881, an unprecedented unveiling of billboard technology occurred in Strobridge's hometown of Cincinnati when Matt Morgan crafted the first large, multiple-sheet outdoor poster. By piecing together 16 sheets, Strobridge was able to go beyond the usual size of theater posters—28 by 42 inches—and make a large billboard eight times larger than anything ever mounted before.[21] This innovation gave Strobridge the technological edge: "In the old craft shop days such a thing would scarcely have been feasible; with the inception of power machinery, however, and the possibility of handling large stones quickly and in greater numbers it was a natural development."[22] The large lithographic billboard—the first of its kind—was a technological unveiling not unlike Apple's iPhone. Indeed, Strobridge dominated U.S. printing with innovative design much like Apple does today in the computer industry. America's first billboard, designed by Morgan, profoundly touched the river city of Cincinnati, whose Ohio River provided the border between North and South, or rather "between the two civilizations," as George S. McDowell put it in 1895.[23] The outdoor poster, called *Eliza Pursued by Bloodhounds* (see fig. 6.1), was exhibited at Cincinnati's Fountain Square when Jay Rial's *Uncle Tom's Cabin* toured in 1881 (each block represents a "sheet" in the billboard; Merten gives 1878 as the date for the billboard on Fountain Square; however, in conferring with art historian Kristin Spangenberg, I believe 1881 is the correct date).[24] At the very heart of the Queen City, but very close to the river, Fountain Square has long been a charged semiotic space, where all kinds of events, from abolition speeches to KKK rallies, have taken place. When the billboard was displayed, crowds were so large that they shut down traffic, requiring police to move people along. Insofar as "lithographic printers and their artists played a primary role in designing pictorial images to capture the public's attention," Strobridge posters—and the world's first billboard—constituted an archival snapshot of a poignant Reconstruction moment.[25]

Very much like the posters, billboards therefore functioned less as archival "*ludus interruptus*," as Christopher Balme has said of their promotional cousins, playbills, and more as dynamic, performative material objects that signified powerfully in their cultural moments.[26] Robin Bernstein's analysis of how material objects "script" human actions is useful here. She suggests "that agency, intention, and racial subjectivation co-emerge through everyday physical encounters with the material world."[27] With a focus on "thing theory" (by way of Heidegger), Bernstein shows how things are not inert "chunks of matter" but rather *active*: "A thing demands that people confront it on its own terms; thus, a thing forces a person into an awareness of the self in material relation to the thing."[28] I'd like to tease out the performative valence of the ways in which the billboard for *Uncle Tom's Cabin* became a kind of "thing-in motion that illuminate[d] its social context," as Arjun Appadurai has written.[29] Specifically, I wish to consider how dynamic groups

Fig. 6.1. The first theatrical billboard: Jay Rial's Ideal *Uncle Tom's Cabin*, Strobridge Lithographing Co., Cincinnati, 1881. (Theatrical Poster Collection, Prints and Photographs Division, Library of Congress, LC-USZ62-17368.)

of people—immigrants, African Americans, whites, working classes, and moneyed elites—gathered at a liminal spatial site (Fountain Square in Cincinnati) to interact with the very pressing (and still ongoing) story of slavery raised by *Uncle Tom's Cabin*. To what extent did "thing and person become unmoored from fixed positions of difference and twirl in sudden mutual orbit, each subject to the other's gravity," to use Bernstein's eloquent words?[30]

The choice to feature *Uncle Tom's Cabin* (also written by Cincinnati native Harriet Beecher Stowe) could hardly be more symbolically charged for this border city, which is perched on the very Ohio River portrayed in the billboard.[31] Most historians of U.S. theater know that *Uncle Tom's Cabin* was the most frequently performed show in nineteenth-century America; indeed, by 1879 no fewer than forty-nine companies were touring Uncle Tom shows throughout the United States.[32] As late as 1898, *Uncle Tom's Cabin* was the most popular book in the Cincinnati library.[33] For Cincinnati, this play—and its billboard—had particular relevance, as the artwork portrays Eliza's melodramatic escape across the Ohio River to Cincinnati. While this scene is not explicitly narrated in Stowe's novel, tableaux of Eliza crossing the frozen river were featured in virtually every dramatic adaptation, and this image became iconic in theatrical posters as well.[34] This scene constitutes moreover a spectacular instance of "showing" both the climatic moment of Stowe's story and the melodramatic weight of slavery. The billboard demonstrates not only skilled scenographic painting but also an intensely layered viewing moment: in 1881, a spectator on Fountain Square would have had an uncanny sort of *mise-en-abyme* in viewing the billboard and the Ohio River virtually at the same time. Decidedly *not* a panorama (the prevailing technology of the early to mid-nineteenth century), the billboard more closely resembles an exaggerated snapshot or film still.[35] Rather than showing the panoramic, comprehensive view from afar, the billboard is more selective, zooming in for a medium shot.[36] A subjective shot. A scene not even featured in the novel. A simulated scene that was, paradoxically, pure Cincinnati.

Time and space—North and South, antebellum and post–Civil War—collide in this moment. But the "things"—in this instance, books and billboards—collide as well. In 1878, Stowe updated her introduction to *Uncle Tom's Cabin* for the last time. As William Barclay Allen has written, this edition was considered "the final comprehensive statement Stowe made in her own name."[37] Morgan's fiercely melodramatic billboard, however, seems strikingly at odds with Stowe's 1878 introduction, which seeks to downplay the horrors of slavery and the Civil War: "Now the war is over," Stowe writes, "slavery is a thing of the past; slavepens, bloodhounds, slave-whips, and slave-coffles are only bad dreams of the night; and now the humane reader can afford to read *Uncle Tom's Cabin* without an expenditure of torture and tears."[38] Morgan's rendering rubs against, and even contests, Stowe's pacifying introduction. The poster brilliantly captures an intensely dramatic moment, suggesting that slavery is hardly a thing of the past. In fact, the centrality of the snarling dogs, which are not bloodhounds at all but mastiffs, points to the ongoing "bad dreams of the night" which plagued the Queen City (and which, to a certain extent, still do).[39] As richly detailed as it is emotionally powerful, Morgan's design shows the moonlight, the frozen river ice, and the fear in Eliza's eyes. In the billboard, the "expenditure of torture and tears" lives on, exaggerating the melodramatic violence as a promotional strategy. For after all, if such spectacular excess makes great advertising, it also taps into the cultural zeitgeist. Significantly, the billboard does not depict the formerly iconic scene between Uncle Tom and little Eva, or a plantation scene, but rather a rendering of the topography that split the nation in two. Viewed from the Northern side of the Ohio (literally and metaphorically), Eliza's escape also offers a glimpse back to the Civil War, offering a temporal perspective.

Matt Morgan's artistry is palpable when his rendering is compared to a competitor from the other side of the river, Donaldson's Lithography Company (undated; see fig. 6.2).[40] Most apparent is the limited use of color in Donaldson's *Eliza Crossing the Ice*, giving it a flat appearance. Even though Donaldson's version contains all the key elements that Morgan's poster does—Eliza being pursued, the ice blocks, the dogs, the moon, and slave hunters on the Southern bank—it lacks the melodramatic flair that Strobridge delivers. Donaldson's lithography is more indebted to older woodcut technology than the vibrant painterly quality that became Strobridge's trademark. Even the title of Donaldson's poster is less dramatic than Strobridge's: Eliza is crossing the ice, not being pursued by bloodhounds.

Strobridge's billboard moreover packs a punch with the intimacy of the scene—the dogs bite her cape, the moon hovers close to the horizon, and the ice chunks heave in the foreground. The framing moreover highlights the proximity of slavery in Cincinnati's riverfront history. The scene portrayed in Morgan's billboard is tactile, emotional, and excessive—giving Strobridge the competitive edge in more way than one.

In addition to constituting grand, if not excessive, scale, advertising, the Strobridge billboard extended the theater's public sphere, as Balme puts it, "that is located temporally and spatially outside the heightened enchantment of the 'event.'"[41] The *Uncle Tom's Cabin* billboard on Fountain Square was part of a broader promotional scheme that included posters displayed in taverns, posting areas and businesses.[42] As Harry Birdoff recounts in his study of *Uncle Tom's Cabin*, lithographic posters functioned as promotional scenery in advance of the arrival of the troupe:

> With the coming of Spring they blossomed forth—covering barns and fences, and in flaming colors overrunning stone walls; the "three sheet" lithographs could not be read from a distance, but there wasn't a boy who didn't recognize immediately the familiar figures: [such as] Eliza pursued across the ice by the hounds.[43]

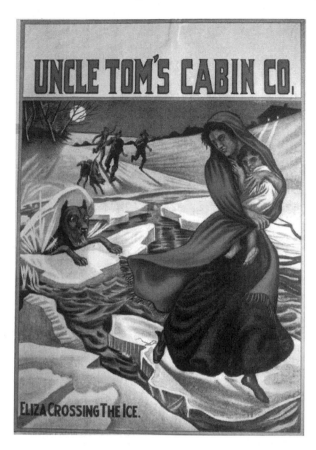

Fig. 6.2. Color lithograph poster for stage production of *Uncle Tom's Cabin*. (Donaldson's Litho, Newport, Kentucky. Harry Birdoff Collection, Harriet Beecher Stowe Center. [46.43].)

According to historian David Reynolds, promotional posters were part of a multipronged publicity event: "For many towns, the arrival of the show [*Uncle Tom's Cabin*] was a big event, trumpeted by posters and enlivened by a Tom parade."[44] Indeed, as John W. Frick has observed in *Uncle Tom's Cabin on the American Stage and Screen*, with the exception of newspaper ads, "the most potent weapon in the advance agent's arsenal when he arrived in a new town were lithographic posters depicting Eliza crossing the ice or Legree beating Tom."[45] If the figures from three-sheet lithographic posters, especially Eliza crossing the river, were recognizable to all, even to youngsters as Birdoff claimed, then the enormous billboard on Fountain Square significantly extended proximity and visual literacy.

Largeness—both of subjects and of the medium itself—was a valuable attribute in the promotional machinery, leading to "mammoth" Tom shows. Jay Rial's "Ideal Production," as it called itself—the production featured in the billboard—was known for introducing large live dogs onstage (previously, actors barked offstage to create the effect of dogs): "During the 1880s . . . when Tomming was already rooted deeply in American culture, the Jay Rial Ideal Company enhanced the shows' circus parade tradition by adding animals to the productions: hunting dogs barked ferociously as Eliza fled with her child."[46] Even though bloodhounds were not featured in the novel, as historian Jo Ann Morgan notes, stage adaptations featured "bloodthirsty hounds lapping at the heels of the runaways." [47] For melodramatic effect, dogs were not only added but also supersized: "On the stage, the beasts of choice were not even the lop-eared bloodhounds of legend but huge mastiffs or Great Danes."[48] Preperformance Tom parades were central promotional tools that were likely modeled on the circus parade "which was the culminating event in a weeks-long publicity campaign."[49] It is not clear whether the dogs were a part of the Cincinnati Tom parade, but I suspect they were, given their presence on stage.

In an effort to grandstand competing shows, display advertisements for traveling Tom shows often promoted ferocious bloodhounds. For example, a London production that toured Cincinnati in 1881 advertised a "Kennel of Blood Hounds" including a St. Bernard named Sultan, who was valued at $5,000. "This superb dog possesses intelligence to an almost incredible degree," the advertisement boasted, "and his acting in the scene of the Fight in the Mountain Pass never fails to raise an audience to the highest pitch of excitement."[50] Strobridge astutely incorporated the latest bloodhound fad by featuring oversized dogs in their posters. As Reynolds notes, this sensationalist trend of *Uncle Tom's Cabin* productions "going to the dogs" drew on years of persecution during slavery when "more than one escaped African American was torn apart by slave hunters' dogs."[51] Jay Rial's Ideal Productions incorporated bloodhounds in their print publicity, promoting "trained bloodhound chase(s)" or "mammoth trained bloodhounds."[52] A chromolithograph advertising card published by Maerz Lithography Company (from Buffalo, New York) promised "the only Genuine Trained Bloodhounds in the World."[53] Rial's production moreover laid claims to canine authenticity and denounced competing shows that made efforts "to give the appearance of presenting bloodhounds," because, they reasoned, "imitation is never entirely successful. Excellence is only obtained by time and labor."[54]

Returning to the unveiling of the billboard in Cincinnati in 1881, to what extent did the crowds "collide" with a variety of things (the billboard, post-ers, Tom parade, dogs) and how did these things "script" the crowd's behav-ior? To what extent did these artifacts incite a collision with the legacy of slavery at the junction of the Ohio River, the boundary between North and South? Did spectators on Fountain Square register resistant behaviors as they interacted with the billboard? Might the billboard and other promo-tional posters have prompted an interaction that "flipped" the racial imagi-nary, even in the midst of Tomitudes and what Kyla Wazana Tompkins calls "racial kitsch"?[55] Surely Cincinnatians were well aware of escaped slave sto-ries like the well-publicized case of Margaret Garner, the young woman who sought refuge across the Ohio River in Cincinnati only to slit the throat of her own child rather than submit her to slavery again after her recapture.[56] Unlike the historical figure Margaret Garner and the dozens of other re-captured slaves, however, the Eliza of the billboard escapes. It is worth not-ing Eliza's agency in the Strobridge rendition as well. While in most visual depictions, Eliza appears frail as she runs away with her child, in Morgan's version she uses a heavy stick to beat back the dogs who threaten her. Her pursuers are barely visible. Eliza dominates the visual field. With one foot on Northern soil—or ice—Eliza and her child eclipse the anonymous slave hunters. North trumps South. The larger-than-life bloodhounds bite at her cape, just as they may have barked during the Tom parade. The unveiling of the billboard collides with slavery's legacy, performing a disjunctive tension at the very site of Garner's recapture, on the border "between two civiliza-tions."[57]

NERVY GIRLS SWINGING TO THE RESCUE
AND RIDING TO THE FINISH LINE

The boundaries between North and South (and whiteness and blackness) find different articulations in posters that serve as my second case study. In artwork for *Down in Dixie*, a play by Scott Marble that premiered in Cin-cinnati in 1894, Southern identity is at the very core of the melodramatic struggle, though it is couched in racialized and gendered performances.[58] Described in the *New York Times* as both "a new Southern comedy" and a "melodrama of Southern complexion," the play was set in Georgia and South Carolina and featured "a pickaninny band, a cotton-field quartet, and a full-size cotton compress," along with the playwright in the role of "an old country squire."[59] Although Strobridge produced several posters of this play, I am interested in those that portrayed unusual manifestations of racial and gender performativity. This first *Down in Dixie* poster features a "nervy hero-ine," to use the poster's text, who, in typical melodramatic fashion, unveils a character's false identity at a climactic moment. While fabricated identities were common in nineteenth-century melodramas, this poster demonstrates the heroine uncovering a character's "false" racial categorization: she "un-wigs" the "counterfeit Negro" (see fig. 6.3). What gives Georgia ability to see through his racial artifice and expose it? Presumably her racial innocence, Bernstein might say, where childhood virtue is marshaled to manufacture the racial imaginary.[60] Her whiteness, in other words, affords her the ability to unmask deceit, figured here as false racial typologies. Significantly, Geor-gia affects the revelation through touch. Just as Eva is allowed to touch, even love, Uncle Tom, so Georgia may unmask the fake black character, which is amplified by the fake blackface performance of the actor. In "un-wigging" the "counterfeit Negro," the nervy heroine also lays bare the mechanics of racial performance—she un-wigs the very process of wigging. In effect, she also reveals the problematics of blackface minstrelsy, for the construct of the "Negro" is indeed counterfeit—just as actors in blackface roles were.[61] It is a scene that therefore unmasks the artifice of racial authenticity—on stage or off. The poster moreover reverses the trope of passing found in nineteenth-century literature: rather than an African American passing as white, in *Down in Dixie* a white character passes as black. The poster highlights the performativity of racial categories while unsettling seemingly rigid borders. The provocative premise of racial passing, un-wigging, and counterfeiting served Strobridge's need for dramatic moments to portray; I see it as an archive of artists portraying the instability of racial categories.

Another *Down in Dixie* poster stands out noticeably with a different kind of nervy heroine. Whereas the other dozen or so Strobridge posters for *Down in Dixie* are all printed with a recognizable gold-and-red color palette, the poster is noticeably darker, alluring, and exciting. Even the title graphics are more rousing, not only in their use of color but also in denoting a sense of action and movement. The hanging moss on the trees, a quintes-sential Southern symbol, evokes an "authentic" setting (thus providing "local color" constitutive of sentimental literature). However, a closer look reveals that the poster subverts expected melodramatic formulas in terms of gender. How, for example, do we explain the following caption: "Georgia Swings to

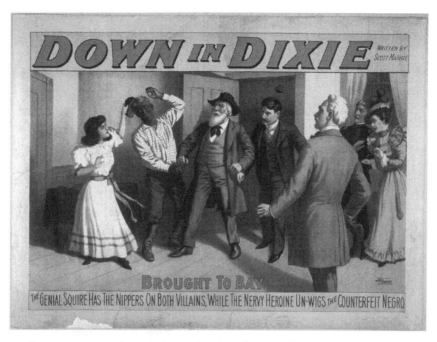

Fig. 6.3. *Down in Dixie* Lithograph poster featuring "the Nervy Heroine" Strobridge & Co. Lith, and Scott Marble. (*Down in Dixie*; New York: Strobridge Lith. Co., c, 1897. Image. Retrieved from the Library of Congress.)

the Rescue"? Moreover, how is it that a *woman* is swinging to the rescue? In striking contradistinction to another version of the poster, where Georgia turns away from her plantation, appearing dejected and weak, here Georgia literally swings from the trees in her efforts to fight for her home. Moreover, she is rescuing *the men*, effectively suggesting an altogether different play. Not only does this poster fundamentally reverse the conventional gender dynamics of melodrama, it also suggests a female action figure. In this poster, Georgia demonstrates "a danger defying, mind-bewildering deed of heroism" as the aubergine text states at the bottom. Did the female protagonist actually swing onto the stage to rescue the men? Was the poster trying to entice female audiences, and if so why did they think that strong women would attract spectators? Or was the Strobridge artist imagining some subversive gender performance—a kind of utopian performative, as Jill Dolan

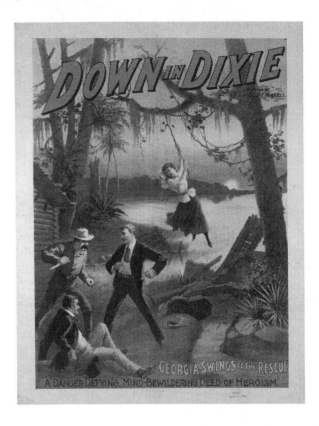

Fig. 6.4.

might say?[62] It is impossible to determine for sure, but I like to think of this poster as flying below the regulatory radar of patriarchy. In such instances, the artist (who is regrettably anonymous) provides us with an extraordinary moment of female agency.

In the world of theater, and especially as depicted in Strobridge posters, women were regularly swinging to the rescue. The swinging gal in *Down in Dixie* brings to mind Mrs. Leslie Carter swinging from the bell clapper in David Belasco's *The Heart of Maryland*.[63] In fact 1895 and 1896 were ringing years for women. Although 1895 was decidedly presuffrage in terms of women's rights in U.S. culture, it was also situated within first-wave feminism. The poster for *The Heart of Maryland*, also designed by Strobridge, focuses on the climax of the melodrama in which Mrs. Leslie Carter's character seeks to prevent the ringing of the bell in order to save the day. Mrs. Carter's physical performance in this scene was extraordinary. As theater historian Kim Marra points out,

Commentators marveled at the sheer physical exigencies of what Craig Timberlake terms Mrs. Carter's "marathonian performance." They wrote over and over of the extraordinary gymnastic ability required to fight off her attacker, stab him repeatedly, scale some seventy-five rungs of the ladder to a height of thirty-five feet above the stage, leap for the clapper, and swing high overhead, trailing her long, red tresses in the breeze.[64]

Marra suggests that Belasco's staging of this scene verged on the pornographic, but I want to focus on ways that the poster resists the voyeuristic urge to look up her petticoat (as Belasco's production did), and instead features her muscular arms. She is portrayed *not* as an object merely to be consumed by the male gaze, but rather as an active, strong subject. The poster's focal point assumes the subjective level of the heroine, rather than the gaze of the (male) spectator thirty-five feet below. Even Carter's signature erotic red tresses are literally cut in half visually by the bell tower.[65] Anticipating what Carol Clover calls the Final Girl of horror film (the lone female who survives and fights back), Mrs. Carter is every bit a survivor and fighter, providing texture to the well-known story about the abusive training method she endured under Belasco.[66] More than this, she "*is* Maryland" as she herself said in publicity for the play.[67] As we have seen with Eliza and Georgia, the resilient women of the South and mid-Atlantic triumph.

When not swinging from trees or bells, women in Strobridge posters were performing other action roles as well. The poster for *In Old Kentucky* brings together the issues of gender performativity, drag, and blackface. The poster seems, at first glance, to portray a stereotypical Southern scene from a melodrama by long-forgotten playwright Charles T. Dazey, which opened on Broadway in 1893.[68] The poster portrays horse racing as a primarily white male enterprise, with white owners, jockeys, trainers, and fans. The few African Americans represented are portrayed in blackface, a common performance practice in nineteenth-century U.S. theater with a vexed history of love and theft, as Eric Lott has suggested.[69] Upon closer inspection we see the text at the bottom of the poster: "Madge, mounted on Queen Bessie, ready for the Race." Madge, featured center of the poster, is a jockey. But Madge is also in disguise—in drag. One of the most popular melodramas of the late nineteenth century, *In Old Kentucky* reverses gender norms: rather than being a spectator at the horse races like Eliza Doolittle, Madge actively rides as a jockey. The composition of the poster places her perfectly center, where virtually all male eyes triangulate on her, giving her focus. In

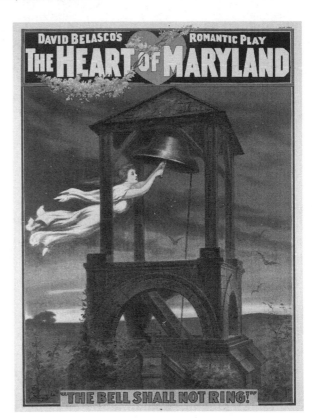

Fig. 6.5. Color lithograph poster for *The Heart of Maryland*, Strobridge Lithograpic Co., Cincinnati. From the Collection of The Public Library of Cincinnati and Hamilton County.

this tableau Madge rides to the rescue and wins the race, offering spectators a resistant moment of gender performance at odds with the image of the passive Southern belle. One review from 1894 noted that the strength of the play was not the tired platitudes of the text, but rather its spectacular scenery.[70] The Strobridge poster, however, chooses to deemphasize scenery (such as the touted mountain scene), and rather portray the complex interactions at the horse races, which appear to have been racially integrated. Can we conclude that Kentucky is a place where women can ride like men and African Americans can engage with whites in business at the track? Or was this poster intended as a visual provocation of a racially mixed public sphere? While we cannot answer those questions, it is clear that the Strobridge artist understood that what would sell tickets was not a mountain tableau, but rather an instance of drag performance and integrated commerce. What sold the show was something beyond the two-dimensionality

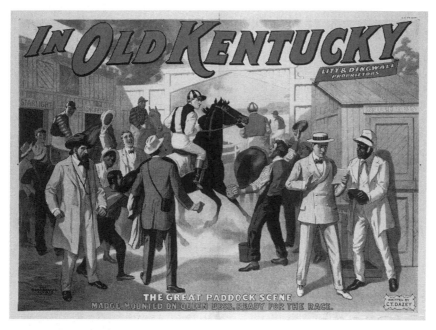

Fig. 6.6. From the Collection of The Public Library of Cincinnati and Hamilton County.

of the plot. Strobridge artists offered a national imaginary that defied traditional boundaries, that experimented with gender and racial norms, and that poked fun at the instability (if not performativity) of those roles.

CONCLUSION

While by no means exhaustive, my analysis of a sampling of Strobridge posters and the first-ever lithographic billboard has attempted to show these artworks as provocative snapshots of nineteenth-century U.S. culture. More than serving as the reigning producer of poster art, the Strobridge Company produced visual artifacts that shed light on crucial cultural dialectics. Whether they were mounted in public spaces, like the *Uncle Tom's Cabin* billboard in downtown Cincinnati, or hung in shop windows or taverns, they invited the public not only to come to the theater, or to interact with the posters themselves, but to also reconsider their positions within

Reconstruction culture. As dynamic "things-in-motion," these posters and billboards also invited spectators to collide with pressing cultural issues (such as slavery, gender hierarchy, and race relations) represented on them or within the play themselves. Within otherwise traditional melodramatic formations, some posters depicted women as exceeding normative narrative frames. These characters are shown as strong, quick thinking, and performing roles often associated with men (as jockeys, rescuers, or detectives). The billboard of *Eliza Pursued by Bloodhounds* prompts us to consider how the image is flanked by the very racialized history that structured postbellum behavior regarding race and gender. To interact with that "thing," that history, that performative moment, is not just great theater or advertising, but rather powerful cultural work.

Notes

1. My analysis draws from the Strobridge Collection in the Cincinnati Public Library. Many thanks to Jeanne De Groote-Strauss for introducing me to the collection and for curating the exhibit in April 2011. Portions of this essay were given as a public lecture to coincide with the exhibit. Thanks also to Mary Jean Corbett, Jim Creech, Elisabeth Hodges, Timothy Melley, Elizabeth Mullenix, and Chris Smith, who provided insightful comments. I am grateful also to the ASTR 2012 Economies of Showing Working Group, especially Natalya Baldyga, Evleen Nasir, and Marlis Schweitzer; thanks also to Catherine Schuler for her stellar editing. For the virtual exhibit at Cincinnati Public Library, see http://virtuallibrary.cincinnatilibrary.org/virtuallibrary/vl_cinciroom.aspx?CityID=17. Duke University and the University of Wisconsin also have collections: http://uwdc.library.wisc.edu/collections/Arts/TheaterPosters

2. Daphne A. Brooks, *Bodies in Dissent: Spectacular Performances of Race and Freedom, 1850–1910* (Durham: Duke University Press), 2006.

3. See Bruce A. McConachie, *Melodramatic Formations: American Theatre and Society, 1820–1870* (Iowa City: University of Iowa Press, 1992). See also David Grimsted, *Melodrama Unveiled: American Theater and Culture, 1800–1850* (Berkeley: University of California Press, 1968).

4. Elijah C. Middleton founded the Strobridge Company in 1847 as a book and stationery store, an enterprise that focused on steel and copperplate engraving. In 1854, lithographer W. R. Wallace and local bookseller Hines Strobridge joined the business and a partnership began. The business was located in the German immigrant section of Cincinnati known as Over-the-Rhine. While there were eventually Strobridge offices in New York and Chicago, Cincinnati was its largest location. The Strobridge Company closed in 1971.

5. Lithography was a Bavarian specialty and Cincinnati—still known as "Zincin-

nati" and for its robust annual Oktoberfest—had a huge German American population throughout the nineteenth century. In fact, all major lithographic printing companies that developed in American cities had large German immigrant populations (including New York, Buffalo, Cincinnati, Milwaukee, and Erie, Pennsylvania).

6. American Federation of Arts, Edgar Breitenbach, and Margaret Cogswell, *The American Poster: A Brief History* (New York: N.p., 1967). See also Jay T. Last, *The Color Explosion: Nineteenth-Century American Lithography* (Santa Ana, CA: Hillcrest Press, 2005); Chalmers L. Pancoast, *Trail Blazers of Advertising: Stories of the Romance and Adventure of the Old-Time Advertising Game* (New York: F. H. Hitchcock, 1926).

7. Invented in 1796 by German author Aloys Senefelder, lithography is a method of printing that uses a slab of stone (lithographic limestone) or metal. A sheet of paper is placed on the stone, passed through a press, and an exact replica of the drawing is transferred to the paper.

8. While this quote references Strobridge circus posters, the economic efficiency applied also to theater posters. See Kristin L. Spangenberg, "The Strobridge Lithographing Company: the Tiffany of Printers," in *The Amazing American Circus Poster: The Strobridge Lithographing Company*, ed. Kristin L. Spangenberg, Deborah Walk, and David Carlyon (Cincinnati: Cincinnati Art Museum, 2011), 88.

9. As Frank Vlastnik puts it, "Probably the best American printing house was the Strobridge Lithographing . . . [which] became the premier theatre poster printer in America." Ken Bloom and Frank Vlastnik, *Broadway Musicals: the 101 Greatest Shows of all Time* (New York: Black Dog and Leventhal Publishers, 2010), 227.

10. "The Founder of a Famous Firm," *Bill Poster*, June 1896, 5. Scholar Mary Henderson has also called Strobridge posters the "Rembrandts of the industry." See Mary C. Henderson, *Broadway Ballyhoo: the American Theatre in Posters* (New York: Harry N. Abrams, 1989), 21.

11. Virginia Frame, "The Lure of the Billboard," *Theatre Magazine* 7 (May 1907), 132.

12. Ibid.

13. Joseph Pennell, quoted in John Merten, "Stone by Stone along a Hundred Years with the House of Strobridge," *Bulletin of the Historical and Philosophical Society of Ohio* 8, no. 1 (January 1950): 15–22, at 1.

14. Frame, "Lure of the Billboard," 134.

15. Ibid.

16. Ibid.

17. Therese Thau Heyman, *Posters American Style* (New York: National Museum of American History, Smithsonian Institution, in association with H. N. Abrams, 1998), 28.

18. Frank H. Atkinson, *Scene Painting and Bulletin Art* (Chicago: F. J Drake & Co, [1916] 1927), 211. For more about Matt Morgan as illustrator and cartoonist, see Tom Kemnitz, "Matt Morgan of *Tomahawk* and English Cartooning, 1867–1870," *Victorian Studies* 18 (1975): 5–34

19. Christopher Kent, "Spectacular History as an Ocular Discipline," *Wide Angle* 18, no. 3 (1996): 1–21.

20. Ibid., 21.

21. Catherine Gudis incorrectly states the billboard was twenty-four sheets. See Catherine Gudis, *Buyways Billboards, Automobiles, and the American Landscape* (New York: Routledge, 2004).

22. Merten, "Stone by Stone along a Hundred Years with the House of Strobridge," 28.

23. George S. McDowell, "Harriet Beecher Stowe at Cincinnati," *New England Magazine*, March 1895, 68. Accessed at http://utc.iath.virginia.edu/redirect.php

24. Jay Rial was an American theater producer. *Eliza Pursued by Bloodhounds*, Jay Rial's Ideal Uncle Tom's Cabin, Strobridge Lithographing Co., Cincinnati, 1881. Credit: Theatrical Poster Collection, Prints and Photographs Division, Library of Congress, LC-USZ62–17368.

25. Spangenberg, "The Strobridge Lithographing Company: the Tiffany of Printers," 20.

26. Christopher Balme, "Playbills and the Theatrical Public Sphere," in *Representing the Past: Essays in Performance Historiography*, ed. Charlotte M. Canning and Thomas Postlewait (Iowa City: Iowa University Press, 2010), 38.

27. Robin Bernstein, "Dances with Things: Material Culture and the Performance of Race," *Social Text* 27, no. 4 101 (2009): 67–94, at 68.

28. Bernstein, "Dances with Things," 69–70.

29. Appadurai, quoted in Bernstein, "Dances with Things," 73.

30. Bernstein, "Dances with Things," 69–70.

31. Near Fountain Square in Cincinnati another landmark—the Underground Railroad Museum Center—engages with similar themes 150 years later. Situated on the Ohio River with its front doors facing *not* toward major roads or downtown, but southerly toward the river's banks, the museum affords a view of the scene portrayed in the lithographic poster of Eliza crossing the ice. The positioning of the museum moreover invites a critical engagement with the passage from Stowe's introduction I cited earlier: "Now the war is over; slavery is a thing of the past; slavepens, bloodhounds, slave-whips, and slave-coffles are only bad dreams of the night." The Underground Railroad Museum Center understood what Strobridge lithographers did in 1881: any meaningful examination of slavery's aftermath must take place on the liminal site shaped by bloodshed and freedom. The museum does in fact house a slavepen (the only surviving one in exhibition in the United States) and while the reach of the museum extends beyond the Civil War to modern trafficking, it becomes very clear that slavery is not a thing of the past.

32. See Jo-Ann Morgan, *Uncle Tom's Cabin as Visual Culture* (Columbia: University of Missouri Press, 2007), 25

33. "Most Popular Book in the Library: All the Year Round *Uncle Tom's Cabin* Is the Work Most Called For—*Ben Hur* is Second," no newspaper listed. February 5, 1898, 2.

34. Ben Brewster and Lea Jacobs, *Theatre to Cinema: Stage Pictorialism and the Early Feature Film* (Oxford: Oxford University Press, 1997), 39–40.

35. It is somewhat uncanny that today Cincinnati has a large LCD screen mounted, much like the large billboard, in Fountain Square where it can broadcast movies and other media.

36. For more on panoramas, see Ralph Hyde, *Panoramania! The Art the Entertainment of the "All-Embracing" View* (London: Trefoil Publications, 1988).

37. W. B. Allen, *Rethinking Uncle Tom: the Political Philosophy of Harriet Beecher Stowe* (Lexington, KY: Lexington Books, 2009), 31.

38. Stowe, *Uncle Tom's Cabin*, liv.

39. In 2001, African American Timothy Thomas was shot by white policeman in Cincinnati, setting off several days of civil unrest in downtown Cincinnati. A review of Cincinnati police procedures led to changes in the police force. See Jane Pendergrast, "2001 Riots Led to Top-Down Change in Cincinnati Police," *Cincinnati Enquirer*, April 3, 2011.

40. Color lithograph poster for stage production of *Uncle Tom's Cabin*. Eliza, three unidentified men, and dogs. Donaldson's Litho, Newport, Kentucky. Harry Birdoff Collection, Harriet Beecher Stowe Center. [46.43]. Printed from *Uncle Tom's Cabin & American Culture* © 2006 the University of Virginia, http://utc.iath.virginia.edu/

41. Balme, "Playbills and the Theatrical Public Sphere," 38.

42. Mary C. Henderson notes that circus made the "first and effective use of the poster," whereby an "advance man" would place posters about the town and villages ahead of the traveling show. I'm assuming that theater followed a similar pattern. See Henderson, *Broadway Ballyhoo*, 19.

43. Harry Birdoff, *World's Greatest Hit: Uncle Tom's Cabin* (New York: SF Vanni, 1947), 1.

44. David S. Reynolds, *Mightier Than the Sword: Uncle Tom's Cabin and the Battle for America* (New York: W. W. Norton, 2011), 177.

45. James W. Frick, *Uncle Tom's Cabin on the American Stage and Screen* (New York: Palgrave, 2012), 143.

46. Barbara Tepa Lupack, *Nineteenth-Century Women at the Movies: Adapting Classic Women's Fiction to Film* (Bowling Green, OH: Bowling Green State University, 1999), 218. A notice from 1883, when Rial's company performed in Washington, DC, observed that the use of animals was still novel: "All the usual attractions are advertised, including eight ferocious bloodhounds, a trained donkey, & c." See "Amusements," *Washington Post*, April 29, 1883, n.p.

47. Morgan, *Uncle Tom's Cabin as Visual Culture*, 50.

48. Ibid.

49. Fred Dahlinger Jr., "After the Posters, the Daily Free Street Parade," in *The Amazing American Circus Poster*, ed. Spangenberg, Walk, and Carlyon, 43.

50. Display Ad for *Uncle Tom's Cabin*, *Cincinnati Enquirer*, October 30, 1881, 5.

51. Reynolds, *Mightier Than the Sword*, 123–24.

52. See, for example, "Amusements," *Cincinnati Enquirer*, May 21, 1883, 4.

53. "Mr. & Mrs. Jay Rial with Jay Rial's Ideal Uncle Tom's Cabin," back of Advertising card. Maerz Lithography Company, Buffalo, NY, n.d. From 19th Century American Trade Cards, Boston Public Library, Print Department. The front of the card features the Rials and two bloodhounds.

54. Ibid.

55. Kyla Wazana Tompkins, *Racial Indigestion: Eating Bodies in the 19th Century* (New York: New York University Press, 2012), 151.

56. Cynthia Griffin Wolff, "Margaret Garner: A Cincinnati Story," *Massachusetts Review* 32, no. 3 (Autumn 1991): 417–40. Toni Morrison uses Margaret Garner's story for her novel *Beloved*. See Toni Morrison, *Beloved* (New York: Plume, 1988).

57. Fountain Square is just a few blocks away from where Margaret Garner was recaptured in Cincinnati.

58. Scott Marble's *Down in Dixie* premiered at the Opera House in Cincinnati on September 2, 1894. See William Davenport Adams, *A Dictionary of the Drama: A Guide to the Plays, Play-wrights, Players, and Playhouses of the United Kingdom and America, from the Earliest Times to the Present*, vol. 1 (London: Chatto & Windus, 1904).

59. "Theatrical Gossip," *New York Times*, August 27, 1894, 8; and "*Down in Dixie* Produced," *New York Times*, September 3, 1894, 3.

60. Here I am using the central premise of Bernstein's book *Racial Innocence*, in which she shows how "performance, both on stage, and especially, in everyday life, was the vehicle by which childhood suffused, gave power to, and crucially shaped these racial projects" (4). To her list of artifacts examined, I would add Strobridge posters.

61. Eric Lott, *Love and Theft: Blackface Minstrelsy and the American Working Class* (Oxford: Oxford University Press, 2013).

62. Jill Dolan, *Utopia in Performance: Finding Hope at the Theater* (Ann Arbor: University of Michigan Press, 2005).

63. Many thanks to Marlis Schweitzer for pointing out this connection to me and for her other comments on a draft of the paper.

64. Kim Marra, *Strange Duets: Impresarios and Actresses in the American Theatre, 1865–1914* (Iowa City: University of Iowa Press, 2006), 200.

65. If Belasco was realigning Mrs. Carter's pelvis in the belfry scene (and in the direction of the emotional school of acting) as Marra notes, the poster also aligns Mrs. Carter's pelvis directly behind the phallic tower beam. Is it penetrating it or covering it up?

66. For more on the intense, if not abusive, relationship between Mrs. Leslie Carter and David Belasco, see Katie N. Johnson, "Zaza: That 'Obtruding Harlot' of the Stage," *Theatre Journal* 54, no. 2 (2002): 223–43; and "John Denson, "Belasco and Mrs. Carter End Their 25-Year Feud," *New York Telegram*, April 10, 1931.

67. Marra, *Strange Duets*, 202.

68. In *Kentucky in American Letters*, the authors report that *In Old Kentucky* origi-

nated as a drama, and was then adapted into a novel. It opened in St. Paul in 1892, and transferred to New York in 1893 where it was "a great success" (68). See John W. Townsend and Dorothy E. Townsend, *Kentucky in American Letters* (Cedar Rapids, IA: Torch Press, 1913). See Charles Turner Dazey, *In Old Kentucky* (New York: N.p., 1893). The play is not listed on the Internet Broadway Database, but according to Wikipedia, *In Old Kentucky* played uninterrupted for twenty-six years in America. See http://en.wikipedia.org/wiki/Charles_Dazey

69. Lott, *Love and Theft.*

70. "Review of *In Old Kentucky,*" *Nebraska State Journal*, December 20, 1894, 3.

CHAPTER 7

Carnival Bands, Popular Politics, and the Craft of Showing the People in Haiti

Chelsey Kivland

For three days in early April 2008, food riots ravaged Port-au-Prince. Thousands of protesters took to the streets demanding an end to the rising cost of living and the hunger it caused. They erected flaming tire barricades to block traffic around the Champs de Mars plaza, where governmental ministries and the National Palace are housed. Accompanied by neighborhood *rara* bands, protesters marched to carnivalesque drumbeats before the palace, demanding that the president come join them in their fight against the "expensive life" (*lavi chè a*). When he refused (citing his lack of tennis shoes), they stormed the wealthier district of Pétion-ville above the city, breaking the windows of businesses, gas stations, and cars and leaving their contents for the taking. All the while they chanted songs and covered the cityscape with graffiti deriding "Clorox," "battery acid," and "paint thinner": pithy monikers that compared their hunger pangs to ingesting toxic liquids. Days later, after police tallied the death toll at five,[1] the prime minister was dismissed, and soon after that, the president brokered a deal with foreign aid agents and food importers to lower the price of U.S. rice, Haiti's staple food, by 16 percent.

Nine months later, as Haitian carnival rolled around, the price of rice had again spiked. A marching brass band, blending the beats of African drumming and fanfare, descended from the poor hilltop shantytown of Bel Air and headed to the city's plaza of governmental ministries exuberantly singing, "Clorox is in my ass, my ass! My misery, I'm trying to deal with it, but I can't support it!" (*Klowòks nan dada m. Mizè m m ap jere. M pa ka sipòte l*). As they approached the plaza, the band dropped into lyrics demanding state officials come out of hiding and respond to their hunger. They yelled: "Where are the country's directors? Where are the ministers? Where is the mayor? Where did the aid go?" (*Kot dirijan peyi yo? Kot minist peyi a? Kot majistra? Kot ed la pase?*) The massive crowd encircling the band responded to each question with a defiant one-liner: "But oh, here are the people!" (*Woy, men noun yo!*) The next week, on the first of three "fat days" (*jou gra yo*) of carnival, a male street performer dressed as a scantily clad woman carried on a conversation with a plastic doll representing Jacques Edourd Alexis, the prime minister who had been dismissed. After simulating various come-ons by the stuffed doll, "the woman" demanded to see what the "prime minister" had to offer. To uproarious laughter, she declared, "too little, too late," a phrase used by parliament to condemn the government's response to the food riots.[2] Moments later, another band from Bel Air hurried by "DGI," the federal tax bureau where Bel Air residents gather to watch the procession of carnival floats, playfully elaborating the Clorox slogan, "Where is Marie Carmel? Where is Marie Lourdes? We put pleasure in her pussy?! But she bleached the dick! Clorox! Fuck your mother!" (*Kote Marie Carmel? Kote Marie Lourdes? Nou mete plezi nan dada l. Men l blanche zozo a. Klowòks. Langèt manman w!*) An array of witticisms, grotesque slander, and politicking converged in this carnival scene around the toxic trope of Clorox. The trope encapsulated the most pertinent and effective political message of that year: that the multiplying food prices—rice alone doubled from January to April 2008—were pricing the people out of life.

Carnival is the most significant urban festival in Haiti,[3] and street brass bands (called *bann a pye*, bands on foot, or *bann madigra*, Mardi Gras bands) represent the voice of the urban poor at carnival. Revelers march out of their neighborhood bases with their loyal followers and amass others along their route as they sing their politicized witticisms to the rapid tempos of the bands. Street bands identify as "engaged" (*angaje*), which means that their music and their performances intervene in political debates and advance the cause of the poor majority—what they call *pèp la*, or "the people." Importantly, popular protests and carnival band processions share the same musical styles, performance frames, procession routes, and punchy slogans, which means not only that protests are permeated by the carnivalesque, but that carnival itself is a genre of politics. Bands' performances interject the populist ambiance of carnival. They socially represent and physically present the popular masses by taking to the streets and elaborating social idioms that define the popular sentiment and political issue of the moment. Band members often articulated what they were doing as "making the people appear in the street," a description that emphasized how their project was oriented around *showing* the people by amassing their bodies, reflecting their plight, expressing their desires, orienting themselves to each other, and situating them against those in power. Yet as much as they were engaged in a project of consensus building among "the people," they were also enmeshed in competition. They competed over musical prowess, lyrical and poetic skill, crowd making, and political efficacy. In many ways, their project of *showing off* the people also entailed *showing up* each other.

This essay is informed by years of ethnographic research on street politics in Bel Air, Port-au-Prince, but it is focused on the 2009 carnival season when I "walked with" (*mache ak*) street bands. Through cultural analysis of bands' activities, I aim to reveal how they illuminate two critical aspects of showing as a performance genre. On one level, I am concerned with examining how the political workings of street bands are dependent on amassing and foregrounding "the people" in the physical and political landscape as a public distinguished from but in need of those in power. As I show, summoning into existence a power capable of redressing the people's shared demands required first manifesting the people in public and as a public. In other words, I am concerned with two ways *showing off* is used to call others to *show up*: to manufacture a public by facilitating consensus and to interpellate those in power by shaming them into action. The circulation of rhythms, slogans, and dance moves was key to this process, and I mobilize Michael Warner's (2002) contention that addressing a public is a form of eliciting participation and poetic world making. It invokes and entails a particular worldview, and demands not spectators but participation among its members. "Run it up a flagpole and see who salutes. Put on a show and see who shows up," he writes (114). Yet on another level, I am concerned with how showing off can be a form of showing up others in the spirit of competition. Bands formally compete for a spot during the culminating carnival processions, and they are engaged in rivalries with neighbor bands—contests decided by their musical and performative prowess and popularity. I approach this tension between popular consensus, interpellation, and competition by looking at three ways, or more precisely, *scales*, in which street bands participated in the articulation of collective and competitive publics. I begin with the amassing of a performance community at bands' rehearsals, then turn to the harmonization of bodies, senses, and movement during street performance, and conclude with the configuration of a public oriented to state power through the fabrication of politicized slogans.

REHEARSALS BUILD CONTESTED PUBLICS

Carnival street bands emerged in the nineteenth century out of the peasant tradition called *rara*, a musical, ritual, and carnivalesque procession dating from colonial times. Akin to urban *rara*, street bands became the popular accompaniment to the elite carnival centered around an organized procession of floats and private balls. Early bands played for a separate public festival held at an outdoor market (Averill 1994), where they entertained poor and working class urbanites. In the 1950s, the dictator François Duvalier, likely appealing for popular consent, integrated them into the formal carnival celebrations held along the Champs de Mars. Today, they remain a fixture of the annual festival; they are responsible for the weekend amusement in the run-up to carnival and they serve as the opening acts for pop music groups during the three fat days. The marching street bands precede the pop groups' truck-floats along the formal parade route. Street bands hail from poor urban districts—the "popular quarters" (*katye popilè*)—and Bel Air, an impoverished and volatile neighborhood dating to the capital's founding, has long fostered a fervent political culture and the city's most popular and acclaimed street bands (Laguerre 1976). From Titato in the early twentieth century to Leloup Party Cool today, Bel Air bands have attracted large followings and become national carnival stars. Most bands, however, tend to be neighborhood sensations. While oriented toward the municipal (and national) carnival stages, bands are best known and most celebrated at their home *baz* (literally, "base"). The term *base* identifies their meeting locale, the home of the core members, and their base of support.

Throughout December 2009, bands held weekly rehearsals at and among their base. Here bands aspired to facilitate what was called a *ti kominote pèp la*, "small community of the people." This phrasing identified how they saw themselves as engaged in a project to build a communal base that was situated within the larger national public of the poor majority. Such groups were akin to localized counterpublics: *localized* because they took shape within a particular area and *counter* because the public with which they marked themselves, "the people," was considered more specific than and

Fig. 7.1. My Business Band mural marking their base. (Author photo, 2009.)

also dissident from an elite or even national public (Fraser 1992; Warner 2002). The localized nature of this group challenged conventional understandings of publics as distinct from communities on the basis of their impersonal nature.[4] While the bands certainly addressed indefinite strangers and the state, this was accomplished by relating to those already holding communal ties, treating them as a minipublic, as both of *the* people generally and of *this* people specifically.

The second orientation of the minipublic allowed the bands to be set against each other. A dyadic logic of competition permeated bands' activities. Street bands, like most music groups in Haiti, were organized around rivalries—called *polemik* (polemics)—between neighboring groups: Samba the Best vs. Laloz, Original Cash Band vs. César Band, Tèt Kole vs. My Business Band constituted fierce rivalries in Bel Air. The neighborhood itself was also engaged in a *polemik* with bands from the adjacent Morne à Turf neighborhood. While all bands competed to be among the fifteen bands selected by the carnival committee for the official carnival procession, their personal rivalries were far more significant to them. They determined their song lyrics, procession times and routes, costumes, and feelings of success. This competitive spirit translated into making their rehearsal sessions as much about drumming up communal support and interest in their songs as about appraising and upstaging their rivals.

At rehearsals, held on Thursday evenings, bands were engaged in the project of *balanse bann nan*—literally, "balancing the band." These rehearsals were musically important, since it was common for the makeup of bands to shift from year to year, with some musicians being hired for the season, and also performatively important, since it was there that the dance moves and song lyrics were adopted and learned by the core group of participants. But the rehearsals were also important vehicles for publicizing the band in the neighborhood. The goal of "balancing" entailed harmonizing the group's diverse energies into a choreographed performance and also creating and energizing a cohesive community with performative force in the zone. Bands held rehearsals in exposed yards or open-air Vodou temples in full view and within earshot of neighbors. The musicians played loudly and without respite, saturating the block's soundscape from 4 p.m. until well after dark. Children and youth joined the scene, crowding the yard and perching themselves on rooftops as they added to the music by clapping hands, tapping glass bottles, stomping feet, or at times putting together a makeshift band. The point was to make the band so loud that they drowned out the other bands practicing.

During the final set of rehearsals, this minipublic was even more explicitly put on display in the neighborhood. Early in the evening, the song lyrics were usually distributed on Xerox copies, called "texts" (*teks*), and secondary school children read them through a megaphone to the gathered audience who practiced singing along to the music. Bands with more resources might also play a studio recording of their official song (actual songs vary along the procession route) in order to teach the lyrics to the audience. Learning the lyrics fostered much enthusiasm, making these final rehearsals sensational affairs. They attracted *machann*, or market women, selling snow cones, fried foods, candies, homemade rum, soft drinks, beer, and other snacks and refreshments. The band leadership often took photos of the scene on their cell phones, which they would use to accompany their letters to commercial businesses asking for sponsorship. At 10 p.m. or later, the band took to the streets with their participants and circumambulated the block. A mark of their success was whether they were able to attract even more participants

Fig. 7.2. Children enacting band at My Business Band base. (Author photo, 2009.)

along the route and, with them, street vendors aiming to sell to them. When the band returned, and depending on the largesse of their president and committee members, the musicians shared a meal prepared by the band's godmother. Because communal attachments in Haiti are grounded in the sharing of food, these meals often turned into small portions shared among an ever-expanding group of band members. The size of the dining group not only verified the strength of the minipublic; it also boosted the reputations of the "big men" (*gwo nèg*) and "big women" (*gwo nègès*) that led and sponsored the band.

The publicizing of this expanding minipublic could also extend beyond the rehearsal event itself. The studio recordings of songs, though distributed as compact discs to radio stations, were rarely played. Their purpose was rather to complete bands' submission portfolios for the official carnival committee and, moreover, to allow the bandleaders to blast the songs endlessly from boom boxes into the street during the week, affirming and expanding the minipublic beyond the rehearsal event.

Taken together, the whole rehearsal period was a moment for showcasing the band, and using it to build the community of sponsorship and participatory fanatics. Edith, a leader and godmother of My Business Band, one of the bands I followed that year, often talked about rehearsals as the first step toward rearing the crowd that would put force behind their message. Looking at the teenagers who had gathered on nearby rooftops to watch a rehearsal, she once told me, "The dream of My Business Band is to show (*montre*) the force of the people, because we have '*a speech to reveal to the people*' [the opening lyric to their carnival song], but the obstacle is to make this little community of the people turn into a huge *crowd* of the people."[5] At the same time, however, these minipublic shows were also oriented toward evaluating their rivals and other groups in the area, and finding ways to respond to and improve upon others' performances. The band would send out scouts to learn the key lyrics and messages of their rival's songs, the size and amplification of their band, the commercial sponsors they had attracted, and their planning around dance moves and costumes. This scouting enabled the bands to collectively orient their songs around the pertinent issue of the day and to simultaneously compete for the most creative and compelling messaging around that issue. In 2009, the idiom of Clorox saturated carnival, becoming not only the slogan that united the bands, but also the platform through which they could compete with each other. My Business Band, for example, picked up the Clorox slogan from their rival during an early rehearsal and embellished it for their own song.

In an important way, the rehearsals constituted the first stage of the bands' mission to form a public oriented around them. Their rehearsals combined visual, lyrical, and embodied forms of address that called on neighbors and strangers to join in their collective project. Rather than closed sessions aimed at a climatic coming out, these rehearsals were self-consciously public "shows" (*sho*), a word used by bandleaders that articulated spectacle with interaction. Unlike spectacle in the Debordian sense, they were not aimed at passive consumption, but rather at eliciting participation. The point was to use this crowd of ever-expanding participants to create an even grander show that attracted attention, sponsorship, and entrepreneurialism and augmented the reputations of the bands and their leaders. While in theory this minipublic would expand to incorporate all the people into a total public, it had its limits. In practice, it was clear that the real aim was to mobilize its growth as the grounds for boasting about the band to its rivals, thereby creating contested publics.

STEPPING OUT AS A POPULAR CROWD

The outings of carnival bands occur each Sunday following the sixth of January or King's Day (*fèt wa*, Twelfth Night in English) and then for the final three days of carnival. In these outings, bands were concerned with building and displaying a crowd that was excited and in control of the physical and sonic landscape. Crowds were important sources of legitimacy, political power, and competitive edge. A crowd distinguished a "total band" (*bann total kapital*) from weak, fake, or corrupt bands, facilitated the carnival ambiance, put popular force behind the group's political critiques, and decided competitions between bands. Of great significance is that the crowd puts into bold relief the form and core values of popular politics. This was not simply because the crowd was a form of sociality associated with the lower class, but, more fundamentally, because the crowd was itself the leveling mechanism that elides, at least momentarily, the sense of distinction among individuals. The crowds created by street bands resembled a sea of people moving in waves, and they were often compared to an "overflowing river" (*rivye debòde*), "whirlpool" (*toubiyon*), or "flood" (*enodasyon*) (Averill 1994; McAlister 2002). Such hydraulic images symbolized the people and popular power as located in a collective, indivisible subject, setting them apart from the elite power of individualized civil society (Canetti 1984; Stallybrass and White 1986). Marching "on foot" also set the band and its crowd apart from elevated floats and spectator stands, signaling the class hierarchy and the band's role as representative of the urban poor (Averill 1994). Further, the crowd was seen as a site and facilitator of popular sociality and danger, of chaos, ecstasy, and aggression that can spill over into elite worlds. Put in semiotic terms, the crowd as an extension of the band indexed—or referred to—the social class of the people by means of inhabiting an iconic image of mass association. This iconic relation was represented in the concepts' linguistic symbolism. "*Enter the people!*" or "*Enter the crowd!*" directed one to the same place, and the phrase *bann nan*, the band, was often used in songs and popular discourse as a metaphor for the people and its political force.

Most bands underwent a preouting ceremony in their Vodou temple with a Vodou priest (*oungan*) who blessed the band with a special bath that would protect them and impart spiritual and performative force along their route. Before taking to the streets, the priest presided over another ceremony at the main intersection of the bands' base. Here the priest lit a fire of wood planks over a Vodou *vèvè* symbolizing the bands' guiding spirit. The band circled the fire as the priest sprayed it with alcohol, ignited gunpowder, and forcefully whipped a leather cord (*fwèt kach*). The militant ceremony, drawing on an iconography of slavery and war, was meant to *chofe*, or "heat up," the band, protecting and empowering them along their long route to overtake rivals and other malevolent forces. After such electric infusion, the band was often compared to a "fuse" (*priz*), a locus of transduction that used spiritual and social power to synchronize common people into becoming the collective force that they always already were. Although not highly ordered affairs, outings were also not unstructured. Bands desired an outing that, as Gage Averill puts it, "teeter[ed] just short of chaos" (1997, 21), of *almost-but-not-quite* disorder. Band processions reflected not a parade-like progression of rows but a roving spiral, a core center that radiated outward as it advanced in space. The ceremonial fire remained the symbolic center, with the band taking its place as the center of the procession, with the troupe of singers and dancers encircling them, and the crowd constituting the periphery. The committee members were also on the periphery, but usually at the front, a mark of their distinction from "the people." Finally, the flag bearer and "scout" ran farther ahead, signaling the band's approach and scanning the terrain for enemies. Within this circle of affiliates gathered layers of fanatics, singing along as they ran, hopped, and swirled their hips to the beat. In the course of these processions, the whole group aimed to attract more participants through the centrifugal force of the band. Linked to the ritual disembarking of the band, the goal of the moving band was to extend their energy to others and to heat them up.

Generating mass consensus by unifying the crowd though style, movement, music, and texts was a core mission of the band. Usually, bands' meager finances meant that they replaced elaborate costumes with T-shirts (either custom-made or displaying the logos of commercial sponsors) for the ten or so committee members and fifty or so musicians, dancers, singers, and other select posts. The male musicians and (the few) male singers draped their T-shirts over shiny jeans and paired them with a new pair of sneakers, whereas the female singers, dancers, and carnival queens,[6] "designed" (*deziyne*)—that is, slit, tied, and twisted—the bulky T-shirts into flashy, skin-hugging tops that they also paired with jeans and shiny sneakers. Such minimal costumes meant that revelers joined the band in similar getups, making them often indistinguishable from more formal members.

This homogeneity was further signaled in their dance moves. Revelers engaged in undisciplined and exuberant forms of movement that helped contribute to the altered forms of embodiment that produced the crowd. Whereas I was routinely reminded to *"kenbe kò ou,"* literally "hold your body," meaning "pay attention," as I walked the streets of Bel Air, on the days and nights I walked with bands the goal was to *lage kò ou,* literally "let your body go." The art of letting-your-body-go involved becoming sensually inseparable from others, your senses entranced by the rhythm and flow of those around you. This feeling was channeled though a cadenced sway that is also called *balanse* (balancing). Just as the band balances itself before it goes out, once en route they seek to balance the crowd into a harmonious whole, rocking back and forth. Revelers built on this sensual unity by adding forward movement to the side-to-side swaying. They usually progressed down the street in a tight two-step and, when the drum was slapped, in paired jumps. They leaned back with hips jutting forward and slightly bent arms waving overhead. Seasoned dancers instructed the novices or slow movers (like me) to "put their hands in the air," to "advance without looking back," and "to lift your feet and fly." Many picked up the choreographed moves of the dance troupe, which added slight hip and arm variations to this basic step. Ideally, this trend will spread through the crowd and become the newest dance craze, like *"laloz"* or *"gaypay,"* both of which emerged from Bel Air music groups. Yet the goal was more fundamentally to heat things up beyond distinctive movement, enticing the troupe and the crowd to move into what was called *apwiye pa frape*, literally to "lean not hit" (McAlister 2002). The name builds on the dual meaning of *apwiye* as "to slant" and "support," configuring this dance as an embodiment of risk and trust. Revelers leaned back, letting the forward momentum of those behind them push them forward and even raise them off the ground. Set against "lean not hit" was the even more charged dance called *lese frape*, or "to let hit." Here revelers totally relinquished control of their body, letting themselves crash into and bounce off those around them, creating an atmosphere similar to a mosh pit in the United States. With the whole group progressing in this manner, it should now be clear why the participants resembled a rushing river.

While fully embodying the pleasure at stake in "letting go" with others, the *lese frape* style, as McAlister (2002) and Averill (1994) note, also facilitated the more disorderly and dangerous ambiance of the crowd. The movement could instigate shoving matches known as *gangan*, outright brawling, or armed confrontations. In *gangan*, men face each other and hurl their chest at their opponent in an attempt to knock them to the floor. The spot before "DGI," where Bel Air folks watch carnival, was known as *baz men lejè* (the base of light hands), as at any point a match of *gangan* can break out. Beyond *gangan*, people could use the cover of the carnival crowd to confront opponents, engaging in acts of revenge or assassination, or to steal the wallets of cell phones from revelers. Finally, the crowd could become an arena for sexual advances or teasing, such as *pichkannen* (pinching the crotch or bottom), which could instigate *gangan*. Such forms of bodily aggression and violation symbolized the loss of individuality and personal space central to bourgeois conceptions of popular sociality (see Stallybrass and White 1986), and upper-class Haitians often cited them as why they avoided the crowd. In a more general sense, these activities also showcased how realizing mass association was a populist ideal rather than reality, since the crowd created the conditions for its own divisibility. Just as people *let go fully* with others, they risked entering into fights to redraw bodily boundaries.

This combative ethos within the crowd spilled over into the movement of bands through space. Special significance was placed on taking over the physical landscape. The bandleaders were always hoping to "cork" (*bouche*) the street, blockading traffic and sweeping up bystanders with the rush of bodies. The route of small bands, like My Business, would avoid main thoroughfares, strategically entering narrow, neighborhood corridors and pathways that they could fill with people. It was critical that this amassing occurred on the street. "We put everyone on the concrete, and make the people appear!" was a common boast among bands. Echoing the urban topography of class in the city, the site of the street and the performance of bands "on foot" grounded band outings as of the people. These "chronotopes" (Bakhtin 1981) of lowness were especially foregrounded during the final three days of carnival, when the crowds of "bands on foot" marched before DJs and popular bands elevated on truck-beds through a Champs de Mars plaza lined with towering street stands, holding wealthier spectators and public officials, including the government's carnival committee. It was at these moments that the bands' complete control of the street and the sheer force of the common people could be put on display for a more general public. On neighborhood streets this dynamic was realized by distinguishing the grounded band from those residents that watched from the balconies and galleries of their street-side, two-level concrete houses. Set apart from the dirt alleyways and corridors where most residents live in crowed shacks, these houses, like the elevated street stands, were markers of class hierarchies.

Dominating sonic space was equally important. While grounded in the ability of the band to play loudly, command of the soundscape was actual-

Fig. 7.3. Carnival band blocking the street. (Author photo, 2009.)

Fig. 7.4. My Business Band blocking narrow alleyway. (Author photo, 2009.)

ized in crowd noise. As at rehearsals, there are no spectator roles for participants. Those who "walk with" bands were expected to not only sing along
but to also, and moreover, engage in boosting the music's amplitude. This
certainly included keeping the beat with *cha-chas*, but it could also involve
using whatever possible (e.g., yells, stomps, whistles, claps) to make noise
and contribute to the band's sonic expanse. Ultimately, the goal was an "uproar" (*tenten*) that could *pouse son*, or "push" their sound over others. As with
physical space, controlling the soundscape reflected a political imaginary. A
bat tenèb, or beating out the darkness, is a key protest method among the
urban poor. They take out their pots and pans, sticks and bottles, and use
them to raise their voices against forces of oppression. The people are often
configured as silent, inaudible, or, to quote one band's song in 2009, "without a voice." Loud and vibrant modes of expression characteristic of carnival
crowds are, in turn, configured as an assertion of the voice of the people,
their power to drown out others, and to be recognized.

Beyond an assertion of popular force, bands used the performance of
mass association to stage contests with bands encountered in the street, especially with their rivals. A successful outing, in fact, depended on "crushing"
(*kraze*) the rival band. This rivalry reached its apex when the bands' routes
collided and the groups faced each other in the street. The victor was the
band that musically, sonically, and physically overtook the other band and
forced its way forward. The loser would take to the curbs and allow the
victor to continue its path. Winning this battle was decided by the size and
energy of crowd. It depended, as bandleaders would say, on putting forward
"our people" (*moun pa nou*) or "our base" (*baz nou*) above and beyond the
rival. Not just about quantity or mass, the victorious crowd was the one that
was better "balanced," musically, kinesthetically, and sensually. This competition between bands elaborated the fundamental tension between *the* and *our*
people of popular politics, or how the crowd created the conditions for its
own divisibility. Insofar as the crowd was fostered by their abilities to rally a
public this consensus was also the basis for competition.

Still, it was the band's potential as crowd-maker that enabled its political potential as a popular force that extended beyond any singular crowd.
Band leaders did not imagine the crowd in the manner popularized by
crowd theorists like Le Bon (2001) and resurrected, on a regular basis, in
elite panics surrounding carnival and protests in Haiti. It was not an act of
fostering a totally uncontrollable, "savage" mass that could be manipulated to
any end (Williams 1977). Instead, they envisioned navigating between an ex-

cited, worked up, vitalized crowd—what Émile Durkheim called "collective effervescence" (1995)—and executing a performance that created a public focused on key messages. The political potential of carnival entailed tapping into, coalescing, and orienting people's stagnant yet powerful energies and structures of feeling around pertinent issues. As the bandleader of My Business Band once told me, following a rather boisterous outing:

> When we make a crowd, we can realize a lot of things. When we attract people, gather everyone in the zone, [the] band on foot becomes soldiers on foot. That means the crowd can make the band have the force of the army. Like that, we don't fall into total disorder. We *approach* it, and we can create something. It's because . . . without a lot of people worked up, no one takes the engagement. *Anrage fè angaje* (agitation or anger breeds engagement).[7]

This last phrase spoke to engaging people in the crowd as well as the crowd against those in power. In many ways, it encapsulated a political praxis: social engagement began with being "worked up" or "agitated." Grounding politics in shared experiences of heightened affection and sensual unity, this praxis defined the popular power behind carnival (Averill 1994). It also suggested that politics begins with frustration, with being *angered by something*. Hence, public engagement in this view emerged from not only inciting but also directing collective energy. Much like Durkheim's totem, the turning of the crowd toward redressing particular wrongdoings as a public rested principally on creating images that allowed them to recognize latent grievances and desires. This image-work, called "making slogans," was a crucial aspect of what it meant to show "the people" as a collective if contested unit.

SLOGANS AND THE POLITICAL PUBLIC

The invention of slogans is among bands' most serious work. Slogans are emotionally charged lyrics that encapsulate songs' messages and rally the crowd. As a bandleader once put it,

> When the people take to the streets, and make a protest, they carry a "slogan" (*slogan*). . . . It's the same with the band. . . . Slogans can speak about everything, any little thing that disturbs you. But what's important

is . . . Look, everybody brings [their] problems, and you look at all the problems, and everything inside the problem, behind the problem, on the side of the problem, and, now, you gather everything to make one. And *now* you have a slogan. . . . Slogan makes the people hot. It unveils all the things in a single utterance. They say this year . . . *Clorox* will totally bleach carnival [laughing].

The slogan *Clorox*, coined amid food riots in 2008, was an example of what Karen McCarthy Brown (2003) calls "word *wanga*," or word magic, verbal charms, that when revisited through ritualized practice bring about an imagined change in reality.[8] The power of such *wanga* is rhetorical, as they are used "to rewrite the existential narrative at issue" by convincing key audiences of their points of view (Brown 2003, 242). This term *Clorox* and phrases using it were employed in protest and carnival songs in 2008 and 2009 to amass a population, voice grievances, and make demands on state (or state-like) power. Like all word *wanga*, *Clorox* worked by revealing and amplifying particular aspects of a situation while concealing others. For example, rather than attribute the price spikes to technical or coincidental explanations pertaining to the global oil market or bad farming seasons in the United States (whence Haiti imports its rice), the term configured the cost of living as a poisonous and malicious attack against the popular masses by a transnational power elite. In so doing, the neologism set this hunger apart from the ordinary rationing of food intake common in Haiti, and configured this price spike as a toxic weapon waged in a social conflict. It framed the situation in such a way as to shame government officials into responding to the demands now shared by a vocally and sensually united public. Though concerned with consensus and interpellation, however, effective slogans are not static. They are like hot potatoes. A slogan only worked insofar as it enticed people to pass it on by creatively reconfiguring it. At carnival, this circulation occurred by, for example, mobilizing it in fervent political or social critiques, framing the drama as a sexualized scandal, or inserting the slogan into carnivalesque tropes of religious or political irreverence. In all this work, it was essential to not just riff off others' puns but to upstage them in contesting or embellishing their usage.

There was an official carnival theme, selected by the carnival committee: "Hand in hand so life can be beautiful" (*men nan men pou lavi ka bèl*). Yet while some groups worked this theme into their songs to appease judges, most focused on Clorox as the hot topic of the day. Aside from the Clorox riffs noted earlier, there were several others that year. David, the bandleader of My Business Band, learned the slogans of nearby bands during rehearsals and through meetings with the federation of bands. The collection of songs we compiled point to the building of a public of street bands united around the Clorox message and all claiming to speak for the people. The band L'as ou Neuf down the road composed a song that spoke to the need for "those people," or those in power, to respect the abnormal conditions of the popular masses: "Mister, we say this Clorox is not normal. It is a big conspiracy against the impoverished masses. Respect us, those people, respect us. Help! The people are dying standing up" (*Mesye, nou di Klowòks la pa nòmal. Se yon two konplo kont la mas defavoryize. Respekte n, moun sa yo, respekte nou. Amwe, pèp la mouri tou kanpe*[9]). Another nearby band, School Band, compelled people to come together to demand that the state appear: "Clorox, battery acid, he says it won't go away. Because there is no state. Let's put our heads together to get out of these jams. The band advances" (*Klowòks, asid batri pase li di li pa p kite. Paske pa gen leta isi. Ann mèt tèt ansamn pou nou kouri dèyè laron. Bann nan avanse*). This final line takes up the band as a metaphor for the people and urges unity and determination in the face of obstacles. Yet another nearby band, Soro Band, similarly employed the city's three largest slum areas as icons of the popular masses, "Arrive in Cite Soleil, in Bel Air, in Martissant. Ask what's going on. . . . Say for them nothing is happening. Say it's the Clorox that stirs it up (*Rive Site Solèy, Bèlè, Martisan. Mande sa ap pase. Di pou yo anyen p ap mache. Di Klowòks la ap boulvèse l*[10]). Most importantly for My Business Band, their rival sang, "Clorox hunger has become unbridled. We feel we can't go on! We call on God to give us relief! For the problems can be resolved" (*Grangou klowòks fin mande dechennen. Nou santi nou pa kapab ankò. N ap rele bondye pou pote yon sekou. Pou pwoblèm yo ka rezoud*[11]). Lest the reference to God make this lyric appear apolitical, it is important to remember the Haitian proverb: "After God, it's the State." In all instances, these songs were united not just thematically but also through common messaging. They named the suffering of the people as part of a social problem, illuminating their common thoughts, feelings, and plight, and also made a clear demand on more powerful figures to address the problem.

However, as with rehearsals and outings, these common texts provided the platform for not only collective mobilization but also for competition. Embedded in these lines were artful jabs at rivals, as well as subtle competitions surrounding wordplay. David was determined to not only compose his own song using the slogan but to improve upon it. He often told me that the shared use of the idiom made the message "go farther" (*rive pi lwen*), and that "it was a good thing that many bands were talking about this because that gave the message the force of the people." He predicted that after carnival the "tally sheet" (*bilan*) would show that "those people," would have taken a hit from the popular masses. Yet he also assured me that their riff on the pun was "more beautiful" (*pi bèl*), "more interesting" (*pi enteresan*), and would carry the message "farther" than others.

Since My Business Band's song serves as a good example of carnival songs that year, it is worth looking at it in more detail. David, like other bandleaders, called their song "The Clorox Song," but its official title was *Kite Mele Nèg Yo*, of which a rough gloss is "[We] Don't Give a Damn about Those Guys." The song, as David explained, carried a message that "the people could not support what those guys were doing" and that "we have to organize so that they hear our demands."[12] In other words, it was about just how much they *do give a damn*. The song emanated from a respected voice among the people, adopting the collaborative "we" while still speaking from an authoritative position. It opened by asserting that the band's mission was to "unveil to the people all that is not good in their eyes" and to "bring forth a better life." The song continued by drawing attention to the need for local food production, before declaring that "today life is more expensive and the misery is multiplying." The most memorable lines followed,

> Mamit diri vann 50 goud
> Peyi a fin depafini
> Pi gwo k ap vale pi pitit
> O o o . . . Kite mele nèg yo
> Yon ti bwat lèt vann 20 goud
> Tout moun ki rich ap vin pi rich
> Kite mele nèg yo
> Peyi a tonbe nan tchouboum
>
> O Desalin di yon mo pou nou
> 1803 nou te bat lame Napoleon
> 1804 nou vin tonbe endependan
> An 2004 nou pran yon okipasyon moral

Chichi[13] klowòks la blanchi n, wi
Nou pran kou sa
Se yon sipriz wi

A cup of rice sells for 50 goud ($1.20)
The country is ruined
The big are swallowing the little
O o o . . . Don't give a damn about *those guys*
A little box of milk sells for 20 goud ($.50)
Everyone who is rich is getting richer
(We) don't give a damn about those guys
The country turns into a mess

Oh! Dessalines say a word for us
1803 we fought Napoleon's army
1804 we became independent
In 2004 we take a moral occupation

Shoo! The *Clorox* bleaches us, yes
We take this punch/coup
It's a surprise, yes

The recitation of escalating food prices—the price of rice doubling and milk increasing by 40 percent[14]—immediately identified this song as a Clorox song, and the following lines underscored this reading by framing the escalating prices as a political conflict. Here the aggressive term *those guys* worked to juxtapose the people against not just the national but also international power elite. Most poor urbanites attributed the rising cost of living to neoliberal trade reforms imposed by the United States and its allies since the 1980s, as well as to the elevated purchasing power of an expanding population of foreigners in Haiti. And although publicized as an executive decree, the deal that ended the April protests resulted from negotiations among domestic and international stakeholders, including the Haitian government, Haitian importers, U.S.-based exporters, and foreign aid experts. Indeed, part of the appeal of *Clorox* was its ability to use racial innuendo to indict foreign stakeholders. Drawing on the function of bleach as a whitening agent, the moniker served to both blame white foreigners for the cost of living and also accuse them of "whitewashing" the issue as a domestic problem.

The critique of foreign power was driven home by the penultimate verse, which denounced the political crisis of 2004 amid longings for revolutionary glory. Specifically, the line "In 2004, we take a moral occupation" castigated the United Nations peacekeeping mission, which began in 2004, as an international violation of popular sovereignty in Haiti. The mission followed the ouster of the popular (and populist) president Jean Bertrand Aristide in a coup d'état that many among the urban poor contended was the machination of foreign powers. In light of the verse's nostalgic longings for Jean Jacques Dessalines, the former slave turned revolutionary general who defeated the French colonists and claimed Haiti's independence in 1804, the phrase "moral occupation" aligned the peacekeeping mission with colonial domination. Yet the modifier *moral* highlighted how peacekeeping pursued occupation through a more covert, if not less potent, form of power. The point was that the mission undermined the sovereignty of Haiti despite its claims to protecting it. Interestingly, this enabled the phrase "moral occupation" to speak to another kind of ethical abuse among foreigners. As David explained to me, it also suggested that insofar as foreigners were in charge, they failed to provide moral stewardship for the people. Indeed, they enacted a moral violation in the form of a violent hunger—a hunger inflicted on the poor as a way of extracting their life for the enrichment of those in power.

The song's last lines encapsulated this polyvalent critique through a catchy slogan: "Shoo! The Clorox bleaches us! We take this *kou!*" In the first phrase, the lightening powers of bleach are used to invoke the "whitening" of the political community, while the term *shoo* invokes the idea of an unwanted outsider (an animal) in the household. The line played on the dual meaning of *blan* as a category of color ("white") and citizenship ("foreigner"), and hence, commented on the intrusion of white/foreign foods and armies into the country. The second line then played on the dual meanings of *kou* as "punch" and "*coup d'état*," further associating the rising cost of living with the 2004 coup against Aristide. This usage of *kou* has long been in the repertoire of Vodou ritual and protest chants. The ritual song that begins *Yo bay nou kou. Kou a fè ou mal* ("They give us a punch. The punch hurts us") was, for example, used to express disapproval of the 1991 coup against Aristide. Such "dialogic" (Bakhtin 1981) recollection of past uses and its relation to the current debate surrounding Clorox motivated these lines' controversial meaning and constructed the song as a *chan pwen* ("point song"), or a song with an embedded and powerful political message. The message, like that of preceding songs, called on the state to show up and address this situation. It used violent language, nationalist sentiment, moral reasoning, and pleading to build mass consensus around the issue and deliver a message.

While clearly addressing national and transnational concerns, songs could also use broader conflicts to intervene in more local structures of power. This was made clear in one memorable outing of My Business Band. It is customary for bands to perform an honorary salute, or *ochan*, to their sponsors and dignified supporters. This salute, whether performed for governmental agents at the Champs de Mars or local sponsors in the neighborhood, acknowledges hierarchical authority. My Business Band formally recognized their president during their performances. While usually a respectful gesture, on the third precarnival Sunday, this salute took on a new dimension. As usual, the band approached the president's bulk food store and began the salute. The sponsor, a middle-aged, portly man dressed in a pair of basketball shorts and a T-shirt, came to the door and stood on the front steps of the two-story cement building. He looked out at the band and the amassing crowd while gesturing as though tipping an imaginary hat. When the band neared the end of this salute, David, a short, skinny man showing all the signs of lifelong malnutrition, then offered a twist on the *ochan*. He began to recite a small poem that communicated, as he put it, the band's "respect for their sponsor." He sang:

> Bon dimanch Mesye
> Se pèp nou
> Gade granmèsi n ap fè la
> Di nou, di nou, di nou ...
> Kote pèp la ka jwen ti mòso

> Pleasant Sunday, Mister
> It's your people
> Look at the big thanks we are giving
> Tell us, tell us, tell us ...
> Where can the people find a small bite

In this salutation and salute, David can be seen to have enacted what sociologist Erving Goffman (1981) called "footing," the intricate performance of words and gestures by which the band presented who it was relationally and what role it was enacting. Through music and words the band signaled, in other words, their deference and another's duty, or both the social hierarchy and social contract that defined the relationship between the local big man and the people. In this way, they offered their gratitude while also demanding more support. The reference to the "small bite" served to request, as does the very *ochan* itself, that the sponsor (as well as audience members) continue to support the band financially. And amid all the talk of Clorox this phrase was especially charged. It invoked both the stockpiles of food at the warehouse and the hunger of the people. Immediately following the *ochan*, the chorus, in fact, began to sing the pithy slogan, "Shoo! The Clorox bleaches us. We take this *coup*. It's a surprise!" The words would have been difficult to make out over the band noise, but since most locals already knew them, the crowd was able to jump into a vigorous chant. The force of the music grew even more powerful as the group climbed the narrow passageway into the neighboring zone, following two other bands with similar messages. The surge of bodies soon blocked the entire street, providing a powerful visual representation of their collective force. Added to this physical unity was the group's harmonized chanting of the slogan, which vocally and rhetorically signaled their collectivity, a collectivity based in shared feelings and grievances.

Once this procession was complete, we all returned to the band's base. David immediately assessed the outing, claiming that he had to give respect to their rival, but that they had performed better, because they gathered more people into the crowd. After finishing the meal prepared by the band's godmother, I asked David about his remarks to the storeowner. He seemed to brush aside the question with a comment about the importance of the meal the group had just shared: "If we do not distribute (*separe*) the food for everyone then the hunger will remain in the gut. This will make us weak next week." But on further reflection, I realized how this comment echoed an earlier conversation in which he explained the meaning behind the slogan. "Shoo! The Clorox bleaches us," he had then told me,

> The expensive life turns us into animals. The state does not respect us. No work makes one. No school makes two. But Clorox is too much. We say, "Shoo, shoo, shoo . . . !" Animals breed animals. The people will die standing up.[15]

Here again Clorox was invoked as the ultimate expression of the people's deprivation, as the limit of community and personhood, the point where

animality begins. He used Clorox to not only display the physical suffering of the people but to also signal their anger and frustration—and, thus,
to threaten popular uprising. Insofar as the expensive life and its hunger
marked a violation of the people, it also, David seemed to say, provoked a
retaliatory violation *from* the people. "The people will die standing up," a
phrase that conveyed a fight till the end. Yet, however forceful, this performance was less an exemplar of total resistance, of directly resisting the state
or even fleeing it to set up a separate one, than a tactic for producing a moral
community that is *at risk* and *in need of* the protection and patronage of
more powerful others. The point of metaphors like Clorox was to showcase
the people as a suffering and agitated majority in order to summon authority
into being and shame it into action. The local objective was to implore the
sponsor to increase his support, whereas the larger goal was to compel national leadership to create a more just economy. Hence, rather than a logic of
repression and resistance, their politics followed the logic of neglect and engagement, in which, to invert Althussser's (1971) interpellation framework,
state or state-like power was being "hailed" by the people. Though, of course,
this was not always the result. As David put it, "we sing [the] slogan Clorox.
It's for us to protest or reclaim (*revandike*) something. You [speaking to me]
want to know if those people pick up the point? Well, gather it, send it . . . or
rather just leave it. That is their own choice."

Still, songs could have an imagined effect on reality. In the weeks following the outing detailed above, the impression grew among people in Bel Air
that the message behind the many Clorox songs had taken hold, at least pro-
visionally. I was repeatedly told that market women were being more generous with the little bit extra that they routinely added to small cups of bulk
goods, and that vendors of cooked food, where most people got their only
daily meal, were also being more forthcoming. And word quickly spread that
two main storehouses, including the one that sponsored My Business Band,
had (again) lowered the price of a large sack of rice. Insofar as this social
appeasement occurred, it was even more ephemeral than the governmental
price reduction in April. To me, it was practically unquantifiable. However,
what is perhaps more significant is the way this protest movement was perceived to mimic the April protests, so that in the end the processions of
street bands were understood to relive both the force of the people earlier in
the year and also the tenuous and episodic existence of the state and its du-
ties. This was only possible because of two interesting uses of the category of
the state among the popular classes in Haiti. First, the tendency to mark the

shared power of governmental actors and wealthy businessmen by referring to both as "the state" (Smith 2001; Trouillot 1990) and, second, the ability to use the term *the state* as both noun and verb, as both a fixed entity (the government) and a genre of action (acting powerful) (Kivland 2012; Trouillot 2001). Both uses were put to work in reflecting on My Business Band's outing. As David put it once all had passed: "We made the state appear in Bel Air like we did in April. . . . The people can make 'those people' have concern for us again if we organize. That's politics. But, the presence of the state, that's something that's not durable."[16]

CONCLUSION

All performance is concerned with revealing something to an audience. Yet as many of the chapters in this volume have argued, showing as a genre of action extends this concern to include the exaggeration, amplification, intensification, or manipulation of what is perceived as real or natural. The shows of carnival street bands put the accent on showing something that is all too real but usually hidden from perception or reality: the common people. Carnival "shows," as a revelatory, competitive, and participatory genre, are models of and for a politics from below, tying together sensuous bodily excitement with articulate political demands in ways that both unify and distinguish the principal political category of the people. Street bands endeavored to manifest the people as a public with inherent powers by taking to the streets, assembling a crowd, relishing popular bodies and comportment, showcasing popular issues and concerns, and demanding moral and material entitlements.

This public, as they make clear, entailed making a show that would not only call others to show up as participants in their praxis but also to use their presence as the force that would call those in power to show up and respond to their demands. The interpellation of an audience, especially a political one, depended on amassing and presenting a public. At the same time, these shows echoed street performance shows, horse shows, and ballroom dancing in that it concerned another sense of *showing up*—competing with rivals by upstaging them. The two senses of *showing up* were, indeed, intermingled, as upstaging rivals entailed bringing people together to take sides. The competition, in other words, rested on bands' abilities to attract participants, fans, and also political interlocutors. I suggest that the communal and divisive, centripetal and centrifugal pull of bands' performances point to something fundamental about showing as a genre: that showing is about attracting not passive audiences but engaged publics, publics that share interests, issues, and concerns but are also pulled into the camps that best express this common ground. The bands' attention to assembling a local performance base at rehearsals, "balancing" bodies during performances, and embellishing a punchy slogan all point to the construction of publics, to putting on a show and getting folks to show up. But the competitive spirit underlying each of these acts demonstrates how the art of showing is also about out-showing others who are showing the same thing.

Notes

1. Reports on the death toll varied, but Haitian officials put it at five (Schuller 2008).
2. Initially, the government responded to the food riots by promising to invest in national production. Sixteen of Haiti's twenty-seven senators then submitted, on April 10, a letter to the prime minister, who is in charge of the governmental ministries (the president leads the executive), stating, "Too little, too late. That's the feeling that your proposals have provoked" (2008).
3. Haitian carnival has roots in colonial times and in the early history of the republic, when people participated in popular festivity modeled on European medieval and African traditions and slave customs born in the New World. Today's carnival dates from the early twentieth century, when an elite carnival that involved parades and social balls in Port-au-Prince took shape alongside popular fairs at public markets. In time, carnival developed to include a procession of masking groups, marching bands, and floats of pop music bands on municipal squares. The main stage is the capital of Port-au-Prince, though provincial cities also host carnivals, with the southern city of Jacmel offering a renowned festival. President Michel Martelly has altered tradition slightly, hosting the main stage event in a different city each year.
4. Michael Warner, for example, notes that the second defining feature of a public is that it is a relation among strangers. Yet, as Susan Gal (2002) and Susan Gal and Gail Kligman (2000) remind us, the ideal of the public should not be confused with an actually existing corpus of people oriented around and circulating discourse.
5. Conversation, January 16, 2011.
6. Carnival queens are crowned at Haitian Carnivals, and particular women are designated queens within some *bann a pye*. They can wear elaborate colorful silk dresses, though today most simply wear the designed T-shirts and a makeshift crown.
7. Conversation, December 10, 2008
8. In a spiritual context, *pwen* may refer to a charm like a soft, pliable doll fashioned with male genitalia and chained to a chair to correct a wandering husband (Brown

2003), or a pithy nickname, such as *Malgre Sa,* "In Spite of It," to protect a child who has survived a sorcerer's attack (Richman 2005). In a more worldly context, however, *pwen* refer to coded messages, like, on the eve of the 2004 coup, when President Aristide used the proverb "The dew dances wildly so long as the sun has not risen" (*lawouze fè banda tout tan soley pa leve*) to warn the oppositional movement of a fierce battle.

9. L'as ou Neuf Band, 2009.

10. Soro Band, 2009

11. Tèt Kole Band, 2009.

12. Conversation, December 8, 2009.

13. *Chichi* is the sound used to shoo a chicken from the house or yard in Haiti.

14. In Bel Air, the price of a small tin (standard soup can) of rice increased from 25 to 50 goud ($.60 to $1.25) from December 2007 to April 2008. After dropping to 35 goud in April, it was again at 50 goud by the end of the year. The price of milk went from 15 to 20 goud ($.38 to $.50). Beans and cooking oil increased by as much as 50 percent. Gasoline increased less dramatically.

15. Personal conversation, January 2009.

16. Band committee meeting, June 2009.

Sources

Althusser, Louis. 1971. *Lenin and Philosophy, and Other Essays.* London: New Left Books.

Averill, Gage. 1994. "Anraje to Angaje: Carnival Politics and Music in Haiti." *Ethnomusicology* 38 (2): 217–47.

Averill, Gage. 1997. *A Day for the Hunter, a Day for the Prey.* Chicago: University of Chicago.

Bakhtin, Mikhail M. 1981. *The Dialogic Imagination: Four Essays.* Translated by M. Holquist. Austin: University of Texas Press.

Brown, Karen McCarthy. 2003. "Making *Wanga*: Reality Constructions and the Magical Manipulation of Power." In *Transparency and Conspiracy: Ethnographies in the New World Order,* edited by H. G. West and T. Sanders. Durham, NC: Duke University Press.

Canetti, Elias. 1984. *Crowds and Power.* Translated by C. Stewart. New York: Farrar, Straus and Giroux.

Durkheim, Emile. 1995. *The Elementary Forms of Religious Life.* Translated by K. E. Fields. New York: Free Press.

Fraser, Nancy. 1992. "Rethinking the Public Sphere: A Contribution to the Critique of Actually Existing Democracy." In *Habermas and the Public Sphere,* edited by Craig Calhoun. Cambridge, MA: MIT Press.

Gal, Susan. 2002. "A Semiotics of the Public/Private Distinction." *Differences: A Journal of Feminist Cultural Studies* 13 (1): 77–95.

Gal, Susan, and Gail Kligman. 2000. *Reproducing Gender: Politics, Publics, and Everyday Life after Socialism*. Princeton: Princeton University Press.

Goffman, Erving. 1981. *Forms of Talk*. Philadelphia: University of Pennsylvania Press.

"Haiti Senators Call on PM to Quit." 2008. Al Jazeera. Port-au-Prince, Haiti. April 10, 2008. http://www.aljazeera.com/news/americas/2008/04/2008525141842769465.html

Kivland, Chelsey. 2012. "'We Make the State': Performance, Politick, and Respect in Urban Haiti." PhD diss., Department of Anthropology, University of Chicago.

Laguerre, Michel S. 1976. "Bel Air, Port-au-Prince: From Slave and Maroon Settlement to Contemporary Black Ghetto." *Contributions of the Latin American Anthropology Group* 1 (1): 26–38.

Le Bon, Gustave. 2001. *The Crowd: A Study of the Popular Mind*. Mineola, NY: Dover.

McAlister, Elizabeth A. 2002. *Rara! Vodou, Power, and Performance in Haiti and Its Diaspora*. Berkeley: University of California Press.

Richman, Karen E. 2005. *Migration and Vodou*. Gainesville: University Press of Florida.

Schuller, Mark. 2008. *Haitian Food Riots Unnerving but Not Surprising*. Washington, DC: Centre for International Policy.

Scott, James C. 1990. *Domination and the Arts of Resistance: Hidden Transcripts*. New Haven: Yale University Press.

Smith, Jennie Marcelle. 2001. *When the Hands Are Many: Community Organization and Social Change in Rural Haiti*. Ithaca: Cornell University Press.

Stallybrass, Peter, and Allon White. 1986. *The Politics and Poetics of Transgression*. London: Methuen.

Trouillot, Michel Rolph. 1990. *Haiti, State against Nation: The Origins and Legacy of Duvalierism*. New York: Monthly Review Press.

Trouillot, Michel Rolph. 2001. "The Anthropology of the State in the Age of Globalization." *Current Anthropology* 42 (1): 125–38.

Warner, Michael. 2002. *Publics and Counterpublics*. New York: Zone Books.

Williams, Raymond. 1977. *Marxism and Literature*. Oxford: Oxford University Press.

CHAPTER 8

The 2014 Sochi Olympiad Shows Off Putin's (New, Great, Open) Russia

Catherine A. Schuler

On July 5, 2007, like Ermolai Lopakhin in the third act of *The Cherry Orchard*, Vladimir Putin must surely have bellowed, "I bought it!" Rather than a decrepit cherry orchard, however, President Putin had just purchased the dubious honor of staging the 2014 Winter Olympics in Sochi, Russia. Only a few months earlier, this visibly depressed Soviet-era resort city on the Black Sea looked like an implausible competitor in a bidding campaign that pitted Russia, South Korea, and Austria against each other. Unlike the Korean and Austrian cities (PyeongChang and Salzburg), Sochi had no existing sports facilities, inadequate tourist accommodations, and a crumbling infrastructure. As if that weren't enough to discourage the International Olympic Committee's (IOC) bid committee, Sochi, best known in 2007 for its subtropical climate, trash-strewn beaches, and deteriorating sanatoria, is located geographically on the edge of a war zone. Nonetheless, Sochi topped Salzburg in the first round of voting and overcame PyeongChang in the second by only four points. Despite predictions of fiasco and disgrace by doomsters at home and abroad, six-and-a-half years later, on February 23, 2014, Mishka, Sochi's gigantic polar bear mascot, blew out the Olympic flame, thereby signaling the end of post-Soviet Russia's first international sports mega-event. Russian mass media wasted no time in trumpeting the Sochi Olympiad as the greatest ever in the history of the modern Olympics. Few critics on the other side of the Atlantic raved so ecstatically, but many admitted that, against all of the odds and expectations, Putin had pulled off a pretty good show. Given the obstacles Sochi faced, one cannot help but wonder at the process by which a city with so little to recommend it became the site of a comparatively successful international sports mega-event.

A chapter of this length cannot encompass the whole tangled web of the Sochi Olympiad—a tale further complicated by the proliferation, over seven years, of official narratives, opposition counternarratives, and official/ opposition counter-counternarratives. Here, I want to consider Sochi 2014 as a kind of post-Soviet, neo-Wagnerian *gesamtkunstwerk*, a total work of art that employs myth, new technology, space, and concealment to draw spectators into a seductive illusion of national unity and exceptionality. The concept suits the Russian context; indeed, variations on the *gesamtkunstwerk* appear throughout late imperial, Soviet, and post-Soviet society and culture. Among others, Viacheslav Ivanov, Anatoli Lunacharskii, and Pavel Kerzhentsev appropriated not only from Wagner but also from Jean-Jacques Rousseau, Friedrich Nietzsche, and Romain Rolland; so prevalent was Soviet appropriation that literary historian Boris Groys called the practice *Gesamtkunstwerk Stalin*.[1] Giving a postmodern twist to recent developments in festival culture, Mark Lipovetsky calls the post-Soviet tendency *Gesamtkunstwerk Putin*;[2] I will argue that, before war with Ukraine compromised its effect, Sochi 2014 marked the pinnacle of this tendency.

Relying in part on my experiences in the city of Sochi and at the Opening Ceremony, I seek to show how the city "performed" and a performance "showed" the Kremlin's dream of a reinvented Russian nation. Bold letters just inside the Olympic Park proclaimed "Russia—Great, New, Open!" (*Rossiia—Velikaia, Novaia, Otkrytaia!*). If the Sochi Olympiad was intended to show the new Russia, what kind of Russia did it show?

PRELUDE: SOCHI? боже мой!

Carol Martin argues that cities can usefully be regarded as live performances, and if cities perform, no city in recent memory has performed more publicly and spectacularly than Sochi.[3] The Russian elite—Putin's ministers, oligarchs, arrivistes, and industries with economic and political stakes in Sochi 2014—understood perfectly the need for a spectacular show. They may, however, have been thinking more about urban renewal than spectacular athleticism. Sports historian Maurice Roche, who calls the Games a "traveling road show," rightly points out that the term "Olympic city" alludes not just to athletic facilities but also to the entire geographical area—in this

Fig. 8.1. Appearing in English and Russian, this signage inside the Olympic Park hoped to persuade visitors that Sochi 2014 embodied the new Russia. (Author photo, 2014.)

instance, all of Greater Sochi.[4] Thus the so-called Sochi miracle consisted not only of new athletic and media spaces, but also—and perhaps more important—the global resurrection of a once vital Soviet resort area.[5] The state marketed Sochi as a triumph of Russian ingenuity and originality, a model of post-Soviet (post)modernity, a show of national vigor, and an unforgettable, once-in-a-lifetime festive occasion that would even make a substantial profit.[6] No wonder then that the Sochi miracle carried enormous real and symbolic burdens.

In contrast to the citizen-invented and performed cities described by Martin, Sochi was repurposed, redesigned, and produced by the state, which also sought to control what and how it "meaned."[7] In a realignment of power that echoed the Soviets, the state—not its citizens—seized control not only of the physical polis but also of its narrative.[8] Indeed, although important, rebuilding Russian sports was, according to Putin, secondary to revitalizing Russia's international image.[9] In a January 2014 interview, he explained to journalists that, for Russia, the Games had always been a means to a greater end. Sochi's meaning, he asserted, would lie not in Russia's medal count, but in showing the world a new Russia. Being excellent hosts and providing visitors with the biggest, most unforgettable, marvelous, and modern Olympic experience in the history of the Games would achieve that end:

> During the Olympiad, we really want participants, journalists, and people who watch it on television or by means of mass communication to see the new Russia, get to know the country, see its face, its possibilities, to look at it with a fresh, unbiased gaze. And I'm sure that this will happen and will enable Russia to build relations with its global partners.[10]

After the Games, Russians celebrated not only their team's medal count but also Sochi's performance. One sports journalist crowed proudly: "Russia showed the whole world that it's not only civilized, but also an innovative Great Power."[11] Although Russians celebrated their athletes' victories, Putin's larger triumph was premised on Sochi's makeover—its transformation into a "high-tech" place of performance.

Looking back to 2005–06—the planning phase for the Sochi bid—Sochi was not an obvious choice. Indeed, skeptics at home and abroad asked, why Sochi? Why a moldering resort area stuck between the Caucasus Mountains and the Black Sea rather than a better-equipped, and more conveniently located, city or region? What would be the environmental and human costs? Couldn't the money be better spent?[12] Given the opposition, one wonders how the Kremlin sold Sochi to the IOC, the citizens of Russia, the residents of Sochi, and, finally, the international community. Moreover, did Sochi do for Russia what the Kremlin intended it to do? Did visitors leave with the sense of having experienced a sustainably new Russia?

Assume for a moment that Sochi is the face of a new, improved Russia—but what exactly is Sochi? Because the 2014 Games provoked such fierce controversy, the symbolic Sochi tends to prevail in the public's imagination, but Sochi is geographically and administratively tangible. Indeed, there are at least two Sochis: the city of Sochi and Greater Sochi, which includes Adler, Krasnaya Polyana, and several other smaller districts. For simplicity's sake, I will use the Olympic bid book's convention and call the entire Olympic city "Sochi" except when the name of a specific district within Greater Sochi is significant.

Part of a southern Black Sea area once called the Russian Riviera, the geographical and administrative area called Sochi is a place of memory. Home since the Soviet era to a national park and a pristine biosphere reserve, the Black Sea coast has served for more than two centuries as a vacation spot for tsars, commissars, and Soviet citizens seeking healthful recreation on its beaches and in its sanatoria (still Sochi's principal industry). After the Revolution, Vladimir Lenin set the area aside as a workers' retreat and encouraged the construction of sanatoria equipped with medical and athletic facilities. Joseph Stalin maintained a dacha in Sochi, as did Boris Yeltsin. Today, Vladimir Putin often retreats to his palatial holiday home nearby. Although the area grew shabby during Russia's transition to postsocialism, Sochi continued to support a thriving tourist industry and much has been made of its identity as Russia's only remaining southern resort. Thus, when Putin began eyeing it in 2002 for renewal and modernization, land values began to rise. After Sochi won the Olympic bid in 2007, everyone wanted a piece of the area, either for development or for preservation.

Most agreed that this beloved piece of real estate had considerable value for tourism. As the aspiring host of an international mega-event, however, Sochi also presented serious geographical and interethnic challenges. The effect of the region's location just north of Georgia and on the edge of the Caucasus Mountains has been to foster significant ethnic diversity. Although the Sochi bid book characterizes Sochi as simultaneously diverse and peaceful, it has not always been so: the Circassian diaspora remembers the Russian genocide (1864); the Whites, Reds, and Georgians fought over the area during the civil war; Chechnya is uncomfortably close; and in 2008 the war between Russia and Georgia over Abkhazia and South Ossetia touched Sochi's southernmost border. Environmentalists aggressively opposed a Sochi Olympiad because of the monstrous construction projects that promised to encroach on the national park and damage the fragile biosphere reserve.[13] Finally, although once a favorite vacation spot, the region declined dramatically after the Soviet Union fell. To renovate and modernize an area barren of the requisite Olympic and tourist facilities would require billions of rubles. Not surprisingly, through all stages of bidding and construction, friends and foes of Sochi engaged in a bitter war of words and images. If critics shaped the Sochi narrative outside of Russia, the Kremlin molded it internally.

Opposing sides in the Sochi polemic painted the region in starkly contrasting colors. Protestors from the Circassian diaspora created a website and Facebook page called NO SOCHI 2014.[14] Graphic images of Olympic athletes skiing down bloody slopes and over the skulls of Circassian ancestors killed by the Russians made their point. The United Nations Environmental Program, World Wildlife Fund (WWF) Russia, WWF International, and Greenpeace published photographs of, and reports on, the damage caused by enormous construction sites to endangered species and the environment. The editors of the *New Gazette* (*Novaia gazeta*) excoriated the "new Sochi law," which allowed the state to evict hundreds of citizens from privately owned land, while radio station Echo of Moscow (*Ekho Moskvy*) provided independent analysis and commentary. The Western press not only criticized but also relentlessly mocked Putin's ambitious plans for Sochi.

Because the Kremlin controls not only the Duma but also most television—still the only widely available communication technology in Russia—it could more easily invent and disseminate Sochi's dominant narratives. Thus, from bid book to closing ceremony, the Kremlin orchestrated Sochi's transformation from seedy resort into an international showplace. The bid book's title, *Gateway to the Future*, conveys the Kremlin's vision: 158 pages of carefully composed text set out ambitious designs for Sochi's future, while stunning photographs of snow-capped mountains, pristine rivers, quaint architecture, and happy children sell Sochi on the basis of its natural beauty.[15] The images, however, bore little resemblance to many residents' actual living conditions in 2007, which included black water, smoking dumps, inadequate roads, decrepit hotels, constant traffic jams, waste-strewn beaches, and toxic sewage pollution. While rightly extolling the area's spectacular mountains, forests, and rivers, neither text nor image reveals its designation as a protected national preserve or its nominal winter sports facilities. Paradoxically, the book uses spectacular nature photography to create one kind of narrative, while using the language of dynamic, high-tech, neofuturist repurposing and redesign to create an almost contradictory narrative of the Sochi miracle.

The miracle involved time, space, architecture, and technology. The Kremlin proposed a fantabulous "one-city" futurist assemblage built from scratch over seven years. Calling the Olympiad a "national priority" and claiming overwhelming popular support for the bid, the Kremlin promised to create a "modern, world-class, year-round destination for sport, tourism, and commerce" and an "elite alpine sports training and competition infrastructure." Readers of the bid book are asked to imagine a revolutionary system of highways, trains, and other modes of transportation that would carry athletes, officials, and visitors swiftly from one state-of-the-art venue to another. An Olympic cluster located on the spectacular Black Sea coast and replete with four-star hotels would host ceremonies, skating events, and the media, while a mountain village "nestled among the peaceful forests in 4-star lodges and chalets" would host skiing and snowboarding events. Add eleven enormous Olympic objects and imagine this byzantine assemblage as compact, manageable, economical, sustainable, environmentally friendly, and safe from terrorism. Then imagine all of this accomplished with overwhelming support from a warm and loving Russian people living in a prosperous, economically stable, representative democracy. Lastly, imagine that they will unite around and find common identity in this enormous national/international/transnational event. In a word, the 2007 bid book's imaginative hyperbole encapsulated Putin's Sochi *gesamtkunstwerk*.

If the bid book's Sochi was compact, sustainable, environmentally friendly, and economical, a different Sochi emerged during the construction process. Although efficient, the one-city solution cost billions; indeed, excessive spending and unapologetic hyperbole marked the whole project. By project's end, the $51 billion price tag seemed a matter of pride rather than a cause for concern: for Putin, the higher the cost, the bigger and more impressive the festival. In his January 2014 interview, he boasted:

> [A]s you and I know, for the last several years, the Sochi Olympic project has been the biggest, most important construction site in the world. Without any exaggeration—this is the most massive building site in the world. . . . Where else in the world would you find construction workers who could do all of this high-quality work on time and at minimal cost? You can't name one country. Do you understand, not one such country in the whole world.[16]

Sochi's image as a massive construction site seemed to thrill Putin, but did the Sochi residents who would shortly be performing on the international stage share his enthusiasm?

In 2007, many locals supported the Olympic project, but support diminished as massive construction sites began to inconvenience city residents. Average citizens did not, after all, conduct a plebiscite on Sochi 2014, thus only after the fact did protests against annihilation of their property and constitutional rights begin. Mounting tensions meant that the state had not only to create an appearance of local enthusiasm for the Olympic project but also to motivate local participation in the city's performance. In Putin's Russia, such conundrums call not for dialogue with the people, but for marketing and spin (*reklam*). Tensions between them gave birth in 2009 to *The Lights of Greater Sochi* (*Ogni bol'shego Sochi*).

Lights, a government-subsidized, glossy monthly magazine, revealed the depth of official Russia's concern for uncooperative locals whose discontent, if not curtailed, would surely spoil Sochi's performance in 2014. Distributed free, this Chamber of Commerce–like publication used a curious bricolage of neo-Soviet, neoliberal visual and written texts to inspire pride of place and fire enthusiasm for the allegedly unprecedented entrepreneurial opportunities presented by the Games. Motivational articles, colorful ads, and inspirational commentary suggest that senior editor Ol'ga Taruta was charged to stoke a Stakhanovite-like sense of mission and urgency in an unhappy and increasingly disobliging citizenry. The ugly mood in Sochi seems to have inspired *Lights*, the sole purpose of which was to sell the Olympiad and the city's revitalization to its own citizens.

No citizen complaints about Olympic authoritarianism marred its pages. *Lights* spun accusations of incompetence and corruption into cheery narratives of corporate devotion to local interests. Articles and interviews with construction bosses, investment entrepreneurs, and government officials prevailed; they spoke glowingly of *stroitel'stvo* (construction), *investitsii* (investment), and government (*vlast'*). Accompanied by humanizing photographs, articles like "We Must See the Future and Program (*programirovat'*) It" and "The Meaning of Our Own Lives Lies in Their Value to Others" saturate every issue. A 2010 interview with Anatoli Pakhomov, Sochi's Kremlin-allied mayor, entitled "Everything in City Management Is Important and I Investigate All of It Thoroughly," exemplifies the genre.[17] Bedecked with photographs of Pakhomov toiling for his community, the interview enumerates his contributions to development projects since 2009. I govern, he claims, according to "principles of honesty, professionalism, and love." Like others who appear in *Lights*, Pakhomov evinces sincere concern for his city and its residents. Could such a decent man be a crook? Could he be performing for the Kremlin's image-making apparatus?

Taruta carried out her mission with gusto. Alongside pedagogic articles instructing her notoriously rude countrymen and women in the fine art of European hospitality, Taruta's editorials called on citizens to believe in the Sochi miracle.[18] Suffering from a sense of helplessness learned in the Soviet Union and still enacted in post-Soviet Russia, Russians had to shake off their ennui. Taruta tried to inspire optimism, convert inertia into civic activism, and dispel citizens' feeling of powerlessness. "Spring," she tooted in March 2010, "and the spirit blossoms. Harmony, spiritual tranquility, and love arrive with spring." Forget Vancouver and "turn the page." It's time for Sochi![19] May, she promised readers, is "a month of dreams, hopes, new ideas, and optimism."[20] In June, she assured them that "the citizens of Sochi are a sovereign people" who "live in an exciting time of difficult tasks and unprecedented opportunities." But, she admonishes, the citizens of Sochi do not understand tourist hospitality: "service personnel demonstrate a total lack of culture."[21] "Citizens," Taruta seemed to command, "build the scenery, sew the costumes, find a role, and rehearse, rehearse, rehearse! Show off Russia's new, flush, progressive, high-tech face to the West!" In September 2014, she urged them to finish brilliantly: "our country's reputation," she intoned, rests on Sochi. Finally, in December 2013, Taruta concluded her four-year jeremiad against citizen apathy: "We're at the finish line! We won!"[22] But what did winning mean?

BEING THERE

While many Russians derided Putin's inflated, image-driven *gesamtkunstwerk*, they also worried about Sochi's performance. In "Sochi smiles on everyone," *Kommersant* correspondent Marina Akhmedova described the city as a place "on show": a revitalized Russian Riviera made up and decked out in Armani for its date with the West. [23] The random foreigners she'd interviewed had so far been cool, limiting their remarks to "nice city." Tepid (and occasionally hostile) responses disheartened Akhmedova, who wanted foreigners to rave about Sochi so that they would return to partake of the city's post-Olympic attractions. Already set against Russia, foreigners, Akhmedova complained, seek out faults in its Olympic city. Sochi, she wrote, is like a lady in a hat:

> [D]espite the brightness of the paint, the cleanliness, and the infrastructure which . . . succeeded in reaching European standards, the city is tense. Tense like a person on whom all eyes are focused. The city is like a lady wearing a hat at the dockyards. She gets all dressed up to go out, but the looks directed at her aren't all friendly.

Although Akhmedova eventually encountered foreigners who enthused over the city, reports on Sochi 2014 by U.S. correspondents indicate that Sochi did not, in fact, cause many of them to smile. Some called Sochi a Potemkin village, while others amplified the city's allegedly spectacular flaws, calling attention to shoddy construction, brown water, rude Russians, mass extermination of stray dogs, homophobia, and censorship. Competing Sochi narratives cause one to wonder what the average visitor to Putin's "celebration of sports" (*prazdnik sporta*) experienced there. What did we—the "we" being those of us who spent thousands of dollars on travel and tickets— actually get for our money? While I cannot claim that mine is the authoritative account, I have traveled to Russia many times since 1991 and experienced its rough ride from post-Soviet destitution to oil-nourished opulence. For better and worse, and in ways both big and small, Sochi—the city and the Games—both astonished and puzzled me.

In the narrative that follows, I describe my experience of the coastal cluster, as well as the stylistically brilliant, but conceptually thin, cultural retrospective staged by Konstantin Ernst and George Tsypin at the Opening Ceremony. One question particularly intrigues me. How could Sochi 2014 succeed as a splendid, richly mimetic, densely symbolic show of Russian greatness, but do so little to alleviate misgivings about the substance of Russia's transformation? Was it all illusion? Following on the heels of the Games, Crimea and Ukraine disrupted Putin's immediate plans for Sochi— but even so, could Sochi have sustained an ideologically coherent illusion of Russian resurrection?

I arrived at the newly enlarged and renovated Sochi/Adler airport just after 10 p.m. on February 5, 2014. My first encounters with friendly, smiling passport control officers and a polite taxi driver driving a clean, new official taxi astonished me. More delightful surprises awaited at my hotel spa, the Green Grove (*Zelenaia roshcha*): gracious reception personnel who spoke English and, with unprecedented generosity, allowed me into my room three hours early; a large, sparkling clean hotel room decorated in gentle shades of pink and furnished with a refrigerator and coffeemaker; and smiling hotel staff. An enormous continental breakfast greeted me in the morning and a spanking new Mercedes minibus drove me to the Matesta hub to pick up the train to Sochi. I had been traveling between Russia and the United States for twenty-two years and although the conditions of travel have improved, I had never experienced anything quite so welcoming. Was this the Sochi miracle?

Wanting to experience the Olympic city more directly, on day one I disembarked from the train at Adler station (a showplace of Sochi renewal) in order to walk to Olympic Park. I moved through security with surprising ease to find respectable shops lining the station's bustling interior. At the Adler station, Olympic visitors could board the new electric trains and brightly colored Olympic busses that shuttled between venues and ride for free. Although temperatures didn't feel subtropical, a bright sun warmed my walk along several miles of newly laid sidewalks, roads, cloverleaf overpasses, gardens, and newly planted trees and grass until I reached an impasse: a more typically Russian shopping area replete with dilapidated kiosks and outdoor markets. After exploring it, I boarded a rickety city bus crammed with shoppers, and eventually disembarked at the Olympic media center, located about a mile from the Park. While trekking between venues, I grasped more fully the breadth of Sochi's transformation: clean streets, plentiful signage, new shop fronts, Olympic banners fluttering in a sea breeze, and multilingual volunteers in colorful Bosco uniforms. Rather than fifteen miles from the Georgian border, I might have been in any wealthy coastal resort in the United States or Europe. Everything along official paths bespoke of the new Russia, as the Kremlin wanted us to see and experience it.

As noted above, Russia sold Sochi to the IOC on the basis of a "unique" one-city solution, but compact hardly describes the 145 kilometers along the coast occupied by Sochi 2014. The space contained two Olympic clusters, one on the Black Sea coast and the other in the Caucasus Mountains; a distance of sixty-eight kilometers separated Sochi from Krasnaya Polyana, while forty kilometers separated the mountain and coastal clusters and twenty-eight kilometers separated Sochi from Adler. Because the area lacked the necessary transportation infrastructure, workers drilled through whole mountains in the Sochi national park for connecting highways and a high-speed electric train. Spreading for several miles along the coast, the coastal cluster included an athletes' village, an enormous, glass-walled media center, and the Olympic Park. To make space for these, the state pulled down entire private residential neighborhoods. In addition to various stages and food tents, the Olympic Park contained five skating venues, two training/practice venues, Fisht Stadium, an enormous, square-ish, silver-swathed souvenir store, and an unfinished Disney-like theme park. In other words, the magnitude of Sochi's task dwarfed all previous Olympiads, including the traditionally larger summer Games.

A grand stairway from the Olympic Park station funneled spectators into the Park's exterior vestibule and enormous parking area. Tight security prevented entrance into the Park without tickets for that day's events. In point of fact, security prevented casual spectating anywhere in the clusters. Although political protest had been relegated to an area miles from either cluster, Sochi's vast security apparatus did not prevent U.S. evangelicals from proselytizing just outside the Park's gates. Some chatted cheerily with me about Jesus; others shouted about salvation and shoved flyers on passersby. Police did not interrupt or remove them to the authorized protest zone in Khosta.[24] Apparently Sochi 2014 welcomed foreign Protestant proselytizers into its space, but not Russian and international human rights and environmental activists.

On February 7, armed with a ticket for the Opening Ceremony, I spent the day inside of the Park. Its size, feeling of emptiness, and the pervasive presence of transnational enterprise struck me. Olympic television coverage conceals the escalation of Olympic commerce, but being there is a revelation. Transnational sponsors include, among others, Coca Cola, Visa, and McDonald's. Monopolies on marketing inside the Park allow these companies to spread their brands visually and materially throughout the space: visitors must eat McDonald's, drink Coke, and pay for it all with their Visa card.[25]

Nonsports structures dotted the Park's landscape, including fan "houses" built by wealthy nations with highly competitive winter sports teams. My favorite building, the "Main Olympic Store" (*glavnyi Olimpiiskii magazin*) added to the Park's postmodern ambiance. Gilded with silver and topped by an enormous, brightly colored Olympic glove, this popular venue sold official Olympic tchotchke. Only the towering, purple, phallus-like Olympic flame rivaled it for sheer eccentricity. Olympic parks have long had a theme park aura, but Sochi had an actual (albeit unfinished) theme park.[26] Located alongside the Olympic Park, its brightly colored rides and tents gave the Park a fairground (*narodnoe gulian'e*) atmosphere.

Although I spent most days and evenings in the coastal cluster, I eventually traveled to both the city of Sochi and Krasnaya Polyana. Along the route, I admired the magnificent mountain landscape, but not the massive destruction inflicted on it. Seeing this confirmed what many already know about the region. For that reason, I want to highlight a commonplace, but to my mind more significant, episode—an urgent stop at Estosadok, a railway station along the route. Only readers who've never experienced public facilities in Russia will wonder why I pause to extol the cleanliness, modern toilets, and wheelchair accessibility of the Estosadok facilities. Paradoxically, that restroom showed Russia's new face more vividly than anything I'd encountered so far.

No athletic events happened in the city of Sochi, but the state nonetheless sank billions into its revitalization. Along the stretch of highway leading into the city, smartly signed sanatoria peeked out from dense, green foliage lining the path. Arriving in the town center, I saw little to recall the Russia

Fig. 8.2. Construction rubble partially concealed behind a Sochi Olympic banner. (Author photo, 2014.)

I had come to know over twenty-two years of travel. Nice on the Black Sea seemed accurate.[27] The bus stopped at a quaint, Italianate railway station encircled by a grassy central square and small, clean shops. More modern, but considerably less European, were the new resort hotels and the enormous shopping center replete with a U.S.-style supermarket. Missing from Sochi were the stray dogs so ubiquitous in Adler, at my hotel in Matesta, and even at the airport. More so than Adler, Sochi felt like a city that had been "cleaned up"—or in the dogs' case, cleaned out—for foreigners.

Complaints after the Games about unfinished rooms, loose knobs, brown water, and rude Russians missed the point. We—the ticket-buying visitors to Sochi—experienced a magnificent, low/high tech illusion. Huge stadiums, new highways and railways, elegant ski resorts, modern hotels, supermarkets, sparkling boulevards, European restaurants, Wi-Fi, clean public restrooms, wheelchair accessibility: in this context, those constituted an urban *gesamtkunstwerk*. The illusion, however, was incomplete, thus the affect fell short. Traces of the apocryphal Potemkin village were clearly visible: colorful banners masked construction trash; new fences concealed old houses; hired exterminators poisoned stray dogs; and the shabby kiosks, rowdy markets, rickety, packed buses, and idle, cigarette-smoking, stubble-faced men of old Russia were just a step away.

A SHOW WITHIN A PERFORMANCE:
SOCHI'S OPENING CEREMONY

Producers of Olympic Opening Ceremonies generally strive to maintain secrecy regarding the particulars of the show until opening night, but Russian media leaked just enough tidbits to stoke an appetite. On February 5, during a broadcast on Channel One, a newscaster stated the Opening Ceremony's aim: "to astonish the whole world," starting with the grandeur of Fisht Stadium. The Ceremony's "sparkling dynamism," he raved, will dwarf all previous opening ceremonies; Sochi's Opening Ceremony will be so dynamic and spectacular that three hours will pass in the blink of an eye. Before Sochi, he implied, all opening ceremonies lacked imagination, but Russia will show the West how to stage a *real* Opening Ceremony![28]

Fisht Stadium, the largest built object and principal signifier of Russian greatness, served just one purpose: to contain the spectacular opening and closing ceremonies. Required by the IOC, the ceremonies meld ritual and theater into a very long, but in Sochi's case, astonishingly entertaining event. The IOC stipulates the ritual elements, leaving local hosts to organize an "artistic programme." They are tasked to "find creative ways to combine Olympic protocol with just the right amount of entertainment, cultural references, and technological innovations."[29] As early as 1980, however, the balance of ritual and entertainment had already begun to tip toward the latter, rendering the meaning of "right amount" proportionally more opaque. With respect to the Winter Games, changes in the kinds of spaces used for the ceremonies have encouraged spectacular excess.

In 2010, Vancouver was the first to stage an Opening Ceremony in an indoor arena; the Russians followed Vancouver's example. As I discovered after four hours of sitting in Fisht Stadium, indoor venues aren't necessarily designed for spectator comfort or warmth. The indoor space does, however, offer opportunities for theatrical spectacle unachievable outdoors. The Russians, who have for several centuries created vast spectacular events indoors and out, took full advantage of Fisht Stadium. Konstantin Ernst, a television producer and director for state-owned Channel One, and Russian American opera designer George Tsypin collaborated to create an Opening Ceremony that, according to some, eclipsed Beijing's.[30]

I should admit here that I traveled to Sochi specifically for the Opening Ceremony. Recently, I've been writing about the theatricalization of Putin's presidency and, in point of fact, a fantasy that Russia's puissant president might ride into the arena on a chariot of fire motivated my desire to attend the Games. If Putin failed to fulfill my dream of an eyewitness encounter with his spectacular masculinity, the Opening Ceremony did not disappoint. Visually and aurally stunning, the show often left me not only breathless but also with many questions about the makers' signifying intentions and the ceremony's effect/affect on spectators. One question was foremost. What did the state hope to achieve with this postmodern romp through Russian culture and history?

Space played a crucial role in the production's affect. Equipped with the latest stage technology, Fisht's massive ovoid interior space accommodated 40,000 spectators. Although not the world's largest stadium, Fisht's capacity more than doubles Madison Square Garden's. For $1,828, I sat in the front row of the second tier on the far side of the oval; while better than many others, in my view such a pricey seat should have been in the first row facing Putin. Apparently other foreigners agreed. A gentleman sitting above me, who'd also paid $1,828, remarked unhappily: "These must be the American seats." The cotton swag bags on our seats contained a plastic medal and a dual-language program. The medals, color-coded in red, white, and blue, lit up at designated moments during the ceremony, making us participants in the spectacle.

Never having attended a live Olympic ceremony, I didn't know what to expect from Sochi's except for one thing: a show of myth in mythical proportions. A preshow, probably targeted to youth, launched the Ceremony. Lasting just under an hour, this dynamic (in the sense of speed, noise, and light) performance featured two hyper-animated emcees (male and female) traversing the arena floor in a golf cart, live popular music, and lots of flashing colored light. In what was surely a scrap thrown to the LGBT community, t.A.T.u., a faux lesbian girl duo, performed the last song. Then, abetted by instructions to hug each other projected onto the arena floor, the emcees prodded spectators to show a transcendent spirit of Olympic love. The directive to hug heralded an applause meter urging the audience to earsplitting expressions of fan frenzy. Finally, when the crowd reached fever pitch, the projected figure of UN Secretary General Ban Ki-Moon appeared to congratulate the "Olympic family" for setting an example of harmonious, international cooperation. Although a perfect segue to the Opening Ceremony, Ban Ki-Moon's appearance—projected, like the applause meter, onto the arena floor—felt incongruous amid the largely pop culture celebrities.

After the preshow, the stadium filled quickly for the ceremony. The lights dimmed and the Opening Ceremony—*Dream About Russia* (*sny o Rossii*)—commenced. Integrated into obligatory Olympic ritual and unfolding over thirteen scenes, the dramatic narrative followed Russian history and culture from ancient and medieval folklore and myth through the imperial, Soviet, and late Soviet eras. The program explained that spectators would experience Russian history through the dream of a young girl called "*Liubov*" (Love). Flying through the clouds of fog filling the arena, she functioned as a sort of framing device or leitmotif. While the sentimentality of this image probably surprised foreigners accustomed to Russia's aggressive posturing, it surely satisfied the Russians, who see themselves as a warm and loving people. As the ceremony progressed, however, connections between the symbolic Liubov/Love and her selectively panoramic dream of Russian history became increasingly vague.

Scenery began flying at us from above and below. Three enormous floats, replete with primitive huts, reindeer, horses, trees, and totem poles, appeared in the air behind me. Flown in from the opposite side, Liubov floated above a host of performers in theatrically heightened, white and gold, historical costume. A startlingly surrealistic moment of Olympic pageantry interrupted her dream of Russian history as a living red, white, and blue flag of the Russian Federation moved smartly onto the arena floor—and thus began the IOC's prescribed ritual. All at once, Liubov's pastoral dream yielded to a lively scene of dancing schmoos,[31] elegant, neofuturist women, and a parade of national teams emerging from beneath the arena's floor. The athletes entered to a relentless drumbeat, which intensified in tone and tempo for the Russians. Finally, Sochi's gigantic mascot puppets skated into the arena to welcome visitors to Russia's Olympiad. Despite occasional moments of stationary presentation, this ritual interlude felt more like a ramped up neo-Soviet mass festival or European football championship than a dignified presentation of athletes and Olympic VIPs. Following the presentation, Liubov's fantastic postmodern collage of Russian cultural history picked up where it had left off.

Ten visually stunning, kinesthetically affective scenarios nipped along,

Fig. 8.3. Liubov imagine Russian history. (Author photo, 2014.)

one after the other. The first three—"Russian Odyssey," "Sacred Spring," and "Maslenitsa"—alluded to ancient and medieval myth and folklore, while the next four—"I Love You Peter the Great," "Natasha Rostova's First Ball," "Time Forward! A Suprematist Ballet," and "A Walk around Moscow"—cited imperial and Soviet history. In the eleventh scenario, "Dream," Liubov reappeared to mark the end of our journey "between past and future." The Olympic fantasy, however, continued apace: the penultimate scenario featured a leading ballerina in a "Dove of Peace" ballet, while the last, "Olympic Gods," a "dynamic installation" of sparkling figures suspended in the cosmos, signified the godlike athletes who compete in the modern Winter Olympic Games.

I said "the last," but Russians like both big and long; thus, frozen spectators remained seated until tennis star Maria Sharapova carried the Olympic torch into the arena. Having traveled 8,000 miles—farther than any other Olympic torch—it arrived to be passed around the space by six prominent Russian athletes (including Putin's rumored paramour) before lighting the enormous, purple phallus planted just outside Fisht Stadium. Fireworks boomed above the stadium, marking the climax of Sochi 2014's Opening Ceremony. Volunteers dressed in their color-coded uniforms

Fig. 8.4. Cultural touchstones: Stravinsky's *Rite of Spring* accompanies Gogol's troika. (Author photo, 2014.)

herded 40,000 visitors efficiently past the flame and toward the Olympic Park station where they boarded the world's most modern train to travel safely home.

The next day, media across the globe agreed that the Russian spectacular was amazing. Writing in the state-controlled *Russian Gazette*, Nikolai Dolgovolov extolled the Sochi miracle: "Sochi's creators did in seven years what other countries would have taken fifteen years to achieve," he raved. "We showed that we were just as good as London and Beijing, and better than Vancouver. . . . Let's keep the celebration going!"[32] Konstantin Ernst enthused: "I've seen every Olympiad for the past twenty years and so I speak with absolute certainty—there's never been one like ours."[33] The *Russian Gazette*'s Il'ia Peresedov added, "The start of the Olympiad presented us with a celebration beyond our dreams." The ceremony was, he glowed, "original, sweeping, and fresh."[34] The Russian media crowed that Sochi 2014 marked Russia's return to great power status.

While Western media allowed that the Russians had produced an impressive Opening Ceremony, many correspondents put a rather more critical spin on the event. David Herszenhorn of the *New York Times* wrote:

Fig. 8.5. The monster purple Olympic phallus. (Author photo, 2014.)

What unfolded in the Fisht Olympic Stadium . . . was sheer pageantry and national pride, with all of the homespun promotionalism, myth-making and self-aggrandizement that are the modern trademark of such ceremonies."[35]

His colleague, Juliet Macur, looked for "the darkness behind Sochi's spar-kle." She wrote of the Opening Ceremony: "It was so entrancing and ran so smoothly, that it was tempting to forget what was behind the pageantry and sparkle."[36] In the *Washington Post*, Russian correspondents Kathy Lally and Will Englund wrote: "Every part of the program was written in the superla-tive." "The scale," they continued, "bordered on the colossal. If London on its small isle would do buzz, Russia would do big."[37] This largely positive review sat next to sports writer Sally Jenkins's article, "A Heart-Seizing Place of Deep Complexities," a much bleaker piece of reporting on the Sochi miracle. Observing (rightly) that "[t]he grim and the gorgeous coexist side by side at the Sochi Olympics," Jenkins enumerated the iniquities of Putin's Russia in general and the Sochi Games in particular: gay scapegoating, poor construc-tion, inefficiency, construction blight, and so on. She summarized:

Putin's Olympics is preposterously outsized, but by the end of the Opening Ceremonies, it was hard to call it artificial. These Games at once overreach and super-deliver: The torch relay traveled to the North Pole and into outer space, a journey so epic it obscured the fact that it frequently guttered out. . . . Yet when it finally flamed at the Olympic Park, the spectacle was frighteningly large. And that effect is precisely what he is after.[38]

Repeated boasting by Putin and his acolytes about Sochi's extravagant scale confirms Jenkins's impression, but size alone cannot account for the event's affect. Ernst and Tsypin directed and designed a monumental patchwork beholden for its style and affect to television, theater, and opera. Richard Wagner and Walter Gropius might have seen in Sochi's Opening Ceremony a total work of art that drew on music, movement, dance, rhythm, color, and all available stage technology to lure spectators into an ideal, sensual world of national myth. The dramatic images created by Tsypin moved with the intensity and rhythm of a gripping television drama. Accompanied by stirring music from Russia's greatest composers, the images and dramatic narrative created the overwhelming sensual experience proposed by Wagner as the goal of the *gesamtkunstwerk*. So powerfully affective was the performance that the various mythologies embedded therein appeared only retrospectively.

After sinking billions into an Olympiad, hosts naturally want to show off their exceptionality, but the IOC discourages nationalist display. The ceremonies, however, which rely for their affect on symbolic imagery, are always vulnerable to charges of nationalist posturing. Can a host nation divorce national feeling from a spectacular public performance of its cultural heritage—especially a former great power still recovering from its plummet to second-world status? No wonder that Sochi's Opening Ceremony seemed to critics to be driven in form and content by a nationalist agenda. While plenty of posturing happened during the ceremony, I argue that the national idea driving its substance and aesthetic was more opaque than its critics suggest. If Putin hoped for an Olympic ceremony that would function ideologically like a Stalin-era mass festival, Tsypin's postmodern bricolage of ancient, medieval, imperial, and Soviet imagery could hardly have satisfied the regime's propagandists.

The ceremony aimed to show off not only Russia's historical greatness but also Putin's modern, progressive, high-tech Russia. Considered individually, each scenario did show a history and culture of which Russians could justly be proud. Collectively, however, they exposed a nostalgic, post-Soviet historiography that underscored contributions to Russian society and culture by a few accomplished, highly Europeanized white men. *Russian Odyssey* connected Sochi to Greece, thereby erasing its Circassian heritage and links with other peoples of the Caucasus Mountain region. Among the Romanov tsars, only Petr I, the great Westernizer, merited a scenario, and among prominent writers and artists of the nineteenth century, only Leo Tolstoi's most iconic novel warranted representation. Twentieth-century scenarios were visually, aurally, and kinesthetically dazzling, but while the first, a biomechanical futurist ballet, acknowledged Kazimir Malevich, it erased Vsevolod Meierkhol'd, whose practices it clearly cited. The second, a vibrant vision of Moscow in the 1950s and '60s, included dynamic, but not entirely coherent, images of Vera Mukhina's Worker and Kolkhoz Woman monument, dancing cars and people, a skyscraper, and a parade of motorcycles. With that, Russian history and culture seemed to end. The Ceremony omitted most of the imperial period, the Bol'shevik Revolution, Lenin, Stalin, and all of late and post-Soviet history and culture. Women appeared only twice as idealized, fictional characters and only European Russia warranted representation; serfs, the proletariat, and communism vanished from the historical landscape. Even the Cossacks, a Caucasus Mountain staple, remained invisible in the ceremony's rendition of Russian history. While no one expected a comprehensive representation of the historical record, including the most unjust and bloodiest episodes, some surely hoped for more diversity. Putin, after all, tirelessly touted Sochi 2014 as an opportunity for visitors to experience the new, progressive Russia. Judging by the Opening Ceremony, "progressive" alluded only to the ceremony's high-tech production values. Not surprisingly, signs of a new *socially* progressive Russia remained for the most part hidden.

My reading of the Opening Ceremony would be incomplete without a brief interpretive foray into the Sochi mascots because, in microcosm, the hare, bear, and leopard selected to represent Russia epitomized the show of Putin's Russia as it manifested in Sochi 2014. Consistent with the usual function of mascots—or talismans, as the Russians call them—the Sochi mascots functioned symbolically. Like so much in Sochi, however, process and product conspired to create symbolic incoherence.

Olympic organizers concocted an allegedly democratic process for selecting the mascots, which included an open design competition and online voting. Like most Russian elections, however, this one wasn't what it seemed.

Fig. 8.6. A biomechanical ballet minus Meierkhol'd. (Author photo, 2014.)

First, an official committee cut the field to eleven designs: a dolphin, snow leopard, hare, snowman, Zoich, a matryoshka doll, Father Frost, Pedobear, two tiger cubs, an elf, and a hedgehog. Zoich, a comic psychedelic-blue toad (*zhaba*), won a large percentage of the vote, but suddenly disappeared from the list of finalists.[39] Soon, Pedobear's rumored dalliance with pedophilia caused him to vanish.[40] Father Frost went next when the organizers discovered they would have to cede the image's copyright to the IOC. Among the banished designs, Zoich caused the greatest bitterness among voters.

Conceived by illustrator Igor Zhgun, Zoich quickly became a popular antimascot. Trusting Zhgun's radical sensibilities, disaffected citizens gave Zoich a large, enthusiastic constituency. Indeed, seeing their vote as a kind of protest, Zoich's fans agreed to participate in a process that they might otherwise have boycotted.[41] Imagine, then, their feelings of betrayal when Zoich proved to be fraudulent. Ordered from Zhgun by the Organizing Committee, Zoich did precisely what she was intended to do: stimulate interest and increase voting among dissident youth, Russia's primary Internet users. When the toad looked like a winner, the Committee pulled her. Committee chair Dmitrii Chernyshenko admitted:

Despite Zoich's popularity, we never for a second forgot our main goal: to choose a mascot for the mass national audience (*dlia massovoi narod-noi auditorii*). A shaggy toad couldn't have pretensions to the role of an official mascot.[42]

Thus, to the chagrin of Zoich's supporters, the election of Olympic mascots, like so many other Russian elections, turned out to be imaginary.

Eventually, voters—or someone—selected three animals to represent the Games: a bear, a snow leopard, and a doe hare. Intriguingly, designs for the winning animals bore little resemblance to the cuddly polar bear, chubby bunny, and grinning leopard that eventually skated into Fisht Stadium. Their choice and generic redesign raise still more questions about the mascots; at some point in their formation, a perceived need for environmentally progressive imagery supplanted democratic process entirely.

New mythologies of Russian environmentalism began to emerge soon after Sochi won its Olympic bid—a strategic state response to international outcry against impending environmental disaster. Needing an environmental counternarrative, in 2008 the Kremlin PR office concocted a wacky scheme to transform Putin into an environmentally enlightened outdoorsman. Was the timing of his bare-chested, mountain man, PR offensive coincidental? What about the appearance on his prime-ministerial website of endangered species initiatives and photo ops? Did Putin's sudden interest in polar bears signify a new concern for global warming? Did his need for a vendible local environmental initiative in the Sochi region account for his sudden support for the snow leopards, which joined the polar bear on his website? As a symbol of Russianness, bears make perfect sense; indeed, a brown bear actually won first place in the voting. But why did it become a polar bear? Because polar bears, like the Sochi region's snow leopard, are endangered, and expressions of concern for endangered species and global warming signify "Russia, new, great, and open." Sadly, behind the environmentalist façade habitat destruction in the Sochi national park and reserve continued apace.

The un-endangered hare remains puzzling. The mascots' Facebook page explains that hares are ubiquitous and run fast, which says nothing about their symbolic suitability for Sochi 2014.[43] Perhaps to balance the geographical specificity of the polar bear and leopard, organizers needed another more universal symbol. The hare's gender reassignment also raises questions. The unmarked bear and leopard were assumed to be male, but

Fig. 8.7. Bear, bunny, and leopard: Sochi's environmentally friendly national mascots. (Author photo, 2014.)

the obviously male hare of the original design became an obviously feminine doe. A scrap to the gentler sex? Like so much connected with Sochi, the mascots' equivocal heterogeneity compromised their signifying function. No respectable Russian would rally around these cuddly critters as symbols of national resurrection.

SOCHI: A TOTAL WORK OF ART?

Can Sochi 2014 usefully be understood as a kind of post-Soviet, neo-Wagnerian *gesamtkunstwerk* with many of the attendant features and affects of unified production? Did the city perform and the performance show a resurrected Russian nation? Did it create new—or reify old—national mythologies? If so, did spectators buy in to them? My response is an equivocal yes and no.

To conceive of the city as a total work of art seems the more difficult task. Obviously, Wagner had in mind not the open space of a city, but a proscenium stage and the closed space of a theater building. Thus, in its more familiar, theatrical sense, the *gesamtkunstwerk* happens on a proscenium stage and creates affective illusion through limiting sight lines, dimming the lights, and concealing backstage machinery. Nonetheless, as noted above, Russians have for decades reimagined and repurposed the *gesamtkunstwerk*; Malte Rolfe's application of the concept to the Soviet mass festival may help to illuminate my own understanding of Sochi as a post-Soviet *gesamtkunstwerk*.

> The idea of the Soviet celebration incorporated much of Wagner's vision. . . . The Soviet holiday was a day when the entire Soviet Union was to celebrate. . . . It blended the huge community of celebrators in an act of creative synthesis. The official celebration—as one thoroughgoing work of art—was itself made up of many smaller festivities in local and regional milieus. According to the propaganda experts' plans, these many simultaneous festivities were supposed to help the "whole country" to not only pitch in collectively to make the grand projects of communism a success but also to come together on a Soviet holiday as one great community of celebrators.[44]

Rolfe might be describing Sochi 2014: not just the Games, but also regional revival, months of pre-Olympic sporting and cultural events, and relentless PR. As tensions over human, economic, and environmental costs grew, the Kremlin increasingly characterized Sochi as a celebration, a national holiday (*narodnyi prazdnik*) for the Russian people. Naturally, Team Russia's gold medal count pumped public enthusiasm, but for more than seven years, Team Kremlin pressed Russians to embrace the Sochi project as a victory for the nation. Sochi, the Kremlin PR apparatus maintained, would unite citizens into "one great community of celebrators." Indeed, both before and after the Games, the Kremlin professed an involvement by "the people" that bordered on fiction.

In point of fact, the Kremlin produced the city's revival the way a Wagnerian master artist produces theatrical illusion in the service of national myth. Using Sochi as its political and aesthetic compass, the state—not the people—created the illusion of a resurrected Russian nation, while reviving the myth of Russian exceptionalism. It not only made Sochi, but also made Sochi "mean." Unfortunately, Sochi's master artist faced two insurmountable obstacles: the media, which kept the machinery visible throughout the production process and performance, and skeptical visitors anxious to peek backstage. No wonder that the Kremlin struggled to maintain the illusion.

Fig. 8.8. The author
with a close friend.
(Author photo, 2014.)

How could it be otherwise? Post-Soviet Russia is not, after all, "new, great, and open," a reality that left Sochi's makers with a conundrum: how to show a deeply divided, increasingly authoritarian nation that still suffers from post–great-power trauma as an economically powerful, socially progressive, democratic nation prepared to function as an equal partner with the West. As bad luck would have it, the Crimean invasion further undercut the illusion Sochi strove to create.

To understand the Opening Ceremony as a neo-Wagnerian *gesamt-kunstwerk* presents fewer obstacles. Music, dance, rhythm, space, scenery, and performers synchronized to produce a unified *Dream About Russia* that drew spectators into a spectacular—albeit dubiously historical—narrative of Russian greatness. But did the absence of fact trouble spectators? Wagner would surely argue that a total work of art relies not on fact, but on myth, for its affect. Thus, it mattered not that invention, illusion, and spectacle shaped audience response to Liubov's *Dream*. Spectators willing to suspend their disbelief experienced a resurrected great power, while the less willing enjoyed the spectacular excess, but rather than resurrection, saw a Russia wallowing in selective moments of imperial and Soviet nostalgia and still deeply invested in regressive sociocultural practices. After all, despite the brilliance of the images, the *Dream's* narrative attributed innovation very narrowly: representing Russian cultural history as white, masculinist, and European, it erased Sochi's much-vaunted multiculturalism, Central Asia, and, for the most part, women. Liubov's postmodern *Dream* intended to remind spectators of Russian greatness through historical citation; what it did instead was to show off Russian stage technology and artistic conception at their commercial best.

In a word, the state produced and Sochi performed an astonishing illusion of "Russia, New, Great, Open."

Notes

1. Boris Groys, *The Total Art of Stalinism*, trans. Charles Rougle (London: Verso, 2011; original publication, 1992).

2. For accounts of Wagnerian influences on Russian, Soviet, and post-Soviet culture, see, among others, James von Geldern, *Bolshevik Festivals, 1917–1920* (Berkeley: University of California Press, 1993), 30–39; Malte Rolfe, *Soviet Mass Festivals, 1917–1991* (Pittsburgh: University of Pittsburgh Press, 2013), 64–65; Mark Lipovetsky, "Anything Goes: How the Russian News Became a Postmodern Game without Rules," *Calvert Journal*, March 10, 2015, http://calvertjournal.com/comment/show/3736/political-steampunk-postmodern-game-mark-lipovetsky, accessed December 12, 2015. In this chapter, I appropriate freely from all of these theorists and scholars.

3. Carol Martin, "Performing the City," *TDR: The Drama Review* 58, no. 3 (Fall 2014): 10–17.

4. Maurice Roche, *Mega-Events and Modernity* (New York: Routledge, 2000), 135–38.

5. Oleg Galitskikh, "Olimpstroi," *Rossiiskaia gazeta*, August 15, 2007: http://www.rg.ru/printable/2007/08/15/sochi.html, accessed June 2, 2014.

6. "Podemnik na Olimp," *Rossiiskaia gazeta*, August 8, 2007: http://www.rg.ru/printable/2007/08/08/tyagachev-sochi.html, accessed June 2, 2014.

7. The Soviets also rebuilt cities as showplaces of innovation. See Rolf, *Soviet Mass Festivals, 1917–1991*, 80–83.

8. The liberal *Novaia gazeta* published many pieces on the new Sochi laws. See, for example, "'Olimpiiskie popravki' pozvoliat bez suda izymat' nedvizhimost' u rossiian," *Novaia gazeta*, September 14, 2007; "Strana v olimpiiskom rezerve," *Novaia gazeta*, September 24, 2007; "Prishli, uvideli, snesli," *Novaia gazeta*, October 8, 2007.

9. But Russia wanted gold. See Sam Dolnick, "Russians with Deep Pockets Adopt Teams Going for Gold," *New York Times*, January 25, 2104, A1.

10. "*Interv'iu Vladimira Putina rossiiskim i inostrannym SMI*," January 19, 2014. Readers can find a transcript of the interview at www.rg.ru/2014/01/19/putin-site.html. All translations are my own.

11. Anastasia Bogdanov, "Olimpiada stala obediniaiushchei ideei dlia Rossii," *gazeta.ru*, February 24, 2014: http://www.gazeta.ru/sochi2014/2014/02/24/a_5925433.shtml. The sports writer was Vladimir Gomelskii.

12. Levada Center polling indicates that although Russians saw the Olympiad as an image-making scheme, they generally supported it. They also thought that it was too expensive and corrupt. See, among many others, "Rossiiane o zimnikh olimpiskiikh igrakh," *Levada Center*, July 19, 2007; "Obshchestvennoe mnenie o izderzhkakh Olimpiady," *Levada Center*, June 27, 2013. Just before the Games opened, Maksim Glikin wrote in *Vedomosti* that no one wanted another Olympiad in Russia ("Olimpiad bol'she ne nado," February 5, 2014) and on February 12, 2014, Levada's Lev Gudkov said, "Only 23% of Russians consider the Olympiad important" (*Tol'ko 23% rossian schitaiut Olimpiady vazhnoi*).

13. The World Wildlife Fund Russia published too many documents to cite all of them here. Readers can find them at www.wwf.ru. Published by the United Nations Environment Programme, "Sochi 2014—Otchet Vyezdnoi Gruppy Iunep," is useful; www.unep.org. *Novaia gazeta* also published many articles critical of Sochi environmental policy; among the best is "Za fasadom Olimpiady—2014," *Novaia gazeta*, July 4, 2008: http://www.novayagazeta.ru/society/39502.html?print=1

14. https://www.facebook.com/NoSochi2014

15. An English version of the Sochi bid book can be accessed at https://web.archive.org/web/20080602124904/http://sochi2014.com/sch_questionnaire?PRINT_VIEW=YES

16. "Interv'iu Vladimira Putina rossiiskim i inostrannym SMI."

17. "Vse v gorodskom khoziaistve iavlaetsia glavnym, poietomy vo vse vnikaiu," *Ogni* 8, no. 16 (2010): 64–71.

18. "Malyi biznes kruphym planom," *Ogni* 5, no. 35 (May 2102): 7.

19. "Zima zakonchilas' . . . da zdravstvyet vesna!," *Ogni* 3, no. 11 (March/April 2010): 5.

20. "Mai—prekrasnoe vremia dlia samorealizatsii," *Ogni* 4, no. 12 (April/May 2010): 5.

21. "Suverenyi narod—Sochinitsy, *Ogni* 5, no. 13 (May/June 2010): 5.

22. "U kazhdogo svoi p'edestal," *Ogni*, 12, no. 51 (December 2013): 9.

23. Marina Akhmedova, "Komu ulybaets' Sochi," *Kommersant*, February 10, 2014; http://www.kommersant.ru/doc/2398749?isSearch=True, accessed June 21, 2014.24.

24. David Herszenhorn, "A Russian Protest Zone Where Almost No One Registers a Complaint," *New York Times*, February 13, 2014. http://www.nytimes.com/2014/02/14/world/europe/a-russian-protest-zone-where-almost-no-one-registers-a-complaint.html?_r=0, accessed October 10, 2014.

25. For an eye-opening account of Olympic commerce and commercialization, see Jules Boykoff, *Celebration Capitalism and the Olympic Games* (New York: Routledge, 2014).

26. Roche, *Mega-Events and Modernity*, 135–38.

27. See "Komu ulybaetsia Sochi." One of Akhmedova's subjects called Sochi Nice on the Black Sea.

28. David Frimen, "Udivit' ves' mir," *Pervyi kanal*, February 5, 2014.

29. For the development of protocol, see Roche, *Mega-Events and Modernity*. Current IOC protocol for the Opening Ceremony can be found at http://www.olympic.org/Documents/Reference_documents_Factsheets/Opening_ceremony_of_the_Olympic_Winter_Games.pdf; accessed November 6, 2014.

30. For more images, see Tsypin's website at http://georgetsypin.com/www/?page_id=1592; accessed September 3, 2014.

31. Schmoos were little, rotund white creatures that appeared in Al Capp's serial cartoon, *Lil' Abner*. Costumed in thick white vests and caps, these dancing extras looked from a distance like schmoos.

32. Nikolai Dolgovolov, "Sochi: Belaia noch'," *Rossiiskaia gazeta*, February 8, 2014, 1.

33. Quoted by Anna Kozina in "Liubov' v bol'shom gorode," *Rossiiskaia gazeta*, February 10, 2014: https://rg.ru/2014/02/10/geroinya.html, accessed November 24, 2014.

34. Il'ia Peresedov, "Kuda letit 'Lastochka,'" *Rossiiskaia gazeta*, February 11, 2014.

35. David Herszenhorn, "Olympics Opening Ceremony Offers Fanfare for a Reinvented Russia," *New York Times*, February 7, 2014.

36. Juliet Macur, "The Darkness behind Sochi's Sparkle," *New York Times*, February 7, 2014.

37. Kathy Lally and Will Englund, "Games Open with Dazzling Spectacle," *Washington Post*, February 8, 2014, A1.

38. Sally Jenkins, "A Heart-Seizing Place of Deep Complexities," *Washington Post*, February 8, 2014, A1.

39. "Egor Zhgun iznachal'no sozdaval Zoicha dlia Orgkomiteta 'Sochi 2014,'" *Sostav.ru*, June 15, 2011; http://www.sostav.ru/news/2011/06/15/doc2. Slate also covered the Zoich scandal. See http://www.slate.com/blogs/five_ring_circus/2014/02/07/zoich_sochi_olympics_2014_meet_the_futurama_themed_faux_viral_sochi_mascot.html, accessed December 2, 2014.

40. For the Pedobear scandal, see "Kaliforniiskaia politsiia napugala roditelei 'medvedem-pedofilom' iz interneta," *Newru.com*, September 13, 2010; http://www.newsru.com/world/13sep2010/pedobear.html, accessed December 2, 2014.

41. See, for example, Iaroslav Zagorets, "Oni ubili zhabu," *Novopolitika*, June 23, 2011; http://novolitika.info/news/45916, accessed December 11, 2014.

42. "*Egor Zhgun iznachal'no sozdaval Zoicha dlia Orgkomiteta 'Sochi 2014,*'" *Sostav.ru*, June 15, 2011; http://www.sostav.ru/news/2011/06/15/doc2/, accessed December 11, 2014.

43. https://www.facebook.com/Sochi2014.olympic/info?tab=page_info

44. Rolfe, *Soviet Mass Festivals*, 64.

SECTION III

Provocation and Titillation
To Show Off the Unshown

Section III most powerfully illustrates one of the least expected distinctions of showing off and up: hiding, promising, and teasing. Authors challenge the idea that showing off and up must be spectacular and shiny, or have artistic, political or commercial intent. Their essays endeavor to show how the quotidian and unremarkable can be made visible in remarkable and unexpected ways, thereby revealing social truths that might otherwise be concealed, disguised, or only insinuated. Showing moves from the private into the public sphere, and from intimate into invited. Here, authors describe intangible, processual, promised, or forbidden shows and performances that are distinctly mediated. Context becomes an even more crucial marker in the experience. What is generated or "hastened into being" might be highly subjective experiences of the paranormal, fervent nationalism, tolerance of diverse sexual practices, or a false start in the performance art scene. The possibility of the unexpected is essential to these shows' success. Asking whether subtle, more elusive genres of showing can, like their more spectacular cousins, be experienced viscerally, these essays demonstrate the latent power of invisibility, imagery, signs, and symbols.

CHAPTER 9

The Intimate Provocations of Showing Religion in Secular France

Elayne Oliphant

Debates around the "*burqa*"[1] reverberated in the French public sphere during the two years I spent in Paris between 2008 and 2010. They called out from the headlines of newspapers, they were deliberated on radio talk shows, and they were the subject of many conversations I overheard and in which I participated. This audible racket, however, always contrasted sharply with the visual absence of these sights on the streets of Paris. As I moved, lived, researched, and worked in the twenty *arrondissements* of the French capital between 2008 and 2010, I never, in fact, encountered a single *niqab*. This haunting omnipresence made me take note when, on two occasions, my eyes caught sight of women dressed in long, dark, flowing robes. Each time, I was surprised enough to want to confirm that my eyes had not deceived me. On both occasions, I pursued the women in order to catch a glimpse of them from the front. After running to position myself ahead of them on the street, however, I realized that the women I saw were not dressed in *niqabs*, but in the very similar garb that is nuns' clothing. And each time I was struck by how the presence of these garments in the streets appeared to cause very little reaction from those around me.

Legislation aimed at limiting and regulating the presence of the *niqab* in the French public sphere has been justified with reference to the particularity of the country's commitment to *laïcité* (secularism). According to discourses in the media and the National Assembly, *laïcité*—which originated in but has been updated numerous times since 1905—both requires and produces a public sphere in which all signs of religion are absent. "Immigrants" (a word which, in France, often also conveys an image of practitioners of Islam), such discourses tend to claim, do not understand the importance of *laïcité* in France. Their dress confirms their outsider status (whether or not this mode of dress in fact aligns with the wearer's citizenship). By inappropriately rendering their internal religious beliefs externally visible, those who bear these signs muddy the neutrality of public life. The solution requires these "immigrants" to "integrate" by accepting the importance of *laïcité* in France and ceasing to display their religious identities.

One way to account for this particularly strident interpretation of *laïcité* is to see it as a local expression of what might be described as the conservatism of the public sphere. In public life, theorists such as Michael Warner (2002) have noted, one is rewarded for blending in, or at least not shocking through displays, gestures, or expressions of distinctiveness. Warner's important argument hinges on the fact that structures of power allow certain subjects to blend in more easily than others. Those who move freely in the public sphere of the modern West, generally, are "implicitly, even explicitly, white, male, literate, and propertied. These traits could go unmarked, even grammatically, while other features of bodies could only be acknowledged in discourse as the humiliating positivity of the particular" (166). The concept of showing off provides us with a framework through which to explore how this process of normalization is locally produced and reproduced. Determining which acts, sign, and gestures stand out in public life in fact requires two forms of social work: first, is the power to *ascribe* the act of showing off—an intentional and provocative act of display—to others; and second is the work required to make other actions, signs, and gestures blend in, of formulating an unmarked norm against which the marked is forced to stand apart.

In what follows I examine a number of public acts of the ascription of showing off—on the streets of Paris (as observed through newspapers and a human rights organization's report), in a site of orchestrated and televised debate on the relationship between clothing and subjects, and in an online forum on "national identity." I then explore these discursive ascriptions of showing off in light of the simultaneous work of normalization.[2] The power to accuse groups and individuals of suspect acts of showing off, I argue, obscures the equally powerful acts of normalizing inherent within such statements. In France, the distinction between the marked and the unmarked is often described as that between "religious" and "secular." Rather than taking the distinction between religious and secular for granted, in this chapter I demonstrate how ascribing suspect and inappropriate acts of showing off to bearers of the *niqab* creates and re-creates the boundaries between religious and secular. I argue that the ascription of "religious" to particular objects and signs in France is, in fact, the power to mark particular signs as provocative acts of showing off. I will conclude by demonstrating how, in contrast, signs of Catholicism are able to circulate unmarked and unseen in the French public sphere; such an imbalance, I argue, forces us to rethink the self-evident and naturalized distinction between religious and secular in France.

According to Talal Asad, it is the secular state that has "the final authority to determine whether the meaning of given symbols . . . is 'religious'" (2006, 500). In analyzing earlier claims made against "Islamic" signs in France during the Stasi Commission,[3] Asad points to the French state's power to define the headscarf as an exclusively religious sign. This capacity to limit the headscarf as an "eternally fixed" sign of Islam is not "some historical *reality* . . . but *another sign* . . . which, despite its overflowing character, is used to give the 'Islamic veil' a stable meaning" (502). Similarly, following Judith Butler (1990) and William Egginton (2003), I will explore how ascriptions of religious to certain objects (and not to others) are "performative" in that they "affect or even produce what they purport merely to describe" (Egginton 2003, 5). The *niqab*, rather than an always-already religious sign, is produced as such through proclamations of the need to forbid it in a public sphere replete with architectural and festive signs of Catholicism. In this highly unequal public sphere, bearing Islamic signs is presented as showing off in excess, while those associated with Catholicism are able to pass as secular when they do not appear as demonstrative displays, but instead go unseen, unregulated, and unmarked.

ENFORCING *LAÏCITÉ* IN THE PUBLIC SPHERE

An article published in the *Guardian*, a British paper, in September 2011[4] recounts the story of Hind Ahmas who was born in France to nonreligious Muslim parents of Moroccan origin. When she was in her thirties Ahmas decided to don a *niqab* in her daily life. She explained to the reporter that the man who is now her ex-husband played no part in the decision to renew her faith with a veil that covered much of her face (but not her eyes), long flowing gowns, and gloves. While dressing in such a way was never "simple" or straightforward in France, since the law banning "full-face veils" was proposed in June 2009[5] her situation has become increasingly untenable. Her employment contract at a telemarketing firm was not renewed and she has encountered the anger of many in Paris who have taken it upon themselves to enforce the state's newest law aimed at renewing France's commitment to *laïcité*.

The *Guardian* reporter describes her arrival with Ahmas at a café in the suburbs of Paris. The atmosphere altered as they entered; outrage and disgust were evident on many of the faces of the men gathered around the bar, sipping their morning coffee. The waiter behind the bar demanded that she account for herself: "wait a minute, isn't this banned?!" In response, Ahmas declared that if she were indeed committing a crime he could call the police. But she also backed down by turning and exiting the café in favor of another across the street. At this second café she described to the reporter some of her experiences in recent months: a man and a woman approached her on the streets, "punched her in front of her daughter," and demanded she "return to Algeria"; bus drivers refused her access to public transportation; and she has been uncertain as to whether she would be served at cafés or in offices of the state. Quoting a French politician who described *niqabs* as "walking prisons," she explained that—thanks to the law—this is precisely what they have become.

Ahmas's story, unfortunately, is not unique. In April 2011, the Open Society Foundation published a study of French women who wear a *niqab*. According to the study, "the day following President Sarkozy's main speech[6] on the full-face veil in June 2009, members of the public tried to physically assault two of the study's participants. One of these women, who had been wearing a *niqab* for over ten years, was confronted by a man who threatened her with a knife" (Open Society Foundation 2011, 17). Of the thirty-two women interviewed for the study, passers-by verbally or physically assaulted thirty in the months following the president's speech. While many in France had condemned the *niqab* prior to Sarkozy's address at the Palais de Versailles, its explicit denunciation by the president gave these critiques new authority. The *Guardian* reporter notes that anti-Islamophobia organizations have reported a

> worrying increase in discrimination and verbal and physical violence against women in veils. There have been instances of people in the street taking the law into their hands and trying to rip off full-face veils, of bus drivers refusing to carry women in the *niqab* or of shop-owners trying to bar entry. A few women have taken to wearing bird-flu-style medical masks[7] to keep their face covered.[8]

The article concludes that, rather than reducing the number of full-face veils in France, the law's only real effect seems to have been to legitimate expressions of Islamophobia in daily life.

An alarming amount of evidence points to a rise in Islamophobia in recent years in France[9] and Europe[10] alike. As the experience of Ahmas suggests, increasingly heavy-handed legislation has exacerbated physical and verbal attacks on Muslims. The sociologist Nilüfer Göle (2010) has argued that legislative restrictions on the visibility of Islam in Europe have had the unintended consequence of affirming the undeniable *presence* of Muslims throughout the continent. For Göle, rather than the signs they work to prohibit, it is laws such as the 2011 ban on full-face veils that threaten the very existence of the lauded European public sphere (famously described by Habermas [1991]), because they limit both freedom of movement in public space and call into question the ideal of an abstract space of rational debate. The state's heavy-handed legislation, that is, has determined and limited discourses and debates surrounding the incorporation of sights, identities, practices, and people connected to Islam.

While visual signs displayed on women's bodies have occupied public attention, such anxieties around visibility are not a self-evident response to a perceived threat. It is not obvious that signs such as *burqas*, *niqabs*, and veils[11] should receive the brunt of Islamophobic anxieties. Elsewhere (Oliphant 2012) I have explored the contradictions that accompany semiotic ideologies (Keane 2005) that simultaneously insist upon and deny the agentive power of visible signs. Here, I argue that while broadly accepted semiotic ideologies in France may insist that that objects do not have agency, as strangers remove veils from women's faces, and presidents describe this mode of dress as a walking prison, such assertions betray an underlying assumption that while certain objects can remain passive, others must be confronted as dangerously active. A woman who shows off a full-face veil in the streets of France today is frequently described as both choosing to offend the secular sensibilities of the French public sphere and unwittingly revealing the limitations of her subjecthood wrought by the oppressive terms of her culture and religion. As a remedy, in forbidding the wearing of the *burqa* and *niqab*, the French state is both refusing a presumably provocative act of showing off and arguing that, by removing particularly active signs, it can produce properly modern and secular subjects.

RELIGION AS INTIMACY

I now want to turn to a televised debate on the relationship between dress, subjects, and agents held at the Catholic cultural center recently opened in the center of Paris.[12] I conducted two years of ethnographic research at the Collège des Bernardins. A quick glance at the soaring vaults and columns of the central nave may appear to land one squarely in the cultural apex of the Middle Ages. Closer scrutiny, however, could call attention to how certain details—such as the designer chairs that fill the Collège's café—nod to current-day markers of wealth and sophistication. The French Catholic Church succeeded in securing funding from the municipal, regional, and national governments—as well as donations from major French corporations—in order to renovate the building. While the 1905 law of *laïcité* prohibits state funding of religious spaces, because the Collège is presented as a "cultural" rather than "religious" space (no masses are held under its vaults) it was able to receive public funds and invite the minister of culture, former presidents, and the mayor of Paris to the building's inauguration, which included a speech from Pope Benedict XVI. I worked here as a mediator (médiatrice)[13] for the contemporary art exhibitions it displayed between 2009 and 2010. Long days in front of exhibitions that did not always see a lot of traffic provided numerous opportunities for conversations of all sorts with my fellow employees. One topic to which we turned with some frequency was the "ostentatiousness" of the *burqa*. In these conversations that punctuated our work of demonstrating the relevance of Catholic "culture" in France's history and present in a space that had received funding from the secular French state, my interlocutors insisted that showing the *burqa* in public was simply "too much." In objecting to these supposed acts of showing off, these critics implicitly took on the mantle of representatives of unmarked public subjects.

Linguistic anthropologist Susan Gal has described the implications of the slippery distinction between the public and private spheres—categories she describes as "fractals"—in the modern West.[14] Like the categories of religious and secular, Gal argues that "public and private do not simply describe the social world in any direct way; they are rather tools for arguments about and in that world" (2002, 79). Actions, persons, or symbols may be variously described as public or private depending on the frame in which they are held. One may create a private space inside a public space, or vice versa, in ways that do not call attention to these contradictions. "The fractal nature of distinctions such as the public/private allows people to experience them as stable and continuous, in spite of changes in the contents of the distinction" (91). Thus, while the archdiocese's purchase of the Collège transferred it from the public sphere to the private (in that it was no longer owned by the city), the Church also claimed that the site merited public funding due to the "cultural," rather than "religious," nature of the Collège's programming. A similar slippage between religious and secular is also occurring. In purchasing the building "back" from the state (it was expropriated following the French Revolution of 1789), the Church was reclaiming this space as its own. Inside of this religious space, however, nonreligious (or secular) activities of "culture" occur, even if they were planned and approved by the archbishop.

In the fall of 2010, the Collège hosted a roundtable discussion entitled *L'habit, fait-il toujours le moine?* The phrase is a somewhat uncomfortable reversal of the phrase *L'habit ne fait pas le moine*, best translated into English as "the clothing doesn't make the man" or, a less common phrase but one that maintains the religious connotations of the French rendering, "the habit doesn't make the nun" (although, in the French version, it is the monk, not the nun, who is the subject). The title of the roundtable discussion reverses this common phrase, asking instead "does the habit always make the monk?" The roundtable was part of the weekly series Bernardins Tuesdays, which brings together a group of experts to discuss current events. The first hour was televised live on KTO (the Catholic television station) and then, once the cameras were turned off, the audience was given the opportunity to ask questions.

To the immediate left of the moderator sat Mehrezia Laidi-Maïza, a scholar on reason and women in Islam and the vice-president of the European branch of the World Organization of Religions for Peace. Next to her sat Jean Baubérot, a professor emeritus at the École politique des hautes études and the research chair of the history and sociology of secularism. Finally, seated facing the moderator was Aude Roy, a former director of two fashion houses in France and currently a "life coach in professional images." Laidi-Maïza, a woman of Moroccan origin, wore a white scarf wrapped around her head, pulled back far under her chin, descending down her neck, and tucked into a loose fitting red sweater over which she wore a black suit jacket. Baubérot, a small, older white man wore a gray suit that was slightly too large for him, sitting with difficulty on his shoulders, and an equally large red and white striped tie, fastened loosely around his neck. Roy, a tall and slender white woman, wore a jacket that was cropped at the waist and made of a combination of black leather and red tweed. Her dark brunette hair was cut evenly just below her ears, and the low cut of her jacket and her shirt revealed her neck and chest (but not her cleavage).

After allowing Laïdi-Maïza and Baubérot a brief moment to introduce themselves, the host of the program then turned to the former director of fashion design houses turned life coach. "You are a woman," he said with a grin, "for whom clothes are very important . . . at least professionally speaking."[15] He then asked her to account for her career shift from consultant in the fashion world to life coach. Her lilting voice, rising ever so slightly at the end of each of her sentences, was punctuated by the gently flowing gestures of her hands. "Indeed, I spent many absolutely *divine* years surrounded by the most beautiful women in the world—that ought to please you, Monsieur," she said with a smile and arched brow to Baubérot—"and the most magnificent artisans who are the treasures of France, of course, who make marvels for women around the world." Roy went on to describe how she had been working the long, strenuous hours required in the world of fashion and then, she shrugged, "I found myself married, and with a son . . . and I wanted, of course, to be more present both for my son, of course, and for my husband as well, to be his wife. So, I decided to bring all that I had learned during these twenty years about beauty in all its forms to those people who either wanted or needed it. Now I am a coach in visual communication, which means that I can both take advantage of my knowledge in terms of clothing, color, and form and also give all the secrets," she paused and lowered her voice to a stage whisper, "that concern gestures. Because our image is not only what we wear, but also the way in which we move. It is everything that we present to be seen."

A number of observations can be made about these introductory remarks. The ease of Roy's speech demonstrated how generalizable she took her experience of the world to be. Her encounters with beautiful women, she presumed, would necessarily pique the interest of the man to her left; the artisans she worked with were capable of designing clothing that are objects of beauty around the world; her desire to be a wife and mother would "of course" require her to be more present in the home and to shift careers accordingly. Statements such as those made by Roy do the work of encouragement, or, in other words, the work of unmarking or normalizing certain kinds of signs, actions, and experiences. Moreover, in her introductory remarks, she also managed to convey the remarkable coherence she attaches to the "selves" that move in public (or professional) spaces. Describing one's image, or one's public persona as "everything we present to be seen" suggests not only that subjects are capable of representing fully consistent selves to others in part through dress and gestures, but that these selves and signs may be clearly read by those we encounter.

The host seemed to quite enjoy Roy's remarks and responded that he liked a certain phrase she has been known to use: *"l'habit ne fait pas le moine mais il le laisse d'entrer dans le monastaire"* (the clothing does not make the monk but it allows him to enter into the monastery). "What does this mean?" he asked with a bemused smile. "Well," she replied, "I find that the monk and the monastery provide an excellent metaphor for me because I can explain to people that, in order to facilitate their professional integration, and this is very French," she lifted her eyebrows suggestively as she paused for a brief laugh, "they need to dress according to the monastery of their choice." Given the violence of the response to signs of Islam in France, the seeming unproblematic way in which the monastery stands in as a proxy for the secular French public or professional sphere in Roy's metaphor is remarkable, especially given the debate's occurrence in a building that once functioned as a monastery. Her presumed authority in being able to describe that which is "very French," moreover, does precisely the sort of work of encouraging and normalizing particular notions of citizenship. Those who are French, that is, know that, rather than showing their religious identities, they have to work to blend into the "monastery" of their choice.

Next, the host turned to Labidi-Maïza to ask how, as a specialist on the role of women in Islam, she could help the audience understand a question currently at the heart of French society. "Because one of the most visible elements of women's Islamic identity, which you are wearing, and I was wondering if you could say, personally, for you, what place you give to the veil and do you think there is an important element of your identity that you would like to express, transmit to your colleagues, to those in the street, to those close to you?" Coming on the heels of the host's friendly conversation about monasteries with Roy, his question to Labidi-Maïza felt abrupt and revealed the true inspiration behind the evening's debate. Furthermore, his question demonstrated how the host took for granted that, in wearing a headscarf, Labidi-Maïza was showing off, purposefully intending to "transmit" her identity to others. Folding her hands and leaning forward, Labidi-Maïza repeated his phrase "an important place? Not really," she said. "That is to say, it is part of an entire manner of living and it is not the essential. . . . In the Qu'ran there are two verses that speak about women's clothing. The first is simply about covering one's breasts; the other is about placing a scarf over the hair." She went on to explain that these verses have held various levels of importance over time and that, at certain moments, "a woman choosing to wear a headscarf would not have to justify herself, just as she would not have to justify praying."

Reinserting herself into the conversation, Roy acknowledged that she found Labidi-Maïza's account of the two verses in the Qu'ran to be very interesting. She always makes clear to her clients is that "no intimate articles of clothing and no intimate parts of the body should be shown in professional life and professional spaces. For, once these are visible, the nature of the conversation changes; the conversation is no longer a professional conversation, but an intimate conversation, that is, seduction. And religion," she continued "is part of intimacy, of the intimate convictions of each of us within ourselves. And so it seems completely logical that this intimacy does not have a place in the professional world either. This intimacy—that which I believe, my religion—is of the order of my intimate convictions."

Labidi-Maïza countered Roy's claim and argued that "there is a difference between the intimacy of the body and the intimacy of religion, of ideas, of philosophy. . . . I could, without shocking others, speak about my religion, my ideas, my philosophy. I could do this without entering into contact with the intimate space of others. I would not use the word 'intimate' to describe that which concerns people's ideas." Roy replied to Labidi-Maïza's position curtly, dismissing her fellow participant's views as those of a foreigner. "In *French* social life," Roy retorted, "we don't discuss our religion or our politics at a dinner party; this is the code here. In France, my religious convictions are part of an intimate sphere that should not be displayed." With these words Roy gave remarkable power to her rather strange equation between a bra strap and religious beliefs and practices by, once again, articulating her position not as particular but as that of the French community at large. In so doing, she also insisted that Labidi-Maïza's position was incorrect by virtue of its particularity, as the opinion of someone who Roy does not include in the national community.

The manner in which Roy accomplished this coup is fascinating. The notion that religion is an "intimate" affair, comparable to showing a "*string*" (the French word for thong, an example which Roy summoned more than once) at a corporate meeting, reveals much about the gendered nature of ideas of public and private as well as secular and religious. Initially, Labidi-Maïza occupied the position of an unmarked (i.e., masculine) scholar, while

Roy stood in for French femininity. The tables turned, however, with the host's question, asking Labidi-Maïza to speak as as a bearer of the headscarf, immediately feminizing the expert by transforming her into an overtly religious subject. This inversion subsequently allowed Roy to take up the position of the unmarked French public, interpreting the "codes" for the benefit of this representative of a particular (i.e., feminized) identity who could not be expected to understand their complexity.[16]

Roy's account of that which is "French," moreover, is a rather generous interpretation of the actual legal conception of *laïcité*. Roy, however, is not the only person in France to make such a claim in recent years. On his blog[17] in September 2012, Roy's fellow debate participant, Baubérot, took one of France's most famous feminists to task for making similar claims. "Believing in God," Élisabeth Badinter declared in the monthly publication *Le Monde des religions*, "must remain a private affair." In advancing this claim, Badinter suggested that the only person who continued to defend secularism in France was Marine Le Pen, the leader of the far-right-wing party the National Front.

Badinter then went on to catalogue a series of the external signs of religion currently polluting French public spaces. As Baubérot notes in his blog, Badinter did not list examples of all religions equally. Instead, she highlighted kosher food and the Kippa, Halal food, and Muslim clothing. While Baubérot acknowledges that Badinter has the right to "detest" religions all she pleases, her insistence that religion only has the right to be "displayed" in the private sphere is, in fact "completely contrary to the law of 1905." He then quotes from Article 1 of the 1905 law: "The Republic guarantees freedom of conscience. It guarantees freedom of worship, subject only to restrictions in the interest of public order." Here Baubérot is pointedly countering the false but widely held assumption in France that *laïctié* is, first and foremost, concerned with the restriction of religious signs. During debates surrounding the creation of the 1905 law, the majority of deputies refused to add an amendment that would forbid the wearing of religious dress in the streets. Those in favor of the amendment, Baubérot points out, also called the clothing of priests and nuns "provocative" and "contrary to human liberty and dignity" and declared that it renders those who wear it "prisoners and slaves" and "separates them" from the rest of men. The perception of those signs deemed too "religious," therefore, change across space and time. Yesterday's habit, it would seem, is today's *niqab*.

A number of feminists in France (see Gaspard and Khoroskhavar 1995), including Badinter,[18] have come out in support of the banning of "full-face coverings" in France, giving credence to the government's claims that the law is intended to liberate Muslim women by legislating equality between the sexes.[19] Similarly, Mayanthi Fernando (2010 and 2014) describes how the Republican state has seized upon examples of a few Muslim women in France who have vocally described their personal experiences of oppression within Islam and have "emerged as vociferous proponents of the ban" (2010, 380). Incorporating some Muslim "others" into notions of French citizenship, Fernando argues, works to emphasize the greater "incommensurability" of broader forms of Muslim difference. Analyses of the symbolic weight women are made to carry in the reproduction of the state and national identity are well known. Paul Silverstein argues that when women wear symbols associated with Islam in France, such acts are perceived as nothing less than a "potential threat to the moral order" (2004a, 142). He insists, furthermore, that it is *laïcité* that is operating as the "national religion" that women are ideally supposed to reproduce in France. In contrast to Silverstein's claims, I would argue that the debate at the Collège demonstrates that secularism in France cannot easily be equated with the absence of religion. As spaces such as the Collège, metaphors of the monastery, and the ease of movement of those wearing nuns' habits demonstrate, the taken-for-granted unmarked against which Islamic signs are thrown into bold relief may also be Catholicism.

VISIONS OF FRENCHNESS:
DEBATING L'IDENTITÉ NATIONALE

One sunny summer afternoon in 2009, I spoke with two elderly visitors on the steps leading into the Collège. The two women remarked on my accent and asked about my origins. In response to my explanation that I was there conducting research for my dissertation, one of the women lamented, how "unfortunately, it just doesn't look the way it used to." "How so?," I asked. "It's really the population that has changed," she replied. Her friend chimed in: "you know, with the immigrants." This observation was accompanied by regretful sighs. "Paris just doesn't look very French anymore," the first woman explained.

Similar complaints became a common refrain when, in the fall of 2009, the elected French government asked the French population to define "*l'identité française.*" In online and town hall forums, the right of center party headed by President Nicolas Sarkozy, the UMP (the Union for a Popular Movement), through the Ministry of National Identity and Immigration provided French citizens with a number of public forums in which to describe the French identity. Despite broad-ranging participation in these debates, the issue itself struck many on both the Left and the Right in France as wrong-headed. For critics, as a political strategy it could be seen, at best, as a method to distract a population mired in high unemployment a year out of the 2008 global financial crisis and, at worst, as an attempt to pander to the extreme Right in France and shore up the more conservative elements of the party's electoral base ahead of regional elections in the upcoming spring. The ruling party defended its efforts by suggesting that "globalization" had made identities of "developed nations" more "fragile" and had created a "crisis of identity" in France that needed to be confronted.[20] As the debate continued, however, the government also acknowledged that some of the online and public forums had been used to express xenophobic or racist opinions that should not be confused with the views held by the French state.

In an op-ed piece published in January 2010, the weekly culture magazine *Télérama* took pity on future professors of history who "will have to explain that in the middle of a global economic crisis, at the moment when the large equilibriums of the world were being redrawn, our dear old country was discussing . . . 'national identity.'"[21] Three months into the debate, it had become the butt of jokes worldwide and a source of embarrassment for many in France. Early warnings that the government was playing with fire by having the minister of the Ministry of Immigration and National Identity, Eric Besson, host a discussion about Frenchness proved rather prescient. Remarks such as "France has become an African colony in an irredeemable manner," "no French person asked to be invaded by foreigners," "to be French is not: profiting from welfare, not working, imposing a discriminatory culture, demanding to be integrated,"[22] revealed once again that ascriptions of showing to others occurs hand in hand with processes aimed at normalizing those signs that go unmarked. While Besson insisted that "the debate on national identity is not focused on immigration and Islam," research by journalists revealed that "38.5% of the [50,000] messages and commentaries" on the debate website "contain at least one keyword connected to immigration or Islam."[23]

This high rate of conflation between immigration, Islam, and non-Frenchness could partly be explained by the ministry's title (the Ministry of Immigration and National Identity). As the op-ed piece pointed out, the government had controversially linked the two since renaming the office in 2007. In addition, the debate came only weeks after a Swiss referendum that successfully banned the construction of minarets in the country, an act that received a fair degree of support in comments on the online forums. "France and our national identity," one participant wrote, "i[s] a cathedral in the center of Paris and not a mosque." "To be French," said another, "is to defend one's identity like the Swiss are doing in refusing the suicide of the nation provoked by an immigration that does not want to integrate itself but wants to impose upon us its customs: *burqa*, polygamy, minarets, a pseudo religion that is attacking us."[24] Throughout the debate, government officials and members of the public expressed Islamophobia ideas in terms that directly and indirectly betrayed assumptions that certain (but not all) religious signs cannot be incorporated into visions of Frenchness.

During the debate, a journalist interviewed Henri Guaino, a close advisor to President Sarkozy. In the conversation, the journalist expertly drew out the contradictions that accompany attempts to differentiate the "secular" French identity from the "religious" immigrants who did not belong. The journalist began by asking if the French population's rejection of the European constitution in 2004 (protesting, among other things, the inclusion of language about Europe's "Christian" heritage) had been inappropriate. While responding in the negative, Guaino also affirmed the place of Christianity in France today. "Were you in favor of the project to inscribe the Christian roots of Europe in the European constitution?" the journalist asked. "No," Guaino responded. "France was fashioned by 1,500 years of Christian civilization. But that, in my eyes, has nothing to do with a constitutional preamble."

The journalist continued to push the presidential advisor. Referring to an op-ed President Sarkozy had published in the centrist paper *Le Monde* in which he had invited practitioners of all religions in France to practice their religions with "discretion," the journalist pointed to how the Muslim community had taken the statement to be a direct attack on the practice of its faith. "No," Guaino insisted, "in the Republic, religious practice must be accomplished without ostentation. This is a principle of respect vis-à-vis those who do not share the same beliefs." "Catholics too?" the journalist interjected. "Of course" the advisor replied. "What would happen then," the journalist pursued, "if a Muslim demanded that church bells shouldn't ring any more in the name of the discretion desired by the head of state?" Guaino's reply to this question is similar to the assertions that helped to fund the Collège. He transformed Catholicism in France, from a "religion" into a "culture" or "civilization" by declaring that "the bells have provided the rhythm to village life for centuries. It is not a religious problem, but a problem of civilization, a problem of society, a problem of tradition."[25]

While religion was never mentioned in the official texts that accompanied this debate, it quickly became a central point of anxiety expressed by those who participated. Yazid Sabeg of the French organization Diversity and Equality of Opportunities suggested that "treating Muslims as a category, as a separate ethnicity is a real risk in this debate. That which I hear coming from the mouths of certain elected officials of the Republic, that which I read, which I see on the Internet, gives me the shivers, makes me afraid, as a Muslim. . . . I see racism, stigmatization."[26] The Islamophobia expressed in the debate was disconcerting enough to demand a critical response; the Left, indeed, seemed well positioned to do so. Many of those on the Left in France, however, refused this important opportunity. Instead, they declared that any attempt to define France's national identity was so problematic that the only possible response to the debate was outright refusal. This debate, a group of scholars and activists announced in an op-ed piece,

> is not free because it is the government who is enacting it, who asks the questions and who controls the responses. It is not pluralist because this formulation reduces the emblem of our national diversity to a single identity. It is not useful because it is a diversionary tactic and a machine of division between French people and stigmatization against foreigners. As a public affair, the nation does not have an identity, which is a private affair. . . . The Republic does not have an assigned, fixed, and closed identity, but political living and open principles.[27]

While it is difficult to disagree with many points made in this statement, it is also notable for its refusal to explicitly include those who had been excluded by participants in the debate. Instead, those critical of the debate insisted upon "identity" as a "private affair." Since the opportunity to describe French identity opened the floodgate to anti-Muslim sentiments, how might those critical of the debate have productively responded to statements that Muslims are not French? Instead of refusing the possibility of speech at all, a more useful response would have been an explicit articulation—or showing—of the opposite sentiment: "Muslims are French; French people are Muslims." These critical voices instead chose to reinscribe the divide between the "public" and the "private," to refer back to the fantasy of a universal citizen that shows no signs of its particular experiences, affiliations, or identities.

Following Joan Wallach Scott, Etienne Balibar, and others, I want to argue that an important category arising out of French political theory—abstraction—has become a "native category" in France in such a way as to make it into something particular. Abstraction—however impossible a political goal—is considered key to the creation of a viable public sphere in France.

> Abstraction, after all, meant disregarding the attributes that distinguished people in their ordinary lives; by this measure any individual could be considered a citizen. Indeed, as Etienne Balibar has pointed out, abstract individualism understands itself to be a *fictitious* universality: "not the idea that the common nature of individuals is given or already there, but rather the fact that it is produced inasmuch as particular identities are relativized and become mediations for the realization of a superior and more abstract goal." (2005, 15)

Thus, in order to be politically efficacious, abstraction must always remain a fiction—a utopic horizon toward which one is always moving, without ever fully arriving.

The fiction of the abstract citizen lacking any fixed identity has problematically become a taken-for-granted nonfiction, a place at which France has already arrived. Instead of a fiction that can never be attained but toward which one is always making strides, critiques of the debate on national identity demonstrate how the abstract citizen is presumed to already exist, is legible, and can be clearly identified by those ("and this is so French") who know how to do so. That is, by arguing that a debate on national identity was unnecessary, those on the left implied that Republican Frenchness was self-evident. Instead, critical voices should have acknowledged the impossibility of abstraction. Such voices, that is, needed to do more to demonstrate how ascriptions of showing off to others are always accompanied by acts of encouragement. The work of making certain signs stand out, that is, requires the simultaneous effort of allowing others to blend in.

CONCLUSION

A number of ethnographies of Muslims in France have helped to complicate simplistic accounts of the supposed threat posed by Islam. Anthropologists Mourad Ghazli (2006) and Paul Silverstein (2004a) describe the difficulties of employment, housing, and belonging faced by Arab and nonwhite citizens who are excluded from common perceptions of what Frenchness looks like. Both John R. Bowen (2007) and Jean-Loup Amselle (2003), furthermore, have identified the difficulties experienced by Muslim and Jewish groups who have had to respond to the French state's demand that each religion be represented by a single body with whom it can negotiate. For Amselle, this demand is one example of how all religions in France are, ultimately, asked to become more "Catholic." He argues that the adoption of the law of 1905 did not end but, in fact, continued the conversation between the French state and Catholicism, as it both aimed to limit the institutional power of the Church and took it for granted as the religious form par excellence. Because the French state historically understood religion through the lens of Catholicism—a process that now goes overlooked—it has, according to Amselle, subsequently required that all religious forms become more like the Catholic Church by creating representative hierarchies that can more easily be identified and regulated. The effacement of this history, I argue, also allows for Catholicism to transform from the paradigmatic religion to the unmarked secular.

Images of Paris and of Frenchness, as the debates at the Collège and on national identity demonstrate, are littered with images of Catholicism. These images move in ways that do not induce calls of "ostentatious," "inappropriate," or, even, "religious." Cathedrals and the Collège, like the fractals described by Gal, may be categorized as "religious" or "secular," "public" or "private," "civilizational" or "cultural," depending on the context of such articulations. The slipperiness of these cultural and religious signs, furthermore, does not result in reexaminations of the distinction between religious and secular. Instead, they are effaced in acts of normalization that tend to accompany those of the ascription of showing to signs of Islam.

In this chapter, along with white, male, literate, and propertied (or middle class), I have argued that the category of Catholic may also be added to the list of abstractable or invisible identities in France. In order to identify how secularism is operating in particular ways in different spaces and times, rather than seek out those spaces in which religion is absent, I have argued that we should instead pay heed to how the work of ascribing acts of showing off to certain symbols and actors occurs alongside of processes through which other symbols are produced in ways that do not appear to demand our attention.

Notes

1. The word "*burqa*" is often used in France to describe what is elsewhere called a *niqab*. The *burqa* is a particular form of full-face covering that cloaks the eyes with mesh netting. Occurrences of the *burqa* in France are negligible at best. The *niqab* is a more general term to describe veils that cover the hair and face to varying degrees.

2. My argument bears similarity to Talal Asad's (2006) account of French secularism, in which he demonstrates how discipline can occur in one of two ways: through discouragement (making something suspect), or through encouragement (making something natural). I use the concept of showing off to demonstrate how the two may occur simultaneously.

3. The Stasi Commission was established in 2003 in order to assess the "challenges" to secularism at the beginning of the twenty-first century. The Commission's report proposed a series of changes to the French legal and education systems; only one recommendation of the Commission was eventually adopted by the government: the ban on headscarves and other "ostentatious" religious signs in state-funded schools in France.

4. Angelique Chrisafis, "France's Burqa Ban: Women Are Effectively 'Under House Arrest,'" *Guardian*, September 19, 2011; http://www.guardian.co.uk/world/2011/sep/19/battle-for-the-burqa, accessed January 15, 2012.

5. In July 2010, the National Assembly passed a proposed bill banning full-face veils, with approval coming from the Senate in September of that same year. The law came into effect in April 2011. An individual caught wearing a full-face veil can be fined up to 150 euros. In addition, a relative found to be forcing an individual to wear the garment may serve time in prison or pay a fine of up to 30,000 euros, or both.

6. In this speech Sarkozy declared that the "*burqa*" was "not welcome in France. In our country, we can't accept women prisoners behind a screen, cut off from all social life, deprived of all identity. That's not our idea of freedom." See Angelique Chrisafis, "Nicolas Sarkozy Says Islamic Veils Are Not Welcome in France," *Guardian*, June 22, 2009; http://www.guardian.co.uk/world/2009/jun/22/islamic-veils-sarkozy-speech-france, accessed July 1, 2009.

7. The ability of women to wear medical masks instead of *niqabs* highlights the remarkable tension that surrounds this particular sign and clarifies how little such concerns are related to the actual visibility of a women's face in the public sphere. The fact that the law has only rarely been enforced, furthermore, suggests that despite the ferocity of the debates and discourses surrounding the law, the *niqab* is not a significant public safety concern.

8. Angelique Chrisafis, "France's Burqa Ban: Women Are Effectively 'Under House Arrest,'" *Guardian*, September 19, 2011; http://www.guardian.co.uk/world/2011/sep/19/battle-for-the-burqa, accessed January 15, 2011.

9. For ethnographic accounts of communities on the receiving end of this disconcerting trend, see Fernando (2005, 2010, and 2014) and Silverstein (2004b); for an anthropological analysis of some of the extreme voices perpetuating Islamophobia in France and elsewhere, see Holmes (2000).

10. The first decades of the twenty-first century have certainly seen no shortage of legislative acts banning signs associated with Islam. In 2011, the government of Belgium prohibited the wearing of *burqas* and *niqabs* in all public spaces. A number of state-level legislative acts in Germany forbid female teachers from wearing Islamic veils. In January 2012, the Dutch parliament passed an anti-*burqa* law similar to that in France. In 2009, a successful referendum allowed for a rewriting of the Swiss constitution to forbid the construction of minarets throughout the country.

11. Many anthropologists have produced nuanced accounts of the use of the veil and *niqab* that call into question assumptions about its effect on a subject. Saba Mahmood (2005) has pointed to the multitude of reasons women may wear a veil, arguing against those who see veils as signs either of a failure of "modernity" (Roy 1994) or a protest against it (Esposito 1992). Thus, these laws also participate in broader contradictory discourses surrounding the relationship between subjects, objects, and agency.

12. For more on this cultural institute—the Collège des Bernardins—see Oliphant (2015).

13. This is a common term used in contemporary art spaces in France. It contrasts explicitly with tour guides who are thought to offer explicit, didactic accounts of the meaning of art objects. The job of a mediator, instead, is to help facilitate or mediate an encounter between an art object and visitor, without having any singular destination in mind. I discuss the concept of mediation in more detail elsewhere (Oliphant 2015).

14. Matthew Engelke (2012) has also relied upon Gal's formulation of fractals to point to the slipperiness of religion and secularism, and religion and culture in England.

15. All translations from the French are my own, unless otherwise noted.

16. In identifying the feminized as marked against the unmarked masculine in France, I am relying on the work of Joan Wallach Scott (1996, 2005) in which she explores the limited means available to French feminists to make political claims in the nineteenth and twentieth centuries, given the particularized status of women against the universal status of men as actors in public life.

17. http://jeanbauberotlaicite.blogspirit.com/

18. Élisabeth Badinter,, "Un peu de Kantisme dans notre société serait bienvenu: Le Mondes des Religions," September 28, 2011; http://www.lemondedesreligions.fr/entretiens/elisabeth-badinter-un-peu-de-kantisme-dans-notre-societe-serait-bienve-nu-28–09–2011–1894_111.php

19. While discourses such as those articulated by Roy explicitly describe the religious-ness of the *burqa* as the reason for its inappropriateness in the public sphere, the gov-

ernment came up with a number of other justifications for the law, including equality between the sexes and the need for face-to-face engagement in the public sphere. The European Court of Human Rights referred to this latter argument as an "essential" aspect of French culture in its decision to uphold the law in 2014. The actual framing and the law (as well as its practical enforcement) are, interestingly, somewhat incidental to its interpretation and effects in the broader public sphere.

20. Charles Jaigu and Paul-Henri du Limbert, "Identité nationale: Le plaidoyer d'Henri Guaino," *Le Figaro*, December 12, 2009; http://www.lefigaro.fr/politique/2009/12/23/01002–20091223ARTFIG00012-guainoes-pere-une-nouvelle-conscience-nationale-.php, accessed February 11, 2009.

21. Thierry Leclère, "Nous sommes tous de mauvais Français," *Télérama* 3133, January 27, 2010.

22. Cited in Soren Seelow, "Sur le site d'Eric Besson: Le pire du débat sur l'identité nationale," *Le Monde*, December 4, 2009.

23. Thierry Leclère, "L'islam a bon dos," *Télérama* 3133, January 27, 2010.

24. Cited in Soren Seelow, "Sur le site d'Eric Besson: Le pire du débat sur l'identité nationale," *Le Monde*, December 4, 2009.

25. Charles Jaigu and Paul-Henri du Limbert, "Identité nationale: Le plaidoyer d'Henri Guaino," *Le Figaro*, December 12, 2009; http://www.lefigaro.fr/politique/2009/12/23/01002–20091223ARTFIG00012-guainoes-pere-une-nouvelle-conscience-nationale-.php, accessed February 11, 2009.

26. Samuel Laurent, "Identité nationale: Les Français reservés sur le débat," *Le Figaro*, December 21, 2009; http://www.lefigaro.fr/politique/2009/12/21/01002–20091221ARTFIG00374-identite-la-moitie-des-francais-dit-stop-au-debat-.php, accessed February 11, 2009.

27. Taken from the open letter posted to the website of the organization "Mediapart," http://www.mediapart.fr/node/69735, where it was signed by 202 French intellectuals. Accessed February 11, 2009.

Sources

Amselle, Jean-Loup. 2003. *Affirmative Exclusion: Cultural Pluralism and the Role of Custom in France*. Translated by Jane Marie Todd. Ithaca: Cornell University Press.

Asad, Talal. 2006. "Trying to Understand French Secularism." In *Political Theologies: Public Religions in a Post-Secular World*, edited by Hent de Vries and Lawrence E. Sullivan, 494–526. New York: Fordham University Press.

Bowen, John R. 2007. *Why the French Don't Like Headscarves: Islam, the State, and Public Space*. Princeton: Princeton University Press.

Butler, Judith. 1990. *Gender Trouble: Feminism and the Subversion of Identity*. New York: Routledge.

Egginton, William. 2003. *How the World Became a Stage: Presence, Theatricality, and the Question of Modernity.* Albany: State University of New York Press.

Engelke, Matthew. 2012. "Angels in Swindon: Public Religion and Ambient Faith in England." *American Ethnologist* 39 (1): 150–65.

Esposito, John L. 1992. *The Islamic Threat: Myth or Reality?* New York: Oxford University Press.

Fernando, Mayanthi. 2005. "The Republic's 'Second Religion': Recognizing Islam in France." *Middle East Report* 235: 12–17.

Fernando, Mayanthi. 2010. "Reconfiguring Freedom: Muslim Piety and the Limits of Secular Law and Public Discourse in France." *American Ethnologist* 37 (1): 19–35.

Fernando, Mayanthi. 2014. *The Republic Unsettled: Muslim French and the Contradictions of Secularism.* Durham: Duke University Press.

Gal, Susan. 2002. "A Semiotics of the Public/Private Distinction." *Differences* 13 (1): 77–95.

Gaspard, Françoise, and Farhad Khoroskhavar. 1995. *Le foulard et la République.* Paris: La Découverte.

Ghazli, Mourad. 2006. *Ne leur dites pas que je suis Français, ils me croient Arabe.* Paris: Presses de la Renaissance.

Göle, Nilüfer. 2010. "Rethinking Secularism: Mute Symbols of Islam." *The Immanent Frame.* http://blogs.ssrc.org/tif/2010/01/13/mute-symbols/. Accessed March 15, 2010.

Habermas, Jürgen. 1991. *The Structural Transformation of the Public Sphere: An Inquiry into a Category of Bourgeois Society.* Translated by Thomas Burger and Frederick Lawrence. Cambridge, MA: MIT Press.

Holmes, Douglas R. 2000. *Integral Europe: Fast-Capitalism, Multiculturalism, Neofascism.* Princeton: Princeton University Press.

Keane, Webb. 2005. *Christian Moderns: Freedom and Fetish in the Mission Encounter.* Berkeley: University of California Press.

Mahmood, Saba. 2005. *Politics of Piety: The Islamic Revival and the Feminist Subject.* Princeton: Princeton University Press.

Oliphant, Elayne. 2012. "The Crucifix as a Symbol of Secular Europe: The Surprising Semiotics of the European Court of Human Rights." *Anthropology Today* 28 (2): 16–19.

Oliphant, Elayne. 2015. "Beyond Blasphemy or Devotion: Art, the Secular, and Catholicism in Paris." *Journal of the Royal Anthropological Institute* 21 (2): 352–73.

Open Society Foundation. 2011. "Unveiling the Truth: Why 32 Women Wear the Full Face-Veil in France." *An At Home in Europe Project.* New York: Open Society Foundation.

Roy, Olivier. 1994. *The Failure of Political Islam.* Cambridge: Harvard University Press.

Scott, Joan Wallach. 1996. *Only Paradoxes to Offer: French Feminists and the Rights of Man.* Cambridge: Harvard University Press.

Scott, Joan Wallach. 2005. *Parité: Sexual Equality and the Crisis of French Universalism*. Chicago: University of Chicago Press.

Silverstein, Paul. 2004a. *Algeria in France: Transpolitics, Race, and Nation*. Bloomington: Indiana University Press.

Silverstein, Paul. 2004b. "Headscarves and the French Tricolor." *Middle East Report Online*. http://www.merip.org/mero/mero013004

Warner, Michael. 2002. *Publics and Counterpublics*. New York: Zone Books.

CHAPTER 10

Not-for-Profit Pornography and the Benevolent Spectator

Joy Brooke Fairfield

Annually since 2005, the Seattle-based amateur pornography festival "HUMP!" has invited brave northwesterners to take off their clothes, turn on their cameras, and create their own short porno films. HUMP! is the brainchild of syndicated sex columnist Dan Savage, who produces the festival through his role as editor for Seattle's free weekly newspaper *The Stranger*. Local sex educators, activists, and *The Stranger* staff members act as judges, vetting the submissions and choosing around twenty to screen in the festival and compete for prizes based on votes cast by the audience. The submitted materials are destroyed after the event and no biographical information is released, allowing the amateur stars and filmmakers to return to anonymity after their short burst of intimate fame. Some may choose to sell their films online, but most will never be available for purchase, and the full festival experience—a two-hour smorgasbord of diverse sexual imagery—is limited to those in the physical audience. Because of the necessity of audience presence at the festival and the films' fleeting presence onscreen, HUMP! is more accurately described as a *live* event rather than a filmic one. Immediate, intimate, and guaranteed to disappear, the festival exists outside the context of mass reproduction and consumption that characterizes commercial pornography. As such, HUMP! creates the market demand for a different kind of porn: films that address time-specific and region-specific viewers who pay not for a product that will get them off, but for the participatory experience of a sex-positive live event. Created for a primarily local audience outside the economic structures of commercial porn, HUMP! films are not beholden to the same conventional expectations. HUMP! performers show off not for money, but for personal reasons as unique and varied as the films themselves. This chapter argues that the production conditions of this "not-for-profit" porn offer a partial, provisional freedom from the market, making possible stylistic innovation. What pleasures can be found in performing erotic acts for a limited public outside of an established scene of economic exchange?

In addition, HUMP!'s exhibition context generates a spectatorial experience distinct from both commercial porn and nonpornographic short film festivals. Far from being a dirty little secret, HUMP! is well known, well publicized, and well situated in respectable film and performance spaces in downtown centers. What began in 2005 as a single screening in Seattle has grown into a multiweekend affair, expanding into Portland, Oregon (in 2010), Olympia, Washington (in 2012), and San Francisco, California (in 2016). Unlike consumers of commercial porn, HUMP! viewers are implicated in the films they watch through geographic and corporeal proximity to the creators, who in many cases hail from their hometowns and may be sitting beside them in the theater. Commanding a relatively high ticket price more akin to theater than the movies, this porn plays to consistently sold-out houses and is consumed by what could be called "a polite public." Savage and the festival producers take a strong hand in curating not just the films themselves but the overall atmosphere of the event. Audience behavior in the theater is regulated explicitly and implicitly to align with a standard of sexual tolerance. Prior to each screening, Savage addresses the audience in person, giving an overt lesson in manners. This preparatory performance conveys to the viewers the notion that as they watch the bodies showing off onscreen, they too are being watched. This disciplinary regulation of the audience's bodies and voices counterbalances the traditional disempowerment of sexually objectified performers. Reminding the viewers that they too can be seen results in a heightened self-awareness of the role of spectator. The audience may have shown up to see the provisional porn stars show off, but the festival's structure requires that they, too, perform a role. This chapter offers analysis of the audience's performance within the exhibition context of not-for-profit porn, paying particular attention to how spectatorship is sculpted by the producers of the event. The ideal viewer at HUMP! enacts a kind of benevolent spectatorship—a term chosen for the way it challenges the paradigm of the adjudicatory gaze. Unlike the Judeo-Christian all-seeing eye of moral judgment, named "malevolent spectatorship" by Slavoj Žižek, benevolent spectatorship suspends immediate judgment of the object presented for examination. Can this form of embodied civic witnessing resist recapitulating the separation between viewer and viewed, subject and object, sexualized and sexualizer?

The producers of HUMP! hail benevolent spectators as part of their socio-political project of sex-positivity. The term sex-positive refers to a loosely defined contemporary cultural philosophy with roots in various forms of sex and gender activism from the 1960s onwards. The term came into use in the United States in the 1980s during what is known as the "feminist sex wars" as a way for some feminists to distance themselves from a negative feminist standpoint on porn and its effects on heterosexual relations. A sex-positive belief system rejects the stigmatization of any sexual behavior as long as all parties involved are conscious, rational, and consenting adults. Carol Queen and Lynn Comella, in their essay "The Necessary Revolution," explain that "sex-positivity allows for and in fact celebrates sexual diversity, differing desires and relationship structures, and individual choices based on consent" (2008, 279). HUMP! audiences are asked to "allow for and in fact celebrate" representations of diverse sexual practices that may be labeled as "deviant" within a society that has enshrined monogamous, romantic, hetero-domestic sexuality as the norm. I suggest that the relationship fostered between porn creator and porn spectator at HUMP! can be likened to an elementary school "show-and-tell." Just as the show-and-tell can reveal to school children the priorities and values of their peers and thus contribute to a more informed and empathetic classroom, HUMP! provides a venue through which sexual priorities and values can be transported from the private sphere into a public forum. The unique content of each show-and-tell is highlighted, but the performative structure of community witnessing extends across individual enactments, rehearsing a respectful relationship between viewers and viewed that disrupts the traditional divisions between subject and object. Kids cannot be too unkind to their fellow students during show-and-tell because one day it will be their turn to stand in front of the class, gripping something personal and prized. At HUMP!, as in the classroom, the ideal benevolent spectator is a nonjudgmental witness, collaboratively creating an environment of tolerance and community sharing.

But benevolent spectatorship is always an ideal complicated by the material conditions of the viewers' lived experiences. To the degree that this sexual show-and-tell is able to achieve the pedagogical and community-building goals of the producers, it is not via perfect performances of benevolent spectatorship, but through the collectivized experiences of awkward precarity when bodily responses erupt into the collective space of viewing. Asked to bear witness to the fantasies of their friends and neighbors, the audience members at HUMP! do not simply watch porn, they confront in real time the lived experience of their own desire and repulsion, all contained within the disciplinary place of the theater. In what follows, I will first examine the stylistic innovations of this not-for-profit porn, then the viewing constraints of the exhibition context, the polite public. Next, I'll analyze how the philosophical ideal of the benevolent spectator is complicated by the embodied realities of porn viewership. Finally, I'll touch upon the mock-civic act of voting that concludes the event. Within a framework of acceptance and tolerance, how does the competitive element of a popular vote compromise the possibility of purely benevolent spectatorship?

NOT-FOR-PROFIT PORN

The form and content of the films at HUMP! vary widely. Due to the politics of the festival producers, the audience is guaranteed a dramatically diverse array of sexual acts. The only rules regulating content maintain that no children, animals, or feces are allowed in the films, and all performers must provide proof-of-age and release forms to ensure their legality and consent. Queer sex usually gets at least equal screen time as hetero films, though trans and gender-queer entries remain less common. Puppetry and animation break up the flow of real skin flicks, and highly conceptual films challenge preconceptions about what constitutes porn. In 2007, because humorous submissions had outnumbered the earnestly explicit, the award categories were divided up into "Best Humor" and "Best Hardcore" in order to try to encourage more entries containing actual intercourse. BDSM (bondage, discipline/domination, sadism, masochism) and kink films are healthily represented every year, and in 2010 a separate prize category for "Best Kink" was added. Due to this variety, many viewers find themselves exposed to something new or unfamiliar over the course of the two-hour screening.

Because of the confidentiality of the event, it is difficult to discern who initiated individual films. With few exceptions, most HUMP! films are creative collaborations between performers and those responsible for writing, shooting, and editing the final products. This blurring of the line between talent and producer is part of what makes these works unique and separates them from commercial pornography in which roles are more clearly delineated and hierarchical. I use the term "creators" to refer to both the filmmakers and the performers affiliated with each film. Conversations with creators reveal that HUMP! films are instigated by a wide variety of people with diverse goals. Local filmmakers use the opportunity to turn their lens towards erotic subject matter. Theater and dance professionals create scripts to showcase their talent and find someone to film them. Sex workers and activists create pieces that align with their philosophies, and part-time or independent pornographers take this opportunity to share their trade with their community. Many projects are spearheaded by nonperformers who want to share their unique sexual practice or experience the thrill of being watched in flagrante delicto. Starting in 2010, the festival organizers offered a "want-ad" section on the HUMP! website to help connect would-be participants. A brief perusal of the list revealed headshots of actors wanting to participate, audition calls from directors, and offers from editors and cameramen to work cheaply or for free. Because the event repeats annually, audience members from prior years can heed the call to participate more directly, the want-ad site thus becoming a venue for local collaboration between strangers. Money is sometimes exchanged over the course of the film's life cycle—some of the listings on the site offer to pay performers or give them a cut of future profits—but most people involved in HUMP! do not identify as pornography industry professionals.

HUMP! is publicized as an "amateur-and-locally-produced porn festival."[1] While the term "amateur" captures well the labor-of-love quality of the films, the appellation is confusing. For a brief period after the release of the consumer video camera in 1981, real-life couples created actual "amateur" videos and traded them noncommercially through subscription-based organizations (O'Toole 1998, 180–81). The nonprofessional styles of these home movies became so popular that studios began to imitate the form: "The slap-dash hand-held camera style of true amateur porn was recycled by commercial companies to become something of a new mode of production offering fresh possibilities for fantasies of identification and spectation" (Uebel 1999, 23). The term "amateur porn" entered the American vernacular in the early 1980s, and has risen in usage ever since.[2] However, as the new style was co-opted by the studios, "amateur" ceased to refer to a mode of production and began to reference a slightly grungy video aesthetic that seemed to promise greater authenticity. The notion of "amateur porn" was further complicated by the revolution in porn distribution resulting from the rise of the public Internet in the 1990s. Increasingly simple modes of recording and sharing do it yourself (DIY) porn resulted in a landslide of videos made by nonprofessional, enterprising "amateurs" with no connection to porn production or distribution companies. It remains true that most of this so-called amateur porn available on the Internet is mediated through an exchange of money. The aesthetic and distribution modality might be "amateur," but the intention is to create a sexual product for a generalized public that will pay to consume it. To differentiate the works in this festival from the amateur porn genre made by studios or individuals for the purpose of generating revenue, I describe the films of HUMP! as not-for-profit porn. Like other not-for-profit endeavors, HUMP! is a noncommercial venture dedicated to a particular vision of a social world. Participants may dream of winning a grand prize, but the small sum is trumped by the pleasure of community recognition.

In addition to nonprofessional, HUMP! advertises itself as a "locally produced" film festival. Contributors participate in what is essentially an annual civic happening, knowing their erotic work will seen by friends and strangers in their region. Most HUMP! films are shot in the Pacific Northwest, many specifically for the event. With the call for submissions, the event producers provide a list of optional inclusions that prove a film was made expressly for the festival, mostly referencing local people, places, and things. Judges give bonus points to submissions that feature these imbedded codes, which in the past have included the name of an ironically conservative suburb of Seattle or the famous ferries that scuttle in and out of the harbor. Because including these visual nods increases a film's chances of inclusion in the festival, HUMP! creators are given an incentive to reference their own community rather than attempt a generalized "everywhere/nowhere" aesthetic that characterizes much of commercial pornography. Choosing to incorporate these often-silly elements requires the creators to actively consider the regional specificity of their future audience. Inside knowledge of their community provides filmmakers a competitive advantage in the festival.

These two qualities—noncommercialism and geographic proximity between creator and viewer—facilitate stylistic innovation within the films and make possible a unique relationship with the audience. The absence of commercialism allows porn creators to follow more freely their own desire rather than their projection of the imaginary consumer's desire. Viewers may be able to appreciate the sex acts featured with less concern that performers are being physically or fiscally exploited. Also, while video and Internet porn must aim for a wide and general audience of paying consumers from around the globe, films in HUMP! are made for a local and temporally specific audience made up of an imagined community of proximal friends and strangers. So what exactly is being shown off here, why, and to what end? Why do people show up for it? Rather than considering the films pornographic *products* ripe for consumption, I suggest we read them as texts speaking to and from a specific community. Whether aiming to arouse, shock, amuse, or educate, the films invite the spectator to join in a collective experience rather than consume a pornographic product. To illustrate this, I'll discuss two submissions from 2008. The first was an award-winning submission named *Trolley Tryst* that mobilized the power of local referentiality. The second was a notoriously explicit kink-focused submission called *Our Ruinous Love* that highlights the stylistic diversity possible within the noncommercial, show-and-tell ethic of HUMP!

The first example reimagined a famous scene from the film *Risky Business*, where Tom Cruise and Rebecca DeMornay make love on a moving train. *Trolley Tryst* was shot on location on the then-brand-new streetcar in the rapidly gentrifying South Lake Union district known colloquially as the "South Lake Union Trolley" for the amusing acronym produced: "SLUT." Tying their film into a contemporary meme (there were already T-shirts being sold emblazoned with the words "Ride the S.L.U.T!"), the creators of *Trolley Tryst* took a local inside-joke a step further. In a scene just over a minute long, the characters, played by a real-life couple, move swiftly from kissing to exchanging oral sex on an empty but apparently in-service trolley. With shared knowledge of the production conditions of this low-budget project, many in the audience may understand that this was an illicit film shoot—and may be left wondering how the couple got away with it. This question is answered at the end of the film when a brief "bonus feature"-style shot shows the performers scrambling for their clothing and looking behind them with an expression of concern. Text then appears on the screen saying: "And yeah, we were busted . . . by a transit cop." If the HUMP! festival itself can be read as a dare to Pacific northwesterners ("Will you do it?"), *Trolley Tryst* seems to be a resounding answer: "Yes, we will!" The creators of this film offer as part of their show-and-tell performance not just their sex itself, but also their sexual audacity.

Pornography always traffics in the fantasy of intimacy: whether viewing porn on a laptop, a magazine, or a film screen, the viewer brings the sexual images into his or her sphere, collapsing the distance between production and consumption with the energy of observation and desire. In the case of locally made porn, the sense of proximity between performer and audience is more than just an illusion. People in the audience have ridden that trolley themselves or seen it rolling down the streets. The difference between the audience members and the film creators is slim; in fact, the creators had participated as audience members at prior years of the festival. In the seconds-long bonus feature shot, the couple (who had just appeared in the film as daring, sexy, porn stars) are then revealed as everyday people just like the audience, vulnerable to the same laws and social mores. This moment of humorous vulnerability invites identification from the audience and begins to collapse the distance between viewer and viewed.

Because they need not appeal to a wide, paying audience, HUMP! films are not accountable to commercial porn standards such as the appearance of models, specific sexual practices, and the traditional pornographic narrative typically concluding with orgasm. One of the most talked-about films of 2008, *Our Ruinous Love*, was a BDSM/kink-focused video that mobilized few tropes from commercial porn, and contained no orgasms at all. More clinical than erotic, the film consists of a single long shot of a woman lying on her back on a table, her face unseen. The camera is focused directly between her legs as if from the perspective of a doctor administering a pelvic exam. A man, also face unseen, inserts a variety of large and oddly shaped items into her orifices, beginning with traditional sex toys, moving to more uncommon objects like a handheld egg whisk and a small orange traffic cone. The finale is a curved metal hook almost a foot long that is inserted, seemingly improbably, into her anus. The film is almost silent: there is no soundtrack, and the woman makes small sounds but nothing resembling the climax to orgasm. At the end, after pulling out the hook, the man says: "So—yeah! This is just what we do." With the financial exchange out of the equation, it is easier for the audience to trust the veracity of this claim. The viewer assumes that if the performers are not making money, it is more likely that these uncommon sexual practices represent their actual desires. While a thorough analysis of the power and pleasure dynamic of this couple is impossible, the film is read by the audience as a truthful transmission of their unusual kinky play rather than a commercial performance aimed at economic gain. They seem to be doing it for themselves, not for the approval or financial validation of a viewing audience. The show-and-tell object presented in *Our Ruinous Love* is a sexual practice that they find pleasurable and wish to share despite the possibility of negative judgment. Like the student presenting her teddy bear in front of the potentially ridiculing eyes of her classmates, this couple chose to value the possible pleasure of self-exposure over the possible stigma of such intimate revelations.

While *Trolley Tryst* was humorous, *Our Ruinous Love* induced gasps and even screams from the audience. Obeying Savage's injunction against heckling even in this intense moment of shock, there are no reports of disparaging comments being made during the screening. The anal-hook moment was widely commented upon in blogs and reviews, and even led to a semiserious moratorium on the use of anal hooks in the following year's festival. The invitation to identify with these performers may be less comfortable for some than the playful couple on the trolley, but it is still an offering of vulnerability, and the structure of the festival attempts to ensure that it will be received as such. Inclusion in HUMP! is an indication that this couple is also a part of the community. Watching the almost unbelievable stretching of the woman's orifices, the audience is asked to stretch their own boundaries of acceptability and expand their vision of what constitutes "normal."

THE POLITE PUBLIC

The festival attempts to mitigate the audience's potential experience of shame in attending a pornographic event through various structural innovations. Savage cites as his inspiration for HUMP! a similar event, known as You Oughta Be in Pictures, which was held annually in Boston from 2000 to 2005. Created by adult-boutique owner Kim Airs, this event was relatively low budget and low profile with very little press encouraging people to submit or attend. The one or two screenings played to full audiences in a local art-house cinema, but due to that cinema's association with a sex shop and a former porn star, the film's audience was limited to a demographic for whom such social notoriety was either acceptable or part of the thrill of attending.[3] Hosted by a newspaper rather than a sex shop, HUMP! benefits from the sense of civic legitimacy affiliated with the free press. It also receives a great deal of publicity; tens of thousands of people see the advertisements in the paper encouraging readers first to submit films and later to attend the event.[4] After years of such publicity, it has achieved a certain level of social acceptability simply through familiarity. If so many people know about it, how can it be wrong?

The festival takes place in high-brow art establishments in Seattle, Portland, and Olympia. The primary venue is a center for contemporary performance in Seattle called On the Boards (OtB), which frequently presents the work of internationally renowned artists. For example, the weekend after HUMP! in 2008, OtB presented the West Coast premiere of OBIE award-winning director Young-Jean Lee's new work *The Shipment* and a month before the 2013 festival, esteemed choreographer Mark Morris presented a world premiere (Czaplinski 2013). As the sole venue in Seattle that hosts this caliber of contemporary performance, OtB is associated with aesthetic sophistication and discrimination. Holding the festival in this venue aligns it with certain markers of class, taste, and worldliness, signaling in advance to the audience that what they'll see has recognized artistic significance and may employ formal innovations. This won't just be smut; it will be highly curated, culturally significant smut. And, as with Young-Jean Lee's work, if you don't like it, it might just be because you didn't *get* it, which speaks, perhaps, to the importance of insider knowledge on the part of spectators and not just producers. Audience members, thus, might not admit it if they didn't get it.

At OtB as well as at the other venues, the films are viewed without the additional personal or interpersonal sexual activity that sometimes characterizes pornography viewed in public. Attentive ushers herd the large audiences in and out, and the full houses make impossible the custom of empty seats separating patrons at traditional porno theaters in red-light districts. Prior to and after the show, bright houselights expose the patrons to one another and the back-to-back screenings result in audiences encountering a new crop of strangers as they enter and exit the theater. In this polite public, there is no cruising, no masturbating, and no illicit acts of shared sex under jackets or in aisles. The viewing conditions create the expectation that audience arousal must be concealed and contained—it cannot be shown.

The "polite public" is invoked implicitly through the festival's relationship with the free press, with high-class art establishments, and with audience management techniques of independent cinema and live performance. However, certain rules and regulations for behavior are explicitly communicated in the welcome speech given by Savage prior to each screening. He lays out three rules. One is that, by state law, liquor is forbidden in the theater. In 2011, Savage mocked this rule, saying: "The state doesn't think you can handle sex and alcohol at the same time and we have to go along with them." He is more sincere about the other two rules. Due to the ubiquitous camera function, cell phones are forbidden, and Savage points out the large, bouncer-like figures standing on both sides of the theater who will confiscate them permanently from violators. Apparently the audience has taken this rule to heart; confiscations happened several times in the early years of the festival, but have not occurred in recent years.[5] This rule protects the privacy of the participants from what W. J. T. Mitchell calls "the new panopticon" of consumer electronics: "At any time, there's probably someone around you with a camera phone, and a record of your activities might instantly end up on the Web" (Jones 2006, 176). This regulation enforces the confidential, impermanent nature of the festival and emphasizes that this porn is to be appreciated in the live space of the theater only; it is not to be played later or further disseminated.

In his third and most serious injunction, Savage addresses audience response. He invites the crowd to feel free to react audibly to the content of the films, but warns them to refrain from derogatory comments. In 2008 he "deputized" each audience member to "punch their neighbor in the face" if he or she was being rude. Perhaps realizing that the threat of physical violence set the wrong tone, he has changed the language of the warning in recent years. In 2011, he said:

> Here at HUMP! the only assholes allowed in the theatre are on the screen. Feel free to laugh, gasp, hang your heads in your hands and cry, but you may *not* make disparaging comments about anyone's body, sexual choices, behaviors, etc. The people who made the film that grosses you out might be sitting right next to you. Assholes, like cell phones, will be confiscated and removed from the theatre.[6]

Based on his experience as a sex columnist, Savage is aware that people can respond negatively to representations of sexuality they find undesirable. As the producer of the event, he endeavors to create an environment that protects the vulnerable act of the sexual show-and-tell. In the attempt to create a safe space for the film creators, the public is overtly regulated. The bodies onscreen show off their sexual expressiveness, but the bodies in the audience are subject to the threat of discipline. The relationship between discipline and observation explained by Michel Foucault in his description of Jeremy Bentham's Panopticon is at play: spectators are reminded that in this space they are not just the watchers, but also the watched. Audience members are subjected to the surveillance of the ushers and the "deputized" audience members surrounding them. This contextualization creates a relationship between audience and image quite distinct from that of traditional porn-viewing environments, either at home alone or in a public cinema. Instead of occupying a position of authority from whence to judge the representations of sex as pleasing or displeasing, the HUMP! viewer is in an ambivalent position: both gazer and gazed-at. The film creators take certain social risks in choosing to share with the public their sexual fantasies or exploits. However, audience members too are rendered vulnerable through the implicit and explicit regulation of their bodies within the theatrical environment. They must comply with the social conventions or risk being thrown out. This mutual precarity sets the stage for a unique kind of spectatorship.

THE BENEVOLENT SPECTATOR

HUMP! creators share not only the fantasy of what gets them off, but the fantasy that someone cares enough to watch them. Žižek describes the psychoanalytic notion of fantasy as this very idea of being watched:

> Fantasy proper is not the scene itself that attracts our fascination, but the non-existent imagined gaze observing it, like the impossible gaze from above for which old Aztecs draw gigantic figures of birds and animals onto the ground, or the impossible gaze for which details of the sculptures on the old aqueduct to Rome were formed, although they were unobservable from the ground. In short, the most elementary fantasmatic scene is not that of a fascinating scene to be looked at, but the notion of "someone out there looking at us." (2008, 225)

Žižek defines the bearer of the fantasmatic gaze as the "malevolent spectator" (2008, 40:00 minute of the video). This is the imaginary viewer that compels self-censorship and in whose name state-sponsored censorship takes place. Like Santa Claus, the malevolent spectator knows when you are good and bad. This gaze can feel disciplinary and dangerous, unmoored from an individual viewer like Bentham's Panopticon—yet it is also highly desirable: "We are afraid of being observed all the time but we are more afraid of not being observed at all, that is the ultimate horror" (2008, 24:00 of the video). Žižek cites reality television shows and the popular movie *The Truman Show* as further examples of how much we want to be watched. The existence of not-for-profit porn seems to provide additional evidence for this strong desire to be the focus of the fantasmatic gaze. At least some of us—for example, the couples in *Trolley Tryst* and *Our Ruinous Love*—want to be seen having sex, not for money, but in exchange for the pleasure of showing off. In this way, the films of HUMP! are doubly revelatory: they feature not only the specific erotic content that arouses the creators but also their intense desire to be seen.

Unlike the fantasmatic malevolent spectator, the audience at HUMP! has been compelled by the unusual viewing context into a performance of benevolent spectatorship. At a basic level they embody a polite public, watching with tolerance the parade of sexual fantasies marching before them; however, the larger fantasy at play—that of being seen by distant eyes—requires more active participation. In the manner of the Aztec figures and the Roman sculptures that direct their beauty at the sky, the films shared in HUMP! can be viewed as offerings. These not-for-profit films require spectators to do more than just consume a product; they are hailed as active witnesses in the performance exchange. A term usually reserved for traumatic or high-stakes situations, "witnessing" seems appropriate given the threat of punishment that accompanies public sexual display as well as the sheer difficulty of enduring certain scenes. For example: we are all witnesses to the minor crimes committed by the creators of *Trolley Tryst*, and the physical intensity of *Our Ruinous Love* seems to merit witnesses in the same way that dangerous acrobatic acts require a "spotter." Witnessing also implies an emotional, empathetic connection with the subject and a willingness to turn one's primarily receptive position as spectator into a more active future role: "To witness an event is to be responsible in some way to it" (Peters 2001, 708). The HUMP! audience becomes involved, through the act of viewing, with the representations of sexuality onscreen. From a purely pedagogical perspective, most audience members leave the theater knowing more about the sex practices of people with orientations and proclivities different from their own. In this way, the festival cultivates tolerance toward forms of desire and embodiment less frequently represented in other cultural products, including mainstream pornography. A witness is a kind of vehicle, someone who transfers knowledge from a place of close proximity to those with a more distant connection to the event. "Witnesses serve as the surrogate sense-organs of the absent" (709). If these witnesses do their job, they will remember these films the next time they encounter prejudice or injustice toward sexual minorities. As witnesses with increased understanding and compassion based on their experience of shared vulnerability in the theater, perhaps they will feel compelled to speak on behalf of those minorities to those who were not present in the audience.

However, each witness has a uniquely personal and embodied response to the sexual imagery shown in the festival. The intensity and intimacy of the filmic content render it impossible to immerse oneself in the experience as one might at a Hollywood film. The viewer is constantly impinged upon by his or her own sexual proclivities and sensitivities, reminded frequently by feelings of arousal or disgust of his or her own embodied spectatorship. The HUMP! viewer is asked to attend to the vulnerable offerings of the sexual show-and-tell while simultaneously being aware of his or her own body and its specific desires and fears. Because of the diversity of the films presented, most people are made uncomfortable at some point by the content, and unlike other porn viewing circumstances, there is no pausing, fast-forwarding, or clicking onto a new site if what's being presented does not please. Audiences yelp or gasp, and audible moments of fear or disgust frequently ripple across the crowd. A woman reportedly fainted, and in another notorious incident an audience member had to run out of the theater to vomit. On the other hand, sexual imagery that succeeds at provoking arousal also has the potential to be chaotic within the polite public of the theater. Feeling turned on in a crowd of strangers can be uncomfortable, particularly if it is in response to new sexual stimuli. As they attempt to abide by the code of the polite public, benevolent spectators are challenged by the reality of their diverse discrete bodies and their vast capacity for stimulation through filmic representation. Whether aroused or horrified, amused or uncomfortable, the spectator is ultimately not simply the pupil of the porn. Acted upon by forces of both discipline and desire, the HUMP! spectator is in a state of physical and emotional vulnerability that mirrors in many ways the public exposure of the amateur porn actor they watch on the screen. The benevolent spectator is also an amateur, in the sense of the word meaning "novice" or "inexperienced." She is called upon to manage the physical sensations of having a body, with all its desires and aversions, with the social requirements of existing in community. In an attempt to discipline into existence an audience of "benevolent spectators" HUMP! in fact creates an intersubjective crucible where the edges of the self are experienced vividly at the same time as their porousness is revealed. These incidents of irruption when the sensing bodies of viewers resist their benevolent role are some of the most interesting and provocative moments of the festival. Surrounded in a crowded theater by other bodies, the audience is stuck with the images on the screen, as well as the titillating proximity of other bodies. While they may not be participating directly in the public show-and-tell, audience members also find their sexuality on display as well: their embodied reactions to erotic input startlingly present in the public space of the theater.

Despite being hailed as benevolent spectators committed to a practice of nonjudgmental witnessing, on the way out of the theater each attendee is asked to fill out a ballot to determine the prizes. While compulsory tolerance regulates your responses within the theater space, personal preferences can be operationalized through the voting process. The mock-civic act of voting asks viewers to reflect upon what they have just witnessed, invoking the participatory nature of politics. With its emphasis on participation, HUMP! proposes the notion that sexual values—often considered the most private of issues—should be included in civic conversations.

Replacing the malevolent spectator with the benevolent—if awkward—spectator charged with witnessing both the desire of others and his or her own embodied desire, HUMP! creates a space where fantasies can be displayed and later discussed. After the festival, many people retire to surrounding bars and restaurants to eat, drink, and talk about the show and their own personal favorites. The films' merits are debated online on personal blogs as well as on the sponsoring newspaper's official blog. Throughout this discourse, a major thread is the question of future participation. "Will you make one next year?" asks the reporter to the man who declared that he didn't see anything he liked. In many cases, people decide to make a film because they don't see their preferences or proclivities represented onscreen. For example, after a dearth of lesbian films in 2006, there were many submissions of woman-on-woman sex in 2007. People who identify strongly with their sexuality see the absence of "people like them" as a lack of public representation and step up to fill that gap. I interpret HUMP! as helping expand the boundaries of the cultural conversation about sexual diversity within local communities. As an event, HUMP! was birthed from the observation that public discourse on sexuality is often circumscribed by shame and fear. While there is some movement from within existing civic structures to change this, there is still an overwhelming belief that issues around sexuality should remain private.

But why? A similar argument for exclusion based on privacy could be made for conversations about "family values," yet they are openly debated in the public sphere, and politicians are expected to serve (or pay lip service) to them. Nation-states take on the responsibility of supporting healthy family values, including engaging in political discussions about what constitutes these values. More than just a pornography festival, HUMP! presents the radical proposal that the similarly private "sexual values" also benefit from public display and debate, and that notions of good sexual values can expand past the Judeo-Christian framework into real conversations about pleasure, power, consensuality, and desire. Freed from the constraints of the market—where most public visions of sexuality in mainstream media remain fettered—HUMP! invites you to show off your personal fantasies, attempting to create a new participatory spectatorial experience benevolent enough to contain them.

Notes

1. http://www.thestranger.com/seattle/Hump2013/Page
2. Google N-gram Viewer: http://books.google.com/ngrams/graph?content = a m a t e u r + p o r n & y e a r _ s t a r t = 1975 & y e a r _ e n d = 2008 & c o r p u s = 0 & smoothing=3
3. I lived in Boston during this period of time and learned about "YOBIP" only through posters displayed at the store and through conversation with a store employee. Since this time, Grand Opening has been bought by San Francisco–based company Good Vibrations. More information is available online at the following sites: http://www.newtopiamagazine.org/issue04/columns/bent4.php, http://www.evolution102.com/newsletter/vol1/news4.html
4. The Stranger has a weekly circulation of 80,000 paper copies with 1.5 million website hits monthly: http://www.voicemediagroup.com/The_Stranger
5. Conversation with bouncer, "On the Boards," November 4, 2011.
6. Dan Savage, verbatim, "On the Boards," November 4, 2011.

Sources

Czaplinski, Lane, ed. 2013. *On the Boards* website. Seattle. www.ontheboards.org
Jones, Caroline, ed. 2006. *Sensorium*. Cambridge, MA: MIT Press.
O'Toole, Laurence. 1998. *Pornocopia, Porn, Sex, Technology*. London: Serpent's Tail Press.
Peters, John Durham. 2001. "Witnessing." *Media Culture Society* 23: 707.
Queen, Carol, and Lynn Comella. 2008. "The Necessary Revolution: Sex-Positive Feminism in the Post-Barnard Era." *Communication Review* 11, no. 3: 274–91.
Savage, Dan, ed. *The Stranger*. Seattle. Online edition and blog: www.slog.thestranger.com

Uebel, Michael. 1999. "Towards a Symptomology of Cyberporn." *Theory and Event* 3, no. 4: 120–29.

Žižek, Slavoj. 2002. "Big Brother, or the Triumph of the Gaze over the Eye." In *CTRL (SPACE): Rhetorics of Surveillance from Bentham to Big Brother* edited by Thomas Y. Levin, Ursula Frohne, and Peter Weibel, 224–27. Karlsruhe: ZKM.

Žižek, Slavoj. 2008. "The Spectator's Malevolent Neutrality." Public lecture, June 8. Accessed October 10, 2011. http://www.youtube.com/watch?v=4QhRxhzVU7Y

CHAPTER 11

A Paradoxical Show of Hunted Ghosts and Haunted Histories

Robert C. Thompson

> They want to see a ghost. Come right up on the porch and they say, "if we come on your tour can you guarantee that we're going to see a ghost?" And the answer to that is "no." Can't guarantee that. Nobody can. If they do, they're lying. This house, some of the other spots near town are slightly more likely opportunities for somethin' like that to happen. You've just gotta maintain the mind and see what happens. Sometimes it does. Sometimes it doesn't.
>
> —MIKE LYONS, GHOST TOUR GUIDE

As Mike Lyons explains in this introductory monologue for his ghost tour in Gettysburg, Pennsylvania, showing ghosts presents certain challenges. Ghost tours bring tourists through purportedly haunted streets, fields, cemeteries, and buildings, accompanied by a guide, costumed to allude to the town's American Civil War history. At various stops along the tour, the guide performs narratives of tragic deaths and subsequent hauntings in order to make the case that ghosts—that is, the continuation of an individual's consciousness after her or his bodily death capable of manifesting itself in perceptible ways to the living—are present at the site and that it is possible for tourists to encounter these ghosts. Tourists expect that the tickets they have purchased will allow them into genuinely haunted spaces; they anticipate an authentic experience with the paranormal that will satisfy their expectations. But, even supposing that ghosts exist to be seen, the chances of their manifesting in some perceivable way are entirely random. As Lyons says, a tour guide should not promise to show ghosts, but tourists pay good money for a ghost tour that seems to promise exactly that, at least on the surface. Thus each tour's ability to market, sell, and provide a paranormal experience convincingly is central to the tour entrepreneur's and performer's survival in a highly competitive tourism market.

In Gettysburg, tourists eagerly seek out ghost tours for their evening entertainment: not surprisingly, the popularity of the form breeds intense competition between and among individual tour companies. I began my ethnographic research into Gettysburg's ghost tourism industry in 2007, and, as part of my research, I trained and performed as a ghost tour guide for the Sleepy Hollow of Gettysburg company. I interviewed guides and tour owners, attended ghost tours with every company in town, and surveyed audiences. My formal period of research ended in 2008, but I continued to perform as a guide intermittently through 2014. During those seven years, between twelve and twenty ghost tour companies sold their services up and down Baltimore Street and Steinwehr Avenue—the relatively small main thoroughfares running through the center of town. Some tours, including Sleepy Hollow of Gettysburg and Ghosts of Gettysburg, have continued in business for well over a decade. Others come and go in a single season. In their quest to win tourist interest and dollars, companies have experimented with a range of amenities designed to enhance the individual tourist's experience—bus and trolley tours, bawdy "adult" tours featuring foul language and dirty jokes, a specially staged Victorian-style mourning parlor complete with a coffin, and the distribution of electronic sensors meant to discern physical disturbances caused by paranormal forces. But the tours with the greatest commercial viability, and therefore longevity, tend to avoid these gimmicks, focusing instead on the ghost tour's most basic elements— storytelling and the implied possibility that an actual ghost may show itself to the tourist.

Showing ghosts requires a subtle touch. Rather than a flashy, theme-park-approach to winning tourism dollars, the most sustainable tours are the least contrived. In *Simulacra and Simulation*, Jean Baudrillard (1994) argues that there are no authentic objects or experiences in postmodern culture. Tourists encounter simulations of reality but never the real thing; perhaps for that reason, they have come to prefer well-constructed representations over the genuine article. The ghost tourist, however, seems to represent the polar opposite of Baudrillard's postmodern subject. Ghost tours are notable for their simplicity. A group follows a guide through what are often very unremarkable and poorly lit spaces and listens to stories. Despite the fact that ghosts are the central concern, the tour company makes little effort beyond the narrative performance to show ghosts to its tour groups. As Lyons's brief monologue suggests, ghosts surface in the form of chance sensations that happen only occasionally and are very much open to interpretation. If frightening figures were to pop out of bushes or ghostly lighting effects appear in tree tops, tourists might have a more spectacular experience, but would it satisfy their expectations? Probably not. Generally speaking, Gettysburg's ghost tourists reject ghosts that are all show, preferring something genuine. They often ask their guides about the possibility of experiencing a ghost while on tour or which tours have the most ghosts. They also share mysterious sensations and narratives of their own possibly paranormal experiences and attempt to photograph ghosts in areas that guides point to as hotbeds of paranormal activity. In this way, they seem to support tourism scholar Dean MacCannell's (1976) seminal theory that tourism is, essentially, the search for the authentic.

Given the fact, however, that ghosts can be difficult to believe in, let alone discover, satisfying tourists' quest for an authentic paranormal experience presents ghost tour guides with an especially formidable task. Although tourists may be inclined to believe, few completely trust in the legitimacy of their potential paranormal encounters. Ghosts remain a scientifically dubious phenomenon in Western culture, and reports of paranormal experiences are often greeted skeptically. Historian Jean-Claude Schmitt (1998) defines belief in ghosts as "a never-completed activity, one that is precarious, always questioned, and inseparable from the recurrences of doubt" (7). Folklorist Linda Degh (1996) argues that "belief is fluctuating, hesitant and selective, not consistent or absolute" (39). In a similar vein, philosopher Colin Davis (2007) imagines the internal monologues of a paranormal believer and disbeliever respectively: "I know ghosts don't exist, but I still believe in them; or, alternatively, I don't believe in ghosts, but I don't entirely believe my lack of belief" (8). Every ghost encounter, real or imagined, comes with a healthy dose of doubt. Even those who want desperately to believe in the paranormal origins of their mysterious photograph or sensation cannot escape the possibility that it does not. I have watched countless tourists approach their tour guide, uncertain of a potentially paranormal encounter, in search of confirmation. They hedge their experience, saying things like "I think I heard a drum playing" or "it looked like there was a figure moving in the shadows," and they often preface their ghost sensations with some variation on "this might sound crazy, but . . ." ending with "it's probably just. . . ."[1]

Ghost tour guides find themselves in the paradoxical position of having to show ghosts without betraying tourists' sense of an authentic paranormal presence at the tour site by showing ghosts. To show, after all, implies fabrication or exaggeration. And, given the fragile nature of paranormal belief, any intimation of fabrication threatens the legitimacy of the supposed haunting. Using only narrative, the guide must activate tourists' feeling that "real" ghosts are present in the tour sites such that the slightest sound, scent, or blip on a camera screen can become a cross-dimensional event of dramatic proportions for the increasingly anxious tour group. Financially, a great deal is at sake in the guide's ability successfully to walk the delicate line between *merely* showing and *genuinely* showing ghosts. Ghost tour guides, after all, rely on the income provided by the tours, at least in part, for their livelihood. Their ability to satisfy tourists' paranormal desires has a direct financial impact insofar as tips go to make up as much as half of a guide's earnings in an evening, and tour owners regularly fire guides who come back with dissatisfied groups. The fact that many guides have enjoyed extended careers in the profession (some as long as fifteen years) suggests that they have discovered a way to show ghosts without undermining tourists' desire for an authentic paranormal encounter. The question becomes: How?

It may be, as Edward M. Bruner (2005) suggests, that we need to rethink authenticity as a subjective rather than an objective judgment. Bruner argues that "the vocabulary of origins and reproductions and of the authentic and the inauthentic may not adequately acknowledge that both are constructions of the present" (164). Guides cannot point out and show authenticity to tourists; tourists must discover it for themselves in the spaces visited by tours. Bruner suggests that the quest for authenticity is in fact motivated by a desire for subjective rather than objective truth: the site's meaning is "emergent in the social context of the visitor's experience of the site" (165). Guides push tourists to look beyond what is being shown into the unseen. In order to have this experience, tourists must open themselves to embracing the purely subjective nature of the ghost quest. The ghost tour acknowledges and utilizes this by reframing tourists' desire for the authentic as desire for the possibly authentic.

I argue that the ghost tour opens a space for an emergent truth within the immediate present of the live performance in which tourists can choose to have an experience that they deem to be a real or authentic encounter with a ghost. The relative reality of these ghosts depends on the guide's ability to show history as a flexible and contingent narrative, constructed in part by the tourist's own emotional connection with the pain and loss memorial-ized at Gettysburg. Rather than an approach that imagines the ghost encounter to exist somewhere "out there" in the tour site, I locate the authentic paranormal experience within the tourist's own subjective interaction with the site. The guide's narrative performance provides the context in which tourists might show themselves the ghosts they seek. In order to show the unshowable, the performer must seem to not be showing anything at all while provoking the audience to create their own personal encounter with a secret presence.

THE POLITICS OF POPULARITY AT A HAUNTED SITE

The demographics of Gettysburg's tourists vary from season to season. In the summer when tourism is at its peak, visitors come from across the country. Many of them are Caucasian but their allegiances—which can be relatively passionate even a century-and-a-half after the Confederacy's surrender—are mixed between the Union Army of the Potomac and the Confederate Army of Northern Virginia. Summer tourists often spend the day visiting sites on and around the battlefield and learning about the history of the battle; a ghost tour occupies their evening hours when the battlefield's vast vistas are covered in darkness. In the autumn, a larger contingent of tourists come from the surrounding area specifically for the ghost tour as a form of seasonal Halloween entertainment. Because Pennsylvania winters discourage leisurely outdoor activity, tourism lulls after the anniversary of the Gettysburg Address on November 19 until early March when school groups start to arrive. Like the summer tourists, school groups hail from across the United States. They spend their day touring the battlefield and commission a ghost tour in the evening. Unlike the summer tourists, the school groups are more ethnically diverse and, aside from their chaperones, under the age of eighteen.

These factors shape the tours in several significant ways. First, the audience shifts the motive of the performance toward entertainment. Touring the battlefield may be primarily about education and cultural enrichment, but touring ghosts is another story. Summer and spring tourists, many of whom spend a full day exploring military tactics and the material circumstances of soldiering, often seek a release at the day's end; and fall tourists seek an experience that will put them into the spirit of Halloween. During the course of my research I surveyed tourists on several different tours, asking why they chose to attend a ghost tour. They talked about looking for ghosts, having a new experience, or seeking fun and enjoyment: few wanted to learn more about the battle.

Still, Gettysburg's popularity depends on its Civil War history and guides always incorporate historical data—selected and tailored to the specific demands of the ghost tour—into their narratives. The fact that Gettysburg's tourists sympathize with either the Union or the Confederacy (coupled with the tour's necessary preoccupation with death and dying) shifts the guide's emphasis away from exploring or even referencing the meaning of the war— that is, ending slavery or Confederate sympathizers' claim about defending states' rights—to the human cost of the war itself. Guides rarely take sides, and their stories are devoid of any sense of Gettysburg's soldiers defending or advancing a particular cause. When stripped of meaning, the soldiers' sacrifices feel more tragic, an effect heightened by the guides' focus on the gruesomeness of nineteenth-century warfare. Guides show Gettysburg as a site of mass tragedy, emphasizing the pathos of soldiers dying too young and overlooking the political complexities of the conflict. After all, Gettysburg is a kind of "dark tourism" destination,[2] visited because of its connection to a bloodstained historical event. The tour's truths emerge in the overlapping space between the tourist's desires and the guide's knowledge and skills. In this context, showing actually conceals the contentious. Guide Nancy Pritt brings tourists to a small cemetery where she tells the story of a boy who was buried there when he stepped on an unexploded artillery shell in a farm field after the battle. The boy's death served neither the Union nor the Confederate cause. Pritt shows his gravestone to illustrate the tragic consequences of warfare—all the more tragic for being unintended. Like many other guides Ed Kenney begins his tour with a narrative of the stench of rotting bodies that filled the streets of Gettysburg after the battle—a stench that tourists might smell themselves in an olfactory paranormal encounter.

This method of showing war as tragic and macabre is particularly conducive to showing ghosts because it cites a familiar trope of restless ghosts with unfinished business, whether lost opportunities or physical and psychological torment. The most popular protagonists in Gettysburg's ghost narratives tend to be young privates, field nurses, or civilian casualties who either do not realize they have died or continue to seek a reunion—interrupted by death—with loved ones. On High Street near the center of town where several buildings had served as field hospitals, Kenney, asking his tour group if they can smell baked bread, tells the story of Agnes Barr. Barr, a citizen of

Gettysburg during the battle, brought bread to the men and boys being operated on and recuperating in the hospitals immediately after the battle. The smell of bread suggests that both Barr and the wounded soldiers continue to haunt the spaces where she witnessed their suffering and where many of them died.

With very few exceptions, nearly all of Gettysburg's ghosts can be tied in some way to the battle. Jim Weeks (2003), a scholar of Gettysburg tourism, argues that Gettysburg has been culturally constructed as the memorial site for the entire Civil War. Gettysburg was a three-day battle costing almost 20,000 casualties: a major defeat that ended General Robert E. Lee's invasion of the North. Thus the battle has a plausible, but not inevitable, claim to this status. Very shortly after the battle, historian John Bachelder sought to identify the greatest battle of the war and chose Gettysburg before it had even ended. Bachelder started a movement that culminated with Union— and later former Confederate—states and veterans competing to fill the battlefield with monuments. Even though the Civil War persisted for two years after Gettysburg, Bachelder labeled the battle the "turning point of the war," transforming Gettysburg into a national mecca. Not surprisingly, Gettysburg's large tourism market helped to generate the ghost tours. In 2012, a report by the California University of Pennsylvania estimated that more than three million tourists visited Gettysburg annually.[3] Other popular Civil War destinations like Fort Sumter in Charleston and the Appomattox Courthouse in Richmond draw more modestly, averaging around 200,000 visitors a year.[4]

The cultural elevation of Gettysburg has not only rendered the town sufficiently popular to support a thriving ghost tour industry, but also established the strong presence of a dominant, federally sanctioned historical narrative that excludes the paranormal as a matter of course. During my interviews with them, battlefield guides and personnel stated unequivocally that Gettysburg's ghosts are personae non grata in the battlefield's official tours and performances. Untested and unproven, ghosts are the product of a spurious, purely oral local history. Ghost tours cannot tour Gettysburg National Military Park—the fields and monuments that serve as the focal point of a Gettysburg vacation. The center of the park is the "high-water mark" of the Confederate charge, the closest that the Confederate Army came to winning the battle and, arguably, the Civil War. The federal government has done its best to preserve the land surrounding this spot, including the areas where the two armies formed their battle lines preceding and during that fateful charge. Tourists are sometimes disappointed that ghost tours do not visit the battlefield, and stories circulate throughout the town of freelance guides who have gotten into trouble for taking tour groups into battlefields. Since the federal government funds the national park, ghost tour companies cannot bring for-profit tours onto park land. They travel on the margins of the battlefield, often coming right up to the edge of federal property but never crossing the boundary.[5] Most tours travel the streets of the town, a marginal tourism space compared with the battlefield, and the noise of the traffic and interruptions from local hecklers shouting to surprise tour groups as they drive past have driven tours even deeper into the margins. The Sleepy Hollow of Gettysburg tour company, for example, travels up a back alley that runs alongside Baltimore Street, and the Haunted Gettysburg tour company uses the parking lots and alleys behind Steinwehr Avenue. Indeed, all of the tours use parking lots, shortcuts, and public lots off the main streets in order to tell their stories.[6] Gettysburg tourism is centered in the battlefield and ghost tours usually happen in the town. Ghost tours don't choose this separate status: it is thrust upon them. Separation, however, enhances the tours' appeal and helps to establish a seemingly authentic haunted world. The park might usefully be considered as the "staged" region of Gettysburg and the town as the "unstaged" or "back regions."[7] Sociologist Erving Goffman's (1959) theory of "regions" is significant here: "accentuated facts make their appearance in what I have called a front region; it should be just as clear that there may be another region—a 'back region' or 'backstage'—where the suppressed facts make an appearance" (112). In Gettysburg, the accentuated fact is Gettysburg's historicity. Gettysburg stresses its significance as a Civil War battle site by directing tourists to areas that have been restored and restaged as battle sites or memorialize the battle itself. These sites not only make Gettysburg "special," but also mark it as a tourist destination. The town's "suppressed" facts are those pedestrian elements that show the town as typical of small American towns: the library, the firehouse, the high school, the hospital, parking lots, and alleyways; the same quotidian sites frequented by ghost tours. In many ways, Gettysburg's functioning sites challenge the preserved ones. Tourists come to experience something other than home, but the backstage areas of the town identify Gettysburg as familiar, or, "just like my home town."

By showing off Gettysburg's back regions, ghost tours create a vacation from the vacation: a departure from difference in order to tour the familiar. But guides are not showing familiarity. Rather, they are drawing on the cultural associations of back spaces to give their audiences the sense that they are being shown secrets. The journey into back regions is a journey into increasingly secret and intriguing spaces. MacCannell (1973) argues that "just having a back region generates the belief that there is something more than meets the eye" (591). Tourists are not barred from Gettysburg's back regions, but they are dissuaded from entering into and looking on them.[8] Thus, ghost tours foster the impression that those regions harbor "secrets" and exploit it by identifying those secrets as ghosts. While I would not suggest that tourists are naturally interested in Gettysburg's back regions, if ghost tours did not illuminate its backstage sites, few tourists would acknowledge them. By moving through back regions, ghost tours accentuate their natural capacity to convey the impression that they bear secrets.

Showing hidden mysteries on a public tour relies on a necessarily paradoxical performance of secrecy. Through the act of touring, back regions become the front regions of the ghost tour performance, which threatens the guide's claim to an authentically covert display.[9] The spaces themselves may not be staged like a theatrical production, but the guide's performance works to stage them through narrative. In other words, the sites are (usually) selected and shown because the guide has a ghost story that she or he can share about the space: thus they are part of a preset plan developed by the guide. Guides do not conceal the fact that they have a plan. In fact, by calling themselves "guides," they claim responsibility for knowing the best places to visit. This is the point at which the realness or authenticity of the back region breaks down. The fact that guides purposefully choose to show particular spaces calls into question the presence of any authentic object. Guides must break the mundane façade of their sites by transforming them into performance spaces, and, through the performance, fill these ordinary sites with extraordinary specters. The quotidian nature of the ghost tour site suggests to tourists that they are not intended to have an experience with the site as such. The site may have historical significance, but—unlike the battlefield—the façade of a functioning twenty-first-century town conceals its history.

THE SUBJECTIVITY OF PARANORMAL PERFORMANCE

Unlike a backstage tour at a theater, museum, or landmark, the secrets revealed on a ghost tour can never be shown fully by the guide because they cannot appear unless the tourist makes a concerted effort to discover them.

The ghost's invisibility suggests the degree to which ghosts are the province of subjective experience and therefore not amenable to objective inquiry. Proponents of the paranormal argue that ghost encounters are idiosyncratic, happening at the will of forces that human beings cannot control. According to sociologist Eric Goode (2000), "[f]irst-hand, personal, anecdotal evidence persuades in the world of the paranormal" (58–59). Consequently, these forces cannot be subjected to the sort of scientific experimentation that would validate them empirically. Since ghosts are strictly confined to the realm of the subjective, their truth or authenticity can only ever aspire to a possible existence. The same might be said of any object or experience claiming the status of absolute authenticity, but ghosts are unique in that, from a strictly scientific standpoint, they are unable to make claims to objective validity. Thus, in order to avoid raising or foregrounding tourists' doubts, guides never suggest that ghosts are objectively valid. Rather, the attitude they take both toward and within their narrative performance rests firmly on the prospect of the ghost as a possibility.

The relative veracity of a ghost story depends on a community of guides and tour operators, circulating tales without any discernible method: a distinctly folkloric system. Bob Wasel, author of a series of books containing purportedly true ghost stories in Gettysburg and operator of ghost tours based on his stories, told me that if a story recurred enough times in letters sent to him by tourists, this was proof enough of the story's validity. He also suggested that if a story grabbed him and seemed honest, he would consider including it regardless of verification. Guides understand the haphazard nature of their narrative collection, but remain largely unconcerned. When I performed as a ghost tour guide for the Sleepy Hollow of Gettysburg tour company, the central aspect of my training was to attend three tours by three guides already working for the company. My first narratives were supposed to come from those tours. Two other companies in town produce books of ghost stories, which serve as sources for their guides' narratives. When I asked if his tours were scripted, Mike Lyons explained that "all of us are given a set of folklore and legend . . . but anyone who works with us builds up their own repertoire of personal experiences and guest experiences." Every company in town works this way.

A guide's narrative performance emerges out of a constellation of sources, including tourists themselves. Guides are a kind of magnet for paranormal stories. I have pages of stories collected during tours. These stories came from tourists who approached me before, after, or during the tour to share their personal narratives. One evening before my tour began, a woman told me about a Civil War nurse who had visited her husband in his sleep and threatened to amputate his arm: "He was talking in his sleep, saying 'Let go!' He had never talked in his sleep before. The next morning he tells me there was this woman dressed like she was from the nineteenth-century pulling at his arm and saying 'we've got to take it.'" Later that same night, a young couple approached with a story about an experience they had staying in a building that I had talked about on the tour: "We had an eerie feeling staying there like someone was with us. . . . We heard noises all night." Both of these experiences ultimately became part of my narrative performance.

Guides will tell stories that may or may not be true, but they will not tell stories that they know to be untrue. Knowingly false stories go against the guide's ethic and are bad for business. As Mike Lyons said of his tour groups, "they don't pay money to go on a tour of things that probably didn't happen here." Tourists want to hear stories that guides are willing to believe in. According to guide Ed Kenney, "if you are a firm nonbeliever, I think that you would be losing some of the enthusiasm needed because you know you're shoveling a load at these people. If you are at least open, this thing may have just happened and I think that gets into the person's voice when telling the story." Kenney is typical of ghost tour guides in that he does not demand an absolute belief from himself. Rather, he wants to remain open to the possibility that his stories are true, and so he limits his tours to stories that, from his perspective, are potentially possible.

This folkloric approach to showing history stands in stark contrast to the official, government-sanctioned narratives of the battlefield. Ghost tours have self-consciously subverted the battlefield's more academic historical narrative in their effort to show history as haunted. Official battlefield tours show a meticulously researched and carefully presented history: the product of strict standards that exclude the paranormal because of its inherently subjective nature. On a ghost tour, foregrounding ghosts forces history into a supporting role, which changes the way it is shown. History becomes fluid, folkloric, and contingent, shifting according to the needs of the storyteller and the audience. Nancy Pritt is one of many guides who joke that tourists can ask any questions they like and if she doesn't know the answer she will make one up. As storytellers, guides brag about their ability to invent, exaggerate, and otherwise bend the truth—explicitly informing their audience that the truths they show are inherently suspect. In this way, the ghost tour undermines or circumvents established narratives, showing a secret and unofficial history that tantalizes because of its marginality.

Demographically, Gettysburg guides are mostly white, gender balanced, and range in age from eighteen to eighty. Many hail from the middle class and tour as a part-time occupation; thus touring supplements, rather than constitutes, their income. Guides include full-time college students, retirees, teachers, writers, hotel clerks, living history actors, history tour guides, sutlers (craftspeople who make historical clothing), office managers, sales associates, and massage therapists. Occasionally, I encountered guides who self identified as paranormal investigators, Civil and Revolutionary War reenactors, and psychics. Many guides held bachelor's degrees in a number of fields including history, theater, and education. One guide had a master's degree in American history and another was pursuing a master's in art education. Guides were intelligent, well spoken, and forthcoming individuals, and I had little difficulty getting them to talk at length about their jobs, lives, and experiences. On or off the tour, these often charismatic and engaging guides liked to tell stories.

The level of education among guides and the fact that many work professionally in the fields of history and education suggests that they have at least a basic understanding of the difference between academic history and folklore. They know that they are presenting an intentionally skewed version of Gettysburg's history in order to entertain and tantalize tourists with the possibility of ghosts. Their open-ended, folkloric meta-communications about their narratives allow them to show ghosts as a potential rather than absolute reality (Babcock 1977). Guide Ray Davis concludes a ghost story concerning the mysterious movement of his lantern by wondering rhetorically, "So how did it happen? I don't know. Was it a ghost? Maybe, but I didn't see anything reach up out of the ground. . . . I have no idea how that happened" (Davis 2006). Guides rarely tell groups that their stories provide certain evidence for the existence of ghosts. Rather, they relate them as strange occurrences that happened and may, if the tourist chooses to believe, be attributed to ghosts.

A guide's uniform also indicates the flexibility of historical truth. The costume invokes Gettysburg's history in a way that is neither strictly accurate nor dismissive of its role as a signifier of nineteenth-century culture. At all but one Gettysburg company, female guides wear hoop-skirt dresses and male guides wear military uniforms or less formal period "civilian" clothes. Unlike reenactors, guides place no premium on material authenticity. Rather, the requirement to wear period-style dress is balanced against the practical demands of guiding outdoors in all kinds of weather. Guide Steve Anderson noted that, although he wears "very formal outfits" for his job performing living history, "I *don't* use them for tours . . . if any nasty weather should happen to come up, I can't be freaking out about letting my best wool get wet." Footwear is almost never accurate to the period because guides must walk for as many as three hours a night across various terrains. In these conditions, period shoes would be uncomfortable at best and treacherous at worst. That being said, I have never seen a guide in sneakers. Costumes do not portray historical character but rather allude to the history of the space in which the guide performs. Like the narratives, historical costuming is fluid, balancing historical fact with the practical and creative demands of the storyteller.

The fluid and flexible truth of the ghost tour is, as Bruner suggests of cultural tourism in general, emergent. The ghost surfaces as an authentic possibility or experience based on the tourist's subjective determination of the likelihood of the performance's and site's overlapping claims to haunting. By this I do not mean to suggest that the ghost tour argues both sides of the debate. When tourists elect to attend a performance calling itself a ghost tour in which a guide foregrounds the paranormal as a possible interpretation of unusual phenomena that occur at specially selected sites, they understand that the tour is clearly claiming paranormality.

Even when they fail to have a paranormal encounter on a tour, tourists tend to be content with the idea of ghosts as a possibility. I often surveyed tourists, asking if they enjoyed the tour; they usually wrote about enjoying the stories, the storyteller, or finding the tour "interesting." None judged the tour on the basis of experiencing or failing to experience a ghost. I asked ghost tour guides about compliments and complaints they had received and had similar results. One guide indicated that "the only complaint that anyone has ever voiced to me directly was that the walk was too far." Tourists want the guide to allow them to entertain the possibility that they may encounter a ghost—to make ghosts *real enough* that they may manifest at a tour site—but they do not insist that the ghost actually make an appearance in their adjudication of the tour's success.

DIGITAL PHOTOGRAPHY AND THE CHALLENGE
OF SEEING GHOSTS

Tourists described various potentially paranormal encounters to me including hearing sounds of gunfire and cannon shots or the music of flutes and drums, smelling perfume or smoke, feeling chills, sensing phantom hands pulling at their ankles and hair, and feeling that they are being watched or stared at. Tour narratives prompt, at least in part, the kinds of experiences tourists report. Sociologist Gillian Bennett (1999) argues that paranormal experiences shape the ghost stories people tell each other just as "knowledge of the [ghost] stories is part of the shape we give to our supernatural experiences" (5). Guides—who build their stories, in part, from tourist experiences—will often tell tourists what sensations to expect—implicitly or explicitly—by developing their tales around paranormal happenings at the sites they visit. Tourists' notion of the ghost encounter also comes through popular culture, including reality television programs based on ghost hunts and franchise horror films. The space, in concert with the guide's suggestive performance of ghostly probability, leaves tourists free to interpret their experience as somehow paranormal.

The most desired paranormal encounter is visual. Both performing and attending tours, the question I most often heard before the performance began has been some variation on the question "Am I going to see a ghost tonight?" (Thompson 2010). In rare instances, tourists have described seeing ghosts with the naked eye. These sightings have consistently taken the form of shadowy figures passing between obstructions at a distance. I gave a tour several days before Halloween, and as the group moved between sites by Gettysburg High School, a man and his girlfriend approached me. He told me that during my narrative, he had a spotted a figure moving in the shadows: "I felt a nudge that I thought was my girlfriend, but it wasn't. So I looked up and I saw it. I think the nudge was meant to point out the presence of this figure that was moving by the school." The tour group as a whole rarely shares in these sightings, which tend to be limited to a couple of tourists. This gives them the air of subjectivity even within the context of the tour.

Much more common are visions mediated through digital cameras. Tourists photograph a range of purportedly paranormal images with their cameras, including fogs, spectral faces, swooping lines of laser-like colored light, and smoke (fig. 11.1). Digital cameras tend to capture "orbs," which look like simple circles of light, usually white (fig. 11.2). In each case, these images appeared on the cameras' viewfinders in spite of the fact that no visible corollary existed in the photographed space. Guides suggest that digital cameras capture ghost images better than conventional cameras. Guides rarely attempt to explain why digital cameras are more sensitive to the paranormal than their film predecessors, but tourists seem to accept the idea that

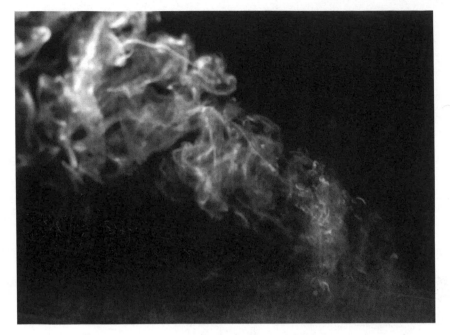

Fig. 11.1. Spectral smoke in the Gettysburg battlefield. (Photo courtesy of Betty Roche.)

technological advances place them in closer proximity to the paranormal. Popular television shows like *Ghost Hunters* and *Paranormal State*, which show electromagnetic meters, infrared cameras, and specially tuned sound devices detecting signs of otherworldly entities, tend to support this impression. This new digital power explains why ghost photographs have become much more prevalent in the last ten to fifteen years.

On almost every tour that I attended or guided, one or more tourists brought cameras in order to photograph ghosts. The prominence of the camera as a tool for amateur paranormal investigation within the context of a tour has become so popular that one company, Ghostly Images Tours, markets specifically to tourists interested in ghost photography. On the "Haunted Orphanage Tour" I followed a tour group into a basement where we were invited to photograph the room in the dark. The guide, Bob Michels, suggested that a particular back corner was a popular spot to capture ghostly images, and, although the corner was extremely cramped, several in the group bent awkwardly into the space in hopes of capturing a digital ghost image.

Paranormal photographs provide a uniquely potent means of showing

Fig. 11.2. Orbs beside a nineteenth-century building. (Photo by Tracey Craley.)

ghosts. Unlike the other, more fleeting, sensations that tourists might experience on their tours, photographs allow them to possess—and show—their paranormal encounter. The photograph testifies to the tourist's presence in the ghost's space. Alice Rayner (2006) suggests that "the impulse of the tourist to collect objects from sites visited surely belongs to a desire to possess the durability of the past and future and to feel that other as the same" (82). By capturing digital ghost images, tourists form a permanent and durable identification with the ghost, the otherworldly other. This allows them to subsume a paranormal unknown into the self. In this way, tourists can feel a certain comfort and ownership of what is otherwise a very frightening unknown: death. The ghost photograph also concretizes the subjective feelings elicited by the site. The eerie ambiance of a space where so many died tragically becomes a reproducible image that tourists can take home. The kind of work done by an artist-photographer touring the monuments at sunset, seeking to capture the battlefield's sense of loss, becomes accessible to those who lack the time, patience, or aesthetic sensibility to create a more artistic souvenir.

The ghost photograph allows the tourist an intimate engagement with the paranormal by closing the distance that otherwise separates the ghost from the tourist. According to Walter Benjamin's (1968) theory of photography in "The Work of Art in the Age of Mechanical Reproduction," the need for co-presence with an object endows that object with a ritual significance, which sets it at a distance from the viewer. Similarly, the need for co-presence with the ghost in a haunted space endows the ghost with an "aura," which Benjamin calls "the unique phenomenon of a distance, however close it may be" (222). Benjamin further explains that the "distant object is the unapproachable one" (243n5). A large part of what makes ghosts unapproachable is the tourist's need for a skilled authority, or the guide, to locate them. On a tour with guide Ed Reiner, a woman captured an orb on her camera only when Reiner very specifically directed her to point her lens behind a monument in the field that the group was facing. At the Jennie Wade House's Midnight Tour, guide Bob Michels's narratives about ghosts moving chains and hopping on beds led tourists to photograph those objects rather than others. Haunted spaces are not immediately identifiable. Ghosts must be located and revealed by experts, which lends the ghost an elevated status.

But the photograph itself diminishes that distance because the photograph does not possess an aura. According to Benjamin, an aura requires the presence of an original, and there is no original in the world of photography. For the ghost photograph, the original is the ghost itself in the haunted space. In the moment that a photographer takes a ghost photograph, the viewfinder displays the immediate presence of a ghost, but an instant later that presence is no longer guaranteed. Since the ghost is invisible and, according to the paranormal terms of the tour, can vanish at will, the photograph only suggests that a ghost encounter has happened. Ghost photography marks a presence that has probably passed; an engagement with an aura that no longer obtains. Insofar as the tourist seeks an immediate experience of a ghost's presence it is the ghost, not the photograph, that possesses a ritual aura. In other words, the aura emanates from the invisible presence of the ghost in the haunted space, not the image of the ghost. The photograph replaces the ghost and displaces the ghost's distance, authority, and the authenticity that inheres within its immediately uncertain presence.

Although the photograph's materiality might seem to move the ghost experience away from the subjective into a more objective dimension, its lack of ritual aura guarantees that even a photographic encounter remains largely subjective. The photograph relies on the emergent authenticity of the moment that it represents, which in turn relies on the liveness of the experience. Without an aura of its own, the ghost photograph looks to the haunted space to lend it authority, and the space looks to the guide to show its paranormality. John G. Sabol Jr. (2007) explicates this point in his book *Ghost Culture*: "the meaning of a photograph comes from making sense of the physical environment . . . a potential haunted space needs to establish connections which work within and outside the frame of the image" (88). In other words, the ghost photograph must return to its original context and borrow its legitimacy from the ritual aura of the haunted space. Tourists take their images home as souvenirs, but, relying for their legitimacy on particular moment and place, such images deplete exponentially as their makers distance themselves from the encounter in both space and time.

In order to assure that a paranormal photograph will effectively show a ghost to the tourist photographer, ghost tours will often attempt to reconnect ghost photographs to the authoritative aura of the haunted spaces by hanging them in those spaces. The walls of the basement of the "Haunted Orphanage" are lined with pictures of spectral fogs and smoke taken in the room. Similarly, the Jennie Wade House features a back room full of ghost photographs taken by investigators and tourists in the building. Showing the photographs in the site where ghosts are meant to materialize (show themselves) emphasizes a paranormal interpretation of both the photograph and the site. This explains why tourists want to share the images they capture on tours the moment they realize they have photographed something unusual, connecting the image to the time and place of its capture in a very immediate sense. The difference between photographs hung at the orphanage or Jennie Wade House and those taken by tourists and shared moments later is one of degree rather than kind. The fact that the immediate context in which the photographs were taken has passed denies the image an authoritative aura; its presence may nonetheless lend greater authority to the haunted aura of the space.

CONCLUSION

The high degree of subjective collaboration required of the spectator makes showing ghosts—invisible and inherently uncertain—a rather unique practice within the broader context of cultural tourism. The complex claims made by reconstructed sites like Colonial Williamsburg and Gettysburg's battlefields ask spectators to invest a certain amount of subjective belief in their performances in order to understand them as authentically historical, but they do not demand as much subjective collaboration as the ghost tour (Handler and Gable 1997). In Williamsburg's colonial city and on Gettysburg's battlefield, audiences must decide if and how to believe in things that they actually see. Even a vanished landmark—a demolished castle or lost battlement—can be understood to be part of the tourist's concept of reality. On the ghost tour, belief precedes seeing: a ghost, after all, may or may not have existed ever or anywhere.

Ghost tours rely on a mirror action of showing: the guide shows the tour group the possibility of a paranormal encounter and then the tourists show themselves the uncertain ghost as a genuine presence. The guide points to the site and the tourist takes the photograph or hears the spectral gunshot or sees movement in the shadows. Together, the guide and the tourist negotiate the paranormality of the tourist's image or experience; this interaction causes the ghost to emerge. The guide performs a paranormal interpretation of sites, sensations, and photographs that not only re-contextualizes the anomalous as a ghost but makes the anomalous itself more possible. Tourists accept the guide's interpretation when they begin actively to explore and seek out potential ghosts at the tour site. If they do not, they will not experience a ghost, but, as the ghost photograph demonstrates, trying out paranormal belief does not mean taking it home.

The authenticity of the ghost encounter is most potent and persuasive in the moment in which it is shown. The aura of authenticity begins to fade the moment the encounter passes: separated from the site and uploaded to a computer (in hopes of discovering dust or light, which might better explain the seemingly inexplicable), its aura further diminishes. Reflecting back on the experience months later, the tourist might begin to doubt whether the movement in the shadows behind the battlefield cemetery was actually a ghost or just the wind in the trees. The power of the performance lies in giving tourists the kinds of encounters that allow for a deeper, experiential understanding of the uncertainty of the ghost. On tour, the possibility of ghosts increases, but nonetheless stops short of asserting itself as a definitive truth. The tour allows disbelievers to entertain the prospect of the paranormal and nascent believers to have their desires complicated and challenged. In this sense, the showing that happens on a ghost tour doesn't necessarily reveal (or want to reveal) the authentic ghost, but rather opens a space for a deeper engagement with the ghost's possibility.

Notes

1. For more on the tenuousness of paranormal belief in the context of the ghost tour, see my article "'Am I Going to See a Ghost Tonight?' Gettysburg Ghost Tours and the Performance of Belief," *Journal of American Culture* 33, no. 2 (June 2010).

2. Dark tourism is a relatively recent concept in tourism research and refers to any site that is visited primarily because of its connection to death and trauma. When I conceive of the battle of Gettysburg as a significant moment in Civil War history, it complicates Gettysburg's identification with dark tourism. Tourists visit for the historical significance of the site, which happens to include large-scale death and the dedication of a cemetery (the occasion for Abraham Lincoln's Gettysburg Address).

3. http://www.destinationgettysburg.com/media/facts.asp, accessed June 26, 2014.

4. http://www.civilwar.org/land-preservation/blue-gray-and-green-2013.pdf, accessed June 27, 2014.

5. Battlefield Memories stands just outside the boundary of the "Brickyard"; the Farnsworth House travels to the end of the parking lot bordering Cemetery Ridge; Ghostly Images brings tourists just outside the gates of the National Cemetery; Farnsworth and Sleepy Hollow travel to the field behind Gettysburg High School just under Cemetery Ridge.

6. The town figured prominently in the second day of the battle, and many of the buildings in the town were used as field hospitals immediately following the battle, but the federal government never purchased land from the town. As a result, the town progressed and changed while the fields purchased by the park service were preserved as "special" spaces.

7. Weeks (2003) suggests that the town itself is also to a certain extent "staged" because many buildings are made to look "more historical," like banks and restaurants. Although these efforts are evident, they fall far short of those taken in Colonial Williamsburg, for example. A McDonald's made to fit a certain aesthetic is nonetheless a McDonald's. The park, on the other hand, models itself on a more Williamsburg-like aesthetic.

8. There are a few notable exceptions. The first is Ghostly Images' Haunted Orphanage Tour. This tour brings tourists into the basement of the Soldier's National Museum after the museum has closed. During the museum's daytime hours, tourists are not allowed access to the basement. The basement and attic of the Farnsworth House are also inaccessible unless the tourist pays for a ghost tour ticket.

9. According to MacCannell, "it is always possible that what is taken to be entry into a back region is really entry into a front region that has been totally set up in advance for touristic visitation" (1973, 597).

Sources

Babcock, Barbara. 1977. "The Story in the Story: Metanarration in Folk Narrative." In *Verbal Art as Performance*, edited by Richard Bauman, 61–79. Love Grove, IL: Waveland Press.

Baudrillard, Jean. 1994. *Simulacra and Simulation*. Translated by Sheila Faria Glaser. Ann Arbor: University of Michigan Press.

Benjamin, Walter. 1968. "The Work of Art in the Age of Mechanical Reproduction." In *Illuminations*, edited by Hannah Arendt, translated by Harry Zohn. New York: Schocken Books.

Bennett, Gillian. 1999. *Alas, Poor Ghost! Traditions of Belief in Story and Discourse*. Logan: Utah State University Press.

Bruner, Edward M. 2005. *Culture on Tour: Ethnographies of Travel*. Chicago: University of Chicago Press.

Davis, Colin. 2007. *Haunted Subjects: Deconstruction, Psychoanalysis, and the Return of the Dead*. New York: Palgrave Macmillan.

Davis, Ray. 2006. "Seminary Ridge Tour." Unpublished manuscript. Author's collection.

Degh, Linda. 1996. "What Is a Belief Legend?" *Folklore* 107: 33–46.

Goffman, Erving. 1959. *The Presentation of Self in Everyday Life*. New York: Doubleday.

Goode, Eric. 2000. *Paranormal Beliefs: A Sociological Introduction*. Stony Brook: State University of New York.

Handler, Richard, and Eric Gable. 1997. *The New History in an Old Museum: Creating the Past in Colonial Williamsburg*. Durham, NC: Duke University Press.

MacCannell, Dean. 1973. "Staged Authenticity: Arrangements of Social Space in Tourist Settings." *American Journal of Sociology* 79, no. 3: 589–603.

MacCannell, Dean. 1976. *The Tourist: A New Theory of the Leisure Class*. New York: Schocken Books.

Rayner, Alice. 2006. *Ghosts: Death's Double and the Phenomena of Theater*. Minneapolis: University of Minnesota Press.

Sabol, John G., Jr. 2007. *Ghost Culture: Theories, Context, and Scientific Practice*. Bloomington, IN: Authorhouse.

Schmitt, Jean-Claude. 1998. *Ghosts in the Middle Ages*. Chicago: University of Chicago Press.

Thompson, Robert C. 2010. "'Am I Going to See a Ghost Tonight?' Gettysburg Ghost Tours and the Performance of Belief." *Journal of American Culture* 33, no. 2: 79–92.

Weeks, Jim. 2003. *Gettysburg: Memory, Market, and an American Shrine*. Princeton: Princeton University Press.

CHAPTER 12

Strip-Showing and the Suspension of a Naked End

Daniel Sack

"FALSE START"

Or, the Problem of Beginning

In the corner of one of the notebook pages in which the Belgian-Mexican artist Francis Alÿs sketched out his proposition for the performance *Rehearsal II*, a small yellow Post-it note states: "false start painting by J. Johns." The painting in question, which the American artist Jasper Johns completed in 1959, announces bright and loud a disjunction between sign and signified: swathes of color splayed across the canvas are named by contradictory texts so that the word "white" is stenciled in the color red atop a thicket of yellow paint, the word "blue" written in yellow on a scramble of white and blue, and so on. *False Start* displays a disjointed economy: the values of the colors shown and the colors written do not correspond—one chases after the other. If the name "red" were to arrive at its proper place we would not know it: "red" written in the color red and on the color red cannot be read. To show, the image requires a disjunction that puts the medium of showing at odds with the thing shown. Such showing is a disjunction that over, or in, time diverts the direct correlation of means and ends.

Strip away the linguistic description laid atop Johns's painting and one sees an exemplary piece of abstract expressionist art. Just as Jackson Pollock's drippings were celebrated as marks of the artist's presence, the base layer of brushstrokes here evidence the gesture particular to Johns himself and

Fig. 12.1. Jasper Johns, *False Start*, 1959. Oil on canvas 170.8 x 137.2 cm (67 1/4 x 54"). (Private collection, New York. Photographed by Jamie Stukenberg, Rockford, IL Art © Jasper Johns/ Licensed by VAGA, New York, NY.)

purport to put his naked authenticity on show. *False Start* theatricalizes the viewer's desire for immediate contact with the artist/artwork by interjecting a linguistic mediation that precedes and eludes one's encounter with the painting. The modernist conviction that an art object revealed the truth of a medium and the truth of the artist-subject is here falsified or set askance.[1] Johns painted his canvas on the cusp of the performative turn in the visual arts, the same year Allan Kaprow staged his *18 Happenings in Six Parts* that would give its name to a performance genre and herald an outpouring of interdisciplinary art in the sixties and onwards. Decades later, the note-taker Francis Alÿs's wide-ranging oeuvre—including painting, sculpture, photography, installation, video, and performance work (and everything in between)—would benefit from this splintering of the discrete arts. In other words, we might say that the *False Start* named by Johns's painting is the start of theatricality's incursion into the realm of the visual, an increased attention to the various processual means of *showing* rather than the art object shown at the end in exhibition.

There is more to this *False Start*. The term resonates in the sporting world, where any beginning before the official "gunshot" is deemed ineligible (a bad showing) and is thus removed from the competitive environment of the race. To keep running after a false start is a waste of energy, a pure expenditure without hope of acknowledgment or reward. It doesn't count or have value. A false start also refers to any linguistic stumble or disruption in fluent speech—a sentence cut off midspeech, a stutter, grunt, or other filler—that may open up an anomalous event in the flow of communication. What are the effects of such a stutter on the clear exchanges of communication, especially on critical writing that aims to show in language what has been experienced bodily? For, if we allow its letters to migrate between words, like the colors migrating beyond themselves on Johns's canvas, "false start" is also the "falsest art," a designation I reserve not for theater with its storied antitheatrical biases, but for criticism. Theater may prey on the real and usurp the other visual, literary, and performance arts under its banner, but criticism—should we be so bold as to claim it an art—is surely the most parasitic of creatures, living its life off the passage of others.

Allow me, a sometimes critic, to feed off of Alÿs's Post-it note a moment longer and ask what performing a false start opens up for an economy of action and an economy of knowledge, those two intersecting fields that those of us who write about performance must inhabit? These are the questions guiding the writing that follows. A false start sets our thought off on an erroneous voyage, unvalued, incomplete, and withheld without ever reaching an end: the race that might be happening right now but has been abandoned. In performance terms, committing to a false start allows us to suspend ourselves in the process of *showing* without ever arriving at the finished thing *shown*. This disjunctive showing takes place on a personal level—between spectator and artwork, writer and event—where one projects an expected end into the imagined future (the finish line, the finished life, the finished object), by forcing one to confront the disappointment of that expectation, a holding back that remains in process. But such showing also works on a sociopolitical level by suspending the capitalistic reliance on the production of ends writ large, perhaps even pointing toward a way of living without a certain profession or object in sight. An investment in showing rather than in a thing to show might provide a model for living in the meantime, rather than in the time of accomplishments, productions, and competitions so often associated with the idea of a "show."

Finally, a false start frees us from the responsibility of beginning in earnest.

"REHEARSAL II"

Or, the Potentiality of Performance

Let me try this again.

A woman rehearses a *Lied* by Schubert with a pianist. She stops in the midst of a phrase and repeats the passage again from the start. Sometimes she interrupts the music to share a few words with her accompanist before the two join up once more, stepping back again a few measures before moving forward. The song stutters on.

At the same time and in the same time, a stripper rehearses her routine downstage. Like the accompanist, she takes her cues from the singer. Whenever the music stops, she, too, stops and then resumes her dance with the song's resumption. Whenever the two musicians converse, she begins to put back on her clothing. So that, for every step forward in the unveiling of her body, the performer enacts a smaller return or rehearsal of the same. The repeated lowering of a strap becomes a kind of stuttering dance between points of arrival and before an ever-receding climax. If a striptease is essentially about the anticipation of arrival and ends with the full reveal, then the ideal striptease would suspend appearance in a constant state of becoming, an increasing arousal without end. The voyeuristic pleasure of both the audience and the scholar writing about performance derives in part from the guarantee of a good show, a revelation of character, spectacle, and any number of sordid secrets. However, the stripper's unstripping proposes an extended showing in place of the final show, even if, by dancing forward three steps and back two, she does eventually arrive at an end. The performer has been following the cues of the musicians behind her, but she is the one that determines the shape of the whole, the inevitable moment of conclusion: fully denuded, the performance is over or, rather, the rehearsal is over. All three performers leave the stage.

The performance just described, *Rehearsal II*, was realized in 2004 under the auspices of New York City's first Performa Festival. The piece exemplifies a certain mode of production that has consumed Alÿs for a number of years, across a variety of media and projects, loosely and explicitly connected. As I've written elsewhere: "His is an investigation of the art of pursuit, but a kind of pursuit reserved for the thing at which one can never arrive, either because the goal is always retreating or, as in Zeno's paradox, half the distance covered always remains uncovered [in this case half the body's

Fig. 12.2. Francis Alÿs, *Politics of Rehearsal*, New York, 2004. In collaboration with Performa, Rafael Ortega, and Cuauhté-moc Medina. Video, 30 minutes. (Courtesy David Zwirner, New York/London.)

"distance" always remains covered]. In Zeno's paradox the arrow somehow manages to find its mark, but it is what happens in the process of becoming this end that sets the mind off and running" (Sack 2015a, 198–99). Re-performing the hunt of the Tehuelche people of Peru for his piece *A Story of Deception* (2003–6), in which hunters pursued their quarry on foot for many weeks, he filmed the seeming movement of the mirages that formed at the horizon, noting how these images vibrated into life with his approach, but stilled with his stasis. As I concluded, "[i]f there is an image that crystallizes these works, it is a form displayed in suspense." Here, we might rather say that it is a form *showing* itself in suspense. For the endless pursuit of the mirage embodies the same poetics of suspension as the erotic extension of the striptease; it is the perpetual distance between the viewer and the viewed that "triggers its life."

Though I've worried over these questions for some time—in a doctoral dissertation and subsequent book, as well as in a number of associated writings—I, too, am playing a game of pursuit here and want to acknowledge the artist Alÿs as my quarry and precedent. I want to see the artist's work as a thing shown that I can only work toward showing, while also exploring the nature of the kind of showing at issue here. My discovery of Alÿs's work a decade ago could only be described as a kind of déjà vu—a sensation of dislocation confirmed by his piece *Déjà vu* (1993–94) in which two nearly identical canvases are hung in different parts of an exhibition, so that an encounter with the first painting is a rehearsal for the déjà vu inspired by one's encounter with the second. I continue in my conviction that this particular artist has preceded my appearance on the scene; he has already said everything that I wanted to say, done all that I meant to do.

This chapter attempts to stage the kind of knowledge that it explores—a knowledge that is always partial, that values the showing more than the thing shown, and that abandons itself to pursuit rather than capture or mastery. As such, I offer a fragmentary series of false starts, each numbered section named after a different work by Alÿs, and each accompanied by a subtitle, as close and as distant from each title as Jasper Johns's naming stands from his painted colors. What follows is a discourse rife with hesitations and restatements. Like the performer in *Rehearsal II*, I strip away texts and put them back on, by circling back to a previous quotation (as I have done in the paragraph above about *A Story of Deception*), all the while showing the figure of that mirage I know as Francis Alÿs, the artist who keeps up his protean dance and keeps retreating with my every approach.

In this way, while reflecting on the philosophical implications of showing in performance and the theater, I hope to stage my own artful pursuit, showing how performative writing can avoid the dangers of resolution that this artist so pointedly rebukes. Thus my opening sally on false starts—and, indeed, this longer game of hesitation now well under way—may be characterized as showing-off in a writerly fashion, and intentionally so. Indulging in a kind of performative showing I hope to attend to the material presence of the written medium as a performance itself, an accumulation of texts in bold and living relief from any thing-like conception of the source event. Showing off in this manner might combat the risk that, in writing about performance, we reduce its processual becoming to an object of knowledge for our control, and thus neglect whatever resistant force it might obtain in an age of late global capitalism. The economic ramifications of this gesture will be discussed further below. Once more: I want to make the medium of writing itself opaque, place its showing center stage so that we might see how it performs.

"SOMETIMES MAKING SOMETHING LEADS TO NOTHING"

Or, some differences between showing and the show

I repeat: "If a striptease is essentially about the anticipation of arrival and ends with the full reveal, then the ideal striptease would suspend appearance in a constant state of becoming, an increasingly attenuated arousal without end. [It] proposes an extended showing in place of the final show."[2] What does this distinction between a *show* and *showing* entail? Let me propose a theoretical circumscription of terms as much as a definition, following a philosopher for whom I have the greatest respect in saying that "terminology is the poetic moment of thought."[3]

One might say that the "show" is the thing seen. To call a performance a "show" is to privilege the sense of sight as the primary means of accessing performance ("spectacle" assumes the same and, of course, the theater, too, derives from "theatron" or "place of seeing"; this imbrication of the seen and scene has been much remarked upon). A show, a performance, must display some*thing*, a fully realized end. It must reveal what is otherwise not shown. And yet to speak of "the show" in these terms is also to suggest the possibility of its opposite, the thing we do not show. This is the supposition behind all shows: that by virtue of seeing this particular framed event, there are other things we do not see. The suggestive presence of these unseen others operates on a spectator's interest in a profoundly erotic manner. For, as Roland Barthes has noted in regard to the dialectic between seen and unseen in the photograph, it is the suggestion of an outside or underside attracting our gaze that distinguishes the erotic photograph from the complete exposure of the pornographic.[4] The striptease relies upon this tension as the driving force behind its interest.[5] So, too, does the entire apparatus of the traditional theater, though often indulging in an erotics of the intellect as much as one of bodily desire (if these two can, in fact, be distinguished). A spatial frame promises an offstage presence constantly encroaching upon and supporting the fragment of a world we survey, from which any number of things may emerge; a temporal frame delineates when we might see and when we might not, the beginnings and ends of an event (the curtain up at 8 p.m., a two-hour run time).[6] Such an exchange inspires a good deal of theatrical interest: who has not felt the desire to follow Nora around the corner at the end of *A Doll's House*, to trail Tuzenbach to his duel in *Three Sisters*, to witness Clytemnestra's revenge in *Agamemnon*? Conventional devices of the theater such as the blackout and the curtain stand as surrogates for this suspension of potentiality, formal figurations that confine the outside and allow us to overlook them. At a further remove, one of these unshown presences is the rehearsal, that wealth of material that lies behind the production of the show. The rehearsal is the means by which the show discovers itself as an end.

The show as thing seen is different from the act "to show." The gerund form—showing—posed without any qualification or object makes the showing itself the show. In other words, the act of showing obscures the thing being shown, as if the finger pointing were center stage and the thing pointed at were relegated to the offstage space. We might even say that "showing" plays at "not-showing." Such showing is grounded in processual movement, not a stationary form or entity; it is the passage (as movement not space) between the hidden and the show(n). Showing is becoming a threshold between the scene and the obscene. Surely a stripper is one of the most literal embodiments of such a becoming-threshold, his or her body playing at the fringe of appearance. It is a garter lowered and raised in one gesture.

In other words, showing is a kind of promise, a promise rehearsed repeatedly that can never be honored without becoming an end, a show. It is the promise to keep promising that Shoshana Felman (2003) has recognized as the purest form of the performative utterance. It is also what Peggy Phelan has described as characteristic of performative writing: "A statement of allegiance to the radicality of unknowing who we are becoming, this writing pushes against the ideology of knowledge as a progressive movement forever approaching a completed end-point" (Phelan 1997, 17). Alÿs's work, and *Rehearsal II* in particular, holds its audience in such a suspended state by uttering long streams of promises that it never really honors. It lets us rehearse "the radicality of unknowing who we are becoming." At least, that is what I am practicing here. If I put this back into the language of an economy of knowledge, this amounts to my renunciation of having any particularly useful or valuable knowledge to show, any final words worth saying.

"THE POLITICS OF REHEARSAL: REHEARSAL II"

Or, the policy of suspended development

Again: "The rehearsal is the means by which the show discovers itself as end." In 2004 *Rehearsal II* was performed live before an audience in New York, but I was not there. The version of the piece that I encountered, with its second title (*The Politics of Rehearsal*) appended like another garment drawn over the performance's body, is a film recording of a rehearsal of that same work: it is *a rehearsal of a rehearsal*. In other words, Alÿs made two versions of the performance—one live before an audience (*Rehearsal II*) and one a video recording of a rehearsal for that live performance (*The Politics of Rehearsal: Rehearsal II*). This reflects a common mode of creation for the artist who, if arriving at an end, will as likely as not return to the beginning and start over, either reenacting the whole or revising it. Nested within the video *Politics of Rehearsal: Rehearsal II* are a series of switchbacks and doubling-overs. First, the event is split into title and subtitle and, secondly, if there is a *Rehearsal II*, then there must be a *Rehearsal I*. Indeed, *Rehearsal I* (1999–2001) is a short video piece similarly concerned with the perpetual distance between beginning and end, showing an old Volkswagen Beetle repeatedly ascending a hill in a dilapidated development outside of Mexico City. Accompanied by the soundtrack of a band in rehearsal, the car will slow to a standstill every time the music stops, rolling back in neutral to the bottom of the hill to restart its climb when the music begins again. Some contemporary descendent of Sisyphus's rock, the car never reaches the peak of the hill, but strives endlessly back and forth. Like Johns's misapprehending colors, the doubles of the music and the Volkswagen are not identical or even particularly accurate resemblances. A preparation, the rehearsal is not the thing itself, but a peculiar version of performance that does not take place, preferring to prepare the place for another. Like the striptease, it is a way of delaying the present as something presentable, something that one can show, but also accepting it as something incapable of arrival. The artist relates this perpetual renewal to a particular logic of Western capitalism endemic to the late-twentieth century.

This is signaled overtly in the recorded version of the striptease piece, *The Politics of Rehearsal: Rehearsal II*, which adds a third and final accompaniment to the two duets already staged in the live performance (singer-pianist and musicians-stripper). An excerpt from President Harry Truman's 1949 inauguration speech now plays in voiceover as an introduction to the piece. The speech represents the first time that the concept of a separate world of "underdeveloped" countries was put forth and with it the expectation that, with the guiding accompaniment of the more "advanced" states, these countries would eventually arrive in a "developed" state of modernity and freedom—or, at least a freedom of the market.[7] It also celebrated the United States of America as the champion of democracy, and by extension capitalism, against the global threat of communism. This third accompaniment develops as the striptease plays out, as we overhear fragments of Alÿs and his cocreator, the curator Cuauhtémoc Medina, converse on the political situation of present-day Mexico.

Alÿs, a Belgian architect-turned-artist, has lived in Mexico City for more than thirty years, and much of his work reflects on the politics of this place and his own place as outsider interrogating its forms. A number of his pieces intervene in the cityscape through the mode of walking or other forms of everyday practice that may be termed *detournements* in the style of the Situationist Internationale, refashioning authorized uses of urban landscape toward unauthorized purposes. He conceives of *Rehearsal II*, and related pieces concerned with this structure of constant deferral, as representations of the country's economic status quo:

> The intention behind these short films was to render the time structure I have encountered in Mexico, and to some extent in Latin America. It also recalls the all-too-familiar scenario of a society that wants to stay in an indeterminate sphere of action in order to function, and that needs to delay any formal frame of operation to define itself against the imposition of Western Modernity. (Alÿs 2005, 10)

Framed as an "underdeveloped" country by the "first world," Mexico is always in what Alÿs describes as a state of arousal.[8] It is unclear exactly who is being aroused by this promise of arrival: on one hand, the artist suggests that the Mexican public is seduced by political voices that propose one inevitably unrealized economic agenda after another, while, on the other hand, those economies that are already modernized desire nothing more than another dancing partner to keep the music playing a little longer. Casting the economic situation of Mexico as a rehearsal also figures the country's position as an inconsequential undertaking, preparing the place that more serious "first world" economies may occupy.

Late arrival that I am, a number of critics, particularly Medina, offer cogent and compelling readings of how Alÿs explores this politics of suspension in terms of the Mexican economy. This represents one possible interpretation of these many false starts, but it is one defined in reference to the end never achieved. In focusing on the failure to arrive at the show, the work stages a poetics of disappointment. I wonder if, on the other hand, a suspended showing can act as an affirmative gesture in itself, without referencing an end that it will never reach. Stated otherwise, what might be gained by showing the process of showing itself without needing to refer to the show at the finish?

"SOMETIMES MAKING NOTHING LEADS TO SOMETHING"

Or, the Performer's Uneconomical Affirmation

And again: "The intention behind these short films was to render the time structure . . . of a society that wants to stay in an indeterminate sphere of action in order to function." Shown in microcosm, what we see onstage is the smallest of societies (two is company, three's a crowd). This party of three—singer, pianist, and stripper—hesitates to perform, to show the thing for which we have paid. Staying in an "indeterminate sphere of action," are they not opting out of the economy of determined and named actions, of playing dramatic characters? Alÿs has assigned a set of tasks to these performers, roles to play, but they possess something of their own capacity as artists within this structure, as if their hesitations were taking back control of whatever part had been assigned them. As such, I hesitate to regard this parable and so many of Alÿs's endless pursuits as *only* an allegory for the perpetual disappointment of Mexico's political economy. From another perspective this presentation of a means without end achieves an emancipatory release from an ends-based economy. "Economic activity, considered as a whole," writes Georges Bataille, "is conceived in terms of particular operations with limited ends. . . . It does not take into consideration a play of energy that no particular end limits" (1989, 22–23). Stepping outside an ends-based economy of production, the stripper in *The Politics of Rehearsal* comes to possess her own potentiality to not-strip or not "to show," to consider that play of energy without translating her appearance into a shown commodity. When she is stripping, the stripper is committed to business as usual, a business that dead-ends in her production as commodity. But in putting back on her garter, she refuses to become an object that can only be shown, and instead invests in showing her *potential to show* as a power and right. Performing potentiality, then, requires a kind of making that Alÿs announces in axiomatic form in the title to one of his other pieces: *Sometimes Making Something Leads to Nothing* (and its companion piece, *Sometimes Making Nothing Leads to Something*). The artist's twin dictums ask not for a named action that could be subsumed under a defined end (in that all actions acquire a name in determining their ends), but rather for an unqualified motion, a "something doing." Is this not the program for a pure means without end, a potential to do that does not lead to a thing done?

Alÿs's art divorces a means from the production of an end, presenting a showing in place of the shown, and revels in what I have taken to calling the sense of *potentiality* at the heart of the live event.[9] What do I mean by applying this word "potentiality" to a live event? In thermodynamics, potential energy refers to the energetic capacity of a form or system before its expression as kinetic energy; everything around us contains potential energy to do otherwise or create change outside of the expected uses or productive ends that a humanized perspective implies. When applied metaphorically to a medium, we might speak of a blank sheet of paper possessing its capacity to be inscribed or the blank canvas its capacity to be painted. Or, as Michelangelo purportedly stated, the block of stone can contain any number of potential statues. To speak of the potential of a living individual is to refer to his or her capacity (means) apart from any particular realization or action (end) presumed in the future. According to philosopher Giorgio Agamben, one maintains one's potential to do by *not* doing a nameable thing, by *not* arriving at an end.

For the last two decades that Alÿs has been exploring the consequences of suspending a means in embodied form, Agamben has also produced an extensive repertoire of essays and monographs addressing these same questions. In his essay "Notes on Gesture," for example, the philosopher writes of the gag or stutter as a revelation of the capacity for language. Swallowing up a word or phrase midexpression, catching our breath on its contours and unraveling the garment of language, the body of speech as a medium is denuded. The speaker exposes his or her potentiality or capacity to speak by withdrawing from a spoken statement: a false start. In embodied terms, the stripper's hesitations between veiling and unveiling, moving in both directions at once, amounts to a similar exposure of potentiality: in not-stripping, she shows her potential to strip (and to do a host of other things). She is showing that she is not-showing.

The fact that the performers in both versions of *Rehearsal II* are masters of a specific technically complex vocation is not insignificant. As John Cage made us realize in his seminal 1952 performance 4'33, in which the pianist David Tudor sat before his opened piano in full concert attire for four minutes and thirty-three seconds without playing a single note, the pianist before the silent piano retains his power to play in a manner quite different from that of the untrained pianist before an instrument. Tudor was showing his potential to play many things by not playing anything at all. In her silence, the singer similarly possesses her capacity to sing at any moment in the immediate future. She holds forth a potentiality in a way distinct from the silence of a nonsinger who would require a change in kind to be able to sing (well).[10] So much for the singer and the pianist retaining their capacity to make music in a manner far beyond my own abilities. In the gaps of the rehearsal's stops and starts, they possess nothing less than a *power* that no spectator or market or political regime may usurp.

But what of the stripper? Is stripping something that exists as a potentiality available to all clothed beings? Clothing, like language, is interchangeable between anthropomorphic bodies—it may not be a pretty sight, but with a little stretching I can fit into your T-shirt—so the potentiality not to strip is akin to some embodied version of the potentiality not to speak. If we put clothing on animals, it is to dress them up as if they were humans, to take pleasure in our own ingenious talent for anthropomorphization. The donning of a particular wardrobe communicates a particular message to others. The French minimalist choreographer Jérôme Bel staged this quasi-linguistic translatability in his 1997 performance *Shirtology*. Here is director/writer Tim Etchells describing the central moment of Bel's antispectacle, when twenty performers (each wearing many layers of secondhand T-shirts) stand in a line at the front of the stage, looking out at the audience and seemingly doing nothing:

> There's a nakedness in the performers, clothed, a presence, a vulnerability and an unease. The public are uncomfortable too, not accused so much as worried, about the ethics of their gaze.
> Only after what feels like five minutes does a performer remove a T-shirt, revealing one beneath: I THINK THEY'RE LOOKING AT US.
> There is a silence again and more looking. And then a further T-shirt is revealed: RELAX. (Etchells 1999, 212)

The nakedness of being shown on stage here reflects back on an audience that is also put on show, hailed in clearly written and read language. In *Shirtology* any such statement belongs to the mass-produced logic of the brand and logo. And yet, for all the meaning expressed in the two shirts with their texts, there are also all those unwritten garments—both visible on the other performers' bodies and submerged beneath their other layers—that act as a kind of support for statements that could be made but are not stated.

I do not mean to say that the stripper's stripping is the same as any clothed person's undressing. Rather, the stripper makes an artful representation out of our everyday action, she perfects its forms and manners as an orator might master the arts of articulating speech or a poet the lines and structures of a shared language. It follows that the stripping in *Rehearsal II* and its descendent, *The Politics of Rehearsal*, are not only an attempt to perfect the common ground of desire's attenuation, but also an attempt to master our belonging to a human community only so far apart from our animal others: the community of those that can be clothed and unclothed in language. Stripped, the stripper is objectified to the gaze of the spectator. But this human being is not professing anything or belonging to a profession that might reduce her to—or produce her as—an object; she is in possession of her potential to be human.

"THE MUSIC LESSON"

Or, Showing How I Have Learned Nothing

"What better way to leave the work alive and living than to sight another storm on the horizon and begin again, the same but differently?" (Sack 2015a, 200). So I wrote not so long ago as the final words in a two-page coda to my book *After Live: Possibility, Potentiality, and the Future of Performance*; this was the last fragment in a series of false conclusions that preferred not to end. There I turned to another suspended performance by Francis Alÿs, where the artist recorded himself as he repeatedly tried to run into the center of the many tornados that form outside Mexico City during tornado season—so many storms whose eyes he sought to see and by which he might be seen. Now, some time removed, I face myself again, suspended in a series of false starts in place of false ends.

Consider this last painting by Alÿs: two similarly dressed men—both wearing dark suits, one in a green shirt, the other in white—sit facing each other across a small table. They are so alike they might be one man doubled over. Between them floats a single sheet of blank white paper. They are blowing with great care to keep the sheet hanging perfectly vertical midair, blowing with such attention that their very chairs and surroundings seem to disappear from view. It is a pure expenditure and will not last; soon their breath will run out, but for this perpetually frozen moment they are showing us that they are here and living, laboring hard without anything to show for their effort. The paper between them could hold any number of excla-

Fig. 12.3. Francis Alÿs, *La Leçon de Musique* c. 2000. Oil on canvas on wood, 8 1/2 x 11 inches, 21.6 x 27.9 cm. (Courtesy David Zwirner, New York/London.)

mations or imitations, but no word or image appears on its unmarked surface. As Alÿs would put it: *Sometimes Making Something Leads to Nothing.* If anything, the page is showing its potentiality to be marked, the voice or breath its potentiality to say or sound. In its title (*La Leçon de Musique; the Music Lesson*) the painting tells us they are only rehearsing for the show that will feature whatever music. The painting also indexes an unheard sensation without a particular object to the lesson, just the passage of a breath between two bodies that requires both in equal measure to maintain the effect.

Is this the lesson? That showing requires a meeting between a spectator and a performer where we cannot tell the two entirely apart? Nothing particularly novel here: indeed, this is the way with much performance—a mutual enactment. Dressed in their matching suits as if for a concert, the two men form a small club (or, as with the musicians and stripper in *The Politics of Rehearsal*, a small society) from which I have been excluded. As a critic, I stand outside the showing, looking for a place at the table where

there is no space for another chair. Isn't this, too, the way with much performance, where the critic presumes to sit removed from the exchange between
performer and spectator, subsumed in a distanced analysis?

And yet it seems that they are not showing themselves so much as the
thing between them, as if they were mutually engaged in the project of displaying this blank and breath-bound sheet specifically for my attention. I
say they are showing the "thing between them," but I know this is a misap-
prehension. There is "nothing" to show there in the space suspended midair:
a blank piece of paper. Indeed, on closer examination it seems that the sheet
itself is transparent, the background bleeding through, as if it were their
breath taking form, transubstantiated. It is showing a music that exceeds
the written or painted medium. If Jasper Johns's *False Start* was committed
to showing a disjoined economy of knowledge to set the sign apart from
its signified, then *The Music Lesson* is showing me an economy completely
divorced from any hope of arrival. And yet (you must excuse my many hesitations), even if I am deaf to the lesson and may not learn the music, it is
showing me a blank page that invites my writing. It asks that I, like the
painter turning breath into image, translate the event into the depiction of
the event. This is, perhaps, the only way for us performance critics to feed
off a music we cannot hear.

One last hesitation. Do we really know the identity of these two men?
Seen and unseen; scene and obscene. Yes, perhaps it is the performer and
his audience, the teacher and his student. But perhaps, instead, that one
with his back turned to us is the artist and that other facing us his representation, both showing themselves in that mutually supported blank screen
for my projection. This could, in turn, mean that I am in fact the one with
the unseen face, looking at the artist who seems so similar to myself in our
common potential to do, to live, to breathe. After all I, too, am rehearsing a
poetics of suspension opposite the artist, some medium held aloft between
us. Or perhaps, in the end, I am the one facing out at you, showing you the
paper between us, here and now, that has nothing to show.

Notes

1. See Greenberg (1986) for the sanctioned version of modernist medium specificity.
2. As I discuss below, I see Alÿs's work as an exemplary exploration of what I have
elsewhere explored as the potentiality of live performance. The paragraph quoted here
is reprinted with very slight modification from the final pages of my book *After Live:
Possibility, Potentiality, and the Future of Performance* (2015) where I look at another

performance by Alÿs. See also my essay "Not Looking into the Abyss: The Potentiality to See" in *On Not Looking: The Paradox of Contemporary Visual Culture*, edited by Frances Guerin (2015). This sense of potentiality derives in large part from the writings of Giorgio Agamben, but also from the work of Gilles Deleuze and Henri Bergson.

3. I am restating the words of Giorgio Agamben who writes in his essay "What Is an Apparatus?" that "a philosopher for whom I have the greatest respect once said, terminology is the poetic moment of thought" (2009, 1). Agamben elsewhere cites this same axiom and attributes it to Walter Benjamin in his essay "*Pardes*: The Writing of Potentiality" (1999).

4. Roland Barthes writes that the erotic photograph "takes the spectator outside its frame, and it is there that I animate this photograph and that it animates me . . . as if the image launched desire beyond what it permits us to see" (Barthes 1981, 59).

5. On the history of the striptease as a mode of performance, see Shteir 2004.

6. On the dramatic theater's use of the offstage space, see Gruber 2010 and Sofer 2013.

7. Harry S Truman's "Inaugural Speech: January 20, 1949," http://www.bartleby.com/124/pres53.html, accessed September 27, 2011.

8. Alÿs says of *Rehearsal II*: "It is a metaphor of Mexico's ambiguous affair with Modernity, forever arousing, and yet, always delaying the moment when 'it' will happen" (Alÿs and Ferguson 2009, 88).

9. A number of critics have employed the word "potentiality" in their discussion of Alÿs's work, but they have generally left their intended meaning unexplained. In the catalog essay accompanying his 2007 retrospective at the Hammer Museum in Los Angeles, for example, curator Russell Ferguson repeatedly uses the word "potential" as an adjective to describe aspects of the artist's work, but never interrogates the significance of potentiality itself. Just a sampling of such usage in Ferguson's essay in *The Politics of Rehearsal* includes "potentially extendable and repeatable" (101), "potentially circulate" (103), "potential story" (106), and "always further potential events to be added" (114), among others. Mark Godfrey, in his essay for the 2010 retrospective exhibition *A Story of Deception* mentions in a footnote that Alÿs's work, particularly *Tornado*, could be read productively as an example of a kind of artwork where "a state of bare life is a form of potentiality" (Alÿs et al. 2010, 33). In connecting bare life, another central concept from Agamben's oeuvre, with potentiality, this is to my knowledge the only time that "potentiality" in the theoretical sense I am calling up is used in reference to the artist's work.

10. I discuss this distinction between the "generic potentiality" of the untrained voice and the "existing potentiality" of the trained and capable singer in *After Live*, 22.

Sources Cited

Agamben, Giorgio. 1999. *Potentialities*. Translated by Daniel Heller-Roazen. Stanford: Stanford University Press.

Agamben, Giorgio. 2009. *What Is an Apparatus? and Other Essays.* Translated by David Kishik and Stefan Pedatella. Stanford: Stanford University Press.

Alÿs, Francis. 2005. *BlueOrange 2004: Francis Alÿs.* Cologne: Walter König.

Alÿs, Francis, Eduardo Abaroa, Klaus Biesenbach, and Mark Godfrey. 2010. *Francis Alÿs: A Story of Deception.* New York: Museum of Modern Art.

Alÿs, Francis, and Russell Ferguson. 2009. *The Politics of Rehearsal.* Göttingen: Stiedl.

Barthes, Roland. 1981. *Camera Lucida: Reflections on Photography.* Translated by Richard Howard. New York: Farrar, Straus and Giroux.

Bataille, Georges. 1989. *The Accursed Share: An Essay on General Economy, Vol. 1, Consumption.* Translated by Robert Hurley. New York: Zone Books.

Etchells, Tim. *Certain Fragments: Contemporary Performance and Forced Entertainment.* New York: Routledge, 1999.

Felman, Shoshana. 2003. *The Scandal of the Speaking Body: Don Juan with J. L. Austin, or Seduction in Two Languages.* Translated by Catherine Porter. Stanford: Stanford University Press.

Greenberg, Clement. 1986. *Clement Greenberg: The Collected Essays, Volumes 1–4.* Chicago: University of Chicago Press.

Gruber, William. 2010. *Offstage Space, Narrative, and the Theatre of the Imagination.* New York: Palgrave Macmillan.

Hardt, Michael, and Antonio Negri. 2004. *Multitude: War and Democracy in the Age of Empire.* New York: Penguin Press.

Hardt, Michael, and Paolo Virno, eds. 2006. *Radical Thought in Italy: A Potential Politics.* Minneapolis: University of Minnesota Press.

Phelan, Peggy. 1997. *Mourning Sex: Performing Public Memories.* New York: Routledge.

Sack, Daniel. 2015a. *After Live: Possibility, Potentiality, and the Future of Performance.* Ann Arbor: University of Michigan Press.

Sack, Daniel. 2015b. "Not Looking into the Abyss: The Potentiality to See." In *On Not Looking: The Paradox of Contemporary Visual Culture,* edited by Frances Guerin. New York: Routledge.

Shteir, Rachel. 2000. *Striptease: The Untold History of the Girlie Show.* Oxford: Oxford University Press.

Sofer, Andrew. 2013. *Dark Matter: Invisibility, Theater, and Performance.* Ann Arbor: University of Michigan Press.

Coda

Not so long ago, while sharing dance and dog stories in the halls of the School of Theatre, Dance, and Performance Studies, Laurie Frederik and Catherine Schuler discovered certain remarkable, and largely unanticipated, commonalities between their extracurricular activities: dancesport (competitive ballroom dancing) and purebred, conformation dog showing. As these hardened theater and performance studies scholars fixed the critical and analytical lens of their trade more closely on their so-called pastimes, the extravagant gestures and flashy, rhinestone-encrusted façades of dance and dog show began to crumble, revealing vast fields of unexamined binaries and ideological impropriety. The future collaborators had to admit that racism, sexism, speciesism, and classism tainted their beloved diversions, transforming them into guilty pleasures. But, as such academics often do, Catherine and Laurie asked themselves whether guilty pleasure could be a way of knowing. Thus intrigued, they began to dig more deeply into relationships between these apparently disparate genres of . . . well, of what?

Early in the project's development, Catherine had the good fortune to see Kim Marra's solo performance, *Horseback Views: A Queer Hippological Performance*, at the annual Performance Studies International conference in Toronto. In her performance, Kim joked that coming out to colleagues as a horsewoman and aficionado of thoroughbreds felt more difficult than coming out as a lesbian. Apparently, Kim's pleasure in a clearly classist leisure activity caused a certain discomfort, making it very like Catherine's and Laurie's guilty pleasures. Recognizing in Kim a kindred spirit, they invited her to collaborate on an initiative they tentatively agreed to call "showing."

Over several years of development, as contributions from scholars across various disciplines enriched the original project, it increased in complexity and moved in new directions. Perhaps that is why the University of Michigan Press prompted the editors to explain themselves—to further illuminate their own intellectual and emotional investments in this thing called "showing." The editors offer their "confessions" in the form of a coda.

LAURIE FREDERIK

So much of life is about showing, even from childhood, though as children we are not embarrassed by it. We crave the attention and the light of pure entertainment. In American society, we are socialized to be seen, to shine, and to always do our best. If a little kid shows off, an adult audience thinks it's cute and that the kid is talented. As a mother, I now understand this and encourage my five-year-old son to demonstrate his special abilities. Then again, some things should simply not be shown off in public, and he has not yet learned that filter. As adults, the assessment of similar showy acts may result in a social critique of being too much of a show-off or showing something that isn't appropriate for our professional world.

I have always been fairly shy and reserved and had to be pushed into the spotlight, but as an athlete I never had a problem with showing off, since it was technical and precisely measured—I either fell off the balance beam or didn't. If I made a big splash upon entry of my springboard dive, the judges took points away from my score. There were "degrees of difficulty" assessed and calculated mathematically. In a track race, I crossed the finish line first or second or sixth, timed to the hundredths of seconds. Even as a contemporary dancer, I was not expected to limit my physical showiness. The higher the leg could kick the better, a lower lunge was more impressive, as was a higher split leap, and turned-out feet were marks of the well trained. However, as a Latin and Ballroom dancer, the competition became more subjective, the performance more guileful than just physical skill, and the scoring, not so clear-cut. Trying to get a professional gig after college graduation, whether on a Broadway stage or a cruise ship, was also a lesson in this regard, since my dancing body in a simple black leotard and ponytailed hair was not given a second glance, regardless of the precision of my double pirouette. I was a total failure at winning such flashy jobs. These experiences made me suspicious when I entered the Ballroom system and made me feel very inadequate, yet dance competition was exhilarating and I loved doing it. Slowly, I learned how to play the game.

For a long time, the easiest way to continue my Ballroom hobby, this guilty pleasure, was to do it without reflexive analysis. I rarely talked about it with my colleagues or nondancer friends. I grumbled about the discomfort of dancing in high heels and tight rhinestoned costumes with fellow competitors, but did not publicly discuss the implications of my chemical-soaked skin—not even realizing until graduate school that it was also politically problematic as an act of racialization. I continue to brown body when I compete in Latin and Ballroom, since to not do it may jeopardize my national standing. I still feel disturbed by it, even more so now, but I have no intention of stopping, addict that I am. This volume gave me the opportunity to analyze just why it is that I am unwilling to give it up, and what it is about competition—academic, athletic, or artistic—that drives us to certain extremes.

KIM MARRA

Although not my first scholarly focus, horses were my first love growing up in a family that bred Thoroughbreds for racing and other equine sports. From a young age in the 1960s, I was taught to understand showing—specifically at equestrian events around the Philadelphia Mainline—as the necessary fulfillment of rigorous daily practice. Exhibiting various breed and performance standards with my horse, I aimed to best the competition in order to move up to the next level. Not only did the work ethic of training for these events help justify the luxury and privilege of the equestrian life style, it also justified prioritizing horses over other WASPy expectations of my social class and gender, such as ballroom dance lessons, dating, and church. While bringing deep pleasure and allowing for subversive tomboy desires, formal English equestrianism nonetheless inculcated strict discipline tested through competition, which appeared to harmonize, albeit unsteadily, with my mother's larger program for turning me into "a proper lady." Ultimately, I failed to measure up, both as a "lady" and as a competitive equestrian. At age twenty-two, I left the horse world governed by my mother's influence and finished college, eventually to forge my own life as a full-time academic and out butch lesbian.

When I returned to horses and riding, post-tenure in middle age, I did so chiefly for love of the animals and recreation; I have deliberately eschewed the pressures of showing and the exacting gaze of judges. But as an American-studies-trained theater historian specializing in the late nineteenth century who happens also to have that equestrian experience, I can read horses in the historical landscape and am compelled to study the U.S. origins of horse shows, which coincided temporally and geographically with the formation of the modern Broadway theater. The juxtaposition of these two once highly influential institutions that shared audiences and aesthetics inspires me to think about the relationship between showing and performance both historically and theoretically. And whereas traditional historiography relegates horses to an obscure, irrelevant background, understanding the horse show alongside the theater via the newer methods of performance studies and animal studies brings the culturally prominent role of these once indispensable creatures into focus. With the perspectives of age and critical training, I want to use my riding now to illuminate how humans and horses so crucially and complexly moved each other's histories through industry, war, and shows of power and identity.

CATHERINE SCHULER

Like a crow, I've always loved the shiny, the showy, and the shallow. As I child, I dreamed the theater major's dream: starring on Broadway, preferably in an extravagant musical. Few dreams are shinier, shallower, or more "show-offy" than that. Unfortunately, it rarely pays off and thus, like most dreamers, I compromised. Nonetheless, once a crow always a crow: the shiny and the showy can seduce even a dull theater historian who's seen the Wizard behind the curtain and knows better.

Having reached late middle-age, my love for spectacular illusion and willingness to be deceived manifest in two extracurricular interests, either of which would have fit comfortably into this volume: conformation dog showing and Vladimir Putin. I confess that "forbidden love" for purebred dog shows, which for many years constituted my topmost guilty pleasure, motivated my original desire to participate in this project. Until, that is, an inexplicable infatuation with international sex symbol and political superstar Vladimir Vladimirovich Putin overshadowed my beloved corgis. Infatuation is not too strong a word, and as a left-wing lesbian feminist with a long history of serious scholarship on Russian theater and culture, I still feel a tad embarrassed about my initial "somatic" enthusiasm for Mr. Putin's carefully crafted image of new Russian masculinity. One might well ask how an otherwise sober, feminist historian became besotted with this unlikely exemplar of post-Soviet showmanship.

I trace it to 2004, during a trip to Moscow where I encountered Vladimir and Liudmilla Putin at an experimental production of Prokofiev's *Romeo and Juliet* at the Bol'shoi Ballet. As luck would have it, I sat no more than twenty-five feet from them in the dress circle. I had no cause to think deeply about this fleeting encounter with post-Soviet political fabulousness until several months later during a haircut at the Bubbles Salon in Bethesda, Maryland. Seeking to keep the conversation lively with Russell, my gay male stylist, I described the Putin episode. To my astonishment, Russell exclaimed: "Putin—he's hot!" I had never imagined a Soviet or post-Soviet leader in those terms and the effect of his enthusiasm was to pique my curiosity about Mr. Putin's erotic appeal. In a word, I became a Putin watcher, which opened up an entirely new world of contemporary political showing, showmanship—and scholarship.

Mr. Putin's modalities of showing manifest variously, from solo performance to mass festival. His individual showmanship, which has been the cause of much merriment and incredulity in the Western press (and among my colleagues and students), pales beside a comparatively new, Putin-generated and Kremlin-financed genre of showing: the spectacular show of post-Soviet revival. The Sochi Winter Olympics, one of Mr. Putin's pet projects, exemplified the genre and it was a mental image of Russia's puissant president flying into Fisht Stadium's enormous arena on a chariot of fire that motivated my desire to reexperience his mythic presence. A serious study of Sochi 2014's sordid history and boastful displays of Russian exceptionality justified the enormously expensive trip. Sadly, Mr. Putin did not fulfill my dream of Russia: although much flew into Fisht Stadium, he did not. Nonetheless, I toured Sochi like a credulous tourist at the Broadway production of *Phantom of the Opera*, ooo-ing and ahh-ing over each new effect and scooping up souvenirs. The truth is that I loved the show—and I'm still a little embarrassed.

Contributors

Contributor biographies are in order of appearance in the volume.
*editors

*Kim Marra is Professor of Theatre Arts and American Studies at the University of Iowa. Her books and articles include *Strange Duets: Impresarios and Actresses in the American Theatre, 1865–1914* (Iowa 2006), winner of the Callaway Prize, and "Riding, Scarring, Knowing: A Queerly Embodied Performance Historiography," *Theatre Journal* 64, no. 4 (December 2012): 489–511, which won the ATHE Award for Outstanding Article and received Honorable Mention for ASTR's Brockett Prize. A former competitor in the cavalry-derived sport of three-day eventing, she continues to ride for recreation and research.

*Laurie Frederik received her PhD in cultural anthropology from the University of Chicago. She is Associate Professor in the School of Theatre, Dance, and Performance Studies and is Director of the Latin American Studies Center at the University of Maryland in College Park. Her book, *Trumpets in the Mountains: Theater and the Politics of National Culture in Cuba* (Duke 2012), won Honorable Mention for Outstanding Book of 2012 by ATHE. Other published works have appeared in *Cuba in the Special Period: Culture and Ideology in the 1990s* (Palgrave), the *Journal of Latin American Anthropology*, *The Drama Review* (TDR), *Gestos*, and in Cuban journals *Conjuntos* and *Tablas*. Frederik is a four-time U.S. Ballroom and Latin Champion and competed in two World Latin Championships.

Jennifer Kokai is an Assistant Professor of Theatre and the theatre program coordinator at Weber State University, in Ogden, Utah. Her essays have appeared in the *Journal of Dramatic Theory and Criticism*, *Journal of American Drama*, and *Theatre and Theatre History Studies*. Her book *Swim Pretty: Aquatic Spectacles and the Performance of Race, Gender, and Nature* is available through Souther Illinois University Press.

Virginia Anderson is Assistant Professor of Theater at Connecticut College. In addition to the history of the circus, her research focuses on the AIDS epidemic and Broadway theater. She has contributed articles to *Theatre History Studies*, *Text and Presentation*, and collections: *The 1980s: A Critical and Transitional Decade*, *The Oxford Handbook of the American Musical*, *The Oxford Handbook of Dance and Theatre*, and the forthcoming *HIV and AIDS in the Twenty-first Century*.

Marlis Schweitzer is Associate Professor in the Department of Theatre and the Graduate Program in Theatre and Performance Studies at York University (Toronto, Canada). She is the author of *When Broadway Was the Runway: Theater, Fashion, and American Culture* and *Infrastructural Politics of Global Performance*, and editor (with Joanne Zerdy) of *Performing Objects and Theatrical Things*. She is the Associate Editor of *Theatre Survey*.

Katie Johnson is Associate Professor of English and an Affiliate of Film and Women's, Gender, and Sexuality Studies at Miami University of Ohio. She is the author of *Sisters in Sin: Brothel Drama in America* (Cambridge, 2006), *Sex for Sale: Six Progressive-Era Brothel Drama Plays* (University of Iowa Press, 2015), and numerous articles and book chapters on theater, performance, film, and U.S. culture.

Chelsey Kivland is a political and urban anthropologist and an Assistant Professor in the Department of Anthropology at Dartmouth College. She writes on street politics, social performance, and gang violence in urban Haiti. She has published articles in, among others, *Cultural Anthropology*, *Political and Legal Anthropology Review*, and *Journal of Haitian Studies*, and she is preparing a book titled *Street Sovereigns: Young Men in Search of the State in Urban Haiti*.

*Catherine Schuler is Associate Professor of Women's Studies at the University of Maryland, College Park. Her books include *Women in Russian Theatre: The Actress in the Silver Age* (Routledge, 1996), which won the Barnard Hewitt Award, and *Theatre and Identity in Imperial Russia* (Iowa, 2009). She is also a past editor of *Theatre Journal*. Her newest work concerns political performance in mass festivals, and media in post-Soviet Russia. An article on Pussy Riot, Russia's notorious punk feminist performance artists, and another on Vladimir Putin's performance of masculinity have recently appeared in *TDR*.

Elayne Oliphant received her PhD in Anthropology in 2012 from the University of Chicago and is Assistant Professor of Religious Studies at New York University. She is a visual anthropologist of religion, secularism, and the public sphere in Europe. Her research examines the flexible role occupied by Catholicism in secular institutions and cultural expressions of western Europe. She has explored how the categories of religion and secularism are applied in unequal ways to different religious symbols in the decisions of the European Court of Human Rights, urban planning, and state funding of religious institutions. Her current book project rethinks the current state of secularism in France through an examination of the transforming place of Catholic symbols and institutions in Paris.

Joy Brooke Fairfield is Assistant Professor in the Department of Theatre at Rhales College in Memphis, Tennessee. Dr. Fairfield received her PhD in the Department of Theatre and Performance Studies at Stanford University where she won the Charles M. Lyons award for outstanding dissertation for her manuscript "Fugitive Intimacies: The Unsettling Vows of Queer Wedlock Performance." Also an actor and director, she specializes in queer and trans theory, feminist themes and methods, and political and protest performance.

Robert Thompson holds a PhD in Theatre and Performance Studies from the University of Maryland, College Park. He is an instructor of theater and the humanities at Chesapeake College and is the executive director of the internationally touring ensemble Odd Act Theatre Group. He has done production work in major cities in the United States, Canada, Scotland, and China. His research focuses on the role of belief in paranormal and religious performances, and he has published in the *Journal of American Culture*.

Daniel Sack is Assistant Professor in the English Department and Commonwealth Honors College at the University of Massachusetts Amherst. His books include *After Live: Possibility, Potentiality, and the Future of Performance* (Michigan 2015), *Samuel Beckett's Krapp's Last Tape* (Routledge 2016), and the edited volume *Imagined Theatres: Writing for a Theoretical Stage* (Routledge 2017). His writings on contemporary performance have been published in a range of journals, magazines, and essay collections.

Index